Satan and the Scots:
The Devil in Post-Reformation Scotland,
c.1560–1700

Satan and the Scots: The Devil in Post-Reformation Scotland, c.1560–1700

MICHELLE D. BROCK
Washington and Lee University, USA

ASHGATE

© Michelle D. Brock 2016

All rights reserved. No part of this publication may be reproduced, stored in a retrieval system or transmitted in any form or by any means, electronic, mechanical, photocopying, recording or otherwise without the prior permission of the publisher.

Michelle D. Brock has asserted her right under the Copyright, Designs and Patents Act, 1988, to be identified as the author of this work.

Published by
Ashgate Publishing Limited
Wey Court East
Union Road
Farnham
Surrey, GU9 7PT
England

Ashgate Publishing Company
110 Cherry Street
Suite 3-1
Burlington, VT 05401-3818
USA

www.ashgate.com

British Library Cataloguing in Publication Data
A catalogue record for this book is available from the British Library.

The Library of Congress has cataloged the printed edition as follows:
Brock, Michelle D.
  Satan and the Scots : the devil in post-Reformation Scotland, c.1560–1700 / by Michelle D. Brock.
     pages cm. – (St. Andrews studies in Reformation history)
  Includes bibliographical references and index.
  ISBN 978-1-4724-7001-0 (hardcover : alk. paper) – ISBN 978-1-4724-7002-7 (ebook) – ISBN 978-1-4724-7003-4 (epub) 1. Devil – Christianity – History of doctrines. 2. Devil – History. 3. Demonology – History of doctrines. 4. Demonology – Scotland – History. 5. Scotland – Church history. I. Title.
  BT982.B736 2016
  235'.409411–dc23
                                                                                              2015027249

ISBN 9781472470010 (hbk)
ISBN 9781472470027 (ebk – PDF)
ISBN 9781472470034 (ebk – ePUB)

Printed in the United Kingdom by Henry Ling Limited, at the Dorset Press, Dorchester, DT1 1HD

Contents

Abbreviations and Conventions   *vii*
Acknowledgements   *ix*

Introduction   1

1   Reforming the Devil   19

2   From the Pulpit   47

3   A Constant Adversary   75

4   Internalizing the Demonic   97

5   Wicked Words and Demonic Belief   125

6   The Devil as Master   149

7   Satan on the Streets   177

Conclusion: Of Monsters and Men   201

Bibliography   *207*
Index   *233*

Abbreviations and Conventions

Adv. MS.	Advocates Manuscripts, National Library of Scotland.
EEBO	*Early English Books Online* (http://eebo.chadwyck.com).
Folger	Folger Shakespeare Library, Washington, DC.
HJ	*Historical Journal.*
Institutes	John Calvin, *The Institutes of the Christian Religion*, 2 vols, ed. J.T McNeill. Philadelphia, PA: Westminster John Knox Press, 1960.
JBS	*The Journal of British Studies.*
JEH	*Journal of Ecclesiastical History.*
KJV	King James Version, The Holy Bible.
NLS	National Library of Scotland.
NRS	National Records of Scotland.
ODNB	*Oxford Dictionary of National Biography*, Oxford University Press, 2004 (www.oxforddnb.com).
RPC	*Register of the Privy Council of Scotland*, ed. J.H. Burton and others. Edinburgh, 1877–1970.
Wod. Fol.	Folios of Robert Wodrow, NLS.
Wod. Qu.	Quartos of Robert Wodrow, NLS.
Wod. Th. MSS.	Theological Manuscripts of Robert Wodrow, NLS.

Spelling, capitalization, names and punctuation in early modern sources have been generally been retained, except when quoted from a more modern edition or version. Unfamiliar Scots words have been explained in square brackets, and readers are also referred to *The Dictionary of the Scottish Language* (http://www.dsl.ac.uk).

Acknowledgements

In reflecting on the arduous yet joyful process of writing my first book, I am filled with gratitude for all of the professional and personal support that I have received over the years from family, friends and colleagues. First and foremost, my doctoral supervisor, Brian P. Levack, has at once been an academic mentor and a dear friend. His enthusiasm for the doctoral project upon which this book is based, the remarkable amount of time he spent reading and discussing my work, and his unyielding confidence in me have been invaluable. If I have any skill as a historian, it is a largely the product of his kind criticism and scholarly example. In graduate school, Neil Kamil and Julie Hardwick were instrumental in informing my ability to think critically about the past. They have continued to be wonderful sources of career advice and moral support over the last few years. Brian Cowan, Jorge Cañizares-Esguerra and Frank Whigham were all generous members of my doctoral committee, and their suggestions for and critiques of my project helped me turn it into this book.

My heartfelt thanks are also due to Washington and Lee University, and my colleagues in the History Department in particular, for the support as this book reached its final stages. The talented editors at Ashgate, especially Tom Gray, Barbara Pretty, and those with the St Andrews Studies in Reformation History series, have been wonderful to work with, and I am very thankful for their guidance and support during the production of this book. Julian Goodare and Roger Mason also deserve special mention for their thoughtful comments and criticisms of my work, and I remain in their scholarly debt. Any errors in the work that follows are, of course, entirely my own.

My personal debts are as vast, if not more so, than my professional ones. First, I must thank my husband Jared, who provided me with seemingly limitless patience and encouragement as this book took shape. Jessica Shore and Anne Proctor have been my constant cheerleaders during the most challenging times of this journey, and for their friendship I will count myself forever lucky. My friends and colleagues in the British Scholar Society, especially Bryan Glass and Martin Farr, have provided encouraging words and invaluable company throughout my academic career. My siblings, David and Kristina, have provided much needed laughter, friendship and a sense of perspective. My father, always willing to listen and give reassurance in all aspects of life, has been an inexhaustible well of encouraging words and advice. My mother, who passed away before I finished the doctoral work that became this book, instilled in me from a very young age a love of reading about people and their stories. She is present on every page. Finally, the unwavering support of my grandparents, John and Louise Hamilton, made my entire education possible. I can never repay them for their generosity. This book is for them.

Introduction

This book is about the Devil, one of the most recognizable figures in Western culture. It is also about persistent, plaguing questions concerning the relationship between evil and humanity that cut across time and space. The pages that follow attempt to address these enormous topics by encountering them in post-Reformation Scotland, a place where Satan, as the Christian personification and purveyor of evil, loomed large in the mental worlds and daily lives of the Scottish people.

As the first history of the Devil in early modern Scotland, this book explores a society in which frequent discussions of Satan in print, from the pulpit, in the courtroom, on the streets and in the intimate pages of personal writings rendered the Devil an immediate, assumed and often terrifying companion. For some, especially those engaged in political struggle, this demonic emphasis produced a unifying effect by providing a proximate enemy for communities to rally around. For others, the Reformed Protestant focus on the relationship between sin and Satan provoked the suspicion that, much to their horror, their own depraved hearts placed them in league with the Devil. In short, the annals of early modern Scotland demonstrate what it meant to live in a world in which Satan's presence was believed to be, and indeed, perceived to be, ubiquitous.

This study contends that post-Reformation beliefs about the Devil profoundly influenced the experiences and identities of the Scottish people through the creation of a shared cultural conversation about evil and human nature. Through its dogged emphasis on human depravity, Reformed theology slowly eroded any rigid divide between the supernatural evil of Satan and the natural wickedness of men and women. This erosion was borne out not only in pages of treatises and sermons, but in lived experience. For many Scots, the battle between Good and Evil was not cosmic but domestic, occurring not in the heavens but in their own corrupted hearts and minds. This perception resulted in a widespread internalization of the relationship between the Devil and mortal sin and an oft-obsessive concern with the darker sides of humanity. The pervasiveness of demonically induced sin in sermons, broadsides and cases of witchcraft carried interest in and anxieties about the Devil beyond the literate populace and into the lives of ordinary Scots. This work thus elucidates the effects of the Reformed emphasis on sin and discipline, a well-trodden subject of scholarly inquiry, through an examination of how connections between Satan and the human condition were regularly promoted from the pulpit, explored in print, and experienced in the lives of Scots of all sorts.[1]

The Devil and Reformed Protestantism

The chapters below are all concerned, to varying degrees, with the ways in which Reformed theology shaped Scottish demonic beliefs and experiences. The events and legacy of the Reformation accordingly undergird many of this book's conclusions. This political and religious revolution of 1560 has a long and rich historiography through which scholars continue to chart and re-chart the course of the Reformation, ask what exactly it achieved, and debate the extent to which it succeeded in reforming Scottish society.[2] Though not without major challenges and setbacks along the way, the Protestant faith slowly overtook the vibrant, sensual Catholicism of medieval Scotland with surprisingly little violence. This is certainly not to imply that there was no substantial resistance to the Reformed church's program of godly discipline. A brief perusal of the ecclesiastical court records reveals regular cases of defiant merry-making, occasional episodes of blasphemous speech and the persistence of ritual, all of which belie any Knoxian mythologizing about a population that uniformly embraced the

---

[1] On the relationship between sin and despair intrinsic to Calvinism, see John Stachniewski, *The Persecutory Imagination: English Puritanism and the Literature of Religious Despair* (Oxford: Clarendon Press, 1991). On the centrality of discipline and controlling sin in Reformed communities like Scotland, see, for example, Michael Graham, *The Uses of Reform: 'Godly Discipline' and Population Behavior in Scotland and Beyond, 1560–1610* (Leiden, Netherlands: E.J. Brill, 1996); Philip Benedict, *Christ's Church Purely Reformed: A Social History of Calvinism* (New Haven, CT: Yale University Press, 2002), chapter 14; and Raymond A. Mentzer, ed., *Sin and the Calvinists: Morals Control and the Consistory in the Reformed Tradition* (Kirksville, MO: Truman State University Press, 2002).

[2] For a few of the most important works on the Scottish Reformation, see Ian B. Cowan, *The Scottish Reformation: Church and Society in Sixteenth Century Scotland* (New York: St. Martin's Press, 1982); Gordon Donaldson, *Scottish Church History* (Edinburgh: Scottish Academic Press, 1985); Jenny Wormald, *Court, Kirk and Community, 1470–1625* (Edinburgh: Edinburgh University Press, 1991); Alan MacDonald, *The Jacobean Kirk 1567–1625: Sovereignty, Polity, and Liturgy* (Aldershot: Ashgate, 1998). For two recent, comprehensive works on the periods before, during and just after the Reformation, see Jane Dawson, *Scotland Re-formed, 1488–1587* (Edinburgh: Edinburgh University Press, 2007) and Alec Ryrie, *The Origins of the Scottish Reformation* (Manchester: Manchester University Press, 2006). For a ground-breaking study of the influence of the Reformation on the Scottish people, especially through the actions of the local kirk sessions, see Margo Todd, *The Culture of Protestantism in Early Modern Scotland* (New Haven, CT: Yale University Press, 2002). For an excellent study of the varied and uneven course of the Reformation at the local level, see John McCallum, *Reforming the Scottish Parish: The Reformation in Fife, 1560–1640* (Farnham: Ashgate, 2010).

rules and regulations of godliness.³ Nevertheless, by the early decades of the seventeenth century, Reformed Protestantism had substantially altered the church, the government and the lives of the Scottish people. In this post-Reformation context, a distinctly Reformed understanding of Satan, based around the principles of divine sovereignty, total human depravity and double predestination, became for many Scots an integral component of lived experience and personal identity.

In re-creating the demonic beliefs of post-Reformation Scots, this book is concerned with highly politicized divides over ecclesiology and theology only in so far as they shaped demonological ideas and personal and communal experiences of the Devil. By the first few decades of the seventeenth century, despite the Reformation's comparative success (or perhaps because of it), the nature of Protestantism in Scotland grew fractured. Heated debates between Presbyterians and Episcopalians – eventually Covenanters and anti-Covenanters – ensued over the ecclesiastical structure of the church.⁴ At times, these conflicts turned violent. And yet, though the relative consensus enjoyed by the church was challenged after 1618 by the influx of 'Arminian' ideas from south of the Border, most Scots remained loyal to the Reformed tradition and doctrine. John Coffey has gone so far as to suggest that 'Scottish Laudians were more Reformed in their pulpit style than were their English counterparts'.⁵ The basics of Reformed theology, though diverse in and of themselves, remained relatively unscathed until the decades following the Restoration in 1660 ushered in new disagreements over Reformed orthodoxy.⁶ In these waning years of the

---

³ For a lively summary and rebuttal of the celebratory mythology about Scottish godliness in the wake of the Reformation, see Jenny Wormald, 'Reformed and Godly Scotland?', in *The Oxford Handbook of Modern Scottish History*, eds. T.M. Devine and Jenny Wormald (Oxford: Oxford University Press, 2012), 204–20.

⁴ On political and religious debates in seventeenth-century Scotland more broadly, see Clare Jackson, *Restoration Scotland, 1660–1690: Royalist Politics, Religion, and Ideas* (Woodbridge: Boydell Press, 2003). On the Covenanters specifically, see John Morrill, ed., *The Scottish National Covenant in its British Context, 1638–51* (Edinburgh: Edinburgh University Press, 1991); David Stevenson, *The Covenanters* (Edinburgh: Edinburgh University Press, 1988). For a wonderful study of the piety of the Scottish Covenanters, see Louise Yeoman, 'Heart-Work: Emotion, Empowerment and Authority in Covenanting Times' (PhD Thesis, University of St Andrews, 1991).

⁵ John Coffey, 'The Problem of "Scottish Puritanism", 1590–1638', in *Enforcing Reformation in Ireland And Scotland, 1550–1700*, eds Elizabethanne Boran and Crawford Gribben (Aldershot: Ashgate, 2006), 86–7.

⁶ For further discussion of religious and political debates in post-Reformation Scotland prior to the Restoration in 1660, see especially the works of David G. Mullan: 'Theology in the Church of Scotland, 1618–1640: a Calvinist consensus?' *Sixteenth Century Journal*, 26 (1995), 595–617; Mullan, *Episcopacy in Scotland: the History of an Idea, 1560–1638* (Edinburgh: Edinburgh University Press, 1986); Mullan, *Scottish Puritanism, 1590–1638* (Oxford: Oxford University Press, 2000). On the diversity of and debates within Reformed theology in early modern Britain, see M. Haykin and M. Jones, eds, *Drawn into Controversie:*

seventeenth century, as Alasdair Raffe has recently demonstrated, some Episcopalians began to reject the orthodox Calvinist emphasis on sin and salvation, as well as the highly introspective piety of their Presbyterian counterparts.[7] Still, even these ecclesiological and theological fissures seem to have little altered the demonic experiences of many Scottish people – at least those who recorded their ideas about and personal struggles with the Devil. Amid important ecclesiastical and political debates, Scots of various persuasions articulated beliefs about the Devil – and themselves – derived from a general embrace of Reformed theology.

In his recent examination of Protestant piety in Britain prior to 1640, Alec Ryrie might well have been discussing Satan in early modern Scotland when he wrote that detailed theological divisions almost 'fade from view when examined through the lens of devotion and lived experience'.[8] Well into the early eighteenth century, after a period that some historians claim witnessed the swan song of Satan's role in Christian theodicy, many Scots continued to articulate a deep and anxious concern for the Devil's involvement in their internal lives.[9] The focus on divine sovereignty and the theoretical decline of Satan's physical prowess in the wake of the Reformation did little to mitigate the profound and frightening reality of the Devil in the lives of Scottish Protestants. Nor was an impotent Satan ever the image projected by the Scottish clergy, for whom constant guardedness and vigilance against the enemy by their parishioners remained critical to the success of the church. In effect, the Reformed emphasis on total human depravity turned the spotlight on the relationship between Satan and 'man's evil heart' and lent the Devil primacy of place in how godly Scots understood themselves and their faith. This lasting focus on Satan, within the context of a community awash in apocalyptic anticipation, makes Scotland emblematic of the interplay between the Devil, lived religion and Reformed Protestantism.

Reformed Theological Diversity and Debates within Seventeenth-Century British Puritanism (Göttingen: Vandenhoeck and Ruprecht, 2011).

[7] Alasdair Raffe, *The Culture of Controversy: Religious Arguments in Scotland, 1660–1714* (Woodbridge: Boydell Press, 2012).

[8] Alec Ryrie, *Being Protestant in Reformation Britain* (Oxford: Oxford University Press, 2013), 6.

[9] Jeffery Burton Russell has, in particular, argued that Protestantism marked the decline of the Devil's role in the Christian world. See Russell, *Mephistopheles: The Devil in the Modern World* (Ithaca, NY: Cornell University Press, 1986), esp. 66–76. Euan Cameron has more recently, and more persuasively, argued that over time, as the sowing of erroneous religious ideas became the Devil's main weapon, the Devil began 'to gradually and imperceptibly slide into the area of metaphor and symbol'. See Cameron, *Enchanted Europe: Superstition, Reason and Religion, 1250–1750* (Oxford: Oxford University Press, 2010), 216.

The findings here complement a number of studies that have traced the development of a Protestant demonology focused primarily on internal temptation and subversion as Satan's greatest weapons.[10] This does not mean, however, that the Scottish Reformation occasioned the abandonment of medieval ideas and the production of a new, exclusively Protestant demonology, or that the demonic beliefs and experiences discussed here were unique to the Scots. Certainly, as a number of scholars have correctly pointed out, Catholic and Protestant demonologies had many similarities, thanks to, among other things, a shared Augustinian heritage and the mutual reliance on Scripture.[11] As with Protestant and Catholic Reformations elsewhere in Europe, the Scottish Reformation provoked a renewed interest in Satan's relationship to humankind, hastened by growing apocalyptic fervour.[12] These important similarities notwithstanding, the introduction of Protestantism to Scotland reoriented demonic belief according to the Reformed emphases on total human depravity and predestination.[13] Despite debates over theology and ecclesiology, both within and beyond Scottish borders, the internalization of ideas about salvation and sin proved formative in shaping how many Scots understood the Devil. The attendant theological, pastoral and experiential focus on the internal temptation of

---

[10] See Nathan Johnstone, *The Devil and Demonism in Early Modern England* (Cambridge: Cambridge University Press, 2006); Johnstone, 'The Protestant Devil: The Experience of Temptation in Early Modern England', *Journal of British Studies* 43 (2004): 173–205; Frank Luttmer, 'Persecutors, Tempters and Vassals of the Devil: The Unregenerate in Puritan Practical Divinity', *Journal of Ecclesiastical History* 51 (2000): 37–68; Darren Oldridge, *The Devil in Early Modern England* (Sutton: Stroud, 2000).

[11] On the shared nature of Catholic and Protestant demonology, see Jorge Cañizares-Esguerra, *Puritan Conquistadors: Iberianizing the Atlantic, 1550–1700* (Stanford, CA: Stanford University Press, 2006); Stuart Clark, *Thinking with Demons: The Idea of Witchcraft in Early Modern Europe* (Oxford: Oxford University Press, 1997), esp. pp. 526–45; Clark, 'Protestant Demonology: Sin, Superstition and Society', in *Early Modern European Witchcraft: Centres and Peripheries*, eds B. Ankarloo and G. Henningsen (Oxford: Oxford University Press, 1990), 45–82. Jeffery Burton Russell has argued, in particular, that Protestant reformers 'uncritically accepted virtually the entire tradition of medieval diabology'. See Russell, *Mephistopheles*, 36.

[12] See, for example, John Coffey, 'The Impact of Apocalypticism during the Puritan Revolutions', *Perichoresis* 4 (2006): 117–147; Katharine R. Firth, *The Apocalyptic Tradition in Reformation Britain, 1530–1645* (Oxford: Oxford University Press, 1979); Arthur Williamson, *Scottish National Consciousness in the Age of James VI: the Apocalypse, the Union, and the Shaping of Scotland's Public Culture* (Edinburgh: John Donald Publishers, 1979); David Drinnon, 'The Apocalyptic Tradition in Scotland', (PhD Thesis, University of St Andrews, 2013).

[13] On the nuances and substance of predestination, see Richard Muller, *After Calvin: Studies in the Development of a Theological Tradition* (Oxford: Oxford University Press, 2003), especially p. 12, and Muller, *Christ and the Decree: Christology and Predestination in Reformed Theology from Calvin to Perkins* (Grand Rapids, MI: Baker Academic, 1988), 79–96.

the Devil ought not be seen as a concerted attempt to do away with any vestiges of medieval demonology or as a rejection of demonic physicality, but rather as a purposeful consequence of Reformed piety's preoccupation with keeping the baser elements of human nature at bay.

Belief and the Scottish People

This book asks not only what people believed about the Devil, but what these beliefs actually *did* – how they shaped the piety, politics, lived experiences and identities of Scots from across the social spectrum. I am interested, then, not just in the formation and articulation of demonic belief in post-Reformation Scotland, but its traction on the ground. In particular, this exploration is concerned with how the unwavering emphasis on the intimacy of Satan and 'man's evil heart' informed the religious experiences and personal and communal identities of the Scottish people. When Robert Louis Stevenson wrote in 1885 that 'man is but a devil weakly fettered', he expressed a view recorded by many Reformed Protestant Scots centuries before him: that all men and women would struggle with Satan throughout their lives on earth, not only as an integral core of the path to salvation, but as an undeniable side of their deepest selves.[14]

Belief, as subject of historical inquiry, is both complex and elusive. As Julian Goodare and Joyce Miller write in their introduction to *Witchcraft and Belief in Early Modern Scotland*, belief 'appears to be about people's inner thoughts, which are not themselves directly accessible; we have only their words, written or spoken, which we must use as indirect evidence for their thoughts'.[15] This poses to the historian an important methodological question: how does one critically consider the available sources when trying to recreate something as intangible and ultimately unknowable as belief? The challenge of this task is only exacerbated by the fact that the texts that reveal such demonic beliefs and attendant experiences are fraught with problems for the historian hoping to sort truth from fiction. Did Satan *really* introduce blasphemous thoughts into the minds of the godly, driving them to despair and suicidal thoughts? Did people *really* practice witchcraft, meet and copulate with the Devil and renounce their baptisms? While these questions are intriguing, they obscure the re-creation

---

[14] Robert Louis Stevenson and Fanny De Grift Stevenson, *More New Arabian Nights: The Dynamiter* (New York: Henry Holt and Company, 1885), 321.

[15] Julian Goodare, Lauren Martin and Joyce Miller, eds, *Witchcraft and Belief in Early Modern Scotland* (Basingstoke: Palgrave Macmillan, 2008), 1. Cowan and Henderson's study of Scottish fairy belief is also instructive in considering how to best approach the beliefs of the past. See Edward J. Cowan and Lizanne Henderson, *Scottish Fairy Belief: A History* (East Linton: Tuckwell, 2001), introduction.

of the place of the Devil in the mental worlds of early modern Scots. If the historian's job is (as I think it is) to interpret and explain the ideas, experiences and events of the past based on the available evidence, then a figure such as the Devil can only been fully understood in the 'context of the perceived realities of past societies'.[16] Otherwise, examining the supernatural suffers from a dearth of any provable, empirical evidence.

In researching and writing this book, I have consciously avoided any approach that reduces religious experiences to medically or psychologically explainable phenomena, such as illness or hysteria.[17] While these approaches are not without merit, to understand as fully as possible the religious experiences of Scots, we need to accept their authenticity. At the same time, it must be acknowledged this authenticity is specific to a set of beliefs, individuals and cultural constructs unique to a past time and place. The aim of this book has not been to assess the reality of the supernatural realm – an unverifiable, impossible task – but rather to describe and interpret people's apparent interactions with it. When I write about Scots encountering or experiencing Satan, I am not making a statement about the existence of the Devil. The historian need not accept or even address the possible reality of the Devil in order to treat these experiences as authentic. Rather, my task, as I have seen it, has been to recognize the reality and authenticity of belief and experience as they pertained to the people being studied.[18] What matters most, therefore, is that Satan was a profound and powerful reality for the early modern men and women discussed below.

Any attempt to examine the beliefs and experiences of a varied and predominantly illiterate population over a large swathe of time will be, in parts, incomplete and uneven. The present work is no exception. While this book explores the demonic beliefs and experiences of Scots from a wide array of backgrounds, it concentrates on the religious lives and identities of the literate, self-identified godly for whom the Devil was an unyielding personal and communal antagonist. The focus is on those who we know, thanks to voluminous historical records, took their interactions with Satan very seriously. This is not, however, a study solely of elite demonological

---

[16] This phrase is borrowed from Jonathan Barry and Owen Davies, *Palgrave Advances in Witchcraft Historiography* (Basingstoke: Palgrave MacMillan, 2007), 1. Here they are speaking about witchcraft, but this same can be said of demonic beliefs and experiences. On this issue of reality and witchcraft, and how these issues have been tackled historiographically, see Malcolm Gaskill, 'The Pursuit of Reality: Recent Research into the History of Witchcraft', *HJ*, 51:4 (2008): 1069–88.

[17] For a discussion of the limitations of sceptical or modern scientific approaches to supernatural phenomena, especially demonic possession, see Brian P. Levack, *The Devil Within: Possession and Exorcism in the Christian West* (New Haven, CT: Yale University Press, 2013), esp. 26–9.

[18] On this point, and for a different but important perspective on how historians ought to approach the religious beliefs of the past, see Ryrie, *Being Protestant*, 12–14.

ideas. Nor is it an examination strictly concerned with 'popular' beliefs. Rather, this book attempts to capture the broader role of Satan in early modern Scotland by taking seriously any description of demonic belief or experience, from the invocation of the Devil during neighbourly disputes to the depiction of Satan in a murder ballad to King James VI's *Daemonologie*. It avoids any assumed existence of a dichotomous cultural understanding of Satan and instead reveals the ways in which post-Reformation Scotland was home to a fluid and shared spectrum of ideas about and experiences of the Devil.

A mutual interest in Satan does not mean, of course, that everyone in Scotland believed the same things about the Devil. Nor does it negate the fact that many Scots continued to believe they lived in a world populated by fairies, ghosts and other supernatural beings.[19] Moreover, this book does not assert that a cultural divide in understandings of Satan or otherwise did not exist in early modern Scotland, though it will suggest that this divide has been overstated.[20] Rather, throughout I have tried to acknowledge divisions in society while also illuminating the continuum of belief through which the demonic ideas and experiences of Scots of all sorts contributed to a varied but collective religious culture. Although some historians have emphasized the severity of Scottish society in matters of religion, this book suggests that it was flexible enough to accommodate a range of ideas about the Devil and the presence of evil in the world.[21]

No history of Scotland should go without recognizing the bifurcation of Scottish society that has existed since the later medieval period. Geographically, economically and culturally, the Highland line has separated Scotland's northern reaches from its more populous and prosperous Lowlands, where the retreat of Gaelic language coincided with the rising tide of Anglicization.[22] The Union of the Crowns in 1603 and the migration of the Court to London further exacerbated these divisions and

---

[19] See Cowan and Henderson, *Scottish Fairy Belief* and Julian Goodare, 'The Cult of the Seely Wights in Scotland', *Folklore*, 123:2: 198–219 and 'Boundaries of the Fairy Realm in Scotland', in *Airy Nothings: Imagining the Otherworld of Faerie from the Middle Ages to the Age of Reason*, eds Karin E. Olsen and Jan R. Veenstra (Leiden: Brill, 2014), 139–70.

[20] With regard to witchcraft in particular, numerous scholars have highlighted the disparity between popular and elite belief. See, for example, the introduction to Goodare, Martin and Miller, eds *Witchcraft and Belief in Early Modern Scotland* and Edward Cowan, 'Witch Persecution and Popular Belief in Lowland Scotland: the Devil's Decade', in *Witchcraft and Belief*, 71–94.

[21] See, for example, Graham, *The Uses of Reform*; Gordon Donaldson, *The Faith of the Scots* (London: Batsford, 1990). In their study of fairy belief in early modern Scotland, Edward Cowan and Lizanne Henderson have explicitly presented Scottish Calvinism as a force that effectively and even intentionally eliminated any supernatural grey area between God and the Devil. See Cowan and Henderson, *Scottish Fairy Belief*, chapter 4.

[22] C.J. Withers, *Gaelic in Scotland, 1698–1981* (Edinburgh, 1984); *Gaelic Scotland* (London, 1988).

led to increased suppression of Highland culture. The Reformation, despite attempts by the Scottish clergy to accommodate the Gaelic language, did not achieve the same success in the Highlands as it did in the Lowlands.[23] This was due in part to the fact that fewer local kirk sessions existed or could meet frequently in the Highlands to enforce the practice of Protestantism, as well as to the efforts of Irish missionaries in Scotland during the Catholic Reformation.[24] That the majority of individuals discussed here are from the Lowlands is not necessarily due to these religious patterns, but rather to the relative paucity of written records left by the primarily oral culture of the Highlands. Whenever the sources permit, important distinctions, as well as common ground, between the demonic beliefs and experiences of Scots living in these regions have been noted.

Gender is another critical element of Scottish society that, though explored in a number of the chapters below, is not a central focus of this study.[25] Obviously, in discussing witchcraft, one cannot overlook the reasons why the vast majority of those accused of and executed for their supposed associations with Satan were women. The scholarship on the gendered dimensions of Scottish witch-hunting is significant and thorough. Historians such as Christina Larner and, more recently, Lauren Martin and Joyce Miller, have greatly augmented our understanding of why Scots associated women with witchcraft, and I have largely left an examination of the gendered dimensions of witchcraft in their capable hands.[26] Other chapters account, where appropriate, for the intersections

---

[23] On the spread of Protestantism to the Highlands, see Jane Dawson, 'Calvinism and the Gaidhealtachd in Scotland', in *Calvinism in Europe, 1540–1620*, eds Andrew Pettegree, Alastair Duke and Gillian Lewis (Cambridge: Cambridge University Press, 1994), 231–53.

[24] It is worth nothing that during the early modern period, while Catholicism in Scotland was practised by only about 2 per cent of the population, it was confined almost exclusively to the Highlands and Islands. See Tim Harris, *Restoration: Charles II and his Kingdoms, 1660–1685* (Penguin, 2005), 29. After the Restoration, episcopacy spread to the Highlands with marked success and actually supplanted Catholicism there. For example, as Alan Macinnes has noted, of the twenty-eight clans that participated in the first Jacobite rising in 1688, fourteen were Episcopalian, six were Catholic, and eight were mixed. See Allan Macinnes, *Clanship, Commerce, and the House of Stuart: 1603–1788* (East Linton: Tuckwell, 1996), 180.

[25] It is here worth nothing that on the occasion that this book refers to Satan and 'man's evil heart' or the relationship between the Devil and 'mankind', this is not meant to indicate a specific focus on men to the exclusion of Reformed ideas about women. Rather, this terminology is reflective of the generally male-focused language used by early modern Scots when discussing Satan's interactions with the human world, including both men and women.

[26] See, for example, Lauren Martin, 'The Devil and the Domestic: Witchcraft, Quarrels and Women's Work in Scotland', in Julian Goodare, *The Scottish Witch-hunt in Context* (Manchester: Manchester University Press, 2002), 73–89; Christina Larner, *Enemies of God: The Witch-hunt in Scotland* (London: Chatto & Windus, 1981); Joyce Miller, 'Men in Black: Appearances of the Devil in Early Modern Scottish Witchcraft Discourse', in Goodare,

between gender and demonic belief, language and experience, while not obscuring the common themes in how godly Scots of all sorts wrote and spoke about Satan. I hope that the gaps in this work will serve to spark ideas and encourage further inquiry into how, beyond cases of witchcraft, gender informed ideas about and interactions with the Devil.

Readers will also notice that the focus here is on personal piety and experience rather than on explicitly political dimensions of demonic belief. The reasons for this are two-fold. First, this book is primarily concerned with understanding the mental worlds of early modern individuals. From the onset, I have been most interested in how, in the wake of the Reformation, personal and communal perceptions of evil shaped how Scots experienced the world and conceptualized their deepest selves. In exploring these topics, an examination of Scottish politics as such has taken a backseat to a focus on religious belief and experience. That said, and to my second reason, I suspect that pulling out and isolating certain material into a designated 'politics' chapter would have been misleading and somewhat anachronistic. Early modern political motivations and religious convictions were wedded, in theory and in practice. From the earliest days of the Scottish Reformation, political goals were informed by and found expression in religious acts, and vice versa. To impose an artificial division between politics and religion when discussing the Devil would obscure the ways in which such ideas about Satan operated in tandem. Throughout the following chapters, I have thus tried to illustrate the ways in which demonic beliefs and experiences shaped how many Scots acted, simultaneously, as political actors and godly believers.

Sources

To recreate, as thoroughly and holistically as possible, the role of Satan in Scottish society and piety is a task that involves the mining of a wide array of sources. For their part, educated elites in Scotland left behind plenty of evidence of their demonic beliefs. Theological writings, manuscript and printed sermons, spiritual diaries, personal covenants, conversion narratives, letters and commonplace books have all been used in the chapters below to illustrate what Scots who were able and inclined to record their beliefs and experiences had to say about Satan.[27] To unearth

---

Martin and Miller, eds, *Witchcraft and Belief in Early Modern Scotland*, 144–65; Sierra Dye, 'To Converse with the Devil? Speech, Sexuality, and Witchcraft in Early Modern Scotland', *International Review of Scottish Studies* 37 (2012): 9–40; Julian Goodare, 'Women and the Witch Hunt in Scotland', *Social History* 23 (1998): 31–57.

[27] The majority of these sources are held at the National Library of Scotland (hereafter abbreviated as NLS) and the National Records of Scotland (hereafter abbreviated as NRS),

the beliefs of ordinary Scots who did not or could not directly record their own demonological ideas, this book examines printed broadsides, cases of witchcraft and ecclesiastical court records. Broadsides detailing murders and the last words of Scots destined for the hanging tree present, in particular, a unique combination of the opinions of educated lay and clerical authors, the preferences of printers and the tastes of a growing Scottish readership. Though these printed pamphlets cannot be accepted uncritically as indicative of popular belief, they should not necessarily be dismissed as unreflective of prevailing ideas about Satan. They suggest, at the very least, what religious ideas appealed to the consuming public.[28]

Satan, as in the instigator of sin and the source of the witches' power, featured prominently in the witch-trials in Scotland. Cases of witchcraft, which involve records of depositions, examinations by the court, confessions of the accused and testimonies of witnesses, provide an important resource for accessing the demonic beliefs from across the social spectrum. As the origins of the demonological ideas found in witchcraft records are often unclear, they require comparison with those found elsewhere. This book is the first to use the records of the Scottish kirk sessions to uncover what ordinary Scots thought about the Devil outside of cases of witchcraft. The hallmark of Reformed polity in Scotland, the kirk session was established during the Reformation and charged with enforcing moral order and implementing discipline in local communities. Most members of a Scottish community could expect to appear before the session, as a defendant, an accuser or a witness, over the course of their lifetime. As Margo Todd has persuasively demonstrated, the local nature of the session and its importance to the early modern Scottish community is difficult to over-emphasize.[29] It is in the voluminous pages of these kirk session records that the demonic beliefs of ordinary Scots are most clearly displayed.

The re-creation of belief, especially across a wide swathe of a mostly illiterate society, is a challenging and messy task. To gauge the beliefs and experiences of Scots to the greatest extent possible, this book asks questions of the relationships between divergent sources and their creators. How did spiritual diaries reflect the prevailing ideas about Satan as promoted from the pulpit? In what ways did popular broadsides contradict or

---

both in Edinburgh. Many printed sermons and theological works from the period are also available digitally at *Early English Books Online*, http://quod.lib.umich.edu/e/eebogroup/.

[28] The majority of these broadsides are housed at the NLS, and many are available on the NLS Digital Collection of Broadsides, 'The Word on the Street', http://digital.nls.uk/broadsides/. Broadsides proliferated as the seventeenth century progressed and the eighteenth century began, as the body of literature Scots slowly grew. Despite this growth, in most areas of Scotland literacy rates remained well-below 50 per cent until the eighteenth century. See R.A. Houston, 'The Literacy Myth?: Illiteracy in Scotland, 1630–1760', *Past and Present* 96 (1982): 89–91.

[29] See Todd, *Culture of Protestantism*, 8–23.

confirm the demonological ideas espoused in theological writings? How did sermons incorporate the demonic beliefs made manifest in court records and cases of witchcraft, and vice versa? In short, I hope to reveal a conversation, not just among the sources, but also between the Scottish voices and perspectives that created them. Despite different nuances in, and consequences of, demonic belief, Scots conceived their ideas about Satan from a combination of personal experiences and, to borrow a phrase from Annabel Gregory, a 'shared pool of cultural meanings'.[30] Of course, the evidence for such cultural meanings privileges elites, and in post-Reformation Scotland's case, this means the self-identified godly. With this challenge in mind, and with a wide array of sources in hand, this book aims to recreate the varied but shared demonic beliefs of early modern Scots and to uncover the profound implications of this belief for their experiences and identities.

Histories of the Devil

During the last few decades of the twentieth century, the Devil was ushered to the forefront of early modern historiography. In the case of Scotland, demonic belief has been addressed in a number of illuminating studies on witchcraft, but has yet to be examined outside of the confines of the witch-trials.[31] Historians of early modern England and Europe, however, have increasingly looked beyond witchcraft to understand the import of Satan.[32] Nearly two decades after its publication, Stuart Clark's *Thinking*

---

[30] Annabel Gregory, 'Witchcraft, Politics and 'Good Neighborhood' in Early Seventeenth Century Rye', *Past and Present* 131 (1991), 52.

[31] See, in particular, Miller, 'Men in Black', and Cowan, 'Witch Persecution and Popular Belief in Lowland Scotland', 144–65 and 71–94; Lauren Martin, 'The Devil and the Domestic: Witchcraft, Quarrels and Women's Work in Scotland', and Stuart MacDonald, 'In Search of the Devil in Fife' in Goodare, *The Scottish Witch-hunt in Context*, 73–89 and 33–50. The classic and path-breaking study of Scottish witchcraft is Larner, *Enemies of God*. For a recent survey of Scottish witch-hunting, see Brian Levack, *Witch-hunting in Scotland: Law, Politics and Religion* (New York: Routledge, 2008).

[32] Studies of the Devil and demonology in early modern Europe include Stuart Clark, *Thinking with Demons: The Idea of Witchcraft in Early Modern Europe* (Oxford: Oxford University Press, 1997); Jonathan Pearl, *The Crime of Crimes: Demonology and Politics in France, 1560–1620* (Waterloo, Ontario: Wilfrid Laurier University Press, 1999); Fernando Cervantes, *The Devil in the New World: The Impact of Diabolism in New Spain*, (New Haven, CT: Yale University Press, 1994); Nathan Johnstone, *The Devil in Early Modern England* (Cambridge: Cambridge University Press, 2006); Johnstone, 'The Protestant Devil: The Experience of Temptation in Early Modern England' *Journal of British Studies* 43 (2004): 173–205; Luttmer, 'Prosecutors, Tempters and Vassals of the Devil'; Oldridge, *The Devil in Early Modern England*. Two useful literary studies of demonology during the Renaissance are Walter Stephens, *Demon Lovers. Witchcraft, Sex, and the Crisis of Belief* (Chicago,

with Demons: The Idea of Witchcraft in Early Modern Europe remains the most extensive and innovative study of demonology in early modern Europe. Drawing from a herculean number of theological treatises and sermons, Clark argues that for Protestants and Catholics alike, demonology was not an aberrant or marginalized field of inquiry, but a central component of early modern thought. Clark's study is primarily intellectual and theoretical; his primary concern is not to trace how demonological ideas actually played out in the lives of early modern men and women. Throughout, Clark treats demonology as a high-culture phenomenon, the concern of educated elites.

Similarly and understandably, most scholars of demonology have focused on elite ideas about Satan. One notable exception to this trend is the work of Fernando Cervantes, which details how Catholic demonology intermingled with the beliefs of the Amerindians of New Spain. Though he relies mainly on literate sources, Cervantes expresses in his introduction the necessity of avoiding the pitfalls of a bipartite model of early modern religiosity:

> There is no question that the idea of the devil belongs equally to both cultures and that it cannot be forced exclusively into either of them without gross simplification and impoverishment. Consequently, the subject of diabolism emphatically requires an approach that transcends the common division into 'popular' and 'elite' groups. Only thus will it be possible to understand early modern diabolism as part of single culture in which both the popular and the educated had a share.[33]

Some twenty years after Cervantes issued this call, few works on the Devil have achieved the aim of presenting the demonic beliefs of educated and uneducated alike and placing these in dialogue as two components of an overlapping and shared whole.

Two important studies of the Devil in early modern England have begun to fill this historical lacuna. Darren Oldridge's *The Devil in Early Modern England* and Nathan Johnstone's *The Devil and Demonism in Early Modern England* broaden the study of formal demonology by analysing

---

IL: University of Chicago Press, 2003) and Armando Maggi, *Satan's Rhetoric: A Study of Renaissance Demonology* (Chicago, IL: University of Chicago Press, 2001). The most prolific scholar in the study of the Devil has been Jeffery Burton Russell, whose five-volume work on Satan spans the full range of European history from antiquity through the modern era: Jeffrey B. Russell, *Lucifer: The Devil in the Middle Ages* (Ithaca, NY: Cornell University Press, 1984); *Mephistopheles: The Devil in the Modern World* (Ithaca, NY: Cornell University Press, 1986); and *The Prince of Darkness: Evil and the Power of Good of History* (Ithaca, NY: Cornell University Press, 1988).

[33] Cervantes, *The Devil in the New World*, 3.

literary works, plays and printed pamphlets intended for the masses. Both studies demonstrate that the ideas of Protestantism led to a concept of the Devil that eschewed demonic physicality in favour of the mental threat posed by Satan. Both persuasively contend that popular ideas about the Devil's physical nature, especially in cases of witchcraft, persisted alongside the new Protestant picture of an internally subversive Devil.

Johnstone's work in particular rejects the binary, conceptual understanding of the Devil as popularized by Stuart Clark. According to Johnstone, an emphasis on contrariety implies that people understood Satan not by what he was, but what he was not. This lent the Devil a contingent reality in which he could be understood, but not felt.[34] Alternatively, Johnstone focuses on the experiential reality of Satan. His conclusions about the centrality of the Devil to the daily lives of the godly bear noteworthy similarities to the experiences of Scots discussed here. However, because he is at pains to counter any assertion that the Devil could be a metaphor or rhetorical tool, Johnstone inadvertently confines Satan to the realm of personal experience and ignores some of the important ways that patterns of demonic belief influenced culture and identity.

This book differs from both that of Oldridge and Johnstone in a few critical ways, beyond its geographical focus on Scotland. First, the pages that follow engage much more extensively with theology, asking how specific components of Reformed thought, such as total human depravity or double predestination, shaped Scottish demonic belief and engendered new ways of conceiving of the self. Second, neither Oldridge nor Johnstone situate English demonic belief in an international context, virtually ignoring Scotland and New England. Yet just as political historians of early modern Britain have embraced J.G.A. Pocock's call for British history that is transnational and inclusive, historians of British cultural and religious history have increasingly begun to look beyond borders to better understand how ways of believing and behaving developed and evolved across time and space.[35] The study of Satan demands the same approach. Thus, throughout the individual chapters of the book, I situate the Scottish demonic belief in its necessary British and Atlantic (and to a lesser extent, European) contexts. Last, while both authors devote much needed attention to the question of 'popular' belief, this they do primarily

---

[34] Johnstone, *The Devil and Demonism*, esp. 17–18.
[35] J.G.A. Pocock, 'British History: A Plea for a New Subject', *Journal of Modern History*, 47:4 (December, 1975): 601–21. A few recent examples of this inclusive British approach are Ryrie, *Being Protestant*; Alexandra Walsham, *The Reformation of the Landscape: Religion, Identity and Memory in Early Modern Britain and Ireland* (Oxford: Oxford University Press, 2011); R.A. Houston, *Punishing the Dead: Suicide, Lordship, and Community in Britain, 1500–1800* (Oxford: Oxford University Press, 2010); Claire Kellar, *Scotland, England, and the Reformation, 1534–1561* (Oxford: Oxford Historical Monograph Series, 2004).

through printed sources such as broadsides and literary works. This book adds ecclesiastical court records to this list to uncover the place of the Devil in the worldview of Scots unable to leave behind written records of their own. The aim throughout is to broaden our understanding of the ways in which demonic beliefs shaped the lived experiences and conceptions of self that pervaded post-Reformation Scottish society.

Terminology

My choice to employ the label 'Reformed Protestantism' over 'Calvinism' reflects both historical accuracy and historiographical consensus. To put it briefly, and to avoid rehashing a decades-old debate, Reformed thought was not the product solely of Calvin's theology, and the term 'Reformed Protestantism' indicates the varied and dynamic heritage of this influential strand of Protestantism.[36] The terms 'Reformed Protestant', 'godly' and 'Puritan' (when discussing England and New England) are also here used to indicate those individuals whose religious views and self-identification placed them in this zealous Protestant camp.[37] These are, of course, messy terms, and within this group there were many disagreements over specific theological, ecclesiological and political issues. For the purposes of the topic at hand, and despite the risk of oversimplification, these imperfect labels will have to suffice.

It should also be noted that though many Scottish Reformed Protestants identified as Presbyterians by the close of the sixteenth century, Presbyterianism in the strictest sense refers to the organization of church government rather than a specific set of theological beliefs. Though the majority of Presbyterians were Reformed Protestants, not all Reformed Protestants were Presbyterians. Thus on the rare occasion that the term 'Presbyterian' is used here, it is intended to denote allegiance to an ecclesiastical system (and increasingly in the seventeenth century, a political party) rather than individual religious belief. Other terminological points are clarified as needed in individual chapters.

---

[36] For the best explanation of why 'Reformed Protestant' is a more accurate term than 'Calvinist', see the introduction to Philip Benedict, *Christ's Church Purely Reformed: A Social History of Calvinism* (New Haven, CT: Yale University Press, 2002).
[37] On religious terminology in early modern Scotland, see Coffey, 'The Problem of "Scottish Puritanism"', 1590–1638'. For complications regarding the terms 'Puritan' and 'godly' when discussing England, see Patrick Collinson, 'A Comment: Concerning the Name Puritan', *Journal of Ecclesiastical History*, 31 (1980): 483–8 and Richard L. Greaves, 'The Puritan-Nonconformist Tradition in England: Historiographical Reflections', *Albion* 17 (1985): 449–86.

Structure

The first two chapters of this book are primarily concerned with the formation and articulation of theological ideas about the Devil in early modern Scotland. To provide the framework for examining how generations of men and women in post-Reformation Scotland understood the nature of the Devil, Chapter 1 begins by surveying the development of Reformed demonology by early Continental and English reformers. The jumping-off point here is John Calvin, but the aim is not to uphold Calvin as the principal figure responsible for Reformed ideas about Satan. Rather, I have chosen to focus on Calvin here primarily for reasons of economy, and also because his demonology typified rather than determined the corpus of Reformed demonological thought. This chapter then traces the adoption and adaptation of Reformed ideas by the early generation of the Protestant clergy within the tumultuous political and religious climate of Reformation Scotland. It suggests that while demonology in Scotland maintained much of its medieval character, the Reformed emphasis on divine sovereignty, double predestination and total depravity dovetailed with the rise of apocalyptic anticipation to realign and intensify demonic belief in post-Reformation Scotland.

Chapter 2 explores how Scottish ministers translated these demonological ideas into pastoral practice in hopes of influencing the beliefs and behaviours of their parishioners. From the pulpit, preachers imbued their warnings about Satan, a well-known figure to educated and uneducated Scottish audiences alike, with the more complex messages of Reformed Protestantism such as predestined election and human depravity. This chapter argues that by focusing on a figure already familiar to Scots, preachers could convey intricate theological ideas as well as political goals in terms that were both understandable and applicable to daily life.

The next chapters of the book ask how Scots of all sorts perceived and responded to Satan's involvement in their daily lives. Chapter 3 assesses the myriad of ways that Scots who were able and inclined to record their spiritual struggles and successes experienced the Devil in their daily lives. By consulting autobiographies, letters, spiritual diaries, commonplace books and personal covenants, this chapter demonstrates how personal encounters with Satan often implicated the questions of sin, self and salvation that comprised fundamental parts of Reformed Protestantism. By briefly comparing the role of the Devil in Scotland with areas of England, New England and France, Chapter 4 explores the darker side of encounters with Satan and identifies the process of 'internalizing the demonic' that occurred throughout Reformed communities in the Anglophone world. This process reveals the close and consequential relationship between the clerical promotion of self-surveillance and the widely internalized belief in the Devil's natural affinity with 'man's evil heart'. Ultimately, these chapters demonstrate the power of demonic belief to determine, in profound ways, how early modern men and women conceptualized themselves and the world around them.

The fifth chapter explores the demonic beliefs of the men and women who left behind few traces of their ideas and experiences. By mining the rich records of the Scottish kirk sessions, this chapter asks what ordinary Scots believed about the Devil and how they responded to the ideas about Satan propounded from the pulpit. It argues that the frequency and variety with which the Devil appears in the speech of ordinary men and women indicates an active blending of traditional and Reformed belief within the framework of a surprisingly accommodating Protestant demonology.

The sixth and seventh chapters explore how beliefs about and experiences with Satan informed Scottish culture and society, often in a very public way. Chapter 6 addresses the role of the Devil in cases of witchcraft and demonic possession. Drawing on the remarkable array of studies of Scottish witch-hunting, it examines the nature of demonic appearances in witchcraft cases, qualifies the oft-assumed division between 'popular' and 'elite' witch-beliefs, and contends that Scottish witchcraft depicted a composite Devil that was the product of Reformed demonology blended with traditional notions about the physicality of Satan. This chapter also examines why, while cases of witchcraft abounded in early modern Scotland, there are records of a mere eleven Scottish demoniacs, all during the later part of the seventeenth century.[38]

Finally, Chapter 7 examines the images of the Devil propagated on the Scottish streets in broadsides recounting both murders and the last words of criminals destined for the hanging tree, as well as accounts of dying Scots immortalized in cheap print. It argues that the primary function of the Devil 'on the streets' was to reify the universality of demonic temptation and to make manifest to a wide audience the admonitions about Satan and sin so often disseminated from the pulpit and experienced in spiritual diaries.

Issues of belief, experience and identity are further united in the conclusion, which asks what this study of the Devil in Scotland, and its comparison with British, Atlantic and European demonologies, reveals about the broader influence of Protestantism on early modern society and culture. While rejecting any teleological narrative about Protestantism as a desacralizing force, it contends that Reformed theology, with its unflinching emphasis on mortal depravity, eroded any rigid divide between the supernatural evil of Satan and the natural evil of humankind. It closes with a few suggestions about the legacy of this rhetorical and experiential focus on the internalization of demonic struggles.

---

[38] On the history of demonic possession in Scotland, see Levack, *Witch-hunting in Scotland*, 115–130; Levack, 'Demonic Possession in Early Modern Scotland', in Goodare, Martin, and Miller, eds, *Witchcraft and Belief*, 166–84.

CHAPTER 1

Reforming the Devil

Satan is the minister of God's wrath, and as it were the executioner, so he is armed against us, not through the connivance, but by the command of his judge.

John Calvin, 1539[1]

O Lord, confirme us in these perillous days and rages of Satan.

John Knox, 1556[2]

During the decades that followed the Scottish Reformation, a spectrum of ideas about Satan developed around the Reformed emphases on the sovereignty of God, double predestination and total human depravity. In educated circles across the country, demonic belief shifted, anxiety about the Devil intensified amid apocalyptic expectation, and perceived struggles with Satan and sin pervaded psyches. For many Scottish men and women, including those outside the clergy, beliefs about the Devil and the nature of his involvement in their lives became clarified and sharpened through the lens of a Protestant theology that was at once prescriptive and practical, communal and personal. This chapter provides a theological framework for examining this evolving role of Satan in early modern Scotland. It begins with an analysis of the demonological ideas articulated by early Continental reformers and then traces the expression and development of these ideas by the first generation of the Reformed Scottish clergy.[3] These discussions about Satan comprised a core component of the Reformation process. In the century that followed, discourses about the Devil in print, from the pulpit, in personal writings, in the courtrooms and on the streets would make manifest to Scots of all sorts Reformed ideas about sin, salvation and the human condition.

By the mid-sixteenth century, the ideas of men such as Martin Luther, John Calvin, Theodore Beza and many others had been gestating in Scotland for several decades. There, Protestantism underwent a series of

---

[1] John Calvin, *Commentaries on the Epistle of Paul the Apostle to the Romans* (1539), trans. Revd John Owen (Edinburgh: Calvin Translation Society, 1849), 305.
[2] John Knox, *Works*, vol. 6, ed. David Laing (Edinburgh: Wodrow Society, 1846), 326.
[3] 'First generation' is here defined as those Scottish divines who, through theological writings and sermons, promoted Reformed theology throughout Scotland from the beginning of the Scottish Reformation through the 1590s.

fits and starts until 1560, when the Scottish church officially and decisively severed ties to Rome.[4] The Scottish Reformation, while often opposed, slow and incomplete, thoroughly reshaped Scottish society, leaving a mark that seems especially pronounced from an international perspective.[5] While the events of the Reformation itself lie beyond the scope of this book, two aspects of its course warrant brief examination. First, the wide adoption of Protestantism in Scotland did not begin with a centralized royal mandate, but developed at the passionate, politically motivated hands of clergyman, lawyers and lesser nobility. This was not a grassroots movement, but nor was it a top-down, act of state, as was the English Reformation. The particularly localized nature of the Reformation was facilitated in no small way by the actions of the kirk sessions – ecclesiastical courts established in parishes in both Lowland and Highland Scotland.[6] Charged with furthering the goals of the Reformation through the enforcement of moral discipline, the kirk sessions disseminated new Protestant ideas to ordinary Scots while also allowing them to participate in the reforming process.[7]

---

[4] On the early struggles to get the Protestant movement successfully off the ground, followed by a revolutionary break in 1560, see Alec Ryrie, *The Origins of the Scottish Reformation* (Manchester: Manchester University Press, 2006).

[5] The consensus, even amid much scholarly debate, is that the Scottish Reformation was more thorough, lasting and peaceful than in other areas of Europe. For a discussion of the nature of the Scottish Reformation and Calvinism from an international perspective, see Philip Benedict, *Christ's Church Purely Reformed: A Social History of Calvinism* (New Haven, CT: Yale University Press, 2002), 152–72; Michael Lynch, 'Calvinism in Scotland, 1559–1638', in *International Calvinism, 1541–1715*, ed. Menna Prestwich (Oxford: Clarendon Press, 1985), 225–56, and Michael Graham, 'The Civil Sword and the Scottish Kirk, 1560–1600', in W. Fred Graham, ed., *Later Calvinism: International Perspectives* (Kirksville, MO: Sixteenth Century Journal, 1994), 237–66.

[6] On the spread of Protestantism to the Highlands, see Jane Dawson, 'Calvinism and the Gaidhealtachd in Scotland', in *Calvinism in Europe, 1540–1620*, eds. Andrew Pettegree, Alastair Duke and Gillian Lewis (Cambridge: Cambridge University Press, 1994), 231–53. Here Dawson argues that though the kind of reformation witnessed in the Lowlands did not occur in the Highlands, there was none the less the creation of a vibrant Gaelic Calvinism achieved through assimilation to Gaelic culture and institutional flexibility on the part of the Scottish church and its Highland ministers. See also Fiona A. MacDonald, *Mission to the Gaels: Reformation and Counter-Reformation in Ulster and the Highlands and Islands of Scotland 1560–1760* (Edinburgh: Scottish Cultural Press, 2006).

[7] See Margo Todd, *The Culture of Protestantism in Early Modern Scotland* (New Haven, CT: Yale University Press, 2002); John McCallum, *Reforming the Scottish Parish: The Reformation in Fife, 1560–1640* (Aldershot: Ashgate, 2010); Frank D. Bargett, *Scotland Reformed: The Reformation in Angus and the Mearns* (Edinburgh: John Donald Publishers, 1989), and Margaret H.B. Sanderson, *Ayrshire and the Reformation: People and Change 1490–1600* (East Lothian: Tuckwell Press, 1997). On the role of ecclesiastical discipline in furthering the Scottish Reformation, see Michael. F. Graham, *The Uses of Reform: Godly Discipline and Popular Behavior in Scotland and Beyond, 1560–1610* (New York: Leiden, 1996).

Second, the Reformation came to Scotland at a comparatively late date. During the 1540s and 1550s, John Knox and his fellow Scottish reformers spent considerable time among Huguenots in France, Calvinists in Geneva and their Protestant colleagues in England. While abroad, they honed their ideas about what the godly Scottish church ought to look like and how they could quickly promulgate Protestantism to the Scottish public.[8] When Knox and company returned home and pushed for revolutionary change in the late 1550s, the way forward had already been paved, at least in certain circles, by the penetration of Lutheran ideas early in the century, the influence of Reformed Protestantism from England since the 1530s, and the preaching of early reformers such as George Wishart.[9] In this context, ripe for reform and buzzing with the zeal of recent converts, Reformed theology began, irregularly but consequentially, to transform how many Scots viewed Satan and themselves.

Calvin and the Devil

The demonological ideas espoused by Calvin and other early Continental reformers built an essential foundation for the later expression of demonic beliefs and experiences in post-Reformation Scotland.[10] In the 1530s, Calvin began to write in earnest about his views on theological reform and the fledgling Protestantism, embedding his ideas about Satan within larger discussions about God, salvation and humanity. His magnum opus, *The Institutes of the Christian Religion*, was first published in Latin in

---

[8] On Knox's time in Europe, see Euan Cameron, 'Frankfort and Geneva: The European Context of John Knox's Reformation', in *John Knox and the British Reformations*, ed. Roger A. Mason (Aldershot: Ashgate, 1998). On the details of the early years of the Scottish Reformation, see Jane Dawson, *Scotland Re-formed, 1488–1587* (Edinburgh: Edinburgh University Press, 2007).

[9] See Ryrie, *The Origins of the Scottish Reformation*, 29–36.

[10] The body of work on John Calvin, in the forms of biography and theological exposition, is vast. The most famous biography of Calvin is William Bouswma, *John Calvin: A Sixteenth Century Portrait* (New York: Oxford University Press, 1988), though this is not a study of Calvin's theology. On Calvin's theology, see François Wendel, *Calvin: Origins and Development of His Religious Thought* (New York: Harper and Row, 1963); Alister McGrath, *A Life of John Calvin: A Study in the Shaping of Western Culture* (Chicago, IL: Blackwell, 1990); Donald K. McKim, ed., *Cambridge Companion to John Calvin* (Cambridge: Cambridge University Press, 2004); Paul Helm, *John Calvin's Ideas* (Oxford: Oxford University Press, 2005); and most recently, Bruce Gordon, *Calvin* (New Haven, CT: Yale University Press). For a discussion of the influence on Calvin's ideas on the religious landscape of Europe, see John T. McNeill's classic *The History and Character of Calvinism* (New York: Oxford University Press, 1954) and the comprehensive work by Philip Benedict, *Christ's Church Purely Reformed*, as well as the comparative studies mentioned in note 5, above.

1536 and marked the beginning of a thirty-year career of theological exploration, preaching and publishing.[11]

Of course, Calvin was just one important member of a large group of Protestant reformers. His theological ideas did not emerge in a vacuum, and many individuals deserve credit for the development of the Reformed tradition.[12] That said, in the case of Scotland, the influence of Calvin's thought can be directly traced through the person of John Knox, who embraced the basics of Reformed theology and Presbyterian polity during his time in Geneva. Though they emerged from divergent political contexts and differed on certain points of theology and practice such as eschatology and rebellion, Calvin directly shaped Knox's understanding of divine providence and God's attending direction of Satan's actions in the world.[13] Concurrently, the growth of French Protestantism spread Calvinist ideas to Scotland through the many political and intellectual connections between the two countries.[14] Though the theology that took root and bloomed in Scotland emerged from a varied confluence of ideas, traditions and individuals, the basic doctrines articulated by Calvin provide an accessible, though certainly not comprehensive, starting point from which to trace the development of Reformed demonological ideas in Protestant Scotland.

An uncompromising belief in the sovereignty of God dictated Calvin's understanding of Satan, as well as his general theology. Calvin's God was no passive clockmaker; divine providence shaped everything that occurred in this world and in the next. As he penned in the first chapter of his *Institutes*:

> [God] is deemed omnipotent, not because he can indeed act, yet sometimes ceases and sits in idleness, or continues by a general impulse that order of nature which he previously appointed; but because, governing heaven and earth by his providence, he regulates all things that nothing takes place without his deliberation.[15]

---

[11] The standard English translation of Calvin's *Institutes*, and the one used here, is J.T. McNeill, *The Institutes of the Christian Religion*, 2 vols (Philadelphia, PA: Westminster John Knox Press, 1960).

[12] For the best discussion of the collective development of the Reformed tradition, see Part 1 of Benedict's *Christ's Church Purely Reformed*. See also Richard A. Muller, *After Calvin: Studies in the Development of a Theological Tradition* (Oxford: Oxford University Press, 2003).

[13] See Richard Kyle, 'John Knox's Concept of Divine Providence', *Albion*, 18 (1986): 397. For a discussion of the points of divergence in Knoxian and Calvinist thought, as well as the influence of other reformers on Knox, see Richard L. Greaves, *Theology and Revolution in the Scottish Reformation* (Grand Rapids, MI: Christian University Press, 1980), esp. 217–24.

[14] For more on the relationship between Scottish and French reformers, see W. Stanford Reid, 'Reformation in France and Scotland: A Case Study in Sixteenth Century Communication', in Graham, ed., *Later Calvinism*, 195–214.

[15] *Institutes*, I.xvi.3.

This emphasis on divine authority found its most potent expression in the doctrine of double predestination. Basing his beliefs about election on Scripture, particularly on Paul's epistle to the Romans, Calvin explained in the *Institutes* that

> We say that God once established by his eternal and unchangeable plan those whom he long before determined once for all to receive into salvation, and those whom, on the other hand, he would devote to destruction. We assert that, with respect to the elect, this plan was founded upon his freely given mercy, *without regard to human worth*; but by his just and irreprehensible but incomprehensible judgment he has barred the door of life to those whom he has given over to damnation.[16]

Men and women, within whom 'nothing appears ... that is not tainted with very great impurity', had no say in the matter of salvation, which lay exclusively in the hands of God.[17]

Within the Reformed tradition, thoughts about predestination differed in terms of presentation and precise definition. Some scholars, most notably Menna Prestwich and R.T. Kendall, have contended that it was Beza rather than Calvin who made double predestination a key doctrine of Reformed theology.[18] Others have downplayed Calvin's commitment to the doctrine, and Bruce Gordon's recent biography of Calvin devotes very little attention to his thinking on predestination.[19] Yet regardless of who made predestinarianism central to Reformed thinking, Calvin undoubtedly advocated the decrees of election and reprobation in his writings. As Leif Dixon has so cogently put it, to Calvin, predestination was not a doctrine that one could simply take or leave: 'it was not a matter of taste; rather it was a Scripturally prescribed corrective to human pridefullness'.[20] The matter was not so much that postlapsarian individuals were completely

---

[16] Ibid., III.xxi.7. Calvin based his beliefs about election primarily on Romans, 9:10–18, emphasis added.

[17] Ibid., I.i.2.

[18] For a summary of historical and theological debates about the doctrine of predestination in Calvinist thought, see Richard Muller, *Calvin and the Reformed Tradition: On the Work of Christ and the Order of Salvation* (Grand Rapids, MI: Baker Academic, 2012), esp. chapter 2. For a further discussion of the development of predestination theology and the Reformation, see Muller, *Christ and the Decree: Christology and Predestination in Reformed Theology from Calvin to Perkins* (Grand Rapids, MI: Baker Academic, 1988), 79–96.

[19] Bruce Gordon, *Calvin* (New Haven, CT: Yale University Press, 2009). For a rejection of the idea that predestination was central to Calvin's thought, see also Richard Stauffer, 'Calvinism in Geneva in the time of Calvin and of Beza', in Prestwich, ed., *International Calvinism*, 34.

[20] Leif Dixon, *Practical Predestinarians in England, c. 1590–1640* (Farnham: Ashgate, 2014), 51.

devoid of goodness, but rather that they could not, on their own accord, resist the urge to sin.

More importantly, as Richard Muller has argued, 'the basic premise of the doctrine, whether formulated as a single or double decree or in infra- or supralapsarian terms, is that salvation rests on the free and sovereign elect of God and damnation results from human sin'.[21] As Calvin wrote, 'when Adam was despoiled, human nature was left naked and destitute ... when he was infected with sin, contagion crept into human nature'.[22] The original, absolute condemnation of mankind was thus 'imprinted on the heavens, and on the earth, and on all creatures', and only through God's undeserved grace, given through Christ, could people be saved.[23]

Beza, a third-generation Reformer and Calvin's hand-picked successor at Geneva, accorded even more importance to the doctrine of double predestination through his development of supralapsarianism. This was the view, most famously laid out in his *Tabula praedestinationis* (1555), that God had chosen the elect and the reprobate prior to his decree of Adam's fall, which itself then provided the just means for the predetermined damnation of some.[24] These ideas were summarized in his *Propositions and Principles of Divinity*, which would be translated and published in Edinburgh in 1591 and again in 1595. With regard to reprobation, Beza explained that God, 'according unto his eternal Predestination,' shall 'adjudge [the reprobate] together with Satan unto eternal punishments, laying open in their just destruction, the glory of his great and most just hatred against evil'.[25] This focus on double predestination would have profound consequences among the godly in early modern Scotland and elsewhere, as ordinary believers were encouraged to look tirelessly within themselves for marks of either grace or damnation.[26]

Calvin, as with most other Protestant reformers, never wrote a treatise on demonology. Discussions of Satan's relationship to God and humankind, however, appeared in many of his writings. Explaining the unequivocal master-servant relationship between the Devil and a totally sovereign God, Calvin wrote in 1539 that 'Satan is the minister of God's wrath, and as it were the executioner, so he is armed against us, not through

---

[21] Muller, *After Calvin*, 12.
[22] Calvin, *Institutes*, II.i.7.
[23] Calvin, *Commentaries on the Epistle of Paul*, 305.
[24] On Beza's predestinarian theology, see Mullan, *Christ and the Decree*, 79–96; Shawn D. Wright, *Our Sovereign Refuge: The Pastoral Theology of Theodore Beza* (Carlisle: Paternoster, 2004). Perhaps most importantly for the purposes of this book, Beza's Supralapsarian view was adopted by English Reformer William Perkins, whose works proved influential in Scotland as well as England.
[25] Theodore Beza, *Propositions and principles of diuinitie* (Edinburgh, 1591), 22.
[26] Benedict, *Christ's Church*, 302.

the connivance, but by the command of his judge'.[27] Though Satan resisted divine orders due to the desire to do all things contrary to God, he could not prevail. As Calvin explained, 'with the bridle of his power God holds him [Satan] bound and restrained, he carries out only those things which have been divinely permitted to him'.[28] In his catechism intended to 'teache children the Christiane religion', printed by the Church of Scotland in 1578, Calvin reiterated the relationship between God and the Devil in a fictional conversation between a minister and a child. 'What sayeth thou,' the minister asked, 'as touching the devils and wicked persons? Be they also subject to him [God]?' The good and godly child would respond, 'albeit that God doth not guide them with his holy spirit, yet he doth bridill them in such sorte that they be not abill to stirre or more without his permission and appointment'.[29] Even children, Calvin insisted, should know that the divine hand directed all the actions of the wicked, human and demonic alike.

In arguing that God willed all of Satan's actions, Calvin and other reformers faced the particularly pressing challenge of explaining the existence of evil in the world. Beginning with the origins of the Devil, Calvin argued that though Satan was of God's making, the wickedness of the Devil's nature 'came not from his creation but from his perversion'.[30] Created by God as angel, the Devil invited his own ruin through greed and pride. Upon his fall from grace, Satan was made an instrument of God's wrath. The key point here, and one on which Catholics and Protestants agreed, was that God himself did not create the Devil as innately and originally evil.

Perhaps Calvin's most useful metaphor in explaining how God willed Satan's actions while remaining absolved of any evil authorship was that of the sun shining on a rotting body: 'And whence, I ask you, comes the stench of a corpse, which is both putrefied and laid open by the heat of the sun? All men see that it is stirred up by the sun's rays; yet no one for this reason says the rays stink'.[31] He clarified that 'though God employs the instrumentality of the wicked', both human and demonic, the divine hand remained 'pure from sin and from taint of every kind'.[32] The problem of evil, then, was not actually a problem at all, for 'all crimes, because subject to God's ordinance, become virtues'.[33] This argument, though complicated

---

[27] Calvin, *Commentaries on the Epistle of Paul*, 77.
[28] Calvin, *Institutes*, I.xiv.17.
[29] Calvin, *The catechisme or maner to teache children the Christiane religion* (Edinburgh, 1578), 12.
[30] Calvin, *Institutes*. I.xiv.16.
[31] Ibid., I.xvii.5.
[32] Ibid., I.i.36.
[33] Ibid., I.xvii. 3.

and often pedantic, allowed Calvin to bolster the formative elements of his demonic belief: Satan operated solely under the yoke of God, Satan was irredeemably evil in contrast to a totally good God, and the Devil's activities – willed but not committed by God – carried out the divine and just plan against fallen and thus deserving men and women.

The doctrine of predestination further directed how Reformed Protestants understood the Devil's role in the world. Satan could lead the elect astray in the world but could never alter God's predestined plan. As Calvin put it, 'all who are planted by the Spirit in the Lord Jesus Christ, are beyond the danger or the chance of condemnation, however burdened they may yet be with sins'.[34] The boundaries between the reprobate and the elect could never be crossed, regardless of the Devil's actions or desires. At first glance, this concept of predestination would appear likely to mitigate concern for the Devil, whose powers had been seemingly castrated by divine sovereignty. Yet Calvin adamantly argued that this was not so. The Devil remained an obdurate, constant presence in the world. Citing I Peter 5:8, he wrote that the Devil 'goeth about like a roaring Lion seeking whom he may deuour, and he is furnished with a thousand craftes and heightes to deceiue'.[35] Beza, too, presented the Devil as 'that great devouring lion, who has spoiled, torn, and swallowed so many'.[36] Though never able to alter salvation, Satan would tirelessly strive to corrupt and hinder the faithful in their earthly lives.

Calvin did not write at length about any physical powers of the Devil, such as the ability to move objects or transform into animals or objects. He did, however, specify that the Devil and his demons were not thoughts, but 'actualities', which he defined as 'minds or spirits endowed with sense perception and understanding'.[37] He did not dwell at length on the topic, for in his view 'this matter does not require discussion among those who have faith in the Lord's Word'.[38] For the godly that would experience demonic assaults in their daily lives, Satan was clearly a reality. Calvin's only interest in including such a definition of demons in his *Institutes* was to 'equip godly minds' against the delusion that Satan and his minions might not exist, 'lest any persons, entangled in error, while thinking themselves without an enemy, become more slack and heedless about resisting'.[39]

---

[34] Calvin, *Commentaries on the Epistle of Paul*, xxxiv.

[35] Calvin, *A harmonie vpon the three Euangelists, Matthew, Mark and Luke* (London, 1584), 221. I Peter 5:8 was a passage used frequently by Scots throughout the early modern period to warn of the Devil's indefatigability. It reads: 'Be sober, be vigilant; because your adversary the Devil, as a roaring lion, walketh about, seeking whom he may devour.'

[36] Theodore Beza, *Christian Meditations upon Eight Psalmes of the Prophet David* (London, 1583), 54.

[37] Calvin, *Institutes*, I.xiv.19.

[38] Ibid.

[39] Ibid.

His musings on the nature of demons constituted a call to action and an impetus for godly discipline rather than the type of sophisticated demonological theory one finds in the writings of Aquinas and other medieval thinkers.[40] Beyond this brief discussion, Calvin had little to say about the physical mechanics of Satan and his demons.

Emphasis on the Devil's spiritual and mental prowess, however, permeated many of Calvin's works. 'For he opposes the truth of God with falsehoods', the Frenchman wrote of the Devil, and 'he obscures the light with darkness, he entangles men's minds in errors, he stirs up hatred, he kindles contentions and combats ...'.[41] Above all, Satan's ability to implant lies and doubts into the minds of all men and women was the most dangerous. Other reformers echoed and elaborated upon these demonic skills of deception. Beza explained the threat of demonic deception during prayer, when 'the devil at all times lies in wait, to seduce us, so does he, especially, at such times, seek to creep into our minds, to divert our thoughts elsewhere, that they may be polluted with many blemishes'.[42] The lies of Satan further corrupted the already doomed souls of the reprobate and attempted in vain – but not without significant social consequences – to damage those of the faithful.

While the Devil created these falsehoods and lies, Calvin maintained that men and women were inherently at fault for believing them. 'If any man doe object that this doth come to passe for the most part rather through errour then malice', he explained, 'wee may easily answere, that no man is subject to the deceits of Satan, *saue only so far foorth as he preferreth lyes before [the] truth*'.[43] Here Calvin affirmed a critical element of his theological outlook: men and women, elect and reprobate alike, were fallen and undeserving of God's grace. They instinctively preferred demonic lies to truth, not simply because of the Devil's powers of persuasion, but because of their own depravity. Second only to the direction of God, demonic activity was predicated upon this postlapsarian human condition. Good, morally upright human behaviour derived not from any free choice to overcome Satan, for total depravity meant that individuals could not keep themselves from sinning. Rather, only God's merciful aid to feeble and fallen hearts could counteract innate human tendencies. This conviction in particular – and the insistence by later divines that the

---

[40] See, for example, *The De Malo of Thomas Aquinas*, trans. Richard Regan, ed. Brian Davies (Oxford: Oxford University Press, 2001).
[41] *Institutes*, I.xiv.15–16.
[42] Theodore Beza, *Maister Bezaes houshold prayers translated out of French into English* (London, 1603), preface.
[43] Calvin, *A harmonie vpon the the three Euangelists, Matthew, Mark and Luke*, 130, emphasis added.

godly must, despite their natures, strive to combat Satan – would have a profound effect on the demonic experiences of early modern Scots.

When Protestant reformers wrote about the Devil, they were often in the midst of addressing a most crucial question: what should a godly life look like? Calvin presented this ideal life in stridently military terms, as a battle in which God and the elect were irreconcilably pitted against Satan and the reprobate. Though salvation was not at stake, the success of the Reformation was, and the elect assumed responsibility for constantly resisting the Devil and all allied with him. Additionally, Calvin averred that Devil targeted the most pious, 'for Satan in some sort trifles where he is not seriously opposed, but exerts all his strength against those who resist him: and again he is never weary with fighting, but, if conquered in one engagement, immediately commences another'.[44] Election, then, by no means lent itself to a life of spiritual leisure.

Accordingly, warfare against Satan ought to define and dominate a Christian life. 'The fact that the devil is everywhere called God's adversary and ours also ought to fire us to an unceasing struggle against him', he clarified, for 'if we are minded to affirm Christ's Kingdom as we ought, we must wage irreconcilable war against him who is plotting its ruin'.[45] Calvin portrayed this war in the *Institutes* as daunting and exhausting, but absolutely necessary:

> Our struggle is not with flesh and blood, but with the princes of the air, with the powers of darkness, and spiritual wickedness ... We have been forewarned that an enemy relentlessly threatens us, an enemy who is the very embodiment of rash boldness, or military prowess, of crafty wiles, or untiring zeal and haste, of every conceivable weapon and of skill in the science of warfare ... Since this military service ends only at death, let us urge ourselves to perseverance.[46]

Such martial imagery abounded in Calvin's works and would find constant expression in the writings and speeches of future Scots who took up the literal and figurative swords of reform.

One might argue that Reformed Protestantism, through its removal of interceding rituals and objects, left its adherents totally exposed and vulnerable to unceasing demonic assaults. This was not so. Protestant reformers maintained that Scripture would forearm the elect against the adversary, for in the words of the Bible they would find a guarantee of their eventual triumph. Despite the danger of the Devil's presence in the world, and their innate susceptibility to his wiles, the elect would ultimately

---

[44] Calvin, *Calvin's commentary on the epistle of James* (Aberdeen: J. Chalmers and Co., 1797), 82.
[45] Calvin, *Institutes*, I.xiv.15.
[46] Ibid., I.xiv.13.

triumph. 'Often, indeed, [the chosen] are distressed', Calvin wrote, 'but not so deprived of life as not to recover; they fall under violent bows, but afterward they are raised up; they are wounded, but not fatally; in short, they so toil throughout life that at the last they obtain the victory'.[47]

This relationship between Satan, divine sovereignty and predestinarian theology raises a perplexing and crucial question about the Devil's role in the Reformed Protestant world: if Satan could never alter salvation, then how does one explain the intense preoccupation with demonic temptation and subversion that plagued a Reformed Protestant area such as Scotland? If good would ultimately triumph over evil, then why should the elect fear the activities of Satan? Partly, the concern for and vigilance against Satan was driven by the pervasive desire among the godly to purify themselves and the world around them. Throughout Europe, the Reformation had provoked a renewed interest in Satan's earthly activities and relationship to humankind. The self-identified godly were concerned with the Devil because it was their duty as the chosen to combat Satan, and because earthly evils and trials reified to them the dangers of Satan as well as God's anger towards a sinful world. Victory was guaranteed, but only in death. Spiritual warfare remained a necessity and a core component of the path to assured salvation.

This promise of victory notwithstanding, Reformed theology also taught that God alone knew who was saved and who was damned. Such knowledge remained too complex and too sacred for humankind to comprehend. As Calvin put it, 'when predestination is discussed, as man cannot restrain himself within due limits, he immediately, through his rashness, plunges himself, as it were, into the depth of the sea'.[48] Of course, some assurance of faith might be gained through a conversion experience, and the doctrine of election could entail a good deal of comfort for the believer.[49] Yet salvation's ultimate unknowability often rendered the pursuit of godliness a very insecure experience. For many Scots, the inability to know, much less control, one's own fate when faced with demonic assaults proved psychologically damaging for an anxious community of would-be elects.[50]

---

[47] Ibid., I.xiv.18.

[48] Calvin, *Commentaries on the Epistle of Paul*, 353.

[49] On the comfort intended in the doctrine of predestination, see Dixon, *Practical Predestinarians*, and Jeremy Schmidt, *Melancholy and Care of the Soul: Religion, Moral Philosophy and Madness in Early Modern England* (Aldershot: Ashgate, 2007).

[50] Scholars have long recognized the psychological consequences of emphasis on the doctrine of predestination. John Stachniewski has argued that Puritanism's uncompromising focus on predestination and damnation isolated its less confident adherents because they worried that their experience of despair would be interpreted by the godly as a sign of reprobation. See John Stachniewski, *The Persecutory Imagination: English Puritanism and the Literature of Religious Despair* (Oxford: Clarendon Press, 1991), 17–61.

This insecurity over salvation combined with a prescriptive awareness of human depravity to carve Satan a powerful foothold in post-Reformation Scotland and beyond. Reformers and later clergy maintained that the Devil most aggressively pursued the elect and deemed active resistance against Satan a demonstration of one's predetermined godliness. Though actions in life were irrelevant to salvation, a man or woman of faith was compelled to act, on God's behalf, against the Devil and against their innate natures. This sense of Christian duty pervaded Calvin's writings, for, as he reminded his readers, those that are 'minded to affirm Christ's kingdom as we ought' must wage 'irreconcilable war against him who is trying to extinguish it'.[51] Suffering at the hands of the Devil was thus an intrinsic part of the godly life and could serve as a troubling but much desired sign of one's election. In Scotland, this focus on warfare would be increasingly married to the assertion that humanity's spiritual corruption, along with divine will, provided both the impetus and the means for demonic activity in the world.

Protestant and Catholic Demonology

In his seminal study of demonology and witch-belief, Stuart Clark suggests that 'if we look at the fundamental ingredients of demonology ... there does seem to be little to distinguish the Protestant from Catholic demonology'.[52] In many respects, Clark is correct. Both Catholics and Protestants believed that the Devil, who they called the father of all lies and a master deceiver, served a sovereign God. Both confessions firmly denounced the notion that God could be the author of evil, and identified men and women rather than Satan as responsible for their sins.[53] Long before Calvin, Catholic theologians had identified the powers and dangers of the internal devices and delusions of Satan. As Aquinas explained in his *Summa Theologica*, the Devil 'always tempts in order to hurt by urging man to sin. In this sense it is said to be his proper office to tempt'.[54] Yet many Catholic thinkers, Aquinas included, placed significant stress on Satan's ability to lead men and women into physical temptations of the flesh or cause bodily harm.[55]

---

[51] Calvin, *Institutes*, I.xiv.15.
[52] Clark, *Thinking with Demons*, 527.
[53] As Aquinas wrote, if 'the human will be determined to an evil counsel, is directly due to the human will, and to the devil as persuading or offering the object of appetite': Thomas Aquinas, *Summa Theologica*, ed. David Bourke, 61 vols (Cambridge: Cambridge University Press, 2006), II.1.80.
[54] Ibid., I.114.2.
[55] On this point, see Hans Peter Broedel, *The Malleus Maleficarum and the Construction of Witchcraft* (Manchester: Manchester University Press, 2003), 40–65.

Conversely, most Reformed Protestants, though they did not deny the Devil other powers, focused almost exclusively on the internal threat of Satan's enticements as manifested in unchristian thoughts and doubts.[56] Despite these differences of emphasis, however, it is important not to create dichotomies where they did not exist. Though Reformed Protestants in Scotland conceived of the Devil's presence and prowess as primarily internal, this did not negate the possibility that Satan might assume physical form and cause bodily defilement and harm.

Like their Protestant counterparts, Catholic demonologists tempered their depictions of the Devil with assertions of the sovereignty of God. The German inquisitor and demonologist Henrich Kramer reminded readers at the beginning of the *Malleus Maleficarum* that 'when they are permitted by God, evil spirits have power over physical objects and over people's imaginative faculties'.[57] The phrase 'with the permission of God' recurs throughout the *Malleus*. Renaissance historian Sydney Anglo has gone so far as to say that in the *Malleus*, the Devil, with divine permission, seemed to have been given '*carte blanche* in terrestrial affairs'.[58] In order to create a sustainable theodicy, late medieval Catholic theologians, in the tradition of Aquinas, drew a distinction between divine permission and divine will. Because God could not be the author of any evil, they argued that the misfortunes and wickedness in the world were products of his passive permission rather than his active will. Correspondingly, Aquinas and other late medieval theologians placed increasing responsibility for the suffering in the world on the Devil's figurative shoulders.[59]

Permission, though, was not enough for many Reformed Protestants, and it is here that perhaps the most discernible difference between Catholic and Protestant demonology emerges. Calvin, who derived much of his theology from Augustine, referred to the Devil being chained to hell, able to exert his influence in the world only 'whenever God loosens the chain

---

[56] For other works supporting the argument that Protestant reformers emphasized demonic temptation and subversion over demonic physicality, see Nathan Johnstone, *The Devil and Demonism in Early Modern England* (Cambridge: Cambridge University Press, 2006); Johnstone, 'The Protestant Devil: The Experience of Temptation in Early Modern England', *Journal of British Studies* 43 (2004): 173–205; Frank Luttmer, 'Prosecutors, Tempters and Vassals of the Devil: The Unregenerate in Puritan Practical Divinity', *Journal of Ecclesiastical History* 51 (2000): 37–68; Darren Oldridge, *The Devil in Early Modern England* (Stroud: Sutton, 2000).

[57] Heinrich Kramer, *The Malleus Maleficarum*, ed. P.G. Maxwell-Stuart (Manchester: Manchester University Press, 2007), 44.

[58] See Anglo, 'Evident Authority and Authoritative Evidence: The Malleus Maleficarum', in *The Damned Art: Essays in the Literature of Witchcraft*, ed. Sydney Anglo (London: Routledge and Kegan Paul, 1977), 15.

[59] Broedel, *The Malleus Maleficarum and the Construction of Witchcraft*, 72–4.

by which he is bound'.[60] Whereas writers like Henrich Kramer, author of the infamous *Malleus Maleficarum*, asserted that God gives the Devil permission to enact his evil upon the world, Calvin insisted that God not only gives the Devil the ability to act, but *wills* him to do so. He eschewed those who 'babble and talk absurdly who, in place of God's providence, substitute bare permission – as if God sat in a watch-tower awaiting chance events, and his judgments thus depended upon human will', clearly referring to the arguments of his Catholic counterparts.[61]

This absolute adherence to the sovereignty of God differentiated Reformed demonology, albeit subtly, from that of many late medieval theologians. As Euan Cameron has argued in his work on superstition in Europe, 'Calvin struck away the conventional prop of medieval demonology, the notion of "divine permission" as the space within which demonic forces could do harm. For Calvin, behind every action of Satan lay the controlling hand of an ultimately benign but also all-sovereign God'.[62] In all cases, the point of departure was the indelible will of God. Unlike his medieval predecessors, Calvin believed that men and women should remain in awe of divine decree and not probe too deeply into God's use of demons and spirits.[63] This is why, in large part, Calvin never felt inclined to write at length on what Stuart Clark has termed the 'mechanics of demonism'.[64] His discussions of the Devil, rather, reiterated core components of his larger theology by illustrating the sovereignty of God, the inescapable necessity of godly warfare and the sinful state of humanity. For Reformed Protestants on the Continent and in the Anglophone world, the true threat of Satan existed in the just wrath of God against deserving men and women. The Devil, therefore, served not only as a frightening experiential reality, but also as a powerful pastoral tool for encouraging good behaviour and creating individual and communal godly identities.

---

[60] Calvin, *Commentaries on the Last Four Books of Moses, Arranged in the Form of a Harmony*, trans. and ed. C.W. Bingham, 4 vols (Edinburgh: Calvin Translation Society, 1950), 429.

[61] Calvin, *Institutes* I.xviii.1.

[62] Euan Cameron, *Enchanted Europe: Superstition, Reason and Religion, 1250–1750* (Oxford: Oxford University Press, 2010), 214–15. Cameron sees this as a downgrade in the Devil's power, relegating the Devil into 'the area of metaphor and symbol'. I suggest, however, that while this consolidation of the Devil's power into the hands of God certainly occurred, this did not diminish the concern for or the power of demonic activity, especially not in the context of apocalypticism.

[63] Christina J. Ross, 'Scottish Demonology in the Sixteenth and Seventeenth Centuries and Its Theological Background', (PhD Thesis, University of Edinburgh, 1962), 73.

[64] Stuart Clark, 'Protestant Demonology: Sin, Superstition and Society', in B. Ankarloo and G. Henningsen, eds, *Early Modern European Witchcraft: Centres and Peripheries* (Oxford: Oxford University Press, 1990), 47.

Reforming Satan in Scotland

Armed with Scripture and encouraged by the spread of Protestantism south of the Tweed, early Scottish reformers set about the work of making their home church a bulwark of Reformed Protestantism. Of the many divines who helped turn Scotland Protestant, few figures had more to say about Satan than John Knox, considered by many to be the spiritual father of the Scottish Reformation.[65] Knox spent the majority of the 1550s in exile from Scotland for his religious convictions, travelling between England, France and Geneva. During these years, his interactions with Calvin and his growing disdain for Scotland's Catholic leadership strengthened his commitment to the beliefs and causes of Reformed Protestantism. When he returned home in 1559, Knox and his fellow reformers, including David Lindsay, John Spottiswoode, John Row and John Willock, among others, began advocating for the theology and practice that would long define the Scottish church. The introduction of Protestantism realigned and intensified demonic belief in Scotland in the generation after 1560, as demonological ideas predicated upon the sovereignty of God, predestination and total depravity were adopted, adapted and promulgated by Scottish reformers.

Within a year of Knox's return to Scotland, the Reformation was well under way, aided by the death of Mary of Guise. In August 1560, Knox and other church ministers (known collectively as 'the Six Johns') drew up *The Scots Confession of the Faith*.[66] After its quick approval by the Scottish Parliament, the break with Rome became official, though the confessional allegiance of the Scottish state remained in flux for the

---

[65] Knox, of course, did not act alone in bringing the Reformation to Scotland, though he did exercise the greatest leadership over the emerging Reformed church. Because of his publications and bold persona, Knox has long been one of the most studied figures in Scottish history. For the most comprehensive collection of his works, see John Knox, *Works*, 6 vols, ed. David Laing (Edinburgh: Wodrow Society, 1846–64). For a few of the many secondary works on Knox, see, most recently, Jane Dawson, *John Knox* (New Haven, CT: Yale University Press, 2015); James Kirk, 'The Scottish Reformation and the Reign of James VI: A Select Critical Biography', *RSCHS*, 23 (1987); Stuart Lamont, *The Swordbearer: John Knox and the European Reformation* (London: Hodder and Stoughton, 1991); Roger A. Mason, *John Knox and the British Reformations* (Aldershot: Ashgate 1998); Richard Kyle, 'John Knox's Concept of Divine Providence and its Influence on his Thought', *Albion* 18 (1986): 395–410; Richard L. Greaves, *Theology and Revolution in the Scottish Reformation: Studies in the Thought of John Knox* (Grand Rapids, MI: Christian University Press, 1980); Richard Kyle, *The Mind of John Knox* (Lawrence, KS: Coronado Press, 1984); W. Stanford Reid, *Trumpeter of God: A Biography of John Knox* (Grand Rapids, MI: Baker, 1974).

[66] For the text of the Scots Confession of 1560, see Arthur C. Cochrane, ed., *Reformed Confessions of the Sixteenth Century* (Philadelphia, PA: Westminster Press, 1966), 159–84. For an analysis of the theology of the Scots Confession, see W. Ian P. Hazlett, 'The Scots Confession 1560: Context, Complexion and Critique', *Archiv für Reformationsgeschichte* 78 (1987): 287–320.

next few decades.[67] From the outset, militant Protestantism characterized post-Reformation demonic belief in Scotland. *The Scots Confession*, a document that was both a declaration of Scotland's embrace of Reformed Protestantism and a melange of the formative beliefs of the nascent Reformed church, exemplified this communal and personal militancy.[68] The confession asserted that when Scots realized their membership in the true church, they would be compelled by their election to engage in a lifelong battle against the Devil and their own corruptions, which operated in tandem. 'Thence comes that continual battle', it read, 'which is between the flesh and Spirit in God's children', whom the confession defined as those 'yet live and fight against sin and Satan as shall live hereafter'.[69] *The Scots Confession* cited the Devil no less than ten times and was unique among other Reformed Confessions in the extent to which it depicted the Scottish church as engaged in an ongoing, apocalyptic battle against the Satan.[70] This was not just a passive declaration of theological convictions. As Ian Hazlett has asserted, *The Scots Confession* comprised 'a manifesto, a zealous proclamation, a prophetic call to action', driven by a vision of demonic struggle in the context of political and religious upheaval.[71]

Behind *The Scots Confession* lay the person and perspective of Knox, whose identity and theology was bound up in the struggle against Satan. Many of Knox's demonological ideas derived from the basics of Reformed theology articulated by Calvin. Most important were the concepts of divine immutability and sovereignty.[72] 'To what miserie', Knox wrote, 'were we

---

[67] The battle to implement Reformed theology throughout Scotland continued to rage during the Catholic reign of Mary Queen of Scots, who was forced to abdicate the throne in 1567. Her son, the future king James VI and I of Scotland, was only thirteen months old, and saw four different regents reign during his minority. It was not until the late 1580s, when James VI began to assert his authority, that some political and religious stability was reached. On the relationship between Knox and Mary Queen of Scots, see Jenny Wormald, 'Godly Reformer, Godless Monarch: John Knox and Mary Queen of Scots,' in *John Knox and the British Reformations*, ed. Roger A. Mason (Aldershot: Ashgate, 1998), 220–41. On the turmoil of the relationship between church and state through in the first generation after the Reformation, see Jane Dawson, *Scotland Re-formed, 1488–1587*.

[68] Philip Benedict has noted that though it was certainly Reformed in character, the *Scots Confession of Faith* was not distinctly Calvinist. He states that it 'sidestepped' the issue of predestination and emphasized ecclesiastical discipline in the tradition of Bucer rather than Calvin. However, various sections on election and good works implicitly, if not explicitly, discussed the issue of predestination, even if it was not the centrepiece of the confession. See Benedict, *Christ's Church*, 162.

[69] Hazlett, 'Scots Confession, 1560'.

[70] Benedict, *Christ's Church*, 162.

[71] Hazlett, 'Scots Confession, 1560', 295.

[72] Richard Kyle, 'John Knox's Concept of Divine Providence', esp. 395–7. As Kyle rightly points out, though Knox and Calvin differed on a number of theological issues, most notably apocalyptic thought and resistance to political authority, there was a 'striking resemblance' between their concepts of divine providence, defined by Kyle as 'God's

exposed, if we should be persuaded, that sathan and the wicked might or could do any thing, otherwiese then God hath appointed ... '.[73] Calvin had actually written to Knox about the issue of divine providence in a 1561 letter discussing the demonically inspired opposition facing the Scottish reformers. Attempting to calm Knox's unease over recent struggles, Calvin reassured him that 'the power of God is the more conspicuously displayed in this, that no attacks either of Satan or of the ungodly have hitherto prevented you from advancing with triumphant consistency in the right course ... unless He who is superior to all the world had held you out from heaven a helping hand'.[74] Such concepts endowed Knox with an unflinching faith in the providence of God and the eventual victory of the faithful, which allowed him to pursue the reformation of religion with uncompromising intensity.[75]

Such discussions of the relationship between the power of the Devil and the will of God found expression in the works of other Scottish reformers who, like Knox, constructed their demonological ideas around the principle of divine sovereignty. In 1581, minister John Craig published a summary of the ideas from Calvin's catechism, intended 'for the greater ease of the commoune people and children'.[76] After a series of questions and answers detailing the creation of man and the sovereignty of God, Craig posed the question of 'who ruleth Sathan and all his instrumentis?' The answer, 'our God also, by his almighty power and providence', mirrored that found in Calvin's own catechism for children published in Edinburgh three years prior.[77]

This confinement of the Devil's powers to the yoke of God by no means undermined the threat of Satan and the necessity of combat. In a world torn between the forces of Good and Evil, perpetual warfare – both externally and internally – was a necessary fact of life. No doubt

---

permanent and universal activity in the world'. The concept of divine providence derived from Knox's (and Calvin's) concept of God, which revolved around divine immutability and sovereignty. Kyle defines divine immutability as 'that perfection of God by which he is devoid of all change, not only in his being, but in his perfections, and in his purposes and promises', and divine sovereignty as God's 'absolute authority over the hosts of heaven and the inhabitants of earth, that he upholds all things in his mighty power, and he determines the ends which they are destined to serve.'

[73] Knox, *An answer to a great nomber of blasphemous cauillations written by an Anabaptist, and aduersarie to Gods eternal predestination* (Edinburgh, 1560), 21.

[74] Calvin, *Letters*, 4 vols, ed. David Constable (Edinburgh: Thomas Constable and Co., 1855), iv.184.

[75] Richard Kyle, 'The Divine Attributes in John Knox's Concept of God', *Westminster Theological Journal*, 48 (1986): 161–72.

[76] John Craig, *A shorte summe of the whole catechisme, wherein the question is proponed and answered in few wordes, for the greater ease of the commoune people and children* (Edinburgh, 1581), 13.

[77] Ibid.

influenced by his radicalization during the violent Marian restoration in England, and perhaps as a product of his own pugnacious personality, combativeness infused Knox's demonic belief.[78] As he stated in a sermon delivered in Edinburgh in 1565, 'there is two heads and captaines that rule upon the whole worlde, to wit, Jesus Christ, the Prince of justice and peace, & Sathan, called the Prince of the worlde, so are they but two armies, that hath continued battaile from the beginning, and shall fight unto the ende'.[79] In his *Fort for the Afflicted*, published in 1580 to comfort for the godly, Knox explained that

> ... from the service of the Devil and sin, [God] hath annointed us Priestes and Kings ... hee hath given you courage and boldnesse to fight against more cruel, more suttle more dangerous, and against enemies that be more nigh unto you, then either was the Lyon, the Beare or Goliah to Dauid: against the Deuil I meane, and his assaultes, against your owne fleshe, and most inwarde affections, against the multitude of them that were (and yet remaine) enemies to Christes religion.[80]

Future generations of Scottish Protestants would structure their ideas around a similar militancy that, in effect, made discussions of warring with Satan intrinsic to discussions of God.[81]

Other Scottish reformers emphasized the unyielding duty of the godly against Satan. David Fergusson, minister of Dunfermline, encouraged Scots to be ever wary of their vigilant adversary. 'Ye knowe planely', he said

> ... if that ye loke ouer the Scripture with humilitie the slight and desait of Sathan (Christes and all Christianes enimies) for to misreule and disturb the trew Kirk and his furious interpryses ... Take head therfore I adiure you welbeloued and Christiane brethren, that ye be not Seduced with his subteltie and craftiness.[82]

---

[78] Jane Dawson has pointed out that Christopher Goodman, who was part of the English exile congregation in Geneva and a very close friend of Knox, greatly influenced Knox's ideas about political radicalism and militancy for the sake of reformation. See Dawson, 'Trumpeting Resistance: Christopher Goodman and John Knox', in *John Knox and the British Reformations*, ed. Roger A. Mason (Aldershot: Ashgate, 1998).

[79] Knox, *A sermon preached by Iohn Knox minister of Christ Iesus in the publique audience of the Church of Edenbrough* (Edinburgh, 1566), 46.

[80] Knox, *A fort for the afflicted VVherin are ministred many notable & excellent remedies against the stormes of tribulation* (London, 1580), n.p.

[81] On this point, see Roger A. Mason, 'Usable Pasts: History and Identity in Reformation Scotland', *Scottish Historical Review* 76 (1997), 58.

[82] David Fergusson, *Ane answer to ane epistle written by Renat Benedict* (Edinburgh, 1563), 19.

Though election protected the godly from the experience of hell, they were nevertheless subject to and compelled to resist the earthly onslaughts of Satan. As Knox had averred, true godliness would require not only the abnegation of sin, but also active combat against the sins of others.[83] This vigilant, unyielding Knoxian mindset, combined with the specific political situation of Scotland, lent a notable immediacy and militancy to Scottish demonic beliefs in the wake of the Reformation. Calvin's Devil had been a necessary instrument of God's divine plan. For the early generation of Scottish reformers and their heirs, Satan proved a more discernible and immediate foe to be combated as part of an ongoing project of godly discipline.

Emphasis on the internal assaults of Satan and their invitation by innate human weakness shaped the demonic admonitions of sixteenth-century Scottish divines. Robert Bruce's series of sermons on the sacrament of the Lord's Supper in 1589 detailed the many corruptions of humanity, which were like a 'canker and venom quhilk [which] the devil hath spued into our hearts'.[84] He explained that the 'devill is so craftie, in this point, that he erects ever ane idol or uther in our saul; and sometimes under the shew of vertue, quhilkof all is maist dangerous'.[85] Near the close of the century, James Melville warned his audiences that 'Sathan seeks by distrust and infidelity, grieuously to afflict & deject the minds of Gods children'.[86] Such language of soul, heart and mind would reoccur frequently in the Scottish sermons of the next century, reinforcing the emphasis on Satan's internal prowess and the inescapable closeness of human lives and demonic presences.

Many Scottish reformers sought to historically and scripturally contextualize these incessant struggles against the Devil by conceiving of themselves and the Scottish nation as the New Israel, with their church as God's chosen covenant. As Michael Lynch explains, it was in these early years that 'the myth of the perfection of the Scottish kirk was born'.[87] This myth gave birth to a Scottish identity that revolved around historicized self-fashioning as elected warriors against the Devil in a battle that was internal and individual as well as communal and political. Using the rhetoric of an ancient struggle, *The Scots Confession* stated that 'Satan has

---

[83] On this point, see Julian Goodare, 'John Knox on Demonology and Witchcraft', *Archive for Reformation History* 96 (2005): 221–45.

[84] Robert Bruce, *Sermons*, ed. by William Cunninghan (Edinburgh: Wodrow Society, 1843), 354.

[85] Ibid.

[86] James Melville, *Ane fruitful and comfortable exhortatioun anent death* (Edinburgh, 1597), 62.

[87] Michael Lynch, 'Calvinism in Scotland, 1559–1638', in *International Calvinism, 1541–1715*, ed. Menna Prestwich (Oxford: Clarendon Press, 1985), 225–56, 232.

labored from the beginning to adorn his pestilent synagogue with the title of the Kirk of God, and has incited cruel murderers to persecute, trouble, and molest the true Kirk and its members'.[88] As its authors averred, only in death, when they would be 'delivered from all fear and torment, and all the temptations to which we and all God's chosen are subject in this life', could the elect finally retire from this inherited battle.[89]

The combative, disciplinary ardour of Knox and other reformers stemmed in no small part from their opposition to the Catholic Church. To them, the 'papists' were Satan's army *par excellence*. In the latter half of the sixteenth century, fears over Scotland's lapsing into 'popery' ran rampant, especially in response to the monarchical turmoil surrounding Mary Queen of Scots. This political context informed discussions of the Devil among Scottish reformers, some of whom referred to the Catholic Church as the 'synagogue of Satan'.[90] Interestingly, this was the same language used in Scotland to describe imagined assemblies of witches, as the Mass itself became viewed as a diabolical act akin to the tacit pact made in servitude of Satan. As Knox wrote in his *Godly Letter to the Faithful in London* of 1554, 'God may not abyd that our bodies serve the devill in joyning ourselves with ydolatrie'.[91] Knox saw himself as a prophet of sorts, issuing a call to arms against Satan broadly and Catholics specifically, calling them 'pestilent papists' and 'sons of the Devil'.[92] Any and all actions of the Catholic Church were viewed as part of Satan's grand attempt to destroy the rebuilding of Zion and establishment of the true religion in Scotland and beyond.

The Privy Council's 1572 description of events surrounding the Saint Bartholomew's Day Massacre made manifest this association between Satan and the Catholic Church. 'The grit murtheris and mair then beistlie crewelteis usit and put in execution in diverse partis of Europe agains the trew Christianis', it claimed, 'proceidit na doubt out of that unhappy devillishe and terrible Counsall of Trent'.[93] Similar rhetoric would be used well into the seventeenth century, when the upheaval of the Bishops' Wars and other events stoked the fearful observation that 'manie ar stirred up by Satan and that Romane antichrist' to hinder, corrupt and 'subvert secreitlie Gods true religion within the Kirk'.[94] The Devil provided an accessible

---

[88] Hazlett, 'Scots Confession, 1560'.
[89] Ibid.
[90] See, for example, Fergusson, *Ane answer*.
[91] Knox, *Works*, vol. 3, 196–7.
[92] As quoted in Goodare, 'Knox on Demonology', 227; for a discussion of the ways in which Knox's identity was bound up in his battle against Catholicism, see Kyle, *The Mind of John Knox*.
[93] *Register of the Privy Council of Scotland 1569–1578*, series 1, vol. 2, 168.
[94] *Register of the Privy Council of Scotland, 1638–1643*, series 2, vol. 7, 69.

vocabulary for Scottish leaders to describe a host of spiritual and political enemies of the church, ranging from the Pope to witches to (later) Charles I, while also lending an immediacy and scriptural imperative to combating these foes.

Scottish reformers took care to remind their audiences that despite this perpetual war, the ultimate victory was firmly theirs. As Fergusson averred, 'Sathan can not take Christes name from you ... I warne you of charitie for your weill and Saluation, that he pluk not Christe him self from you'.[95] Knox asserted that in order to endure demonic afflictions in particular, the godly must hold fast to the knowledge that in the end they would prevail, for, as he put it, 'the knowledge of this is so necessarie to the afflicted conscience, that without the same, it is verie harde to withstande the assaultes of the aduersarie'.[96] Bruce echoed this promise of victory in the face of assaults from without and within when he reiterated that 'being sanctified, in despite of the divell and of the corruption that is in us, this faith shall never perish!'[97] In trying times, early Scottish divines deployed the doctrine of predestination to reassure and comfort their flocks in face of Satan and other obstacles. Comfort this did – at least for the lucky ones confident in their own election.

An anonymous book of prayers and meditations published in Edinburgh in 1591 demonstrates how the above ideas found popular expression in print. Employing a straightforward, suggestive language, this collection addressed diverse issues such as weather, sickness, hope and despair. It included an extended prayer 'against the temptations of Sathan', intended to communicate Reformed demonological ideas and proper godly behaviour to its audience. This prayer commenced with a call to God to 'protect and strengthen us weake and terrible ones, against the tentations of Sathan'.[98] The language of humanity as 'weake and terrible' almost always attended and often pre-empted discussions of the 'unspeakable subtiltie' of Satan who, as the prayer notes, 'layed snares to entrap our soules' and hoped to cast Christians 'headlong into extreme desperation'. Using evocative imagery to highlight the indefatigability of Satan, the anonymous author – very likely a clergyman – detailed how 'night and day, whether we sleepe or wake, hee is about us, and with foaming mouth and open jawes'.[99]

As Reformed theologians had insisted for decades, total human depravity left men and women completely reliant on God for deliverance

---

[95] Fergusson, *Ane answer*, 19.
[96] Knox, *A fort for the afflicted*, n.p.
[97] Bruce, *Sermons*, 151.
[98] Anon., *The sacrifice of a Christian soule conteining godlie prayers, and holy meditations for sundry purposes; drawne out of the pure fountaines of the sacred Scriptures* (Edinburgh, 1591), 211.
[99] Ibid., 211–13.

from these demonic assaults. 'No ayde, prudence, or pollicie is in our nature against so strong and subtill an enemie', the prayer read, for 'our nature is accursed and uncleane, our fleshe is weake, our life transitorie'.[100] The prayer closed with a request that God aid spiritually feeble humans in their struggles against Satan, invoking the militancy that had become a mainstay of Scottish religious thought: 'give us thy whole armoire that like right soldiers wee may resist the evill day and vanquish our Enemie'.[101] This collection of prayers, published three decades after the Reformation, thus epitomized the interdependent elements of human depravity, demonic ubiquity and divine sovereignty that had become central to Reformed Protestant thinking about Satan in Scotland.

The Devil Unloosed

While concern for the Devil's actions in the world comprised a small yet essential component of Calvin's writings, Satan loomed larger and more nefarious in the works of early Scottish reformers and in the minds of future Scottish divines, who increasingly placed demonic activity within the contexts of political turmoil and personal depravity. This intense anxiety about the Devil's involvement in Scotland was evidenced by the feverish witch-hunting that began in the 1590s, driven in large part by the diabolical definitions of the crime of witchcraft.[102] Perhaps even more important than witch-belief, the Scottish clergy explicitly linked the Devil to all manner of spiritual failings, including sexual crimes, religious deviance, moral vices such as drinking or gambling, and to historical phenomena past and present. The prevalence of Satan in post-Reformation Scotland extended far beyond church walls and found expression in the spiritual diaries, personal poetry, street literature and court cases of the late sixteenth and seventeenth centuries.

All of this raises the question of why, beyond a sense of godly duty, Reformed Protestants in Scotland were so concerned with the *imminent* danger of Satan – far more than Calvin himself seems to have been – when their salvation was never at stake. The answer appears to stem, at least in part, from the rising influence of apocalyptic thought in early modern Scotland. As Reformed theology took root and flourished there, reformers adapted Calvin's demonology to fit the Scottish context, informed by their own cultural experiences and facing a mess of political, social and religious issues. Inspired by the turmoil of the age, these Scots increasingly believed

---

[100] Ibid., 214.
[101] Ibid., 216.
[102] See Levack, *Witch-hunting*, 11.

that they were living in the Last Days. As Carol Edington has explained, this apocalyptic explanation appealed to early reformers 'engaged in the hazardous business of rebellion', and also to a great many of the Scottish population who in recent years had 'seen their country devastated by war, plague and political crisis'.[103] According to the faithful, this recent strife resulted from the Devil's ever-increasing action in the world, which was itself the ultimate indicator of the coming of the End Times. In this volatile context, apocalypticism became a formative component of Reformed theology, and in turn, demonic belief in Scotland.[104]

The prevalence of apocalyptic thought was not unique to Scotland, of course. Protestants throughout early modern Britain and Europe increasingly focused on preparing and purifying their respective communities for the impending Apocalypse.[105] In his study of Puritan migration to New England, Avihu Zakai argues that the Protestant Reformation itself made way for a new mode of historical consciousness, based in part on the legacy of Augustine's own eschatology. In *City of God*, Augustine contended that the fall of Adam marked the beginning of a sacred, preordained history defined by the apocalyptic struggle between 'two societies of human beings, one of which is predestined to reign with God for all eternity, the other doomed to undergo eternal punishment with the devil'.[106] This apocalyptic vision of society propelled,

---

[103] Carol Edington, 'John Knox and the Castillians: A Crucible of Reforming Opinion', in *John Knox and the British Reformations*, ed. Roger A. Mason (Aldershot: Ashgate, 1998), 29–50, p. 46.

[104] See Arthur Williamson, *Scottish National Consciousness in the Age of James VI: the Apocalypse, the Union, and the Shaping of Scotland's Public Culture* (Edinburgh: John Donald Publishers, 1979). Williamson has argued that the apocalyptic impulse in Scotland did not form as central a component of Scottish political thought as it had in England. None the less, he recognizes the centrality of apocalypticism to the theology and mission of the Scottish church. On the importance of apocalypticism to the Scottish Covenanters, see Sidney Burrell, 'The Apocalyptic Vision of the Early Covenanters', *Scottish Historical Review*, 43 (1964), and John Coffey, 'Impact of Apocalypticism, during the Puritan Revolutions', *Perichoresis*, 4 (2006): 117–147, pp. 122–5. For a survey of Scottish apocalypticism in the seventeenth century, see David Drinnon, 'The Apocalyptic Tradition in Scotland' (PhD Thesis, University of St Andrews, 2013).

[105] See Coffey, 'Impact of Apocalypticism'; P. Toon, *Puritans, the Millennium and the Future of Israel: Puritan Eschatology 1600–1660* (Cambridge: Cambridge University Press, 1970); Richard Bauckham, *Tudor Apocalypse: Sixteenth-Century Apocalyptism, Millenarianism and the English Reformation* (Oxford: Oxford University Press, 1978); Paul Christianson, *Reformers and Babylon: English Apocalyptic Visions from the Reformation to the Eve of the Civil War* (Toronto: University of Toronto Press, 1978); C.A. Patrides and J. Wittreich, eds, *The Apocalypse in English Renaissance Thought and Literature* (Manchester: Manchester University Press, 1984); Katharine R. Firth, *The Apocalyptic Tradition in Reformation Britain, 1530–1645* (Oxford: Oxford University Press, 1979).

[106] As quoted in Avihu Zakai. *Exile and Kingdom: History and Apocalypse in the Puritan Migration to America* (Cambridge: Cambridge University Press, 1992), 77.

as Arthur Williamson has written, Satan into 'an unprecedented place in Scottish thinking' during the 1590s.[107] The Devil's primacy in Scotland would continue well into the seventeenth century and, in some circles, well beyond.

For his part, Calvin remained wary of apocalyptic preaching that might hint at radicalism, due in part to the turmoil he witnessed during the violent 1535 millenarian uprising in Munster.[108] Among his many scriptural commentaries, he never wrote at length on the Book of Revelation. He did refer to the existence of the Antichrist, whom he identified with the papacy as well as the Turks, stating that Satan had led both groups astray 'for the purpose of setting up a seat of abomination in the midst of God's temple'.[109] Calvin did not speculate as to when Christ would come again or when the world would end.[110] As with many other things, he believed firmly that this was for God, and God alone, to know.

Knox, on the other hand, did not shy away from apocalyptic inquiries. He was one of the earliest reformers in Britain to espouse eschatological concerns in his writings and sermons.[111] During the early years of the Scottish Reformation, he grew increasingly preoccupied with the coming of the Last Days. His apocalyptic thought provided an essential backdrop for how he interpreted both Christian duty and demonic activity. For Knox, the Apocalypse was nigh, and the cosmic struggle between God's servants and those of Satan was coming to a head, fulfilling the prophecies of the Old Testament.[112] In particular, his conviction that the Day of Judgement was imminent helps to explain the intense militancy of his theology.

According to Knox, the Devil had always raged, but his fury seemed to grow in his lifetime more than ever before, a sure sign of the coming End Times. In an early work composed in 1554, he told how 'the whole powers of my body tremble and shake for the plag[u]es [that] are to come'.[113] Elaborating upon the depiction of Satan as increasingly active in the

---

[107] Williamson, *Scottish National Consciousness*, 55. Williamson argues that the rise in witchcraft prosecutions in Scotland and the attending emphasis on the demonic pact indicated the new important of Satan in Scottish thought.

[108] Firth, *Apocalyptic Tradition*, 22.

[109] John Calvin, *Commentaries on the Epistle of Paul the Apostle to the Philippians, Colossians, and Thessalonians*, trans. John Pringle (Grand Rapids, MI: Eerdmans, 1948).

[110] David Holwerda, 'Eschatology and History: A Look at Calvin's Eschatological Vision', *Exploring the Heritage of John Calvin*, ed. David E. Holwerda (Grand Rapids, MI: Baker Academic, 1976).

[111] Richard Kyle, 'John Knox and Apocalyptic Thought', *Sixteenth Century Journal* 15:4 (1984): 449–70.

[112] Ibid.

[113] Knox, *An admonition or vvarning that the faithful Christia[n]s in London, Newcastel Barwycke [and] others, may auoide Gods vengeau[n]ce bothe in thys life and in the life to come* (London, 1554), n.p.

world, and in Scotland specifically, Knox composed a prayer in the 1560s that lamented how his homeland had 'fallen in these latter dayes, and dangerous times, wherein ignorance hath gotten the upper hand, and Satan with his ministers seke by all meanes to quenche the light of thy Gospel'.[114] In an apocalyptic sermon preached in 1565 in Edinburgh, he continued to warn of the coming judgement and of the attendant wrath of God. He told the congregation to 'flatter not thy self, the same justice remaineth this day in God to punishe thee Scotlande, and thee Edenborough in especiall, that before punished the lande of Juda, and the citie of Jerusalem'.[115] With language that was at once historical and immediate, Knox made clear that the elect too would experience the pain and punishment wrought by the Apocalypse, despite their eventual deliverance.

David Fergusson echoed these dangers of the impending Last Days. 'I besech you', he implored his fellow Scots, 'that ye deceaue not your selues, and namely in these last and moste perrellous dayes, of the which the holy write prophecieth and affirmeth ...'.[116] According to a 1591 collection of prayers, at the heart of this peril lay the raging of Satan, 'especiallie in this doting age of the worlde, as he knoweth his time of raigning is but short ... the day of judgement be very nigh at hand, wherein his filthiness shall be made manifest to all creatures ... so now he rageth in a deadlie hatred against thy flock'.[117] These eschatological warnings served four interlocking theological and pastoral purposes: to encourage the public to purify themselves and police the actions of their community in order to avoid additional wrath of God; to augment the reliance of the populace on the church; to warn Scots of the demonic rumblings and rages going on around them; and to historically and scripturally contextualize the turmoil experienced by the Reformation generation.

Scotland's first Protestant king, James VI, contributed in his prolific writings to the development of the Scottish apocalyptic tradition. In 1588, he published *Ane fruitfull meditation*, an extensive theological commentary on the Book of Revelation. Though his ideas were not especially original, the monarchical endorsement of Protestant eschatology was, and no doubt his work augmented the place of apocalypticism in post-Reformation Scotland.[118] In the introduction, James explained that 'of all buikes the holie Scripture is maist necessarie for the instructioun of

---

[114] Knox, *Works*, vol. 6, 347.
[115] Knox, *A sermon*, 11.
[116] Fergusson, *Ane answer*, 18.
[117] Anon., *The sacrifice of a Christian soule*, 211–12.
[118] On this point, see Bernard Capp, 'The Political Dimension of Apocalyptic Thought,' in C.A. Patrides and J. Wittreich, eds, *The Apocalypse in English Renaissance Thought and Literature: Patterns, Antecedents and Repercussions* (Manchester: Manchester University Press, 1984), 102 and Drinnon, 'The Apocalyptic Tradition in Scotland', 20.

a Christiane, and of all the Scriptures, the buik of the Reuelatioun is the maist meit for this our last age, as a prophecie of the latter tyme'.[119] During the final years of the sixteenth century, James believed that the world had entered into its closing days and that the godly should act accordingly. His commentary explicitly cited the connection between the Apocalypse and the augmentation of Satan's involvement in the world, for 'the divel, having bene bound, and his power in his instruments having bene restrained for a long space ... is loosed out of hell by the raising up of so many new ereors and notable evil instruments'.[120] In Revelation, Reformed Protestants in Scotland found a scriptural basis for why Satan appeared so active in the world during their lifetimes.

In particular, James saw the evidence of 'Satan's loosing' in the actions of the Catholic Church, infusing his apocalyptic thought with an overtly political message. He explained that in Revelation, 'by Satan is meant not onely the Dragon, enemie to Christ and his Church, but also with him all the instruments in whom he ruleth, and by whom he ruleth, and by whom he uttereth his cruell and crafty intentions, specially the Antichrist and his Clergie'.[121] Here, by unambiguously identifying the Pope as the Antichrist, James placed the events prophesied in Revelation within the context of the current struggles against 'popery' in Scotland. His apocalypticism also informed his witch-belief; a decade later, he would close *Daemonologie*, the only demonological treatise written by a European monarch, with the admonition that 'the consummation of the Worlde, and our deliverance drawing near, makes Sathan rage the more in his instruments, knowing his Kingdome to be so near an ende'.[122] This preoccupation with the approaching Apocalypse fuelled the ardent desire of James, and many others who came before and after, to rid the world of contaminants like Catholicism, irreligion and witchcraft during its waning days.

In the last decade of the sixteenth century, John Napier, an influential Scottish mathematician and astrologer (among other academic pursuits), composed a study of Revelation titled *A Plaine Discovery of the Whole Revelation of Saint John*. In the epistle dedicatory, he implored his king to move towards 'that great and universall reformation and destruction of that Antichristian seat and citie Rome'.[123] Analysing the text of Revelation within the historicist eschatological tradition, Napier concluded that based

---

[119] James VI and I, *Ane fruitfull meditatioun contening ane plane and facill expositioun of ye 7.8.9 and 10 versis of the 20 chap. of the Reuelatioun in forme of ane sermon* (Edinburgh, 1588), introduction.

[120] Ibid.

[121] Ibid.

[122] James VI and I, *Daemonologie* (Edinburgh, 1597), 81.

[123] Robert Clouse, 'John Napier and Apocalyptic Thought,' *Sixteenth Century Journal*, 1 (1974): 101–14.

on the time elapsed between the foundation of the Roman church and the start of the Reformation, Satan had been bound for over one thousand years. The Devil was thus, according to Scripture, loosed.[124] Using other Protestant commentaries as well as original calculations, he went on to predict that the final 245 years of history would take place between 1541 and 1786.[125] Napier's commentary on Revelation was printed in 1593, 1611 and 1645 in Edinburgh, as well as twice in London and many times abroad. As one of the first works to posit possible dates for the end of world, Napier's commentary accelerated expectations about the coming of the Apocalypse and Satan's attendant machinations by placing this paramount event in the foreseeable future.

As Stuart Clark has pointed out, a major question posed by witchcraft theorists and theologians more generally was why the Devil and his agents were more active at present than in the past.[126] Clark contends that the perception of increased demonic action in the world, manifested above all by witchcraft, propagated among theologians a progressively apocalyptic understanding of their age.[127] In the case of the Scottish reformers, however, the prevalence of apocalypticism also provided a *basis* for viewing the Devil as increasingly active in the world. Belief that the Last Days loomed near served as a precondition of understanding Satan's worldly involvement as much as an explanation for heightened demonic activity. Prior to the Apocalypse, God would keep the Devil completely in check, using Satan as his agent for punishment but restricting his endeavours. The total sovereignty of God could not allow for the Devil's actions to go unmitigated. In the Last Days, however, God loosed Satan's chain, still willing his actions but endowing him with more influence than before. In many respects, the perception that the Apocalypse was nigh allowed Scottish Protestants to reconcile their understanding of the absolute sovereignty of God with the evidently growing power of the Devil and his army.

---

[124] Firth, *Apocalyptic Tradition*, 145. It is worth nothing here that most Scots were, at this time, amillenialists or nonmillenialists who asserted that the thousand years referenced in Revelation were likely symbolic, referring to the history of the Christian church prior to the Reformation. Christ would remain in heaven until Judgement Day, when the elect would be forever separated from the reprobate and the rages of Satan. According to them, to believe in a literal millennium was not only erroneous; it was heretical and potentially dangerous. On the apparent tension between this simultaneous binding of Satan, the reign of the Catholic Church, and the ensuing rise of millenarianism proper in seventeenth-century Britain, see John Coffey, 'The Impact of Apocalypticism'. For a larger discussion of the ways in which Scottish apocalypticism diverged from its English counterparts, particularly over the issue of millenarianism, see David Drinnon, 'The Apocalyptic Tradition in Scotland'.

[125] Ibid., 144.
[126] Clark, *Thinking with Demons*, 315.
[127] Ibid., 321–63.

Apocalyptic thought in Scotland thus influenced demonic belief in three primary ways. First, it provided a scriptural basis for understanding the Devil's augmented power in the world in conjunction with God's divine immutability. Second, apocalyptisicm explained and historically contextualized recent religious, political and social turmoil in early modern Scotland, buttressing accusations of the Pope as the Antichrist and solidifying a view of the world as polarized between warring armies of God and Satan. Third, the belief that they were living in the Last Days caused the Devil to become an all-the-more terrible and tangible figure to godly Scots and served as am impetus for greater individual and communal discipline. In the shadow of the Apocalypse, future Scottish divines would take to the pulpits and set about furthering the Reformation. To do so, they would rely heavily on admonitions about Satan to convey to their varied audiences the Protestant pillars of predestination, divine sovereignty and human depravity. A godly society, they believed, could and would be created, and the Devil would be in vanquished in the end. First, though, the Scottish people needed to know their enemy.

CHAPTER 2

From the Pulpit

In the early years of the seventeenth century, John Welsh, son-in-law of John Knox and a remarkably pious man by all accounts, stood before his congregation at Ayr. He looked into the faces before him, some of whom he must have baptized or married, and some that he might soon bury, and warned them all of an indefatigable adversary.[1] 'He is called Satan', Welsh said, and 'nothing can quench his thirst but the pulling off Christ's crown off his head, and pouring out the blood of the souls of men and women, and the casting them in the everlasting fire of hell, that they may be burnt eternally'.[2] Lest his audience feel safe or sheltered by their faith, he assured them that the Devil 'will not spare thee, for as all the monstrous beasts on earth are not able to express his cruelty of nature, therefore he is compared to a wolf, to a lion, to a dragon, to that mighty leviathan'.[3] In the constant quest to preserve and further the Reformation, such admonitions about Satan proved indispensable to Scottish ministers who strove to inspire the necessary combination of wariness and zeal in their listening and reading audiences.

The Devil figured prominently in the abundant sermons of late sixteenth- and seventeenth-century Scotland. From the pulpit and in print, ministers used discussions of Satan to communicate the more complex messages of Reformed Protestantism to the Scottish public. A highly visible element of later medieval piety, the Devil was a well-known figure to educated and uneducated audiences alike.[4] The ideas of predestined election and reprobation, the indelible sovereignty of God and total human depravity, however, were more esoteric and less tangible. By focusing on a figure

---

[1] Welsh was only at Ayr for five years, but his sermons were said to have been so popular that the burgh council discussed building a larger church to house the increased crowds that he drew. See Alan R. MacDonald, 'Welsh, John (1568/9–1622)', *ODNB*.

[2] John Welsh, 'Sermon XI', *Forty-Eight Select Sermons* (Edinburgh, 1744), 160. Though these sermons were published later in both Edinburgh and Glasgow, they were delivered in the early years of the seventeenth century.

[3] Ibid., 162.

[4] On the role of the Devil in late medieval Christianity, see Norman Cohn, *Europe's Inner Demons: The Demonization of Christians in Medieval Christendom* (Chicago, IL: University of Chicago Press, 1975); Andrew P. Roach, *The Devils World: Heresy and Society 1100–1300* (Harlow: Pearson, 2005); Michael David Bailey, *Battling Demons: Witchcraft, Heresy, and Reform in the Late Middle Ages* (University Park, PA: Penn State University Press, 2003).

familiar to Scots, preachers sought to convey intricate theological ideas in terms that were understandable to their congregations and applicable to daily life. In their attempt to create a godly community in both thought and deed, ministers reinforced the importance of individual responsibility and communal identity in the face of an ever-active adversary. This pastoral emphasis on Satan served not only the didactic purposes of Scottish divines, but also responded to an active interest in and concern for the Devil amongst the clergy and laity alike.

The Sermon in Protestant Scotland

The sermon was the primary regular form of mass communication in early modern Scotland.[5] In the decades following the Reformation, church attendance was made compulsory for all Scots, on Sundays as well as weekdays in many areas.[6] Whole communities filed into their respective parish churches on the Sabbath day, excepting those who ignored the rules and faced penalties from the local ecclesiastical court for doing so.[7] The sessions' efforts to enforce sermon attendance proved at least moderately successful. In many areas, the number of offenders for missing sermons was relatively small compared to those indicted for slander, swearing and fornication.[8] Even in much of the Highlands, church attendance had reached consistently high rates by the seventeenth century.[9] The increase in sermon attendance should not be viewed, however, as simply a result of the kirk

---

[5] The same point is made about New England by Harry S. Stout, *The New England Soul: Preaching and Religious Culture in Colonial New England* (Oxford: Oxford University Press, 1986), 3.

[6] Margo Todd, *The Culture of Protestantism in Early Modern Scotland* (New Haven, CT: Yale University Press. 2002), 24. Todd also notes that the pre-Reformation church had been concerned with low attendance, but they never did put any compulsory attendance programme in place, as they did following the Reformation. See also *Statutes of the Scottish Church 1225–1559*, ed. D. Patrick (Edinburgh, 1907), 127–8 and 138–9.

[7] On the topic of discipline in early modern Scotland, see Todd, *Culture of Protestantism*; Michael F. Graham, *The Uses of Reform: "Godly Discipline" and Population Behavior in Scotland and Beyond, 1560–1610* (Leiden, Netherlands: E.J. Brill, 1996); Graham, 'Social Discipline in Scotland, 1560–1610', in Raymond Mentzer, ed., *Sin and the Calvinists: Morals Control and the Consistory in the Reformed Tradition* (Kirksville, MO: Thomas Jefferson University Press, 1994), 129–57.

[8] Todd, *Culture of Protestantism*, 44.

[9] See Jane Dawson, 'Calvinism in the Gaidhealtachd in Scotland', in Andrew Pettegree, Alastair Duke and Gillian Lewis, eds, *Calvinism in Europe, 1540–1620* (Cambridge: Cambridge University Press, 1994), 231–53, p. 250. Here Dawson tells a particularly interesting but tragic anecdote about the surprisingly high levels of Highland church attendance in some areas. On the Isle of Skye, church attendance was so consistent that the MacDonalds of Uist were able to wipe out their rival clan, the MacLeods of the Waternish peninsula, by locking the church door when the sermon began and setting fire to the building.

sessions strong-arming parishioners into pews, though this was certainly part of it. Ordinary Scots often reported offenders who missed sermons to their session elders.[10] Moreover, ministers and parishioners alike doubtlessly viewed sermon attendance as a metric and a means for godliness. In a theological system where salvation seemed elusive and perplexing, sermon attendance could serve a two-fold purpose. For individuals, the words of the sermon provided the most likely means of achieving a conversion experience and some assurance of faith. For the community, sermon-going could be performative as well as personally fulfilling; by attending regular sermons, Scots hoped to publicly demonstrate their election.

If there was an important message to be spread, therefore, the pulpit provided the means. In a society where many people remained unable read the Scriptures on their own, the sermon served as a centrepiece of worship in Protestant Scotland and a powerful mechanism for continued reform.[11] Of course, as John McCallum has rightly pointed out, the sermon was not the only tool for spreading the faith at local level, especially during the earliest decades of the Reformation when many parishes had yet to obtain a minister who could preach weekly and bi-weekly sermons. The reading of prayers, the singing of psalms and the dissemination of an array of religious texts all helped to introduce and maintain Protestantism among the people.[12] This is also not to say that sermons held a marginal place in medieval devotion; decades of elucidating scholarship on preaching in medieval Europe speak otherwise.[13] Nevertheless, the increased focus on the sermon and the

---

[10] Todd, *Culture of Protestantism*, 32.

[11] On preaching and Reformed Protestantism, see James Thomas Ford, 'Preaching in the Reformed Tradition', in Larissa Taylor, ed., *Preachers and People in the Reformations and Early Modern Europe* (Leiden: Brill, 2001). In Scotland, urban literacy, judged by the ability to sign one's name, hovered around 50 per cent in the 1630s for men, 10–20 per cent in rural areas, and much less for women. So though literacy rates were certainly on the rise in seventeenth-century Scotland, many remained unable to actually read texts as dense and complex as Scripture. See R.A. Houston, 'The Literacy Myth?: Illiteracy in Scotland, 1630–1760', *Past and Present* 96 (1982): 89–91; John Bannerman, 'Literacy in the Highlands', in Ian B. Cowan and Duncan Shaw, eds *The Renaissance and Reformation in Scotland: Essays in Honour of Gordon Donaldson* (Edinburgh: Scottish Academic Press, 1983), 214–35.

[12] See McCallum, *Reforming the Scottish Parish: The Reformation in Fife, 1560–1640* (Aldershot: Ashgate, 2010), especially chapters 1 and 4.

[13] To name a few of the many important studies of preaching in medieval Europe: J.W. Blench, *Preaching in England in the Late Fifteenth and Sixteenth Centuries: a Study of English Sermons 1450–1600* (Oxford: Oxford University Press, 1964); H. Leith Spencer, *English Preaching in the Late Middle Ages* (Oxford: Oxford University Press, 1993); Carolyn Muessig, *Sermon, Preacher and Audience in the Middle Ages* (Leiden: Brill, 2001); Katherine L. Jansen and Miri Rubin, eds, *Charisma and Religious Authority : Jewish, Christian, and Muslim Preaching, 1200–1500* (Turnhout, Belgium: Brepols, 2010); Kimberly A. Rivers, *Preaching the Memory of Virtue and Vice : Memory, Images, and Preaching in the late Middle Ages* (Turnhout, Belgium: Brepols, 2010); Larissa Taylor, *Soldiers of Christ : Preaching in*

attendant removal of the more visually stimulating elements of Catholicism were concerted attempts by the church and its ministers to alter what and how the Scottish people believed. Unsurprisingly, not everyone accepted the changes wrought by the Reformation immediately or without protest.[14] Yet in Scotland, these changes occurred with almost no bloodshed, and the influence of Reformed Protestantism on Scottish worship was remarkably thorough, if not as immediate as some have suggested.[15] By the beginning of the seventeenth century, the sermon had become a major focal point not only of church-going, but also of personal belief.

In the last few decades, scholars from a wide range of disciplines – historians, literary critics, theologians and anthropologists – have begun to mine sermons not just for theology, but as sources with the ability to bring into focus the religions and cultures of the medieval and early modern pasts.[16] As James Ford put it, 'understanding the sermon as "social event" involves knowing something about the style and personality of the preacher, the context of the sermon, the social makeup of the audience, and the events or issues of the day'.[17] This 'social history of preaching' thus seeks to analyse the sermon as not just as a text that expounded theological ideas, but as a social and cultural event.[18]

Late Medieval and Reformation France (Oxford: Oxford University Press, 1992), and Daniel R. Lesnick, *Preaching in Medieval Florence : the Social World of Franciscan and Dominican Spirituality* (Athens: University of Georgia Press, 1989).

[14] During the generation immediately following the Reformation, the newly Protestant church struggled to stamp out stubborn remnants of Catholicism. Organized recusancy was rare, however, and at no point in the seventeenth century did professed Catholics exceed 2 per cent of the population. See Margaret H.B. Sanderson, 'Catholic Recusancy in Scotland in the Sixteenth Century', *The Innes Review* 21(1970): 87–107; Allan I. Macinnes, 'Catholic Recusancy and the Penal Laws, 1603–1707', *Records of the Scottish Church History Society* 24 (1992): 27–63. Well into the seventeenth century, kirk sessions continued to prosecute parishioners for skipping out on church service and even verbally abusing their ministers. See, for example, the detailed excerpts from the Perth kirk session, NLS Adv. MS 31.1.1–1a.

[15] On changes to Scottish sermons and rituals following the Reformation, see Todd, *Culture of Protestantism*, esp. chapters 1 and 2. For a concise discussion of the limits of Todd's arguments, particularly as they might apply to the early decades of the Reformation, see Julian Goodare, 'Review of Margo Todd's *Culture of Protestantism in Early Modern Scotland*', *Albion* 36 (2004): 376.

[16] See, for example, Arnold Hunt, *The Art of Hearing: English Preachers and their Audiences, 1590–1640* (Cambridge: Cambridge University Press, 2010); Muessig, *Preacher, Sermon and Audience*; Taylor, ed., *Preachers and People*; Taylor, *Soldiers of Christ*; John W. O'Malley, *Religious Culture in the Sixteenth Century: Preaching, Rhetoric, Spirituality, and Reform* (Aldershot: Ashgate, 1993); Bruce Gordon, 'Preaching and Reform of the Clergy in the Swiss Reformation', in Andrew Pettegree, ed., *The Reformation of the Parishes* (Manchester: Manchester University Press, 1993).

[17] James Ford, 'Preaching in the Reformed Tradition', 81.

[18] On the sermon as both a text and an event, see Mary Morrissey, 'Interdisciplinarity and the Study of Early Modern Sermons', *HJ* 42 (1999): 1111–23.

This important approach entails its own set of problems. Sermons reveal, by their nature, a one-way street of ideas and speeches. Measuring the reception of these sermons by people no longer living, especially those who were not literate, is an elusive task. Equally problematic is assessing the extent to which the manuscript or printed sermon resembled the delivered version. Lee Palmer Wandel has pointed out, with regard to printed sermons, that one cannot know exactly 'what any one Christian heard'.[19] Happily for the historian, many printed sermons in Scotland were transcribed from auditor's notes rather than the minister's written sermon draft and may provide a clearer picture of the words spoken from the pulpit.[20] Additionally, the pages of Scottish diaries and sermon notebooks, most dating from the second half of seventeenth century, abound with descriptions of sermons and the men who delivered them.[21] These references suggest that many early modern Scots cared quite deeply about the authors, contexts and content of the sermons they heard in the pews. Still, this only reveals what the minority of literate Scots took away, or said they took away, from sermons. These issues notwithstanding, sermons provide unique insights into the beliefs of preachers as well as glimpses into the listening predilections of the public, revealing much about the import of the Devil in early modern Scottish society.

Through their discussions of Satan, Scottish preachers conveyed complex theological ideas to a laity with varying levels of education and religious conviction. The sermons through which they did so run the gamut of early modern Scotland in terms of date and location. This chapter draws from the analysis of nearly 150 sermons composed between 1560 and 1720, about a third of which are in manuscript form and all of which discuss the Devil in some or great detail. The largest numbers of sermons examined here were written and delivered in the Lowlands between 1630 and the 1670s. The increase in both political strife and religious controversy during these years, manifested in the rise of the Scottish covenanting movement and the so-called 'second Scottish Reformation', prompted this mid-century proliferation of sermons.[22] Scottish sermons usually began with the recounting of a biblical text, continued with an analysis of that scripture, and ended with a discussion of the ways in

---

[19] Lee Palmer Wandel, 'Switzerland', in Larissa Taylor, ed., *Preachers and People*, 222.

[20] Todd, *Culture of Protestantism*, 50. See, for example, the introductory note to Andrew Gray's *Select Sermons* (Edinburgh, 1792).

[21] For examples of sermon notebooks, which often contained transcriptions of delivered sermons as well as notes of general themes, see NRS, CH2/21/5; NLS MS V.a.415; MS 2824; MS 3008; MS 5770.

[22] For a discussion of the second Scottish Reformation, see John Young, 'The Covenanters and the Scottish Parliament, 1639–51: The Rule of the Godly and the "Second Scottish Reformation"', in Elizabethanne Boran and Crawford Gribben, eds, *Enforcing Reformation in Ireland and Scotland, 1550–1700* (Aldershot: Ashgate, 2006), 131–58.

which that scripture might be applied to daily life.[23] This final didactic portion of the sermon was the most important, for it explained to listeners why the Word actually mattered to them. It was within this discussion of the scripture's application to daily life that ministers dwelt at the greatest length on the topic of Satan.

In analysing the sermons that span post-Reformation Scotland, the consistency in how ministers explained the nature, threat and immediacy of Satan to their audiences is striking. Certainly, the specific contexts in which sermons were delivered shaped demonic references to persons and events. The personality and preferences of the individual preacher infused the sermons with different nuances and emphases. Yet despite the specificities, the overarching themes of the sinfulness of humanity and the grace of God consistently determined how preachers spoke about Satan to their audiences. This is due, of course, to the fact that the ministers who composed and delivered these sermons were consistently Reformed Protestant in belief, as well as Presbyterian in training. By the mid-seventeenth century, there were certainly Episcopalian ministers delivering sermons throughout Scotland. Fewer of their sermons are preserved, however, and the ones that do exist contain discussions of the Devil similarly shaped by the tenets of Reformed Protestantism. As scholars have pointed out, opinions on church polity did not negate common theological beliefs.[24] For the bulk of the seventeenth century, Reformed Protestantism clearly guided how Satan figured into the composition and delivery of sermons.

The Preacher and the Devil

In the early decades of the Reformation, filling the thousand or so pulpits of Scotland with properly trained ministers proved a major challenge for reformers.[25] As the sermon provided one of the primary tools for

---

[23] Todd also notes this structure of sermons. See *Culture of Protestantism*, 49.

[24] David Mullan, *Scottish Puritanism, 1590–1638* (Oxford: Oxford University Press, 2000); John Coffey, 'The Problem of "Scottish Puritanism", 1590–1638', in Boran and Gribben, eds, *Enforcing Reformation in Ireland And Scotland, 1550–1700*. Many Scottish ministers also switched ecclesiastical allegiances over the course of their careers. See, for example, the works of Andrew Ramsay (1574–1659), who began his career as an Episcopalian but later joined the Presbyterian cause.

[25] According to Philip Benedict, one-quarter of Scottish parishes had an ordained minister in 1567, largely due to the fact only 18–25 per cent of ministers stayed on to serve the newly Reformed church after 1560. See Benedict, *Christ's Church Purely Reformed: A Social History of Calvinism* (New Haven, CT: Yale University Press, 2002), 443. On Scotland's early difficulties providing Reformed ministers, see also McCallum, *Reforming the Scottish Parish: The Reformation in Fife, 1560–1640* (Aldershot: Ashgate, 2010), 16–35; James Kirk, *Patterns of Reform: Continuity and Change In The Reformation* (Edinburgh: T. & T. Clark,

spreading Reformed Protestantism, the dearth of preachers was no small issue. Readers, literate laymen whom Michael Lynch has termed 'the foot soldiers of the kirk in its first generation', stepped in to fill the ministerial void by reading the Scriptures to parishioners.[26] In the early seventeenth century, however, the seminaries that had sprung up across Scotland began producing adequate numbers of trained men. By the 1620s, and earlier in many places, the dearth of ministers was largely abated. This was especially true of the Lowlands, where most parishes received their own minister.[27] At the time of the signing of the National Covenant in 1638, some 150 newly minted ministers stood in line for benefices.[28] In the Highlands, conversely, clergy were assigned to districts, and individuals preached itinerantly throughout those districts in conjunction with a team of ministers.[29]

Entrance into the Scottish ministry was not a task to be taken lightly. Before assignment to a parish, most ministers in Scotland underwent a formal university education and a thorough vetting process. The minister had to prove he knew Scripture and the true doctrine like the back of his own hand, for, as David Dickson remarked to the General Assembly in Glasgow, 'the preaching of errour is like the selling of poysoned Pestied bread, that slays the eater of it, and infects with the breath every man that comes near'.[30] In many places, ministers-to-be had to come before a parish's particular presbytery and expound upon Scripture, then deliver a sermon in the local church considering him for its minister.[31] Proper oratorical style was essential, and most Reformed preachers eschewed florid, excessively wordy sermons.[32] The best way to teach the laity about how to live a godly life was to speak to them in a clear, plain manner. This 'plain speak' must, however, be accompanied by verve and passion.

1989), 96–153; Michael Lynch, 'Preaching to the Converted?' in A. MacDonald, Michael Lynch and Ian Cowan, eds, *The Renaissance in Scotland* (Leiden, Netherlands: Brill, 1994), 307–14; Ian Cowan, *The Scottish Reformation: Church and Society in Sixteenth Century Scotland* (New York: St. Martin's Press, 1982), esp. 159–81; Walter Roland Foster, *The Church before the Covenants: The Church of Scotland 1596–1638* (Edinburgh: The Scottish Academic Press, 1975).

[26] Lynch states that Readers formed as much as 70 per cent of the ministry in 1574. Lynch, 'Preaching to the Converted?', 310.

[27] W.R. Foster, 'A Constant Platt Achieved: Provision for the Ministry, 1600–1638', Duncan Shaw, ed., in *Reformation and Revolution* (Edinburgh: St Andrews Press, 1967), 132.

[28] Benedict, *Christ's Church*, 444.

[29] Dawson, 'Calvinism in the Gaidhealtachd', 246.

[30] These are minister David Dickson (or Dick) words to the General Assembly in Glasgow in 1638 about the errors of Arminianism. *The Records of the Kirk of Scotland*, Vol. 1, ed. Alexander Peterkin (Edinburgh: P. Brown, 1838), 156.

[31] Todd, *Culture of Protestantism*, 24.

[32] Ford, 'Preaching in the Reformed Tradition', 66–71.

As Calvin himself put it, the minister of the Word 'should not only give a clear understanding of scripture, but must also add vehemence so that the message will penetrate the heart'.[33] Moreover, Scottish ministers were expected to be active members of their communities and meet lists of duties that extended far beyond the requirement of preaching on the Lord's Day.[34]

Accordingly, these preachers were not just men of considerable formal learning, but also of charisma and character. To this day, tales abound in Scotland of ministers who could move their audiences to tears, trembling and conversion. The most famous example is perhaps that of John Livingstone, a young and outspoken Presbyterian who had been travelling around southwest Scotland when he stopped at the Kirk of Shotts in North Lanarkshire. Here, on the morning of 21 June 1630, he gave a singularly powerful sermon on Ezekiel 36:25–26.[35] The full content of Livingstone's sermon is unknown, but given the choice of text, it is not unlikely that his sermon contained lengthy discussions of human sinfulness, Satan's influence and the dependence of man on God's grace. As the story goes, he preached for over two hours in the rain, during which time nearly five hundred men and women had conversion experiences. One chronicler even wrote that some, so moved by Livingstone's words, fainted to the ground and laid there 'as if they had been dead'.[36] This story, though presumably exaggerated for political and evangelical purposes, displays the powerful place that ministers held in early modern Scotland. These men did more than preach the Word; they were expected to change the lives of their parishioners as well.

Quite often, the identities of these Scottish ministers were bound up with the belief in and struggle against Satan. They acted as generals, leading their troops to fight in an inevitable and crucial conflict against the forces of evil. For some, the battle against the Devil drove their religious careers and personal piety from the very onset. Robert Bruce, minister and moderator of the General Assembly of the Church of Scotland, explained how his own conversion experience and subsequent call to the ministry in

---

[33] Ibid., 67.

[34] In many parishes, church officials checked up on local ministers to assure that their duties were being performed properly. In Aberdeen, for example, a checklist of duties for ministers and kirk session elders included visiting the ill, staying out of taverns, and the maintenance and promotion of 'peace and love among all people'. See Benedict, *Christ's Church*, 441.

[35] Ezekiel 36:25–26 reads 'Then will I sprinkle clean water upon you, and ye shall be clean: from all your filthiness, and from all your idols, will I cleanse you. A new heart also will I give you, and a new spirit will I put within you: and I will take away the stony heart out of your flesh, and I will give you an heart of flesh'.

[36] Recounted in Leigh Eric Schmidt, *Holy Fairs: Scottish Communions and American Revivals in the Early Modern Period* (Princeton, NJ: Princeton University Press, 1989), 63–5.

1581 began when God directed the Devil to 'accuse me so audibly, that I heard his voice as vividly as I ever heard anything'.[37] One contemporary described how a mid-century preacher named John Welwood struggled in his youth 'with the sense of sin and apprehensions of deserved wrath, yea with very disquieting temptations from Satan'.[38] According to this account, God delivered him from these youthful tribulations, and in return, Welwood 'promised to God that he should imploy his best endeavors for the ruine of Satan's kingdom' by committing himself to the ministry.[39]

Zachary Boyd, minister at Glasgow, preached in 1628 that demonic hatred for the Scottish ministry should come as no surprise, 'seeing Gods word is his appointed meane whereby hee not onlie giveth health to the body, but also to the soules of his children, let vs not wonder that Sathan the enemie of mans salvation bee a great enemie to this word, to the teachers, and to the hearers'.[40] Both the teachers and the hearers of the word were part of the same godly community that was constantly assaulted by the Devil. Though this sermon singled out preachers as particularly noteworthy targets of Satan, it also emphasized to ordinary Scots – 'the hearers' – that they were not alone in their struggles, thus embedding discussions of the Devil with a sense of community. Sermons, and these men who delivered them, informed post-Reformation piety and identity in Scotland in no small way – and it is from the pulpit that ideas about Satan spread to, and were often internalized by, the Scottish people. Discussions of Satan served not only as didactic tools to promote godly conduct and communal solidarity, but also provided a necessary pastoral language to communicate key elements of Reformed Protestantism in an immediate and evocative way.

On Knowing the Enemy

For Scottish divines, the frequent religious, social and political turmoil of the seventeenth century made clear the precariousness of godly life. As one minister eloquently told his congregation

> ... no sooner we come out of the Womb, but we Launch forth into an Ocean of Miserie ... together with our own Infirmities, and encompassed with continual Evils, that, for the most part, follow us unseparably, as the Shadow follows the

---

[37] Robert Bruce, *Sermons*, ed. William Cunninghan (Edinburgh: Wodrow Society, 1843), 7.
[38] NLS, Wod. Qu. LXXV.
[39] Ibid.
[40] Zachary Boyd, *The balme of Gilead prepared for the sick* (Edinburgh, 1629), 201–2.

Body, and never leaves us, till we get beyond the bounds of Time, and enter those interminable Mansions of Eternity.[41]

To prepare the laity for this hazardous landscape of earthly life, ministers devoted considerable ink and breath to preparing their parishioners to war with Satan. The sermon provided the means. First, the Scottish people had to know their adversary, and the Bible afforded many examples of the Devil's abilities, earthly activities and evil aspirations. As II Corinthians 2:11 told readers, such knowledge was power: 'Lest Satan should get an advantage of us: for we are not ignorant of his devices', while 1 Peter 5:8 provided an evocative and tangible vision of demonic threats, advising readers to 'Be sober, be vigilant; because your adversary the devil, as a roaring lion, walketh about, seeking whom he may devour' – a passage that would be quoted and paraphrased by preachers throughout the early modern period.[42]

With Scripture providing the ultimate evidence of demonic prowess and vigilance, ministers sought to impress upon their congregations the earthly reality of Satan. In a sermon given at Ayr in the first years of the seventeenth century, John Welsh emphasized the unrelenting nature of Satan's rage against the godly: 'Is he a meek lamb think ye? Will he have any pity on thee? Nay, as the Lord lives, he will not spare thee, for as all the monstrous beasts on earth are not able to express his cruelty of nature, therefore he is compared to a wolf, to a lion, to a dragon, to that mighty leviathan'.[43] In another sermon, Welsh reiterated the necessity of fighting, asking 'What is the life of a Christian but a daily battle?'[44] Couching the necessity of combat in terms of election, ministers no doubt hoped to spur those concerned with their own salvation into action and proper godly behaviour.

To better explain the nature of Satan and the imminence of demonic threats, ministers often employed metaphors from the more banal aspects of daily Scottish life. Alexander Henderson once told his audience at Edinburgh that 'Ye would think it a very ill thing if the cold winter were coming upon you and ye had neither house, nor fire, nor meat, nor clothes to defend you from the injury of it … But it is worst of all if the devil come against us and we have no armour to defend ourselves from him'.[45] Henderson's words, delivered in the context of the 1638 National Covenant and Glasgow Assembly, anticipated the impending political and religious

---

[41] NLS, Adv. MS 5.2.6, f.17–18
[42] For examples of references to 1 Peter 5:8, see David Fergusson, *Ane answer to ane epistle written by Renat Benedict the Frenche doctor*, 1563; Adv. MS 5.2.6; MS 2206; John Welsh, *Forty-Eight Select Sermons* (Edinburgh, 1744).
[43] Welsh, 'Sermon XI', 162.
[44] Welsh, 'Sermon X', 140.
[45] Alexander Henderson, *Sermons, Prayers and Pulpit Addresses of Alexander Henderson*, ed. Thomas R. Martin (Edinburgh: John Maclaren, 1867), 458.

crises of the first Bishops' War that would begin in the next year. His sermon emerged from a specific context but carried a more general message, echoed time and time again in Scottish sermons: the people, profoundly weak on their own, must turn to God to arm themselves for the battle against the Devil. By comparing the need to arm oneself against Satan to the necessity of preparing for a harsh winter – something pre-modern Scots would have understood all too well – Henderson reified the both the scriptural instruction of Ephesians 6:11 and the threat of the Devil.[46]

Like their theological predecessors, Scottish ministers tried to convey to their parishioners that Satan acted only as an agent of a sovereign God, while at the same time maintaining that God could not be the author of any evil. In a sermon delivered at the beginning of the seventeenth century, Welsh explained that 'when it is said that he [the devil] is powerful, it is true, but his power is limited and bounded, and there are marches and bounds set unto him, that he dare not pass over'.[47] Many explained to their congregations that the Devil acted, with divine instruction, according to his corrupted nature, thus absolving God of direct authorship of evil. Famed political theorist and minister Samuel Rutherford detailed the origins of Satan's malice in sermon published in 1645. 'The Malice of the Devil', he wrote, 'is a natural Agent, and worketh as intently and bently as he can, [like] the Fire putteth forth all its Strength in burning, the Sun heateth and enlighteneth as vehemently as it can ... The Malice of Hell being let loose, it worketh Mischief by Nature, not by Will'.[48] While Rutherford attributed some agency to Satan, probably more than Calvin would have allowed, he carefully maintained that the Devil could not act according to his own independent will. The core idea here was that God willed Satan to act, but within the space of this divine will, the Devil moved according to his nature, or, to use a phrase of Knox's, by his own 'inward motion'.[49] Such rhetorical clarifications (and, occasionally, obfuscations) gave Scottish preachers a way to attribute the evils of the world to demonic actions while still keeping the Devil under the yoke of God.

At times, sermonic warnings of God's wrath became so intertwined with descriptions of the rage of the Devil, who acted as 'the currier sent of God

---

[46] Ephesians 6:11 reads 'Put on the whole armour of God, that ye may be able to stand against the wiles of the devil.' On the biblical armour of God and references to Ephesians in Protestant British sermons, see Alec Ryrie, *Being Protestant in Reformation Britain* (Oxford: Oxford University Press, 2013), 243–5.

[47] Welsh, 'Sermon XI', 166.

[48] Samuel Rutherford, 'Sermon V', *The Trial and Triumph of Faith* (Edinburgh, 1645), 43. *Trial and Triumph*, published again in London in 1652, was a collection of 27 sermons delivered in the early 1640s amid the turmoil of the Wars of the Three Kingdoms.

[49] John Knox, *An answer to a great number of blasphemous cauillations written by an Anabaptist, and aduersarie to Gods eternal predestination* (Edinburgh, 1560), 179.

to put his wrath in execution', that the two functioned interchangeably.[50] Robert Baillie portrayed God's anger with imagery of fire and terror often reserved for depictions of Satan, when he told his audience to

> ... consider the exceeding great terror of God when he is angry, his wrath burneth like fire ... it maketh the most godly to become like a bottle in the smoak ... it turneth their moisture into the draught of Summer, knowing the terror of the Lord be not persuaded to make peace with him in time; venture not his hot displeasure.[51]

Interpreting a recent fire as a clear sign of God's wrath, James Webster warned an Edinburgh congregation in 1700 that those afflicted 'have been under the sense of God's Wrath, under great fears of a provoked God that is pursuing a terrible controversy with Scotland. When the Lyon roars who will not fear?'[52] Here the lion likely refers to Satan, the ultimate instrument of God's displeasure. Admonitions of divine wrath and demonic rage served the same purpose in Scottish sermons: to warn the faithful of the impending punishments for their personal sins and the sins of their community. Combining the two in sermons allowed ministers to demonstrate both the awfulness of God and the subservice of the Devil in orchestrating punishment for great human sin. The goal was to incite parishioners to alter their beliefs and behaviours accordingly.

Scripture, theological writings and lived experiences attested to the fact that Satan was a master of deception and temptation. Accordingly, Scottish ministers went to great lengths to assure that their parishioners were cognizant of and prepared for demonic lies and assaults. First, men and women had to protect their thoughts from Satan, who could enter the mind unnoticed, planting doubts and impure feelings at a whim and leading even the most pious headlong into sin. As one late seventeenth-century minister warned, 'when Satan gets one thought, he will get another thought, and then the man is all blown up with filthy lusts'.[53] John Brown advised his audience in 1660 not to give heed 'to the lying Injections and temptations of Satan: It is not safe to entertain discourse with such an enemy ... He is too great a Sophist and Disputer for us'.[54] As another minister put it, Satan 'is that subtle serpent that deceives all the world; he is that seven-headed dragon that has such wit and wisdom that no wisdom

---

[50] Welsh, 'Sermon XI', 195
[51] Robert Baillie, *Satan the Leader in chief to all who resist the reparation of sion* (London, 1643), 39.
[52] NLS, MS 2206.
[53] NLS, MS 5770, f.69.
[54] John Brown, *Christ in believers the hope of glory being the substance of several sermons* (Edinburgh, 1694), 90; probably delivered in 1660.

can come about it but only the wisdom of God'.[55] Here again, preachers expounded on the powers of the Devil while giving the obligatory nod to the supremacy and ultimate victory of God.

Ministers took equal pains to impress upon their parishioners that Satan most easily preyed upon open and unguarded minds – a natural state for naturally depraved individuals. As Alexander Henderson explained to his audience, 'the devil, he knows every man's disposition, how it is set; if he see him to be a voluptuous man; if he be one whom he sees to be ambitious; or if he be one whom he sees to be covetous. And he knows also the complexion and constitution of man's body ... and he has temptations fitted for all these'.[56] Ministers emphasized these mental dangers of Satan in hopes that their parishioners would use prayer and divine dependence to shield their minds from impure thoughts or doubts that might be demonic in origin. For the Reformation of Scotland to succeed and the wrath of God to be avoided, the Scottish people had to be disciplined not only in word and deed, but in their thoughts as well. Though the human mind was ultimately uncontrollable, ministers intended their sermonic warnings to have substantive influence on how their listeners both thought and acted.

Through preaching, Scottish divines communicated to their congregations that the struggle against the internal temptation of Satan served as a necessary component of the godly experience and identity. As many examples from Scripture made plain, the relationship between God's children and the Devil was an ancient one. Satan, congregations were reminded, precipitated the fall of humankind. As one mid-century minister put it, 'it is a very wily sin, at first forged solely and subtly in our first Parents, by the father of liars, the Devill himself ... for he [Satan] having thus poisoned the root purposes also to poison the branches; wherefore study to lay aside this old man of original sin and put on the new man of grace'.[57] Echoing this reference to Genesis, John Livingstone told his flock at Ancrum in 1661 that 'truly it is very probable that Satan thought after he had gotten Adam and Eve in the snare, he thought he had all mankind ... as his own, in possession under lock and key'.[58] Just as the Devil had easily beguiled God's first creations, he would surely attempt the do the same to ordinary men and women.

Even Christ, congregations were reminded, had been subject to demonic assaults. As John Brown told his audience at Wamphray in 1660, 'We know with what temptations the devil set upon Christ himself; After that he had tempted him, with the foulest Idolatry, *To wit*, to worship the devil ... What will he not then attempt against the poor Followers

---

[55] Welsh, 'Upon Christian Warfare', *Forty-Eight Select Sermons*, 165.
[56] Henderson, *Sermons*, 477.
[57] NLS, MS 5769, 'Sermon by Mr. W. Jack', f.133.
[58] NLS, Wod. Qu. LXVII., 9rv.

of Christ? Why should his Followers think it strange, when long troubled with such injections?'[59] The lies and temptations of the Devil thus were, and always had been, an inescapable component of godly life. By emphasizing the universality of demonic assaults, ministers further instilled a sense of community in their parishioners; they were all in it together, with Satan and his followers as the common enemy. The failure to guard one's heart against demonic incursions, however, belonged above all to the moral weakness of the individual believer.

The Enemy Within

The Scottish people faced another enemy that was distinct from but intimately related to Satan: themselves. Preachers had no qualms about reminding their audiences of their innate, postlapsarian corruption. As one mid-century minister bluntly put it, 'our original and natural corruption, which sticks exceedingly close to us, being an universall disease and poyson runing throw, and infecting both the utter and iner man, defiling all the faculties of our souls, and members of our bodies ...'.[60] Only through this corruption could Satan operate effectively; humanity's 'Corrupt Nature' was 'the Devill's Agent, loading us like as many dogs in a Leish to provoke the Lord'.[61] A generation after the Reformation, the relationship between the corruption of human nature and Satan had become a frequent and central theme of Scottish sermons. Such orations echoed a theological conviction prevalent in Reformed Protestant thought: though external threats certainly existed, made manifest by the political enemies in league with the Devil, they often paled in comparison to internal temptations and corruptions.[62] This emphasis on the innate susceptibility of humans to demonic wiles was central to how Reformed ministers throughout the seventeenth century conceptualized Satan.

From the pulpit and in print, human corruption and the actions of Satan were presented in tandem; one could not exist without the other. As Charles Hammond put it in a 1671 sermon delivered in Edinburgh, 'a true Christian hath always three enemies to deal withall, the world, the flesh and the Devil; and these three seek all opportunities to lay hold and

---

[59] Brown, *Christ in believers*, 98.
[60] NLS, MS 5769, f.133.
[61] Ibid.
[62] On the focus on internal temptation, see Nathan Johnstone, *The Devil and Demonism in Early Modern England* (Cambridge: Cambridge University Press, 2006); Johnstone, 'The Protestant Devil: The Experience of Temptation in Early Modern England' *Journal of British Studies*, 43 (2004): 173–205; Frank Luttmer, 'Persecutors, Tempters and Vassals of the Devil: The Unregenerate in Puritan Practical Divinity', *Journal of Ecclesiastical History*, 51 (2000): 37–68.

conquer'.[63] Here, the world refers to the corruptions of others, and the flesh denotes temptations and lusts from within. Both worked with the Devil to ruin the work of God. Echoing this sentiment, David Willingham advised his congregation to 'be zealous, for there are snares without, and corruptions within.'[64] John Welsh couched this message within militaristic and dualistic language, explaining that 'the godly, because God and the devil, light and darkness, righteousness and unrighteousness, a Jacob and an Efau are within them, therefore they cannot be without warfare'.[65] The necessity of eternal, earthly warfare came, at least partially, from the fact that men and women existed in an inherent state of total depravity.

Some ministers went so far as to claim that humans had a natural affinity, even a sordid love, for Satan. Samuel Rutherford stated that while men and women hate the Devil for the pain he inflicts upon them, there existed 'in all Men an inbred moral Love of the Devil, as he is a fallen Spirit, tempting to Sin; here every Prisoner loveth this Keeper, like loveth like, broken Men and Bankrupt flee together to Woods and Mountains ... '.[66] Without divine grace, ministers insisted, humans would fall into a spiritual abyss, subject to every whim of Satan. Andrew Gray warned his mid-century congregation at Glasgow that

> ... if your heart were left one hour to your selves to keep, you would commit more iniquity, than ye can imagine or dream of ... there is many of us that hath two hearts in our bosom ... a man that hath two hearts, a part of his heart goeth to God, and a part of his heart goeth to the devil: And I think, if we were all well searched, it is to be feared that many of us would be found two hearted men.[67]

The emphasis on the corruption of humankind continued well into the eighteenth century. John Mclaurin, a minister in Glasgow, wrote in 1723 that 'we should reflect in the first place, that the Devil and our own corrupt hearts are such notorious imposters, that the Experience we have of their Deceitfulness are innumerable, and so also are the Evidences we have of God's holiness'.[68] Far from being strange bedfellows, humans and Satan possessed an innate link, established at the Fall. Through preaching and

---

[63] Charles Hammond, *God's Eye from Heaven* (Edinburgh, 1671), n.p.
[64] NLS, MS 5770, f. 119.
[65] Welsh, 'Sermon X', 144.
[66] Rutherford, *Trial and Triumph of Faith*, 39.
[67] Andrew Gray, *Directions and instigations to the duty of prayer how, and why the heart is to be kept with diligence.* (Edinburgh, 1669), 95.
[68] NLS, Wod. Oct. XXXI, Part of the diary of Sir John Chiesly, 1667; Personal Covenant of Marion Stewart. Edinburgh, March 10 1716, 247v.

spiritual guidance, ministers strove to sever, or at least override, this internal connection.

Above all, ministers impressed upon Scots that they must rely upon God in order to resist the base desires of their natures. In a letter to the Presbytery of Irvine in 1641, Robert Baillie warned that the members of the church must collectively 'pray to God for our cause and Church: God will help us against all, men and devills: No man is to be trusted; the best is naturallie false'.[69] As Alexander Henderson told his congregation in 1638, 'our hearts they are contrary to God; they are proud, disobedient, rebellious, and he who sees and knows his own heart sees all this to be in it'. Yet believers ought not be 'dismayed nor discouraged, albeit thou sees thou has no strength of thy own', Henderson reassured his congregation, 'for where is there strength to be found in any against the devil and the world? The stoutest natural courage will be overcome by these; but our strength must be in God allanerly [only]'.[70] This particular sermon explained why Satan so prevailed over human hearts while also offering potential for relief, through prayer and ultimate reliance on God, from these internal struggles. As Robert Rule explained in 1688

> ... it is true that the Lord makes use of the fears of his people to stiff up their hearts to vigilance, and watchfulness against sin, and to provoke them to diligence and care about their eternal Salvation. But the Devill makes a sad use of it, for he makes use of their fears to cast them into despondency, and unbelief and distrust of his promises, and turning them out of [God's] way for his way for help.[71]

Such ministers went to great lengths to explain to their parishioners that God was eager to help them, if they would only get out of their own way.

The sermonic connection between Satan and human depravity left a clear mark on the self-perception of many lay Scots, at least those able to leave behind accounts of their experiences. The spiritual diaries of the period, discussed at length in the subsequent chapters, made frequent references 'the devil and man's evil heart'. Many Scots espoused a remarkable obsession with personal depravity in connection with the actions of Satan, which drove some individuals so far as to contemplate suicide in response to the religious despair that this obsession could cause.[72] Archibald

---

[69] Robert Baillie, *The Letters and Journals of Robert Baillie, 1637–1662*, 3 vols, ed. David Laing (Edinburgh: The Bannatine Club, 1841), 350.

[70] Henderson, *Sermons*, 464.

[71] NLS, MS 5770, f.3.

[72] See, for example, 'Mistress Rutherford's Conversion Narrative', ed. David G. Mullan, *Scottish History Society, Miscellany xiii* (Edinburgh: Scottish History Society, 2004), 146–88; NLS, Wod. Oct. XXXI Part of the diary of Sir John Chiesly, 1667; James Melville, *The*

Johnstone of Wariston, a lawyer famous for his radical Presbyterianism, wrote in 1650 'O let not, let not the devil, world, sin, our corrupt hearts, ever be able to outsay, unsay, gainsay God in this, what thou says of us, that we shall be thine. Let nothing in hell or earth, within us or without us, be able to say, We shall not be thine …'.[73] James Nimmo, a layman and self-identified Covenanter, bemoaned how, throughout his life, 'sathan and my corruptions and ivel heart being desperatlie wicked of it self strove to crush me'.[74] In the early eighteenth century, schoolteacher Thomas Locke explained in a letter that 'by nature we are of our father the devil, and his works we will do as natively as fire casteth forth heat …'.[75] These examples are a few of the many instances in which lay Scots demonstrated reception and adoption of the descriptions of close cooperation between Satan and human nature that they heard from the pulpit or read in printed sermons.

Expositions of human depravity could not have been pleasant things for parishioners to hear. Tellingly, after an extended stay north of the Border in the 1610s, an Englishman opined that all Scottish sermons were 'nothing but railing'.[76] Still, the emphasis on human corruption during discussions of Satan served three distinct pedagogical purposes. First, by explicitly connecting human weakness to the actions of Satan, ministers buttressed one of the central doctrines of Protestant theology. To fully grasp the doctrine of double predestination, a marked change from salvation by good works, Scots needed to understand *why* they were unable to achieve salvation through their own actions. Ministers sought to reify theoretical discussions of human spiritual malaise by pointing to specific, more tangible acts of the Devil. Temptation to sin was something relatable for the vast majority of Scots. In explaining that Satan was

---

Autobiography and Diary of Mr. James Melville, ed. Robert Pitcairn (Edinburgh: Wodrow Society, 1842); James Nimmo, *The Narrative of Mr. James Nimmo: Written for his own Satisfaction to Keep in some rememberance the lords way dealing and kindness towards him, 1654–1709*, ed. W.G Scott Moncrieff (Edinburgh: The Scottish History Society, 1889); NRS, CH12/18/6 Diary of John Forbes of Corse; CH12/20/9 Religious diary, 1679–1692.

[73] Archibald Johnston of Wariston, 'Diary', in David Mullan, ed., *Protestant Piety in Early Modern Scotland: Letters, Lives and Covenants, 1650–1712* (Edinburgh: Scottish History Society, 2008), 44.

[74] Nimmo, *The Narrative of Mr. James Nimmo*, 9.

[75] NLS, Wod. Qu. LXXXII, Thomas Locke, 'To the parents of the children of Eastwood', c. 1706, f. 159. In this description of this folio he is described as the 'parish catechist', which traditionally describes a Catholic position in the community. However, in a letter by Locke found in the same Wodrow volume, he admonished the episcopacy of the English church and wrote a treatise in favour of federal theology and predestination. Clearly, he was a Presbyterian, and likely the label of 'parish catechist' meant that he was a religious teacher in the community.

[76] Anthony Weldon, *Early Travellers in Scotland*, ed. P. Hume Brown (New York: 1970), 100. It should be noted that the authorship of this work is disputed. See Joseph Marshall and Sean Kelsey, 'Weldon, Sir Anthony (*bap.* 1583, *d.* 1648)', *ODNB*.

the source of this temptation, and that he acted through innate human corruption, ministers killed two birds with one stone, as both the nature of Satan and of humankind were clarified through these discussions.

Second, by informing their audiences that all men and women were spiritually infirm, sermons reiterated the importance of relying on both God and the church for deliverance. Over the course of the seventeenth century, many Scottish ministers came under fire from Erastian monarchs and internal factions. By insisting that Scots needed a clear understanding of the divine word to achieve spiritual peace, ministers solidified their own place in a tumultuous society. They provided, above all else, a link to God's will, thanks to their exceptional command of the Bible. Last, if Scottish men and women wondered why they struggled so much with temptation to sin, these sermons informed them that they needed to look no further than the mirror for the answer. Preachers emphasized human sinfulness in hope that their parishioners would do just that. As one sermon put it, 'Christians should be full of eyes within to examine themselves and to see their own corruptions. There are many who have eyes without to take notice of other peoples carriage, but they have no eyes to look within to themselves'.[77] The sermonic discussions of human depravity in the context of demonic activity thus championed an internal, introspective turn that ministers hoped would result in a more pious, self-aware population.

Enemies Without

As the seventeenth century progressed, the church and many of its ministers became consumed with the spiritual backslide of their country. They worried that Scots of all sorts had grown complacent, losing ardour in the battle against Satan. Worse yet, evidence of demonic influence was rampant at the very top of British society – particularly in the person of Charles I and, later, his son Charles II. Ministers, especially those of the covenanting persuasion, found themselves engaged in warfare that was at once spiritual and political.[78] In their eyes, the success of the Presbyterian cause equalled the success of the Reforming mission itself. Because Satan

---

[77] Gray, *Directions and Instigations*, 113.

[78] There are many works that deal with religious controversy and the Covenanters in seventeenth-century Scotland. To name a few: Louise Yeoman, 'Heart-Work: Emotion, Empowerment and Authority in Covenanting Times' (PhD Thesis, University of St Andrews, 1991); Clare Jackson, *Restoration Scotland, 1660–1690: Royalist Politics, Religion, and Ideas* (Woodbridge: Boydell Press, 2003); John Morrill, ed., *The Scottish National Covenant in its British Context, 1638-51* (Edinburgh: Edinburgh University Press, 1991); David Stevenson, *The Covenanters* (Edinburgh: Edinburgh University Press, 1988); Tim Harris, *Restoration: Charles II and His Kingdoms, 1660–1685* (New York: Penguin, 2005).

lay behind all hindrances to the true faith, demonic belief provided a conceptual framework to understand political and spiritual turmoil as inextricably linked, as well as a language to communicate the severity of Scotland's crises to a wider audience.

Overtly politicized discussions of Satan escalated during the beginnings of the Wars of the Three Kingdoms and reached a climax during the Restoration. In 1638, a group of Presbyterian clergyman composed and signed the National Covenant, a document that opposed what its authors saw as Charles I's imposition of the English liturgy upon the Scottish church.[79] This document laid bare the aims of the church and its objections to the recent actions of the government, which the authors believed had been 'stirred up by Satan, and that Roman Antichrist'.[80] The men who promised to uphold the National Covenant became known as Covenanters, and self-identified as such.[81] The Covenanters faced their most intense period of political persecution during the reign of Charles II, who reinstated episcopacy in Scotland and actively sought to imprison and even execute the radical Presbyterian rebels. In the sermons of these Covenanters, one finds some of the most passionate and urgent discussions of Satan.

In explaining their angst about the spiritual decline of their country, these ministers told their congregations that the Devil worked in conjunction with an assortment of enemies, all poised to subvert the mission of the true church of Scotland. The question of who comprised the enemy shifted according to political and religious tensions, incorporating many enemies in Rome and beyond. Around 1630, John Livingstone told his congregation at Ancrum that the Pope was the supreme instrument of the Devil against the godly, for 'Satan has many engines, but there is one that is the master piece ... And he is rightly called the antichrist because he is both a enemie to Christ and ... has ordinances very like the ordinances of god, sits in

---

[79] This was not the first national covenant signed in Scotland; the first major covenant was composed in 1581 and bound those who signed it to uphold the reforms of the newly Protestant church against any and all Catholic incursions. Endorsed and signed by James VI, who hoped that the document implied loyalty to the king as well, the covenant of 1581 was also known as the King's Covenant. Though this covenant did not contain the theological implication of a contract with God, as did 1638 National Covenant, it none the less laid important groundwork for future covenanting documents. For a further discussion of the lead-up to the signing of the National Covenant of 1638, see David Stevenson's brief but very useful *The Covenanters*.

[80] Church of Scotland, *The National Covenant of the Kirk of Scotland and the Solemn League and Covenant of the Three Kingdoms* (Edinburgh, 1660). The National Covenant was signed in 1638 but was not printed in Scotland until 1660.

[81] It should be noted that those who were self-described as Covenanters after 1660 were wedded to the Solemn League and Covenant of 1643 as much as to the National Covenant of 1638, making the Covenanter movement a British endeavour, not a purely Scottish one. Thanks are due to Roger Mason for this insight.

the temple of god as god ...'.[82] During the wars of the mid-seventeenth-century, Scots used the framework of demonic activity to understand yet another foe. In a sermon delivered to the House of Commons on 28 February 1643, Robert Baillie averred that 'the great and chief leader of all those who oppose the Reformers of a Church or State, is the Devill'.[83] This sermon insisted in unambiguous language that Charles I, Archbishop Laud and their supporters were in league with Satan. During the period of the Restoration, when Presbyterians came under increasing fire from the government of Charles II, John Brown of Wamphray delivered a sermon which explained the contemporary plight of the Church in demonic terms:

> It is wonderfull to see how variously Satan doth assault the Churches of God, some one way, some another ... Against some, Satan doth raise cruel & bloody persecutions, others he endeavoureth to draw away from their stedfastness & zeale, by ensnareing allurements: a third sort he invadeth with all his troupes & forces at once: And thus is the lately glorious Church of Scotland tried this day.[84]

Clearly, ministers emphasized the demonic association of their enemies to further vilify any opposition, but in so doing they also expressed a genuine belief in the Satanic allegiance of their earthly adversaries.

On occasion, the diaries of lay Scots indicate an awareness of Satan's role in instigating the political conflicts that dominated the lives of many Scottish ministers. Quinton Dick, an Ayrshire farmer, observed in his diary the political tumult around him, including the conflicts between moderate and radical Presbyterians during the late 1670s and '80s.[85] Discussing the Cameronians and the assassination of Archbishop James Sharp in 1679, Dick lamented that 'some of that partie (instigat by the divel, I may say) to the dishonour of the Presbyterian cause, has put in practice by horried bloodsheds and other inhumane and vile actions'.[86] Mourning the violence of recent years, he wrote in 1684 that 'the divel is aloft in Scotland by one engine or other utterly to ruine the Presbyterian cause and work of reformation in that land'.[87] Throughout his diary, Dick connected political

---

[82] NLS, Wod. Qu. LXVII, 56r.
[83] Robert Baillie, *Satan the Leader and chief*, 33.
[84] John Brown, *An apologeticall relation of the particular sufferings of the faithfull ministers & professours of the Church of Scotland* (Edinburgh, 1665), n.p.
[85] Though a self-proclaimed Presbyterian, Dick refused to take up arms against Charles II, as the militant Cameronians had done. See Quinton Dick, 'A Brief Account', in Mullan, ed., *Protestant Piety in Early Modern Scotland*, 167–96.
[86] Ibid., 179.
[87] Ibid., 180.

infighting with the Devil's desire to overturn the true faith in Scotland, reflecting the language of contemporary sermons.

Political documents also mirrored the demonic language of sermons when explaining the religious and political plight of the Scots throughout the seventeenth century. An act passed by the Scottish Parliament in 1645 authorizing the *Directory of Public Worship* to replace the common prayer book revealed a familiar and intensely militaristic attitude about faith. The act proclaimed that 'all who are baptized in the name of Christ, do renounce, and by their baptism are bound to fight against the devil, the world, and the flesh ...', and implored God to strengthen the elect 'against the temptations of Satan, the cares of the world, the hardness of their own hearts, and whatsoever else may hinder their profitable and saving hearing'.[88] The fact that many political documents waxed sermonic is hardly surprising, given that their authors were often also clergymen. The line dividing the political from the spiritual was thread-thin at most, and discussions of the Devil comprised a crucial means of interpreting and conveying the intertwined political and religious struggles in post-Reformation Scotland.

This association of the Devil with enemies of the church was, in effect, a political tool. Yet behind the overtly political messages laid the potent and experiential fear that Satan was enjoying easy success in overturning the work of God. As Andrew Gray wrote in the mid-seventeenth century, 'I confesse the devil needs not to be at much pains in these dayes, there is many which gives the devil work and imployment, yea, and if he seeks not them, they will seek him!'[89] While earlier reformers like Calvin and later Knox certainly cautioned the faithful about the danger in 'resting', seventeenth-century Scottish ministers were increasingly fervent in their admonitions against 'contentment'. They sensed that the religious fervour and commitment to reform had waned after Protestantism had been firmly established in churches throughout the country. In response, ministers across Scotland used their pulpits to deliver sermons aimed at dismissing any misconceptions that the battle with Satan might be over. By at times attaching a literal call to arms with discussions of concern for the spiritual welfare of the Scottish church and people, ministers hoped to awaken their congregations to Christ's battle cry and their godly duty.

In one particularly evocative exhortation delivered at Inverness in 1638, Andrew Cant lamented the recent spiritual backslide of Scotland and painted Satan as the maestro of this decline:

---

[88] Parliament of Scotland, *Charles I. Parl. 3. Sess. An Act of the Parliament of the Kingdom of Scotland approving and establishing the Directory for Publick Worship* (Edinburgh, 1645).

[89] Gray, *Directions and Instigations*, 156.

> Long ago our gracious God was pleased to visit this nation with the light of His glorious Gospel, by planting a vineyard in, and making His glory to arise upon Scotland. A wonder! that so great a God should shine on so base a soil ... But alas! Satan envied our happiness, brake our ranks, poisoned our fountains, mudded and defiled our streams; and while the watchmen slept, the wicked one sowed his tares ... Truth is fallen in the streets, our dignity is gone, our credit lost, our crown is fallen from our heads; our reputation is turned to imputation.[90]

To ministers like Cant, Satan lay behind all of Scotland's political and religious troubles. This message of Satan's envy and attempts at ruin mirrors that of later Puritan divines who averred that demonic malice was especially directed at the 'brave souls' who had colonized New England, which in their view was a heathen world once under the domain of Satan. As Cotton Mather wrote in *The Wonders of the Invisible World* (1692), 'never were more *Satanical Devices* used for the Unsetling of any People under the Sun, than what have been Employ'd for the Extirpation of the *Vine* which God has here *Planted* ...'.[91] As for their Reformed Scottish counterparts, Satan was a favourite topic of Puritan ministers who, finding themselves in a both figurative and literal wilderness, viewed the struggles of the New England community as part of the larger cosmic battle between Good and Evil, God and Satan.[92]

Alexander Henderson emphasized the persistent necessity of spiritual warfare in Scotland in a 1638 sermon by which he chastised his audience for being so foolish as to expect spiritual rest. 'Ye should not imagine', he explained

> ... that ever the kirk, so long as she is here, shall be free of afflictions ... No, I will assure you it would not be so, for the devil is not dead yet, and he has evermore his awin supposts, and malignant spirits anew to raise up to trouble his kirk ... And therefore think not that ye sail have a heavenly peace so long as ye are here ; but ye must put on the whole armour of God, and resolve to fight ... .[93]

---

[90] *The Covenants And The Covenanters: Covenants, Sermons, and Documents of the Covenanted Reformation*, James Kerr, ed. (Edinburgh: R.W. Hunter, 1895), 77–8.

[91] Cotton Mather, *The Wonders of the Invisible World* (Boston, 1693), xii.

[92] For a thorough and controversial discussion of this 'wilderness' mentality as a motive for Puritan emigration to North America, see Avihu Zakai, *Exile and Kingdom: History and Apocalypse in Puritan Migration to America* (Cambridge: Cambridge University Press, 1992); For more on the New England ministry, see David D. Hall, *The Faithful Shepherd; A History of the New England Ministry in the Seventeenth Century* (Chapel Hill: University of North Carolina Press, 1972).

[93] Henderson, *Sermons*, 245.

Samuel Rutherford issued his own militaristic call to arms at Anworth during the turmoil of the mid-century, telling his audience that 'the Devil will not be removed without Blood, Sweating, and Great Violence'.[94] In the same sermon, which was later published in Glasgow and London, Rutherford went on to say that 'the Devil's War is better than the Devil's Peace ...'tis terrible to be carried to Hell without any Noise of Feet: The Wheels of Satan's Chariot are oiled with carnal Rest, and they go without ratling and Noise ...'.[95] In a 1672 sermon delivered in the parish of Carluke, Michael Bruce implored his congregation. 'Is there any noise or shaking in your dry bones? ... is there any thing among you that says ye will be a Living Armie to God or all be done?'[96] Even when the world seemed at peace and Satan appeared to rest, ministers instructed their parishioners not to cease in their crusade. As John Brown put it, 'an unseen and quiet devil, may be more hazardous, than a seen and a roaring devil; Corruptions grownot always most, when they rage most'.[97] This focus on warfare and the need to maintain the Reformation's success in the face of demonic assaults informed audiences of individual responsibility as well as communal obligation to Scotland.

Apocalyptic thought in Scotland, introduced by early reformers like Knox and firmly entrenched by the seventeenth century, drove much of this militarism and obsession with continued reform. As the drama of the Reformation itself had done, the turmoil of mid-seventeenth-century events indicated that Satan raged more than ever before and that the end of the world was correspondingly nigh. Ministers like Daniel Woodward believed that 'the end of all dayes, the end of the world, the consummation of weeks, moneths, and years' fast approached and strove to communicate the immediacy of the Apocalypse to their parishioners.[98] As James Renwick told his audience in the 1670s, 'if ye have any respect to God and his truths, ye cannot but be concerned in this evil and declining day'.[99] Samuel Rutherford described this ongoing turmoil in Scotland as an intrinsic part of Christ's second coming, explaining that 'what wonder is it that Multitudes of Heresies and Sects, and many blasphemous and false Ways arise now, when the Lord is to build up Zion ... Satan raiseth up Storms and Winds in the broad Lake of Brimstone to drown the Church of God: Christ hath not fair weather when he goeth to Sea'.[100] These eschatological

---

[94] Rutherford, *Trial and Triumph*, 401.
[95] Ibid., 402.
[96] Michael Bruce, *The Rattling of Dry Bones* (Edinburgh, 1672), 4.
[97] Brown, *Christ in Believers*, 97.
[98] Daniel Woodward, *An Almanac but for one Day, or the Son of Man reckoning with Man* (Glasgow, 1671), 5.
[99] James Renwick, *Christ Our Righteousness* (Glasgow, 1776), 8.
[100] Rutherford, *Trial and Triumph*, 461.

ideas infused discussions of Satan and his activities in the world with renewed urgency, and minister took great oratorical and written strides to communicate this urgency to a wider audience.

A warning from the General Assembly in 1645, addressed to the 'Noblemen, Barons, Gentlemen, Burrows, Ministers, and Commons' as well as the armies of Scotland, reified to Scots of all sorts the urgency of this apocalyptic conflict:

> Satan is full of fury, because he knowes he hath but a short time to reigne. The Cockatrice before hatched, is now broken forth into a Viper. The danger was before feared, now it is felt; before imminent, now incumbent; before our division, now our destruction is endeavored; before the Sword was fourbished and made ready, now the Sword is made fat with flesh, and drunk with Bloud, and yet it hungreth and thirsteth for more.[101]

In the Last Days, more than ever before, the Scottish people ought not be surprised about the trials facing them. As Scripture foretold, Satan would be loosed from his chain in hell during the Apocalypse in order to carry out God's divine justice. In surveying the ongoing political and religious tumult of the seventeenth century, evidence of the Devil's loosing seemed to many to be undeniable.

Amid this apocalyptic anxiety, ministers commonly gave sermons on the Book of Revelation that included discussions of the impending wrath of God and furious actions of Satan. As Andrew Gray told his congregation, 'believe it, the day is coming, that either that contract between you and Christ, shall be eternally confirmed, or that contract between the devil and you, shall be eternally ratified'.[102] By asserting the immediacy and finality of the Apocalypse in the context of predestined election, Scottish ministers attempted to drive home the absolute necessity of battle with the Devil and his army as part of the road to salvation. In a particularly ominous sermon delivered in the late seventeenth century, Alexander Pethane described Scotland's current state with apocalyptic rhetoric: 'for Scotland shall be drowned with Blood er long ... in that Fearful Day of Treachery and Covenant-breaking with God'.[103] With these words, Pethane hoped to

---

[101] *The Records of the Kirk of Scotland*, 425. Cockatrice, a translation of a Hebrew word used in the King James Bible, referred to a mythical dragon with a rooster's head, supposedly produced from a cock's egg. Modern versions of Scripture use the terms 'viper' or 'poisonous snake'.

[102] Andrew Gray, *Great precious promises* (Edinburgh, 1667), 145.

[103] Alexander Pethane, *The Lords Trumpet sounding an Alarm Against Scotland* (Edinburgh, 1682), 6. Here Pethane was specifically targeting the popish ministers, professors at Oxford, and 'the Bloody Duke of York', all of whom he believed to be in league with the Devil.

enflame his congregation with the desire to combat evil in the Last Days. In so doing, they could be assured that final salvation would bear the fruits of their labour.

Comfort for the Afflicted

Warnings about Satan and his legions, lamentations of man's sad spiritual state, and anxieties about the Apocalypse thus resounded from pulpits throughout early modern Scotland. Yet within these bleaker messages persisted the foundational idea that the elect would eventually emerge victorious. Because salvation was predetermined, nothing the Devil did could thwart God's holy plan. David Willingham explained to his congregation in the late seventeenth century that the death of Christ had given 'the Devill a dead stroke ... He has destroyed him, that had the power of death, that is the Devill. He hath broken the Devills armes: He has cut off Goliah's head with his sword ...'.[104] With the sacrifice of his son and attending salvation for the elect, God eliminated any chance that Satan had to hinder salvation. Reiterating this point in another sermon, Willingham told his audience to take comfort in Christ, even when assaulted by Satan: 'It may be the Devill raise a storme on some of your consciences ... well, then for your comfort Christ has broken the serpents head ... if your conscience be sprinkled by the blood of sprinkling, ye are saved from the destroying Angell'.[105] The use of the word 'conscience' is key here. Ministers like Willingham recognized the internal struggles imbedded in the Reformed Protestant experience and sought to comfort their parishioners with Scripture-based promises of eventual relief from sin and Satan.[106]

This comforting imperative was especially prevalent in the context of apocalyptic thought. During the turmoil of the Civil Wars, for example, when the end of the world seemed undeniably at hand, Robert Baillie assured his congregation that at the end of days, the godly 'at last in all these have become more then Conquerours, the Devill by the mouth of Christ is chased away from further molesting them, the spots of sinne are washed off, as if they never had been on ... they are clothed and made Beautiful with the graces of the Spirit'.[107] The overall message of apocalyptic hope

---

[104] NLS, MS 5770, f.60.
[105] Ibid., f. 110.
[106] See, for example, John Brown, *Christ in Believers*; William Thompson, *The churches Comfort, or a Sermon on John XVI* (Edinburgh, 1661); Boyd, *The Balme of Gilead*, and Rutherford, *Trial and Triumph*.
[107] Baillie, *Satan the Leader*, 7.

revolved around the understanding that the Devil's actions in the world would ultimately be rendered meaningless. As John Brown explained:

> No Devils, nor Instruments or Devils there, to molest or tempt us; no inward stirrings of Corruptions there; no Objects to divert there, no lusting of the Eye, no lusting of the Flesh, nor pride of Life, shall be there. That Glory secures the Soul, and seats it beyond the reach of all spiritual Enemies: There, shall Believers be as Princes, Rulers and Conquerors over the World; And there, shall Satan, with all his Devices and Instruments be utterly routed, and eternally shakled under their feet, and shall never more be unloosed.[108]

This assurance of victory rang especially true for the Covenanters such as Brown, who, after refusing to take the Abjuration Oath at the orders of John Graham of Claverhouse, became a martyr for the covenanting cause in 1685.[109] As Leif Dixon has recently argued, the doctrine of predestination, despite its potential for spiritual anxiety, was pastorally intended as a source 'of comfort and contextualisation for those who risk death or dislocation, and for those who, in war, are forced to kill'.[110]

In these discussions of eventual victory, ministers asserted that earthly struggles, especially those against Satan, served as integral pieces of the salvation process. In Scotland, particularly in times of social, political and religious strife, many people – including members of the clergy – craved assurance that these challenges would not detract from their journey to heaven. Michael Bruce, who had faced intense religious persecution under the reign of Charles II, gave a sermon in which he explained that 'tribulation is a piece of the paved way to the kingdom of God'.[111] He reassured his congregation that 'our Master can borrow the Devils wind to guarantee his ship sail the better to the Harbour; Tribulation shall blow us to the kingdom, and shall not blow us by it'.[112] It is worth noting in Bruce's sermons, and in many others, the constant use of the words 'us' and 'we'. This communal rhetoric stemmed from the self-identity of these Scottish divines; they believed that they, along with their flocks, were the new Israelites, a status that created an important sense of community and solidarity in the face of demonic and other struggles.

The promise of election notwithstanding, sermons emphasized that the godly must not act as passive recipients of divine mercy. Rather, they must reach out to God in moments of need. As Zachary Boyd explained in

---

[108] Brown, *Christ in believers*, 10.
[109] This oath was produced by the government in 1684, and required that all Scots swear allegiance to the King, or be killed.
[110] Dixon, *Practical Predestinarians*, 7.
[111] Bruce, *Soul Confirmation*, 2.
[112] Ibid., 3.

1628, 'troubles make us to crye, bodily afflictions rouse us up to crye: but alas while wee sinne we keepe silence ... While Satan is forcing us with his temptations to offend our God, wee often yeelde thereunto without any crye to our God: It is then especially that wee shoulde crye vnto him'.[113] After highlighting the problem of human silence in the face of Satan, Boyd advised his Glaswegian parishioners on how they might apply his words to their lives. 'The use of this', he claimed

> ... is that whensoever wee shall perceive Sathan comming with force for to deflower, or defile our soule Christs *Damsell*, we incontinent crye with all our force unto GOD. *Lord help mee: Lord leade mee not into temptation: O God, prevent mee and keepe me from these snares: bee thou a shelter for mee, and a strong tower from the enemie.*[114]

This is an apt illustration of how discussions of Satan in early modern Scottish sermons served to move parishioners not simply to believe, but to act.

Whether or not these pastoral assurances of victory actually comforted Scottish audiences is difficult to assess, especially given that comforting descriptions of God's grace and demonic impotence were usually attended by intense warnings about Satan's assaults on the godly and reprobate alike, as well as lamentations of human depravity. The frequency with which ministers aimed to provide assurances of victory to their parishioners suggests that there existed a great deal of fear of the Devil and insecurity about personal salvation. In response, ministers attempted to assure their flocks that fears and doubts were, in fact, key indications of godliness. A common refrain of the day was 'is the devil angry with thee, then God is at peace with thee'.[115] For Scots insecure in their own salvation – and likely many fell into this category – these assurances may have brought little or great relief, or both at different moments in their lives. It can be safely said, however, that from a pedagogical perspective, promises of victory over Satan served a three-fold purpose. First, they reminded the audiences of a foundational component of Reformed theology – the sovereignty and goodness of God in contrast to the evil of both Satan and humankind. Second, these assurances reiterated and reified the doctrine of election. Last, promises of victory and eventual relief from Satan lent insecure and faith-confident Scots alike a grander purpose in and explanation for their daily struggles.

---

[113] Boyd, *The Balme of Gilead*, 123–4.
[114] Ibid., 124–5, emphasis original.
[115] Welsh, 'Upon the Christian Warfare', *Forty-Eight Select Sermons*, 145.

Conclusion

In many respects, the dissemination and maintenance of Reformed Protestantism in Scotland hinged upon the sermon, a powerful tool for communicating theological ideas to the masses. Teaching doctrine was not enough; ministers were charged with moving their congregations to believe and behave like good Christians. Discussions of the Devil figured prominently in the ministerial efforts to explain theology to the laity. By conveying the complexities of Reformed theology, such as predestination, the depravity of humanity and the sovereignty of God through discussions of the Satan, ministers clarified and reified theology for Scots of all sorts. Discussions of Satan served not only as didactic tools to promote godly conduct and communal solidarity; they also provided a necessary pastoral language to communicate key elements of Reformed Protestantism in an immediate and evocative way.

Beyond the theological purposes of such discussions, the prominence of Satan in Scottish sermons also suggests a concern for the Devil amongst the laity. Ministers were not only beholden to the institutions of the church. They were also charged with meeting the spiritual needs of their parishioners, who had a surprising amount of agency in selecting their ministers. Equally significant, ministers consistently cooperated with the lay elders of the kirk session in enforcing moral discipline throughout Scottish parishes.[116] Far from being distant from the needs of their congregations, ministers remained throughout their lives heavily invested in the day-to-day activities and concerns of ordinary Scots. The fact that Satan remained a central feature of sermons throughout the seventeenth century implies that parishioners desired to hear more about the Devil. Even if they did not express this desire explicitly, the immense popularity of preachers like John Welsh, Samuel Rutherford and John Livingstone, whose sermons contain frequent discussions of the Devil, indicates a widespread and vested interest in the activities of Satan.

Perhaps most importantly, by focusing on the Devil in their sermons, ministers instilled their audiences with a strong sense of individual and communal identity and responsibility. Communities came together through the very act of attending a sermon. Preaching about Satan reinforced this collective identity, in both a local and a national sense, by expounding on shared turmoil, responsibility and eventual victory. On a personal level, sermonic discussions of the relationship between the Devil and human depravity profoundly shaped the internal lives and self-perceptions of Scots of all sorts. This influence of Satan on individual and communal identity would inform the society and culture of early modern Scotland in innumerable and consequential ways.

---

[116] See Todd, *Culture of Protestantism*, 361–401.

CHAPTER 3

A Constant Adversary

Tales of spiritual striving and struggle abound in the historical records of post-Reformation Scotland. Many Scots reported a consuming awareness of an ongoing contest between the forces of Good and Evil unfolding around and within them. Despite the promise of eventual victory for the elect, Satan served as an unyielding antagonist in their mortal lives. As the educated layman and self-described 'country-gentleman' Andrew Hay wrote in 1659, 'no place is free of Satans temptations'.[1] This chapter surveys the experiential muddle of emotions and interpretations provoked by personal belief in and interactions with Satan. For those Scots able and inclined to record their religious experiences, demonic encounters could be at once individual and communal, political and spiritual, terrifying and reassuring. For some, these confrontations entailed a good deal of hope and comfort in the decree of election and the community of the godly. For many others, the personal relationship with the Devil was dominated by insecurity and fear. Whatever the nature of Scottish experiences with Satan, they proved formative to how many Scots understood and defined themselves, their communities and the faith that guided their lives.

Along with sermons and theological works, discussions of the Devil in Scotland often appear in 'self-writings', defined here as first-person, usually autobiographical writings that include letters, spiritual diaries, political memoirs and personal covenants of educated Scots.[2] In the nearly one hundred discrete self-writings examined for this chapter, Scottish men and women laid bare their struggles with Satan and demonstrated how such experiences informed their broader religious lives and identities.[3] Some of these accounts were published, while others remain only in manuscript form. All of the diverse genres of self-writing, from the spiritual diary kept only for personal reasons to the autobiography written in hindsight

---

[1] Andrew Hay of Craignethan, *The Diary of Andrew Hay of Craignethan*, ed. Alexander George Reid (Edinburgh: Scottish History Society, 1901), 8.

[2] On the genre of Scottish self-writing, the most comprehensive and important work is David Mullan's *Narratives of the Religious Self in Early-Modern Scotland* (Aldershot: Ashgate, 2010).

[3] Mullan lists about eighty examples of Scottish autobiographical writings that focus explicitly on religion, about a dozen of which were composed prior to 1640. On top of consulting the eighty works noted by Mullan, I have also considered as part of this genre of 'self-writing' about 25 letters (or groups of letters) and political memoirs from separate authors that detailed their religious experiences.

and with the intent of public consumption, are fraught with problems for the historian hoping to sort fact from fiction.[4] These men and women presented their lives, and indeed their encounters with Satan, in a very self-conscious way, trying to fashion themselves as the deserving godly they hoped to be. Yet as David Mullan has argued, in Scottish spiritual narratives, 'self-imagining is very much part of the story – the genre depends upon a strong sense of the self as worthy of exemplification, or at least as representing a story worth telling, under the watchful eyes of a holy God'.[5] Within this self-imagining and sometimes contrived presentation of life events, both the patterns in and specifics of these accounts illustrate what educated early modern Scots fervently believed about Satan's involvement in their personal lives. Demonic encounters may have been purposefully constructed, but those constructions are in and of themselves revealing of the relationship between the Devil and Scottish piety and identity.

Many of the authors of Scottish self-writings were family members and wives of clergymen, or members of the clergy themselves. Ministers promoted the keeping of spiritual diaries and personal covenants as an integral part of godly piety, and lay people from the upper echelons of society also kept record of their religious experiences. Memoirs, usually intended for publication or for family consumption, chronicled the lives of godly Scots as they critically assessed (and fashioned) the trajectory of their spiritual and political lives. Letters, often penned by individuals fleeing persecution in the latter part of the seventeenth century, reveal how the perceptions of Satan featured prominently in the interpretation of personal and political struggle. The men and women who composed these religious narratives in various forms were thus elites and represent only a small slice of a mostly illiterate society.[6] The vast majority of these authors were also committed Reformed Protestants, ranging from moderate, royalist Presbyterians to radical Covenanters. Clearly, this is a wide array of people,

---

[4] See David, *Narratives of the Religious Self*. On the genre of autobiography in Puritan England and New England, see Owen C. Watkins, *The Puritan Experience: Studies in Spiritual Autobiography* (New York: Schocken, 1972); William Matthews, 'Seventeenth-Century Autobiography', in William Matthews and Ralph W. Rader, eds, *Autobiography, Biography, and the Novel* (Los Angeles, CA: William Andrews Clark Memorial Library, 1973); Elizabeth Botanaki, 'Seventeenth-Century English Women's Spiritual Diaries: Self-Examination, Covenanting and Account-Keeping', *Sixteenth Century Journal* 30 (1999): 3–21; Paul Seaver, *Wallington's World: A Puritan Artisan in Seventeenth-Century London* (Stanford, CA: Stanford University Press, 1985).

[5] Mullan, *Narratives of the Religious Self*, 8.

[6] On literacy and education in Scotland, see R.A. Houston, 'The Literacy Myth?: Illiteracy in Scotland, 1630–1760', *Past and Present* 96 (1982), 89–91; John Bannerman, 'Literacy in the Highlands', in Ian B. Cowan and Duncan Shaw, eds, *The Renaissance and Reformation in Scotland: Essays in Honour of Gordon Donaldson* (Edinburgh: Scottish Academic Press, 1983), 214–35.

and yet all of these men and women had a faith rooted in Reformed theology and discussed the Devil in similar ways. Their voices, though those of a minority, provide historians with a complex but accessible glimpse into Scottish perceptions of and experiences with the Devil.

An Internal Enemy

The self-writings of godly Scots often read as reports from the frontlines of an internal spiritual war, depicting a populace perpetually wrestling with demonic temptations and doubts. Temptation and subversion had long been considered powers of the Devil, but following the Reformation, Scottish reformers increasingly emphasized this demonic temptation in its internal, mental form, only sparingly discussing Satan in any material or corporeal terms.[7] The focus on the internal nature of the Devil resulted, in large part, from an encompassing Protestant emphasis on controlling the baser instincts of depraved human hearts and minds. As multiple generations of Scottish divines would aver, Christians ought to live a godly life not only in word and deed, but also in thought – and it was through human thought that Satan proved the most dangerous. The wiles of the Devil became a fixation for many Protestants in Scotland who perceived Satan's presence in nearly every negative thought, misgiving and challenge life presented them.

Of all of the delusions of Satan, the implantation of doubts about salvation specifically and faith more generally was considered the most dangerous. Satan, the clergy warned, would approach the righteous and unredeemed alike with a full arsenal of temptation and spiritual confusion, leading them to doubt their redemption and the grace of God.[8] Such sermonic warnings informed and were confirmed by personal experience. In his memoirs, the minister James Fraser of Brea detailed how, in years

---

[7] On demonic temptation in Catholic theology, see Jeffrey B. Russell, *Lucifer: The Devil in the Middle Ages* (Ithaca, NY: Cornell University Press, 1984), 36–37, 100–101, 202–6; Russell, *Mephistopheles: The Devil in the Modern World* (Ithaca, NY: Cornell University Press, 1986), 50–54. According to Nathan Johnstone, 'a characteristically Protestant demonism emerged from a subtle realignment of emphasis rather than attack upon tradition. The central focus of this change was to emphasise the Devil's power of temptation, especially his ability to enter directly into the mind and plant thoughts within it that led people to sin'. See Johnstone, *The Devil and Demonism in Early Modern England* (Cambridge: Cambridge University Press, 2006), 1–2.

[8] The internal assaults of the Devil were a constant theme of seventeenth century sermons. See, for example, Andrew Gray, *Directions and instigations to the duty of prayer how, and why the heart is to be kept with diligence* (Edinburgh, 1669); John Brown, *From Christ in believers the hope of glory being the substance of several sermons* (Edinburgh, 1694); Robert Baillie, *Satan the Leader in chief to all who resist the reparation of sion* (London, 1643), and Alexander Henderson, *Sermons, prayers and pulpit addresses of Alexander Henderson*, ed. Thomas R. Martin (Edinburgh: John Maclaren, 1867).

gone by, the Devil 'did most cruelly, tyrannically, and furiously batter my soul with objections tending to discourage me, and to create evil thoughts of God in me, and to make me believe that all this while I was living in an unconverted condition and delusion'.[9] An Edinburgh woman named Mistress Rutherford wrote that for six long weeks during her teenage years, she wrestled with fears that she was doomed to hell, as 'the sight and sense of these things put my soul in such torment as is inexpressible, finding myself guilty of every tribunal of God and my own conscience'.[10] The frequent rumination about salvation in the midst of demonic struggles highlights the anxiety and powerlessness provoked by the fear of momentary or permanent estrangement from God. In the context of predestination and human depravity, the perception of closeness to God remained essential for the spiritual confidence of faith-conscious Scots.

When facing demonically induced turmoil and doubt, many Scots reported difficulty in discerning the origins of evil thoughts and unchristian cognitions. Did they arise from their own corrupt minds, or had Satan planted them there? While imprisoned in 1667 for opposition to Charles II, Sir John Chiesly found himself overcome by concerns for the aberrations of his heart and soul. 'O my soul', he lamented, 'thou art become so sloathfull in following the Lord, why dost thou so wander in prayer, and thy heart is not fixed ... '.[11] He wondered whether this spiritual laxity was a result of his own nature and or of God's letting the Devil rouse him to sin. 'O my soul', he implored, 'is the lord become better and thou worse, or doest thou but see more of thy own naughtiness then formerly, or doth the Lord let Satan ever more lose and not restrain thy corruptions as formerly? O what a vast wilderness of sin and wickedness do I see in my heart'.[12] In a 1728 piece of last advice for his children, John Stevenson, a farmer in Carrick, wrote similarly of his sinful nature and the erroneous thoughts that troubled him as a youth. He was, as many other Scots seem to have been, persistently confused about the source of his transgressive thinking. 'These unworthy thoughts of God filled me with horror', he wrote, 'and I neither allowed them nor entertained them, but at the time could not discern that they were Satan's fiery darts, but rather charged them on myself, which still increased my trouble'.[13] According to

---

[9] James Fraser of Brea, 'Memoirs of James Fraser of Brea', in W.K. Tweedie, ed., *Select Biographies*, 2 vols (Edinburgh: Wodrow Society, 1841), ii.212.

[10] Mistress Rutherford, 'Mistress Rutherford's Conversion Narrative', *Scottish History Society, Miscellany xiii*, ed. David Mullan (Edinburgh: Scottish History Society, 2004), 163.

[11] Part of the diary of Sir John Chiesly, 1667, NLS, Wod. Oct. XXXI, f. 41rv.

[12] Ibid.

[13] John Stevenson, 'A Rare Soul-Strengthening and Comforting Cordial for Old and Young Christians: Being the last advice of John Stevenson, in the shire of Ayr, to his children and grandchildren', in W.K. Tweedie, ed., *Select Biographies* (Edinburgh: Wodrow Society, 1841), ii. 417.

both Catholic and Protestant theology, Satan had the power to place evil thoughts into the susceptible minds of individuals. At the same time, the innate corruption of humanity made the mortal mind irrevocably prone to malicious thoughts, independent of the Devil or not.

Darren Oldridge has suggested that the fact that the Devil could inject evil thoughts into human minds provided an opportunity for the godly to profess their secret doubts and desires without the risk of appearing to be the author of these thoughts.[14] Yet even if Satan was identified as the source of such transgressions, men and women in their infinite weakness were still to blame for allowing demonically induced notions into their minds. One letter, anonymously written in Scotland in 1698, explained that while the Devil often introduced blasphemous thoughts, the human heart was equally culpable, for 'there is the root of all sins in [the] heart' that 'yields many times' to the suggestions of Satan. Demonically induced or not, for many Scots, sins and doubts led to intense fears of punishment from God, with the divine sentence often being carried out by the Devil. The Reformation had removed many of the traditional rites and ceremonies that offered protection from the Devil, and now only God could rescue them from demonic assaults. Accordingly, prayer and beseeching of the Lord for aid against Satan appeared repeatedly in Scottish self-writings.[15] In this way, struggles against Satan made manifest a key tenet of Reformed theology – that the spiritual malaise of humankind and the doctrine of double predestination made one's dependence on God absolute and eternal.

Though Scots usually encountered Satan during internal, psychological struggles, the despair caused by the Devil had the potential to wreak not only spiritual harm, but also physical damage. As James Fraser of Brea described, 'the devil rested not in the meantime violently and unseasonably to press some strict duties, seeking to undo my body and spirit at once, driving furiously as Jehu did'.[16] In the early 1650s, after Katherine Collace had entered into a personal covenant with God as a teenager, she was beset with demonic assaults. These assaults, though internal in nature, led to bodily strife. She described how, 'being under a violent fit of sickness', she could not get out of bed. Collace set about praying for relief, but 'Satan in his usual was opposing, to the breaking of my body'.[17] In some of the

---

[14] Oldridge, *The Devil in Early Modern England*, 47.

[15] Alec Ryrie discusses the importance of combating the Devil through prayer as an essential component of this godly path. See Ryrie, *Being Protestant*, 243–7.

[16] James Fraser of Brea, 'Memoirs', 213. This is a reference to Jehu, a king of Israel who killed many and supposedly drove a chariot like a madman: 'the driving is like the driving of Jehu the son of Nimshi; for he driveth furiously': 2 Kings 9:10.

[17] Katharine Collace, 'Memoirs or Spiritual Exercises', in David Mullan, ed., *Women's Life Writing in Early Modern Scotland: Writing the Evangelical Self, c. 1670–1730* (Aldershot: Ashgate, 2003), 399–445.

more dramatic self-writings of godly Scots, such encounters with the Devil resulted in dangerous illness and even thoughts of suicide.[18]

More broadly, the internal temptations or instigations of Satan might lead to the bodily harm and even death of another. To give one brief example, in 1567 Robert Birrel, burgess of Edinburgh, detailed in his diary the events of a tragic and bizarre murder. A man called Peter caught his brother, George, in bed with his sister-in-law. In retribution, Peter stabbed him. As George was dying, his body fell over the cradle of his child and smothered the infant to death. This 'rair and vounderful accident' was no accident at all, according to Birrel; this tragedy had occurred at 'Sathan's instigation'.[19] Here, the internal actions of the Devil in inciting both adultery and a murderous response produced the tragic death of an innocent infant. Though anxiety about demonic temptation had come to supersede concern for bodily harm, internal struggles often manifested themselves in profoundly external ways.

Moreover, while the godly understood the Devil to be a primarily internal foe, they did not altogether abandon the idea that Satan could have a corporeal reality. This was most evident in cases of witchcraft, when the Devil often appeared before supposed witches as a man or a black animal – a physical description that was accepted, if not outright suggested, by the authorities overseeing the trial.[20] In self-writings, however, Scots usually described Satan in the intangible form of an apparition or an illusion. As Mistress Rutherford described in her diary, after her grandfather's death she began to see apparitions of him for twenty straight days, which she believed to be 'the devil in his likeness'.[21] Elizabeth Blackadder wrote in 1684 that when she was young, she was perpetually terrified of apparitions or spirits. She reported that once she was

> ... lying into a room alone, and there came into the chamber a great black dog, which I was tempted to believe this was the devil. But the greater fear overcame the lesser, for being under the terror of an approaching eternity and dead of an angry God, I cried out to the Lord, 'O, I fear no enemy but thyself'. Towards

---

[18] For more information on suicide in early modern Britain, see R.A. Houston, *Punishing the Dead: Suicide, Lordship, and Community in Britain, 1500–1800* (Oxford: Oxford University Press, 2010); Michael Macdonald and Terence Murphy, *Sleepless Souls: Suicide in Early Modern England* (Oxford: Oxford University Press, 1990).

[19] Robert Birrell, 'The Diary of Robert Birrell', in J.G. Daylell, ed., *Fragments of Scottish History* (Edinburgh: A. Constable, 1798), 12–13.

[20] See Joyce Miller, 'Men in Black: Appearances of the Devil in Early Modern Scottish Witchcraft Discourse' in Julian Goodare, Lauren Martin and Joyce Miller, eds, *Witchcraft and Belief in Early Modern Scotland* (Basingstoke: Palgrave Macmillan, 2008), 144–65.

[21] Mistress Rutherford, 'Conversion narrative', 153.

the morning I got ease of my outward trouble and had a very deep sense of the Lord's mercy to me in preventing my utter ruin by death at that time.[22]

In retrospect, both Rutherford and Blackadder acknowledged that the apparition or being they saw was not the Devil, but an illusion caused by Satan or by their spiritual weakness. At the time of their demonic visions, however, they were convinced that Satan had appeared before them, prepared to drag them away to hell. Whether he appeared before Scots in material form or implanted in their minds the desire to sin, Satan's primarily threat remained his ability to cause fear and trembling over personal salvation, sin and estrangement from God, all of which had profound consequences that could be at once psychological and physical.

The Ubiquity of Struggle

The struggle against Satan dominated the lives of the godly, regardless of age, sex or social standing. A life full of unavoidable, persistent encounters with the enemy was both a common reality and a powerful religious expectation that had long existed at the heart of Reformed theology. As Calvin wrote in his *Institutes*

> ... the fact that the devil is everywhere called God's adversary and ours also ought to fire us to an unceasing struggle against him ... If we are minded to affirm Christ's kingdom as we ought, we must wage irreconcilable war with him who is plotting its ruin. Again, if we care about our salvation at all, we ought to have neither peace nor truce with him who continually lays traps to destroy it.[23]

The message of Satan's unrelenting assault on the godly was, as we have seen, repeated time and time again from pulpits across Scotland. The fact that engagement with the Devil was considered a key component of a Protestant life only reinforced the individual, experiential reality of Satan for many Scots, who entered into this unceasing war with the Devil, both consciously and subconsciously, from the very moment they became believers.

Many Scots recalled their youthful years in particular as cesspools of ungodly deeds and demonically induced thoughts. Only God, they averred, had pulled them out. In his late sixteenth-century autobiography, reformer

---

[22] Elizabeth Blackadder, 'A Short Account of the Lord's Way of Providence towards me in my Pilgrimage Journeys', in Mullan, ed., *Women's Life Writing*, 387.

[23] John Calvin, *Institutes of the Christian Religion*, 2 vols, ed. J.T. McNeill (Philadelphia, PA: Westminster John Knox Press, 1960), I.xvi.15.

James Melville described his struggles with Satan while he was a 'vile and corrupt youth' who wrestled, above all, with demonically encouraged temptations of the flesh.[24] These were internal temptations in their inception, but obviously had physical consequences. In his autobiography, Melville describes himself as a handsome man ('not unlovlie', in his words) and 'of nature very loving and amorous'. This, he explained, allowed Satan 'to snare me, and spoil the haill wark of God in me'. The Devil encouraged his sexual pursuits, and he had 'many lovers' on 'many occasiones, in diverse places and sortes of persones'.[25] The godly often attributed unclean sexual thoughts or actions to demonic temptations. This by no means absolved them of their responsibility in sinning, however, for the Devil's success depended on the corrupt nature of humankind, which was especially unchecked during the follies of adolescence.

The autobiography of an educated layman, James Nimmo, exemplifies the cycle of temptation, fear and divine mercy that characterized youthful encounters with Satan.[26] Born in 1654, Nimmo, a self-identified Covenanter, recorded the narrative of his life in his elderly years. His narrative's subtitle, 'Written for his own Satisfaction to Keep in some remembrance the lords way dealing and kindness towards him', made clear the purpose of recording his experiences. The Devil played a leading role in young Nimmo's life, luring him into temptation and highlighting the viler qualities of his nature. Speaking of his boyish follies, Nimmo wrote that he committed sin thoughtlessly and often, with 'the Divel leading [him] captive att his pleasure'.[27] In his school days, he was moody and selfish. To those that followed him with 'fairness and aplaus', he was kind and loyal, but to those who crossed him, his affection turned sour, as 'the verie venom of Hell and nature of Sathan appeared to ane extreame'.[28]

In 1676, at the age of twenty-two, Nimmo fell very ill for eight days. After recovering, he began to contemplate the evil of his ways, and he 'fell into such dreadfull terrors that was insuportabl, apprehending it could not consist with the justice of God but that the earth should open & swallow me up to hell qwick'.[29] After this episode of spiritual angst, fear of the abyss proved a powerful incentive to seek the righteous path, and Nimmo began to try to turn away from things abhorrent to God. He assessed his

---

[24] James Melville, *The Autobiography and Diary of Mr. James Melville*, ed. Robert Pitcairn (Edinburgh: Wodrow Society, 1842), 79.
[25] Ibid.
[26] James Nimmo, *The Narrative of Mr. James Nimmo: Written for his own Satisfaction to Keep in some rememberance the lords way dealing and kindness towards him, 1654–1709*, ed. W.G. Scott Moncrieff (Edinburgh: The Scottish History Society, 1889).
[27] Ibid., 2.
[28] Ibid.
[29] Ibid., 6.

spiritual growth through his ability to resist Satan, claiming that when his faith was strengthened, 'Satan did nott get me so easlie brangled out of my peace, as sometimes before'.[30] He thus used his interactions with Satan as a metric for interpreting his godliness; both increased demonic assaults and the ability to resist them were viewed as signs of God's grace.

In a confession written in the late seventeenth century, another layman, James Gordon, described all of the sins he had committed since his youth. Among the other traumas of his childhood, at the age of seven both of Gordon's parents died, leaving him orphaned. He wrote that shortly after, the Devil encouraged him to run away to a loch in the woods with the intention of drowning himself. When Gordon came to the water's edge, however, he 'wandred off ane other way', having changed his mind about suicide. Reflecting on this incident as an adult, he thanked the 'Lord who preserved me from that evil accident when Satan might have easily forced me to ane untimely and unhappy death'.[31] Here, the entrenched belief in a reciprocal relationship between the Devil and human nature had turned to experiential reality for Gordon, who upon examining his youth found that he had been perpetually and easily led astray by demonic wiles, only to be spared by God's undeserved grace.

Of course, children themselves did not write such accounts of youthful wickedness and deliverance. The authors were adults, reflecting back over their lives and recreating their experiences on paper in accordance with the culturally prescribed expectations for a godly existence. It is thus difficult to discern whether children actually felt the intense anxiety over Satan and sin described in many accounts. Elizabeth Blackadder, for example, wrote that at the age of six she 'had very early conviction of sin and terrors of hell'.[32] Were these the true fears of a six-year-old – and the daughter of a covenanting minister– or the interpretation of childhood events by an adult? Certainly impressionable young Scots were frequently taken to hear sermons on the topics of sin and Satan, as church attendance was compulsory in most areas. It is no coincidence that when demonic possession cases did begin to occur in Scotland during the last decade of the seventeenth century, the vast majority of those afflicted were adolescents between the ages of eleven and sixteen.[33] This was a tender, impressionable age, when Scots seem to have initially become aware of the possibility of damnation.

---

[30] Ibid., 21.
[31] Ibid.
[32] Elizabeth Blackadder, 'A Short Account', 387. Blackadder would have been six years old around 1665.
[33] See Brian Levack, 'Demonic Possession in Early Modern Scotland', in Goodare, Martin and Miller, eds. *Witchcraft and Belief in Early Modern Scotland*, 166–84.

Yet the 'truth' of such childhood demonic experiences is perhaps beside the point. As Alexandra Walsham has suggested,

> ... it is misguided to try to disentangle 'fact' from 'fiction' in these accounts ... Nor does it matter that many stories which have survived are several steps removed from the original experiences from which they emerged. The distorting filters of emotion, memory and ideology through which they were sieved are extremely revealing.[34]

Here Walsham is writing about the search for 'accuracy' in angel stories in early modern England, but her words are equally applicable to understanding stories of childhood demonic encounters. Even in the likely event that the passage of years and distortion of memory by self-conscious adults led to a re-fashioning of actual events, this does not diminish the larger role that Satan played in the consciousness of many early modern Scots, be they young or old. Distortions of memory and interpretation notwithstanding, descriptions of youthful demonic encounters, appearing commonly in print, from the pulpit and in private writings, clearly had cultural cache in early modern Scotland.

Scots of all ages reported experiencing Satan at night more then any other time, when darkness rendered the world more precarious and dreams blurred the line between reality and fantasy.[35] As schoolmaster Hugh Cameron of Lochbroom observed in the mid-eighteenth century, 'every night Satan laid a Snare to discompose me'.[36] He described the perilous dark thus: 'when the sun is out of sight, the wild beasts of the Forrest creep forth ... it is remarkable that all the wild creatures that are hurtful to man and his Interest, commonly come abroad at night being Creatures of Darkness ...'.[37] Katharine Collace described one particularly difficult experience from the mid-seventeenth century, when the night before the daybreak became 'exceedingly dark so as I never remembered to have the like: it was a none-such strong and violent sett of tentations from Satan'.[38] As these Scots lay in bed with their thoughts, perhaps engaged in self-searching and ruminating on the sins of days past, the perception of demonic assaults became more acute and terrifying in the absence of daylight.

---

[34] See Alexandra Walsham, 'Invisible Helpers: Angelic Intervention in Post-Reformation England', *Past and Present* 208 (2010), 87.

[35] On dreams and the epistemology of dreaming, see Stuart Clark, *Vanities of the Eye: Vision in Early Modern European Culture* (Oxford: Oxford University Press, 2007), chapter 9. See also Ann Marie Plane and Leslie Tuttle, *Dreams, Dreamers, and Visions: The Early Modern Atlantic World* (Philadelphia: University of Pennsylvania Press, 2013).

[36] NLS, Adv. MS. 34.6.30, Hugh Cameron, 'Remarks on Providences and the Lords dealings with me in my tender years, and progressively carried on since', 1746–1763, f. 21.

[37] Ibid., f. 176.

[38] Collace, 'Memoirs or Spiritual Exercises', 53.

In an unusually detailed account composed on 14 March 1679, an anonymous author described how in the midst of a dream, s/he saw 'a dark flood cast forth from the dragon, which was ready to swallow me up ... my alone defence was prayer, crying without ceasing, & saying nothing else for the greatness of my anguish and fear, but O Jesus!'[39] Then, for a brief moment, s/he saw God and Jesus and was filled with an intense calm. Then, thrust back into fear, the author reported seeing 'the Dragon, the Beast, and Babylon lying on this earth. The Dragon was of a long shape, & of a Green color like a serpent, it had four short legs ... it was Terrible to behold; the very thought of has since made me almost to tremble'.[40] While this description of the Devil in a dream was unusually vivid, it illustrates how at night, as in waking life, demonic encounters led to sinful thoughts, fear and the beseeching of the Lord for aid.

The terror provoked by dreams of the Devil usually proved temporary. Upon waking, frightened dreamers found solace not only in daylight, but also in contemplating the inevitable victory of the godly. In 1655, 'a representation of the divell in a dreame' awakened Sir George Maxwell of Pollock from his slumber.[41] Troubled by his demonic vision, he turned to prayer and meditation and soon arrived at the comforting reminder of 'what a change it shall be when divells at whose remembrance or appearance we now tremble shall then tremble before Christ'.[42] At any hour, many Scots found pondering the contrast between the demonic afflictions of mortal life and the eventual, glorious triumph of the godly a reliable source of solace, reflecting confidence in the comforting words they had so often heard from the pulpits.

In another such diary, composed shortly before he died in the early eighteenth century, minister Henrie Duncan described the assaults of Satan while he was asleep and a similar joy upon waking:

> I have never been so capable either of joy or sorrow nor so sensibly affected with the same ever in my life wakeing with respect to any manner of object as I have been sleeping or upon wakeing after sleep. My sorrow hath been non[e] such in sleep when dreaming that I was committing some wicked sin and my joy none such upon awaking and finding that it was but a dream ... *Whence I am ready to conclude that such dreams are more immediately from Sathan rather than the working of natural corruption, altho' also I grant if there were not corrupt nature in me susceptible of such corrupt imaginations, either sleeping or wakeing, Sathan could get no place, not for a moment in me.*[43]

---

[39] NRS, CH12/20/9, f.15.
[40] Ibid.
[41] NLS, MS. 3150, f. 28.
[42] Ibid., f. 29.
[43] Henry Duncan, 'The most memorable passages of the life of Mr. Henrie Duncan, late minister of the gospel at Dunsyre, c. 1710', in David Mullan, ed., *Protestant Piety in Early*

Even in interpreting the dream-world, Scots tended to view the activities of Satan through the lens of their innate corruptibility. In theory and in experiential reality, one could not operate without the other. Dreams, moreover, functioned in the early modern world much as they do today: they were profoundly personal activities revolving around visual representations of an individual's private, innermost thoughts.[44] That the Devil or 'some wicked sin' should appear in such dreams, which might themselves be considered 'devilish delusions', suggests the extent to which ideas about Satan and sin had permeated the godly Scottish psyche.

Fear and Loathing, Hope and Comfort

As will be discussed at greater length in the next chapter, anxieties about Satan, whether in youth or adulthood, waking or asleep, were predicated upon two related components of Reformed theology: the innate depravity of postlapsarian men and women and their total dependence on God. Satan did not just prey on man's spiritual weakness; human frailty provided both the impetus and the means for demonic assaults. James Nimmo articulated this relationship between the Devil and human nature when he described the difficulty of making spiritual progress. As soon as he achieved some assurance of faith, 'sathan and my corruptions and ivel heart being desperatlie wicked of it self strove to crush me and all I had attained of peace by terrors, feares, and discurradgments'.[45] In 1684, for example, his father sent him money when his son was born. Thinking with his pocketbook and not his conscience, Nimmo thought 'to improve it' through an investment, without first consulting God for advice. He lamented that 'Sathan and my coruptiones prevailed too farr, the world coming too much in when ther was not a fit season ... much disqwaietment of minde thereby prevailed, to the braiking of my bodey'.[46] He later observed in his narrative that 'how often may we see what we are by nature wer our eyes open. O hee [God] guides fooles'.[47] For Nimmo and many others, experiences with Satan embodied the spiritual blindness of humanity emphasized in Reformed theology.

The contemplation of human sin in the midst of demonic struggles inevitably led to reflection on the goodness of God, who had bestowed upon an otherwise fallen few eternal deliverance from Hell. Around the

---

Modern Scotland: Letters, Lives and Covenants, 1650–1712 (Edinburgh: Scottish History Society, 2008), 247, emphasis added.
[44] Clark, *Vanities of the Eye*, 302–3; on the Devil in dreams in particular, see 312–22.
[45] Nimmo, *Narrative*, 9.
[46] Ibid., 63.
[47] Ibid., 62.

age of eighteen, the anonymous author of a late seventeenth-century spiritual diary, presumably a minister, recorded his encounter with his own sinfulness. 'All my sins were laid before me', he wrote, and 'my whole life was like ane act of sin, and that Hell was to receive me I said that I have deserved the hottest place in it ... I have nothing that was good in me, a poor sinfull creature, what is there in me that God should pardon me?'[48] Mistress Goodall articulated the relationship between human sin and demonic action in the 1660s when she bemoaned 'the depths of Satan's subtilty, and our depraved nature that he as to work upon'. Imbedded in this lament was an expression of reverent thankfulness, or, as she put it, 'blessed be God that lets not Satan get the victory'.[49] Many Scots articulated this intense gratitude toward God in their self-writings, for only divine providence delivered their feeble souls from the jaws of Satan.

In his examination of English demonic experiences, Nathan Johnstone has argued that while 'diabolic affliction' allowed 'people to express their trust by relying completely on [God] to ultimately constrain the Devil', God did not 'intercede directly' against Satan in times when the godly agonized most.[50] In their self-writings, however, some Scots did describe direct intervention from God in moments of demonically induced despair. One brief but dramatic Scottish example comes from the conversion narrative of Mistress Rutherford. When she was a teenager, she was tormented by guilt and fear at the thought of her own sins and fallen state. For the second time in her life, she considered suicide, detailing how 'Satan tempted me to put violence hands in my self'.[51] Soon after, the Lord dissuaded her from self-destruction by filling her with 'inexpressible joy' during sermon time.[52] While this was not a physical intervention on the part of God, divine intercession quite likely spared Rutherford from a tragic end. Regardless of whether or not God's intervention against the Devil can be labelled as 'direct', what is clear is that the interactions between earnest Protestants and Satan reified through experience the necessity and totality of human reliance on God.

Few actions epitomized this mortal dependence more than the practice of entering into a covenant with God, an act that came to be defining feature of early modern Scottish religiosity.[53] Covenanting provided a partial solution to the taxing and melancholic quest for conversion and assurance. Personal covenants connected individuals to God through a statement of

---

[48] NRS, CH12/20/9, ff.5–6.
[49] Mistress Goodall, 'Memoir', in *Select Biographies*, ii.484.
[50] Johnstone, *Devil and Demonism*, 61.
[51] Rutherford, 'Narrative', 166.
[52] Ibid.
[53] On the practice of covenanting in Scotland, see Mullan, ed., *Protestant Piety*, introduction, and Mullan, *Narratives of the Religious Self*, esp. 309–42.

allegiance and godly purpose, and usually began with an admission of one's sinful nature and the need for reliance on God's mercy.[54] At the turn of the century, the minister William Gordon, driven by the realization of his own spiritual baseness, recorded his personal covenant. He wrote that

> ... having considered as I could, altho' not as I ought, my lost estate and condition by nature and my uncleaness and vileness by nature, all the powers of my soul being polluted by it and the bent of my inclination to sin, as also my innumerable transgressions of the first and second tables of the law and my inability to satisfy the justice of God for any of them, and thus God might most justly cast me out of his sight for ever for these my sins and transgressions ... .[55]

At the centre of these covenants was the renunciation of the Devil, the world and the flesh. In essence and in intent, this constituted an implication of oneself in a lifelong struggle against Satan. Covenants imbued individual Scots with a sense of a purpose and membership in a cause larger than themselves: to combat the actions of Satan and his followers, not as a means to salvation, but as an expression, at once hopeful and insecure, of their membership in the elect.

Though clearly psychologically taxing for many, demonic struggles also often reaffirmed the godliness of these Scots – an identity that entailed the assurance of eventual salvation together with the responsibility of spiritual warfare. The promising theme of election pervades Scottish self-writings alongside cycles of demonically induced fear and self-loathing. When faced with earthly tribulations and demonic assaults, godly men and women clung to the notion that in the end, God's grace alone would render the Devil's actions futile.

This hope was especially powerful for those facing political persecution, who for different reasons and in different guises throughout the seventeenth century conflated the eventual victory of God over Satan with the victory they wished to have over their pursuers. Sir John Chiesly, imprisoned in 1667 for opposition to the Restoration regime, called on Christ to:

---

[54] For examples of personal covenants in Scotland, see John Stevenson, 'A Rare Soul-Strengthening and Comforting Cordial', in *Select Biographies*, Vol. 2; Archibald Johnston of Wariston, 'Diary', in Mullan, ed., *Protestant Piety*; Alexander Brodie, *The Diary of Alexander Brodie of Brodie, and of his Son, James Brodie* (Aberdeen: Spalding Club, 1863); James Cadwell, *The Countesse of Marres Arcadia, or Sanctuarie* (Edinburgh, 1625); GD 18/2093, Sir John Clerk's 'personal covenantings with the Lord' and renewals thereof, 1692–1708; 'An Account of the Particular Soliloquies and Covenant Engagements, past betwixt Mrs. Janet Hamilton, the defunct Lady of Alexander Gordon of Earlstoun', in *Select Biographies*, i.495–508, and Elizabeth West, *Memoirs, or Spiritual Exercises of Elisabeth West* (Edinburgh, 1724).

[55] William Gordon, 'Personal Covenant of William Gordon', in Mullan, ed., *Protestant Piety*, 76.

Redeem Israel, thou who didst cast out a legion of these devils at once out of a man, can ridd these nations of legions that possess it in kirk and state ... thy word can cure the blind, deaf, lame, and raise the dead and cast out legions of devils, O Lord there is need of all this power to be set forth, for my soul, and these nations.[56]

When John Gilry was jailed in the Edinburgh tollbooth in 1638 for his actions against the government of Charles I, he wrote to a friend about the trials he was facing. 'Those floods that the dragon is casting out of his mouth to swallow up all', he penned, 'cannot deceive the elect ... all the wiles of devills and men cannot prevail against them that belong to him nor none can pluck them out of his hand'.[57] In the late seventeenth century, overcome with concern for her husband (an oft-persecuted covenanting minister), Marion Veitch slept 'little or none for several nights'.[58] She found comfort, however, in the words of Revelation: 'Wo to the Earth and the Inhabitants thereof for the Devil is come down with great wrath but his time is short ...'.[59]

This knowledge that God was Satan's master regularly tempered fears of demonic intervention in daily life. This was particularly true for those most learned in theology and most confident in their election, such as the late sixteenth-century minister Robert Blair, who reported in his autobiography that when he was a student at Glasgow, he spent his time studying in a room in which no one would go due to the sighting of apparitions. 'Yet in that same chamber', he wrote:

> I resolved to spend my waking nights, and did so the whole summer, and was never troubled nor terrified a whit ... for this thou taughtest me that devils were chained with chains of darkness, reserved to the judgment of the last day, so that they could not, nor durst not, once appear, far less molest, without thy permission; and that if thou permittest any such thing, thou wouldst make it work for good to one devoted to thee, whom thou hast taken into protection.[60]

To individuals like Blair, trust in God could prove a powerful salve against the fear of Satan.

---

[56] NLS, Wod. Oct. XXXI, Part of the diary of Sir John Chiesly, 59r.
[57] NLS, Wod. Qu. XXXVI, Two letters from John Gilry, 1683, f.165.
[58] NLS, Adv.MS. 34.6.22, Marion Veitch, 'An account of the Lord's gracious dealing with me and of his remarkable hearing and answering my supplications', c. 1670–1680s, f.12.
[59] Ibid. The exact wording of Revelation 12:12, in the King James Version, is 'Therefore rejoice, ye heavens, and ye that dwell in them. Woe to the inhabiters of the earth and of the sea! for the devil is come down unto you, having great wrath, because he knoweth that he hath but a short time'.
[60] Robert Blair, *The Life of Mr. Robert Blair*, ed. Thomas M'Crie (Edinburgh: Wodrow Society, 1848), 8.

For the Scottish Covenanters in particular, the belief that Satan acted only in accordance with God's will offered both an explanation for political and religious strife and a language with which to express fears and hopes about themselves and the precarious future of Scotland. The letters of John Welwood exemplify this relationship between demonic assaults and faith in God's providence.[61] A remarkable preacher according to existing accounts, Welwood was a charismatic man who had an unconventional and circuitous path to the ministry. Though generally confident in his salvation, he lacked sure footing in navigating the precarious landscape of godly life. Despite his resolve to overcome demonic obstacles, Welwood wrestled throughout his adulthood with the dual menace of Satan and his own sinful nature. As he explained in 1676, 'I find it still a great difficulty to be clear of the Lord's call ... and many a time I take mine own way'.[62] Welwood wrote to another friend that same year that he had 'been in sore damps this while bypast, and not yet out of them. Satan labours to hold me in hot water, and hath again put out of my view the life of faith'. 'Sometimes I will be in great confusions and darkness', he explained, referring as so many before him had done to the Devil's implanting of doubts and disorientation in the vulnerable human mind.[63]

In his letters, Welwood reiterated that Satan desired, above all, to destroy the most pious of God's servants. As he told a friend who had recently suffered demonic assaults, 'I am glad (and ye may think it strange) that Satan and his instruments love you not; for it is a token that you are none of theirs'.[64] In another letter to a friend in July 1676, he wrote that 'I am so slothfull and love ease and know pleasures so well. And Satan so jumbles me about my call away that it is a great difficultie for me to goe from one corner of a shire to another. I do indeed sigh and go backward. But I hope the time of refreshing from the presence of the Lord is not far off'.[65] In an era fraught with apocalyptic anxiety, Welwood believed that for he and his fellow Christians, struggles against Satan would be unceasing until death or the Day of Judgement, when the godly would at last have their victory.

This hope for the Day of Judgement pervaded the writings of many radical Presbyterians, whose anti-Erastian ideals subjected them to persecution from the British government, particularly following the

---

[61] When Welwood died young in Perth in either 1678 or 1679, barely forty years of age, he left behind a large collection of letters sent to various friends and fellow ministers throughout Britain composed just before his death: John Welwood, 'Letters, 1675–77', in Mullan, ed., *Protestant Piety*. Original source: NLS, Adv. MS 32.4.4 1r–25v.

[62] Welwood, 'Letters', 100.

[63] Ibid.

[64] Ibid., 84.

[65] Welwood, 'Letters', 168.

Restoration of Charles II. Many Covenanters faced imprisonment and even execution because of their religious and political recalcitrance. As Welwood saw it, Satan's earthly intervention lay at the heart of these hardships. Bemoaning recent events in Scotland, he wrote in 1676 that 'O but Satan be cruel ... he, in his instruments, is so unmerciful'.[66] He stated in 1676 that 'O but a Christian hath much worke while he is hereaway. He hath sin, Satan, dissertion, afflictions, and plagues to debate withal ... we have need of trials and afflictions to purge out our corruptions, and this hath been the lot of all his people in all ages'.[67] Welwood thus accepted his personal difficulties – demonic and other – by biblically and historically rationalizing the struggles of God's chosen people: 'Wee sometimes fear and are troubled, but we are in no hazard, for we are built upon the rock of ages, and our anchor is fixed within the vail, and the gates of hell may terrify us, but not prevail against us'.[68] For the elect, victory may not have been immediate, but at least it was assured.

This conviction that Satan faced predetermined defeat did little, however, to extinguish the fears of many Scots. Henrietta Lindsay, the daughter of a covenanting layman, wrote in her diary in 1687 that she had been 'much slated by Satan's devices ... wherein was discovered the greatest frailty and weakness in yielding to slavish fears, as if Satan were not fettered in chains and under command'.[69] Despite her theoretical and scripturally derived belief in God's control of the Devil, Lindsay could not escape her immediate fear of Satan. According to widely accepted theology, Satan operated only with divine instruction and would be vanquished in the end. Yet ministers used the pen and the pulpit to impress upon Scots that God willed Satan to provide the godly and reprobate alike with daily temptations and harassments. This seems to have created an experiential paradox for many Scots, for the message of eventual victory for the elect was usually delivered amid discussions of the ultimate unknowability of salvation. As we shall see, even for Scots confident in their faith, the perception of demonic assaults dovetailed with anxiety about personal sin to at times override any comfort in the promise of victory.

Demonic Experiences in Protestant Britain

In their studies of the Devil in post-Reformation England, Darren Oldridge and Nathan Johnstone emphasize characteristics of English demonic beliefs and experiences – concerns over personal sin, cycles of fear and relief, a

---

[66] Ibid., 101.
[67] Ibid., 85.
[68] Ibid., 82.
[69] Henrietta Lindsay, 'Her Diary', in Mullan, ed., *Women's Life Writing*, 275.

focus on the Devil's internal assaults and the importance of reliance on God – that often mirror those prevalent in Scotland.[70] English spiritual diaries, like their Scottish counterparts, depict self-identified godly men and women struggling with concerns about internal demonic assaults, which sermons and published devotional writings had conditioned them to expect.[71] As one Elizabethan gentlewoman put it, 'sin and corruption conceived in the heart of man is the spawn of the Devil'.[72] Fear of the Devil's mental, and sometimes physical, intrusions loomed large in the minds of many English Reformed Protestants. Perhaps the most famous example is that of Nehemiah Wallington, a London artisan whose recorded struggles with Satan and sin were particularly detailed and dramatic. In 1619, during one intense episode of inner turmoil, Wallington felt that the Devil would not leave him alone and became convinced that anyone who tried to help him escape his sorry state was Satan in disguise. He told his father that 'the Devil can come in any likeness', and he found himself believing that friends and family members, and even his own shoes, were the Devil in a different guise.[73] In 1621, Wallington's conversion experience brought divine deliverance, albeit temporarily, from the 'eleven sore temptations of Satan' that had so afflicted him in the years prior.[74]

While serious Protestants throughout Britain were, as Alec Ryrie has put it, 'as liable to terrifyingly vivid encounters with the Devil as anyone else', the comparative lack of detailed descriptions of the Devil in Scotland are worth noting.[75] In England, Protestant authors recorded their beliefs about and experiences with Satan in 'a remarkable variety of forms', recounting the sights, smells and sounds of their demonic encounters. In one particularly colourful account, the preacher John Rogers reported how Satan and his helpers had tormented him 'in severall ugly shapes and forms (according to my fancies) and sometimes with great rolling flaming eyes like sawcers, having fire-brands in one of their hands, and with the other reaching at me to tear me away to torment'.[76] In Scotland, however, internal encounters with Satan were generally mental and emotional rather than visual, involving the words and occasionally the sounds of the Devil. Satan often whispered in godly ears, but appeared less frequently as a vision or corporeal entity. When Scots did claim to have seen the

---

[70] Johnstone, *The Devil and Demonism*, and Oldridge, *The Devil in Early Modern England*.
[71] See, for example, William Perkins, *A Case of Conscience* (London, 1592), and John Bunyan, *Grace Abounding to the Chief of Sinners* (London, 1666).
[72] Grace Mildmay, 'Lady Mildmay's Meditations', in *With Faith and Physic: The Life of a Tudor Gentlewoman*, ed. L.A. Pollock (London: Collins & Brown, 1993), 81.
[73] Seaver, *Wallington's World*, 24.
[74] Ibid., 15.
[75] Ryrie, *Being Protestant*, 245.
[76] Cited by Oldridge, *The Devil in Early Modern England*, 41–3.

Devil, they usually did so in a dream or in a fever, providing only terse descriptions of Satan in their accounts.[77]

This divergence comes, in part, from the fact that Scots were exposed to far fewer images of the Devil than were their English counterparts. The hyper-iconoclasm of Reformed Protestantism in Scotland led not only to whitewashed church walls, but also to a dearth of images from the printing press. The only printed image of the Devil in early modern Scotland came from a 1592 pamphlet detailing the North Berwick witch trials of the previous year, which was printed in London rather than Edinburgh.[78] Part of this was logistical, as the Scottish print industry lagged behind England, producing little popular 'cheap print' until the latter half of the seventeenth century.[79] Yet even after 1700, printed broadsides still contained very few images. Scotland thus lacked the persistence of medieval depictions of the Devil and of Hell, which continued to appear in printed woodcuts even after the Reformation in England.[80] This lack of demonic imagery in both print and recorded internal experiences was also likely due to the fact that Scotland's break with the Catholic Church was more abrupt and thoroughgoing than in England. The Protestant de-emphasis of the physicality of the Devil bled into spiritual diaries, as reduced exposure to images of Satan combined with the emphasis on internal demonic threats to create a dearth of colourful descriptions of the Devil.[81]

Perhaps the most significant difference between demonic beliefs in England versus Scotland lies not in kind or quality, but in societal breadth and depth. To a considerable extent, this stemmed from the divergent courses of the British Reformations and the attending fact that zealous Protestantism was, as Nathan Johnstone has pointed out, always a minority culture in England.[82] The Reformed Protestant brand of internal, experiential demonic belief found among the godly in England and Scotland may not have been shared by the bulk of the English population. As Oldridge contends, 'the rest of the population, characterized by the Essex

---

[77] See, for example, NLS, MS. 3150, Diary of Sir George Maxwell of Pollock, 1655–56, f.28; Mistress Rutherford, 'Conversion narrative', 153; Blackadder, 'A short account', 387. One exception is the colourful account of the Devil and hell found in NRS, CH12/20/9, Religious diary, 1679–1692, f.15.

[78] James Carmichael, *Newes from Scotland* (London, 1592).

[79] On printing in Scotland, see Alasdair J. Man, 'The Anatomy of the Printed Book in Early Modern Scotland', *Scottish Historical Review* 80 (2001): 181–200. For a discussion of the proliferation of broadsides in early modern England, see Tessa Watt's foundational work, *Cheap Print and Popular Piety in England* (Cambridge: Cambridge University Press, 1993).

[80] Oldridge, *The Devil in Early Modern England*, 145–7.

[81] Descriptions of the Devil in cases of Scottish witchcraft were also surprisingly terse or quotidian, and very rarely monstrous or grotesque as in elsewhere in Europe. On this point, see Miller, 'Men in Black'.

[82] Johnstone, *Devil and Demonism*, 108.

pastor George Clifford as the "common sort of Christians," retained many pre-Reformation ideas about the devil'.[83] Tellingly, the more thoroughly Reformed Scotland was frequently seen by its southern neighbours as a hotbed of religious adherence and enthusiasm, a characterization that could be positive or negative depending on the observer.[84] Accordingly, the intense preoccupation with sin, salvation and the personal experience of the Devil does not seem to have been as widespread or thorough in England as it was in lowland Scotland, where Reformed Protestantism had planted deeper social and cultural roots.

Conclusion

Struggles with Satan reveal the specificities and complexities of inner piety as well as individual and communal expectations. When considering the large body of demonic experiences found in Scottish self-writings, a distinct pattern emerges. As demonstrated above, encounters with Satan generally adhered to a cycle of demonically induced sin or doubt, followed by fear of God and the Devil, and finally relief provided by God's mercy and the knowledge of election.

What does this pattern reveal about the experiential role of Satan in early modern Scottish society? For the authors of the self-writings considered in this chapter, encounters with the Devil produced two interconnected results. First, beliefs about, and experiences with, Satan both clarified and confirmed key tenets of Reformed theology: humans were irredeemably sinful by nature; godly life entailed a battle against Satan and oneself; salvation lay solely in the hands of God, who was both wrathful and merciful; and election would bring final victory to the true believer. Through struggles with the Devil, these Scots came to understand, in an experiential rather than theoretical way, the components of Reformed Protestantism. By serving as a metric for godliness, symbolizing the innate depravity of humans, and affirming the absolute sovereignty of God, the Protestant Devil buttressed the Reformed theology whence he came.

Second, encounters with Satan helped Scots to define themselves through religious experience. It was in their darkest hours, when confronted with deeply personal fears, that Scottish men and women most ardently sought to embrace their faith. Through this process of spiritual warfare, these

---

[83] Oldridge, *Devil in Early Modern England*, 3.

[84] One telling but probably exaggerated anecdote comes from the early eighteenth century, when several English authors noted that unlike in England, bible ownership was nearly universal in Scotland. See Benedict, *Christ's Churches Purely Reformed*, 516. Benedict rightly notes that these English authors may have spoken with some exaggeration, in the attempt to chide their fellow Englishmen into more usual and zealous reading of Scripture.

Scots hoped to identify their membership in a community of the elect whose roots lay with the Israelites of the Old Testament, a community for which struggles against Satan were inherent and necessary events. Some, it must be said, found more comfort and success in doing so than others. As these self-writings attest, Reformed Protestantism in Scotland entailed an intensely emotional, internal, divinely dependent journey to overcome one's nature and live a good life in word, deed and thought. Though election was predestined, godliness was a lifelong process in which the Devil played a leading part.

When considering the many roles that Satan played in the spiritual experiences of the men and women discussed here – as a tempter, a reminder of human depravity, a confirmation of God's mercy, an agent of divine wrath – it is tempting to functionalize the Devil in early modern Scotland. In many ways, Satan served as a psychological tool that allowed earnest Protestants to better understand themselves, their faiths and their communities. The Devil provided the language necessary to express troubling fears about sin and salvation within the context of pastorally prescribed and cultural expected experiences.

Such observations do not mean that the personal experience of the Devil was not intensely real for, and individualized to, the authors of these accounts. Nathan Johnstone has argued that 'in functionalizing diabolic assault by rationalizing it was a palliative for something else – vulnerability of conscience and devotional weakness – there is a tendency to present the experience of the demonic as largely a retrospective process of narrative creation'.[85] Viewing the Devil as imbued with meanings about sin and weakness, however, does not reduce demonic experiences to narrative tools to highlight broader ideas about human depravity. Experiences with Satan certainly reified the ubiquity and depth of human sin, and this did not negate the reality, for the author, of that demonic encounter. Nor does the retrospective and consciously constructed nature of many self-writings contradict the constant, experiential struggle with the Devil faced by the godly. Rather, the fact that Satan embodied a whole array of early modern preoccupations with sin and salvation made the experience of the Devil all the more present and tangible – and indeed, worth recording for posterity.

---

[85] Johnstone, *Devil and Demonism*, 23.

CHAPTER 4

Internalizing the Demonic

In post-Reformation Scotland, personal, internalized struggles with Satan existed on a spectrum. They could serve as a hopeful metric of one's godliness or as a trenchant reminder of the sad spiritual state of postlapsarian men and women. Though the experiential reality of the Devil usually fell between these extremes, the bleaker, despairing end of the spectrum often prevailed. The perception of humanity as innately depraved, tempted at every turn to yield to the Devil's behests, profoundly shaped how godly Scots experienced Satan and conceived of their inner selves.

This chapter focuses on this darker side of demonic struggles and situates this discussion within its larger British, Atlantic and European contexts.[1] Through examination of the circulation of English texts in Scotland and brief comparison with Reformed communities abroad, it demonstrates how transnational discussions of sin, Satan and human nature informed personal religious experience. Ultimately, this chapter identifies a process of anxiety and self-identification as evil that occurred during introspective, personal engagement with Satan, loosely coined here as 'internalizing the demonic'. This process reveals the close and consequential relationship between the clerical promotion of self-surveillance and the widely internalized belief in the Devil's natural affinity with 'man's evil heart'.

Despite the impressive array of illuminating studies of the Devil in the early modern world, the connections between Reformed theology, self-examination and demonic belief have yet to be fully assessed, not least in the context of Scotland.[2] The term 'internalizing the demonic', admittedly an imprecise phrase, serves as a way to characterize and understand this experiential relationship and its influence on Scottish conceptions of the self. In this context, 'demonic' is used to connote a range of ideas about the Devil, his involvement in earthly affairs and his relation to humankind which were often internalized by Scottish men and women anxious about personal sin and the possibility of eternal damnation. The process of internalizing the demonic suggests that through the embodied experience of temptation, Scots wrestled with concerns not only of the Devil, but also with deeply held and culturally constructed fears about themselves.

---

[1] An earlier version of this chapter has been published as Michelle D. Brock, 'Internalizing the Demonic: Satan and the Self in Early Modern Scottish Piety', *Journal of British Studies*, 54:1 (2015): 23–43.

[2] See for a partial list of these works, see above, Introduction, note 31.

In short, encounters with Satan created, articulated and validated widely internalized ideas about both demonic and human evil – ideas that often proved, in their experiential expression, both dramatic and destructive.

This does not mean that the spiritual malaise that attended demonic struggles could not bear fruit. On the contrary, the recognition of sinfulness and even the self-identification as evil served as preconditions for submission to God, conversion experiences and entrance into the community of the elect.[3] Yet internalizing the demonic remained a mostly painful and passive process, the result of clerical and cultural discussions of Satan and self-examination that were intended, as Louise Yeoman has put it, 'to convince men that their everyday selves were irremediably evil'.[4] In the religious experiences of the godly in Scotland, internal struggles against the Devil were symbiotically connected to the recognition of one's evil nature and spiritual impotence.

The process of internalizing the demonic is revealed primarily through 'self-writings' – examined at length in the previous chapter – composed by an influential minority of literate Scots. Though these men and women experienced Satan according to individual personalities and histories, this process usually entailed four distinct phases. First, the Scottish clergy promoted the necessity of introspection – an idea predicated on human depravity – from the pulpit and in print. Second, the godly (or would-be godly) placed their thoughts, words and deeds, past and present, under intense scrutiny. More often than not, this introspection involved the perception of assaults by Satan and the recollection, at the Devil's prodding, of past transgressions. Third, during these internal struggles against the Devil, the godly began to self-identify as evil or even demonic, feeling helpless, hopeless and sometimes suicidal.[5] Finally, and only through the mercy of divine intervention following moments of prayer and beseeching, this period of internalizing the demonic would come to an end.

---

[3] On the potential spiritual benefits of despair, see Alec Ryrie, *Being Protestant in Reformation Britain* (Oxford: Oxford University Press, 2013), chapter 2.

[4] Louise Yeoman, 'Heart-Work: Emotion, Empowerment and Authority in Covenanting Times' (PhD Thesis, University of St Andrews, 1991), 11.

[5] On suicide in Scotland, see Houston, *Punishing the Dead: Suicide, Lordship, and Community in Britain, 1500–1800* (Oxford University Press, 2010), esp. pp. 292–312. For other works on the relationship between suicide and Reformed Protestantism, see Jeffery Watt, ed., *From Sin to Insanity: Suicide in Early Modern Europe* (Ithaca, NY: Cornell University Press, 2004) and Michael MacDonald and Terence Murphy, *Sleepless Souls: Suicide in Early Modern England* (Oxford: Oxford University Press, 1991). In his study of the Protestant experience in Reformation Britain, Alec Ryrie persuasively cautions against attributing thoughts of suicide to Calvinist theology on the basis of reported suicidal thoughts, many of which were more about expressing temptation than actual contemplation of self-harm. See Ryrie, *Being Protestant*, 30–31.

The process of internalizing the demonic was neither guaranteed nor homogenous. Just as Reformed theology contained remarkable diversity over time and space, so too did the demonic experiences of the godly, even amongst the zealous Protestants that populated the Anglophone world.[6] Some Scots simply recognized the presence of demonically induced doubts, while others became suicidal at the thought of their own reprobation. These experiential differences were thus deeply informed by both personal proclivities and specific communal expectations. Still, interactions with Satan, especially those that turned dark and despairing, were consistently shaped by ideas about human depravity, irrevocable election and the necessity of introspection promoted in print and from the pulpit. The collision of Reformed doctrines with experiential struggles against Satan caused the self-identified godly in Scotland, in moments of intense scrutiny, to believe the very worst: that they were irrevocably evil, even demonic, and destined for an eternity in hell.

Satan and Self-examination in Reformed Scotland

When analysing the role of the Devil in the pre-modern world, scholars have often focused on the language of external demonization – the 'othering' and dehumanizing of religious foes.[7] Elaine Pagels has examined how the

---

[6] For a discussion of both shared theological foundations as well as schisms within Reformed Protestantism in Britain and on the Continent, see, for example, Richard Muller, 'John Calvin and Later Calvinism', in David V.N. Bagchi and David Curtis Steinmetz, eds, *The Cambridge Companion to Reformation Theology* (Cambridge: Cambridge University Press, 2004), 130–49; Philip Benedict, *Christ's Church Purely Reformed: A Social History of Calvinism* (New Haven, CT: Yale University Press, 2002), 293–423; M. Haykin and M. Jones, eds, *Drawn into Controversie: Reformed Theological Diversity and Debates within Seventeenth-Century British Puritanism* (Göttingen: Vandenhoeck and Ruprecht, 2011). For a discussion of religious and political debates in post-Reformation Scotland, especially prior to the Restoration in 1660, see especially the works of David G. Mullan: 'Theology in the Church of Scotland, 1618–1640: a Calvinist consensus?' *Sixteenth Century Journal* 26 (1995), 595–617; *Episcopacy in Scotland: the History of an Idea, 1560–1638* (Edinburgh: Edinburgh University Press, 1986); *Scottish Puritanism, 1590–1638* (Oxford: Oxford University Press, 2000). For an examination of the dissolution of theological consensus after 1660, see Alasdair Raffe, *The Culture of Controversy: Religious Arguments in Scotland, 1660–1714* (Woodbridge: Boydell Press, 2012).

[7] Historians of late medieval Europe in particular have explored the 'demonization' of others as part of the growing power of the Catholic Church and the centralization of European states. R.I. Moore has famously examined how from the tenth through thirteenth centuries, Europe underwent an elite-led transformation into a society, dominated by the Catholic Church, that sought to define itself by marginalizing and 'demonizing' those who did not conform to 'normal' orthodox society. See Moore, *The Formation of a Persecuting Society* (New York: Blackwell, 1987), 64–5, 89–91. Norman Cohn, in his discussion of the beginnings of the European witch-hunts, examines how the growing emphasis on the

very idea of Satan developed, as theologians (Jewish and then Christian) increasingly used Scripture to associate their enemies with the Devil. Soon, the demonization of others – 'first other Jews, then pagans, and later dissident Christians called heretics'– became a foundational component of the Christian mentality.[8] Building upon this concept of demonization, some scholars have explained the concept of the Devil in terms of opposition and contrariety.[9] This understanding of Satan accords with the fact that in many respects, cosmic oppositions governed religious doctrine in the Christian world: Good against Evil, God versus Satan, Catholics opposing Protestants and Christ facing the Antichrist. As John Knox once professed, 'In religioun thair is na middis: either it is the religioun of God ... or els it is the religioun of the Divill'.[10] Militaristic conceptions of the warring of the armies of God and Satan were intrinsic to how Protestant theologians and reformers explained the tumultuous events around them. The language of cosmic struggle resonated with many early modern men and women, who were constantly beleaguered by political, economic and religious hardship.

It is unsurprising, then, that many historians have understood the cultural import of Satan in these oppositional, external terms, suggesting that the crucial function of Satan was to define negatively what was good and human.[11] In examining the experiential function of demonic belief in early modern Scotland, however, it becomes clear that within the religious experiences of individuals, the demonizing of others stood secondary to one's internal relationship with Satan and the ensuing self-identification as evil – a process that we might even think of this as the 'demonization of

---

devil among Christian elites led to the demonization and scapegoating of others through the creation of the stereotype of the witch: Norman Cohn, *Europe's Inner Demons: The Demonization of Christians in Medieval Christendom* (Chicago, IL: University of Chicago Press, 2001, revised edition – original published in 1975), 16–59.

[8] Elaine Pagels, *The Origin of Satan* (London: Allen Lane, 1996), xvii.

[9] The most important scholar who has both employed and promoted this binary understanding of the Devil is Stuart Clark, *Thinking with Demons: The Idea of Witchcraft in Early Modern Europe* (Oxford: Oxford University Press, 1997); Clark, 'Inversion, Misrule, and the Meaning of Witchcraft', *Past and Present* 87 (1980): 98–127. See also Jeffery Burton Russell, *Mephistopheles: The Devil in the Modern World* (Ithaca, NY: Cornell University Press, 1986). As Ethan Shagan has recently pointed out, historians of early modern England in particular have applied this discussion of contrariety, originally used by Clark to explain witchcraft and Satan, to early modern society as a whole. He argues that this dualistic approach, while certainly useful, has led scholars to overlook the importance of the logic of moderation and the finding of a middle way in early modern society. See Shagan, 'Beyond Good and Evil: Thinking with Moderates in Early Modern England', *Journal of British Studies* 49 (2010): 488–513.

[10] John Knox, *Works*, 6 vols, ed. David Laing (Edinburgh: Wodrow Society, 1846), iv.232.

[11] Pagels, *The Origin of Satan*, esp. xxvii–xxx.

the self'.[12] Reformed conceptions of human sin and predestined salvation undergirded this focus on the internal role of the Devil and proved formative in shaping how many Scots understood Satan and themselves.

The doctrine of double predestination, espoused from pulpits throughout early modern Scotland and predicated on both the sovereignty of God and the depravity of man, taught that God alone knew who was saved and who was damned.[13] Some assurance of faith might be gained through a conversion experience, but election remained ultimately (and often frustratingly) unknowable. To aid the search for assurance amid this unknowability, many Reformed theologians averred that the Devil most aggressively pursued the godly – an assertion that only further encouraged Scots to search their hearts and minds for signs of demonic intrusion. The real threat posed by the Devil thus did not lie at the end of salvation, but rather on the road to salvation. On this long and arduous path, interactions with Satan exploited not only anxiety over salvation, but as importantly, struggles with one's innately depraved nature.

The Scots Confession of 1560 epitomized the mandate for internal spiritual warfare against Satan and the self that lay at the core of internalizing the demonic. The writers of the confession maintained that after conversion 'comes that continual battle which is betwixt the flesh and the spirit in God's children; while the flesh and natural man (according to their own corruption) lust for things pleasing and delectable unto the self ... and at every moment are prone and ready to offend the Majesty of God'.[14] Though God bestowed undeserving men and women with eternal life, human 'nature is so corrupt, so weak, and so imperfect, that we are never able to fulfill the works of the law in perfection'.[15] There was little in theory, then, to differentiate the reprobate, who 'act as the devil and their corrupt nature urge', from the elect. The key disparity lay in the actions of the godly, for 'the sons of God do fight against sin, do sob and mourn, when they perceive themselves tempted to iniquity; and if they fall, they

---

[12] The findings here thus concur with numerous studies that have traced the development of a distinctly Protestant demonology focused primarily on the internal role of the Devil. See Nathan Johnstone, 'The Protestant Devil: The Experience of Temptation in Early Modern England', *Journal of British Studies* 43 (2004): 173–205; Johnstone, *The Devil and Demonism in Early Modern England* (Cambridge: Cambridge University Press, 2006); Darren Oldridge, *The Devil in Early Modern England* (Stroud: Sutton, 2000).

[13] For a further discussion of the development of predestination theology and the Reformation, see Richard A. Muller, *Christ and the Decree: Christology and Predestination in Reformed Theology from Calvin to Perkins* (Grand Rapids, MI: Baker Academic, 1988), 79–96. On the pastoral use of the doctrine of predestination in post-Reformation England, see Leif Dixon, *Practical Predestinarians in England, 1590–1640* (Farnham: Ashgate, 2014).

[14] *The Scots Confession of Faith* (Edinburgh, 1560), chapter 13.

[15] Ibid., chapter 15.

rise again with earnest and unfeigned repentance'.[16] In the generations after the composition of *The Scots Confession*, Scottish divines promoted these central ideas in a dizzying array of sermons and devotional literature. It is little wonder, then, that the godly felt compelled to 'sob and mourn' at hints of demonically induced temptation, which revealed above all their own corruption by nature. The internalization of these theological ideas lent the Devil primacy of place in the personal religious experiences of many Scots, sometimes with dramatic consequences.

As we have seen, from the Reformation through the close of the seventeenth century, many Scottish divines predicated their encouragement of introspection, especially in the face of demonic assaults, on the emphasis on the innate and total depravity of all men and women, elect and reprobate alike. This obsession with human sin, which almost invariably directed theological and pastoral discussions of Satan, assumed extreme forms in post-Reformation Scotland. Here, warnings about the Devil – found in sermons, theological writings, spiritual diaries and pamphlet literature, among other sources – almost always coincided with remarks about the evil human heart and the attending need for self-examination and continued surveillance.[17] Many Scots, accordingly, considered their naturally evil thoughts to be as bad as the performance of evil deeds. This led, for the godly, to an intense and sometimes obsessive desire to control their inner worlds.[18] Such control would require not only self-examination, but also constant self-surveillance. It was not enough to recognize past sin; future evils needed prevention as well. This was a daunting task, for it was concurrently asserted from the pulpit that human depravity rendered such control impossible. At the same time, the Scottish clergy stressed that though their audiences could not adequately and independently fulfil the laws of God, this was no excuse for not attempting to do so.[19]

This focus on the sinfulness of humanity and the attending need for self-examination and surveillance had a long heritage. Saint Augustine of Hippo considered human behaviour to be the ultimate evidence of Satan's presence in the world, more than any general mischance or misfortune.[20]

---

[16] Ibid., chapter 13.

[17] See, for example, John Welsh, *Forty-Eight Select Sermons* (Edinburgh, 1744); Charles Hammond, *God's Eye from Heaven* (Edinburgh, 1671); Andrew Gray, *Directions and instigations to the duty of prayer how, and why the heart is to be kept with diligence* (Edinburgh, 1669).

[18] Yeoman, 'Heart-Work', esp. pp. 7–11. See also Yeoman's article on the connections between the process of obsessing about sinful thoughts and witchcraft accusations, 'The Devil as Doctor: Witchcraft, Wodrow and the Wider World', *Scottish Archives* 1 (1995): 93–105.

[19] Ibid.

[20] On this point, see, for example, Hans Peter Broedel, *The Malleus Maleficarum and the Construction of Witchcraft* (Manchester: Manchester University Press, 2003), 47. In

Like Augustine, John Calvin ruminated about demonic activity primarily because of its connection to the sinfulness of all men and women. Even the elect, he wrote, remained subject to 'the flesh, the world, and the devil' because they were 'besprinkled only with a few drops by the Spirit'.[21] As the English clergyman John Downame wrote in 1634, all progeny of Adam were 'made backward unto all good, and prone unto all evill'.[22] Even children, many Reformed Protestants averred, were totally corrupted 'limbs of Satan'.[23] In his farewell address given in the early eighteenth century, Thomas Locke, a Scottish schoolteacher, warned of the susceptibility of children to Satan's wiles. 'Are there not some children', he implored, who 'before they can well speak they have the devil in their mouth? ... By nature we are of our father the devil, and his works we will do as natively as fire casteth forth heat'.[24] The only means of combating such innately depraved tendencies, many ministers avowed, was through extreme self-examination and surveillance. It was during this intense introspection that internalizing the demonic occurred.

The English pastoral tradition was largely responsible for spreading the focus on self-examination north of the Border in printed sermons and devotional guides.[25] The practice of diary keeping in England began in the 1580s and 1590s, thanks to its promotion by the Protestant divine William Perkins. The keeping of spiritual diaries proliferated in England in the early seventeenth century, when Protestants of the staunchly Calvinist ilk increasingly perceived themselves to be in the minority and sought to record their experiences in the face of persecution.[26] This practice spread to Scotland a few decades later and accelerated during the religious upheaval created by the Restoration, as many covenanting Scots took up the pen in hopes of documenting their struggles, finding solace in writing and providing example for others.[27]

---

particular, Augustine's *Confessions* (written AD 397–398) provided the model for examining and recording the sins of one's past in a systematic way.

[21] John Calvin, *Commentaries on the Epistle of Paul the Apostle to the Romans* (1539), trans. Revd John Owen (Edinburgh: Calvin Translation Society, 1849), 308.

[22] John Downame, *The Christian Warfare* (London, 1634), 1041.

[23] John Stachniewski, *The Persecutory Imagination: English Puritanism and the Literature of Religious Despair* (Oxford: Clarendon Press, 1991), 97–8.

[24] Thomas Locke, 'To the parents of the children of Eastwood', c. 1706, NLS, Wod. Qu. LXXXII, f. 159.

[25] On the tradition of Puritan self-examination, see Margo Todd, *Christian Humanism and the Puritan Social Order* (Cambridge: Cambridge University Press, 1987), 30–31 and 192–5.

[26] Owen C. Watkins lists 220 titles of English autobiographical works up to 1725 in his bibliography to *The Puritan Experience: Studies in Spiritual Autobiography* (New York: Schocken, 1972).

[27] Mullan, *Narratives of the Religious Self*, lx.

Perkins, as the most frequently reprinted English author between 1590 and 1620, became the wellspring for much of Reformed Protestant thinking throughout the Anglophone world. His ideas – particularly his focus on predestination and the necessity of introspection – found quick acceptance among the clergy in post-Reformation Scotland.[28] Here, the Perkins brand of practical, reflective divinity undoubtedly influenced the composition of self-writings, a genre to which the Scots appended their particular focus on covenanting.[29] Perkins' *A Case of Conscience* was printed in Edinburgh as well as in London in 1592. In this work, Perkins recognized the fears propagated by the doctrine of predestination, and to this end he offered his readers the advice that they must confess their sins in order to experience any sense of salvation.[30] As he penned in his influential catechism, 'all men are wholly corrupted with in through Adam's fall, and so are become slaves of Satan'.[31] Closeness to God could only be achieved through recognition and confession of this innate depravity.

Lewis Bayly's *Practice of Piety, Directing the Christian how to walk that he may please God* also informed Scottish piety and devotional practice.[32] Originally written in 1611, *Practice of Piety* was perhaps the most popular devotional guide in England during the first half of the seventeenth century. It was reprinted in Scotland at least six times between 1630 and 1667, and it is very likely that copies from London circulated in Scotland prior to these dates.[33] *Practice of Piety* encouraged, in a systematic way, the introspective process that could lead to internalizing the demonic. As Bayly wrote in his introduction, first man had to know God, and then to know his own 'state of Corruption'. 'And forasmuch as there can be no true piety without the knowledge of God', he explained, nor could there exist 'any good practice without the knowledge of a man's own self'.[34] Bayly went on to compare the glories of God's election with the terrible state of man who lived without redemption, whom he described as existing for eternity

---

[28] On Perkins' ideas and preaching about predestination, see Dixon, *Practical Predestinarians*, chapter 2.

[29] Benedict, *Christ's Church*, 521–2. On the practice of covenanting in Scotland, see David Mullan, ed., *Protestant Piety in Early Modern Scotland: Letters, Lives and Covenants, 1650–1712* (Edinburgh: Scottish History Society, 2008), and Mullan, *Narratives of the Religious Self*.

[30] Perkins, *A Case of Conscience, the greatest that euer was; how a man may know whether he be the child of God or no* (London, 1592).

[31] Perkins, *The Foundation of Christian Religion Gathered Into Six Principles* (London, 1641, orig. 1591), 16.

[32] Lewis Bayly, *Practice of Piety, Directing the Christian how to walk that he may please God* (London, 1611).

[33] According to *EBBO*, *Practice of Piety* was printed in Edinburgh twice in 1630 and in 1636, 1642, 1649 and 1667, long after Bayly's death in 1631.

[34] Bayly, *Practice of Piety*, 1.

in a 'bottomless lake of utter darkness', where the reprobate would 'always weap for the paine of the fire, and yet gnash [their] teeth for the extremity of the cold'.[35] English divines such as Perkins and Bayly intended their work not only to encourage readers to recognize and record their own depravity, but also to equip them with the necessary tools, in the form of prayer and general devotion, to combat the inevitable temptations of Satan.

Preaching on Satan, Sin and Self-scrutiny

These English devotional works accorded with the sermons of Scottish ministers who encouraged introspection through recurrent discussions of human wickedness and the need for self-surveillance.[36] One mid-century minister described the tyranny of man's 'original and natural corruption' as a 'universall disease and poyson runing throw, and infecting both the utter and iner man, defiling all the faculties of our souls, and members of our bodies'.[37] To combat this innate tendency towards evil, the Glasgow minister Andrew Gray preached that 'Christians should be full of eyes within to examine themselves and to see their own corruptions. There are many who have eyes without to take notice of other peoples carriage, but they have no eyes to look within to themselves'.[38] The sermonic focus on internal weakness championed among parishioners an introspective turn that ministers hoped would result in a more pious, self-aware population. As John Welsh of Ayr, son-in-law of the famed reformer John Knox, bluntly preached in the early seventeenth century, 'the book of your conscience must be opened or you will go to Hell'.[39] Even James VI and I seems to have taken heed. In his advice to his son, the future king Charles I, he included this telling (and, in hindsight, ironic) verse: 'Looke to your selves, what Conscience you have; For Conscience shall damne, and Conscience shall save'.[40]

To this end, the Devil was a favourite topic of Scottish ministers, who intertwined their discussions of the powers of Satan with the understanding of men and women as irrevocably debased. In a sermon delivered in 1591, Robert Bruce described how demonic temptation could manifest itself

---

[35] Ibid., 64–5.
[36] The clerical emphasis on self-surveillance and inner piety in seventeenth-century Scotland has been explored by Louise Yeoman in her excellent PhD thesis, 'Heart-work'.
[37] NRS, MS 5769, Seventeenth-century sermons, c. 1655, f.133.
[38] Andrew Gray, *Directions and instigations to the duty of prayer how, and why the heart is to be kept with diligence* (Edinburgh, 1669), 113.
[39] John Welsh, *Forty-Eight Select Sermons* (Edinburgh, 1744), 66.
[40] James VI and I, *The fathers blessing: or, counsaile to his sonne* (Printed by B. Alsop for Leonard Becket: London, 1624), 30. This was originally published in 1616. Though James VI and I is cited as the author, it should be noted that *The fathers blessing* was an anonymously written adaptation of *Basilikon doron*, 1599.

in a variety of tangible and intangible ways, all of which collaborated with the pre-existing corruption of men and women. As he put it, Satan 'insinuates himself in our affections by reason of the corruption that is in us'.[41] Alexander Henderson preached in 1638 that 'if so be that we had a right heart, then Satan nor his temptations would not prevail over us. But it is a pitiful thing that he has darts, and shoots them at poor souls, and we are ready to receive them, and then we cannot get them out again'.[42] Satan, then, did not just prey on spiritual weakness; human frailty provided both the impetus and the means for demonic assaults. As the covenanting minister Robert Baillie warned the Presbytery of Irvine, each believer must 'pray to God for our cause and Church: God will help us against all, men and devils: No man is to be trusted; the best is naturallie false'.[43] In highlighting innate depravity in the context of experiences with Satan, Scottish clergymen encouraged their audiences to recognize their absolute dependence on God and the necessity of constant self-surveillance.

Like their Scottish counterparts, Reformed preachers in England sought to convince their parishioners of their 'wretched state by nature' – a phrase common in sermons throughout the Anglophone world – and the attending need for introspection.[44] In an evocative mid-century treatise on Revelation, John Cotton cautioned his fellow believers against spiritual confidence or complacency in their dealings with Satan: 'the Devil, you say you defie him, and did renounce him in Baptisme ... But if there were not a strong power of Satan in us, how comes it that the blood of Christ must be shed, to destroy him that had the power of death ... ?'[45] Such sentiments were likewise promoted across Scotland and internalized by anxious parishioners.

The most interesting element of Reformed sermons on human corruption was the insinuation, implicit or explicit, that Satan was actually *within* men and women. From the pulpit, Scottish preachers frequently used the language of the Devil being inside the individual hearts and minds of men and women, a presence against which they must constantly battle. In a 1589 sermon, Robert Bruce told his audience that they must be vigilant

---

[41] Robert Bruce, *Sermons*, ed. William Cunninghan (Edinburgh: Wodrow Society, 1843), 389.

[42] Alexander Henderson, *Sermons, prayers and pulpit addresses of Alexander Henderson*, ed. Thomas R. Martin (Edinburgh: John Maclaren, 1867), 215.

[43] Robert Baillie, *The Letters and Journals of Robert Baillie, 1637–1662*, 3 vols, ed. David Laing (Edinburgh: The Bannatine Club, 1841), 350.

[44] Frank Luttmer, 'Prosecutors, Tempters and Vassals of the Devil: The Unregenerate in Puritan Practical Divinity', *Journal of Ecclesiastical History* 51 (2000): 39.

[45] John Cotton, *An exposition upon the thirteenth chapter of the Revelation* (London, 1656), 177–8.

... for we have to do with principalities and powers, with spiritual wickedness, which are above us and within us also. For he is not that has corruption within him, but Sathan is in him; So we cannot be half walkrife [wakeful], ever studying to cast out the devill, to renounce our selfs, and to submit to the obedience of Christ.[46]

Alexander Hume echoed these words in a late sixteenth-century treatise on the human conscience when he wrote that 'the devil was never lother to come out of the person whom he possesseth, nor naturall vices will be to come out of mans hart, where they have once taken deepe root'.[47] As Andrew Gray lamented in 1628, 'I think many of us may be afraid that the devil dwels and keeps possession in many of our hearts, and alace! He is like to be a possessor of some of them perpetually...'.[48]

Samuel Rutherford couched this internal presence of the Devil in horticultural terms, stating that 'Satan findeth his own Seed in us by Nature'.[49] James Durham, minister of Glasgow, wrote about this internal demonic presence in his wonderfully titled sermon, *The great corruption of subtile self, discovered, and driven from it's lurking-places and starting-holes*.[50] The English minister Richard Sibbes shared such concerns, warning a London congregation in the 1630s that the Devil aimed to 'build his nest' in the human heart.[51]

The presence of the Devil within the human heart rendered the battle against evil an internal as well as external one. As John Welsh explained, 'the godly, because God and the devil, light and darkness, righteousness and unrighteousness, a Jacob and an Esau are within them, therefore they cannot be without warfare'.[52] Gray echoed this duality when he told listeners that 'a man that hath two hearts, a part of his heart goeth to God, and a part of his heart goeth to the devil'.[53] Such language was not unique to Scotland. In England, Thomas Goodwin wrote that 'a man's heart is like those two-faced pictures, if you looke one way, you shall see nothing but some horrid shape of a devil, or the like; but go to the otherside ...

---

[46] Bruce, *Sermons*, 23–4.
[47] Alexander Hume, *Ane treatise of conscience Quhairin divers secreits concerning that subiect, are discovered, as may appeare, in the table following* (Edinburgh, 1594), 57.
[48] Gray, *Directions and instigations*, 106.
[49] Samuel Rutherford, 'Sermon V', *The Trial and Triumph of Faith* (Edinburgh, 1645), 43.
[50] James Durham, *The great corruption of subtile self, discovered, and driven from it's lurking-places and starting-holes* (Edinburgh, 1686). This was probably delivered mid-century in Glasgow, where Durham was minister.
[51] Richard Sibbes, *The Saints Safetie in Evill Times* (London, 1643), 6.
[52] Welsh, *Forty-Eight Select Sermons*, 144.
[53] Gray, *Directions and instigations*, 95.

and you shall see the picture of an Angell'.[54] Time and again, Reformed clergymen described the opposition and contrariety usually reserved for the demonization of others in a profoundly personal, internal way.

Did these preachers actually mean that Satan was *within* the hearts of their parishioners, or were they using the Devil to connote evil and corruptions more symbolically? According to Reformed theology, the Devil and human corruption both existed and operated in tandem. Reformed Protestant theologians, most notably the Swiss reformer and friend of Calvin Pierre Viret, had long articulated the idea that all human beings, due to their innate depravity, were possessed by the Devil.[55] The implantation and enactment of sin was, after all, Satan's greatest weapon, and people had sinfulness in spades. As such, it is possible that some Scottish divines would have indeed averred that the actual presence of Satan could be found in the hearts and minds of the elect and reprobate alike. This was not, of course, the type of physical, total possession that overtook a very small number of demoniacs – as few as eleven in total – in Scotland at the turn of the seventeenth century.[56] Yet due to their innate sinfulness, demonic possession was, in a spiritually inherent sense, a constant component of the lives of all men and women. To many Scottish clergymen, it seemed that demonic forces resided in the human heart in an ongoing attempt to provoke the unredeemed and chosen few alike to act in ways contrary to God.

Internalizing the Demonic

Given this sermonic emphasis, it is hardly surprising that in their self-writings many Scots identified Satan and their own corruptions as intimate bedfellows. After months, years and even decades of hearing about human depravity and the necessity of self-surveillance from the pulpit, many Scots became acutely aware of and sometimes obsessed with their own sinfulness. Satan, and his ability to impede any spiritual progress or peace, served as a trenchant reminder of personal frailty and failings. In moments of compulsive introspection, many godly men and women began to fear that they were, due to their 'evil hearts', in league with the Devil, even

---

[54] Thomas Goodwin, *Childe of Light Walking in Darknes: Or a Treatise Shewing the Causes, by which the Cases, wherein the Ends, for which God Leaves his Children to Distresse of Conscience* (London, 1636), 193.

[55] On this point, see Brian P. Levack, *The Devil Within: Possession and Exorcism in the Christian West* (New Haven, CT: Yale University Press, 2013), 19.

[56] Levack, *Witch-hunting in Scotland*, 115–30; Levack, 'Demonic Possession in Early Modern Scotland', in Julian Goodare, Lauren Martin and Joyce Miller, eds, *Witchcraft and Belief in Early Modern Scotland* (Basingstoke: Palgrave Macmillan, 2008), 166–84.

themselves demonic and beyond the pale of salvation. Some began to feel that Satan was actually within them, a likely consequence of the sermonic rhetoric discussed above. The self-writings of many Scots thus reveal the profound effect that beliefs about Satan, paired with the promotion of self-examination and conceptions of human sin, could have on how early modern men and women understood themselves and their place in the cosmos.

The recounting of the life of James Fraser of Brea, long-time minister of a parish in Fife, epitomizes the angst experienced by Scots who internalized Reformed ideas about the close relationship between the Devil and humanity. Born in 1639, Fraser underwent a great deal of demonically induced turmoil prior to and even after his conversion experience at age nineteen. In his memoirs, he told how as a youth he had committed 'the dreadful sin of blasphemy' during a heated game of cards.[57] One night after speaking these unspecified abominations, Fraser struggled, and failed, to pray. He wrote that '[I] could not get my mouth opened; there did a number of blasphemies and cursings run in my mind with great horror and against my will, which I thought was like the devil in me'.[58] Though the Lord temporarily relieved his troubles, a year later he heard a sermon that led him to recall and profoundly regret his prior sin of blasphemy: 'I saw in God's countenance terror, wrath, hatred, and vengeance ... I was in an hourly expectation when Satan should come and take me away; and it was beaten upon me with a mighty impression that I was delivered to the devil'.[59]

This language of Satan's overwhelming presence pervades Fraser's memoirs. Even eventual confidence in his election did not bring spiritual ease. At various times, he believed that he 'smellest already of hell', referred to himself as 'a bitter enemy to God, and a toad full of poison and venom', and even wrote that he had 'devil in him'.[60] When Fraser wrote about the presence of evil within his own heart and mind, he conflated his own depravity with that of the Devil, a conflation that married the understandings of human and demonic evil and reinforced the necessity of God's free grace. This created in the godly conscience a sort of feedback loop between sin, the temptations of Satan and divine sovereignty. Far from unique, such experiential language appeared frequently in the spiritual diaries, sermons and theological works of Reformed Protestants for whom internal encounters with Satan embodied beliefs about their own inherent sinfulness.

---

[57] James Fraser of Brea, 'Memories of James Fraser of Brea' in *Select Bibliographies*, ed. W.K. Tweedie, 2 vols (Edinburgh: Wodrow Society, 1841), ii. 89–370.
[58] Ibid., 103.
[59] Ibid., 106.
[60] Ibid., 116, 122 and 103.

Another particularly illustrative example of internalizing the demonic comes from the narrative of Mistress Rutherford, a young woman who in the early seventeenth century chronicled the spiritual successes and failures that had dominated her life.[61] Orphaned early in life and raised in Edinburgh by her strict grandparents, she was from her youth plagued by a profound fear of Satan intertwined with an internalized belief in her own depravity. Rutherford's demonic apprehension was so consuming that she suffered insomnia and even suicidal thoughts: 'I could not sleep for fear of him ... Many a time wished I for wars to come into the kingdom, that I might have been slain so being that I had been guilt of doing it myself'.[62] Later in life, she wrote that the Devil convinced her that she had committed the sin against the Holy Ghost – an unforgivable, eternal sin by which salvation becomes impossible.[63] Tormented by guilt and fear at this thought, she again considered suicide, writing that 'Satan tempted me to put violence hands in my self, making me think it so far from sin, that it would be looked on as good service to God to execut his justice on such a traitor ...'.[64] For Mistress Rutherford, who had her own conversion experience at a young age, faith equalled neither confidence nor spiritual comfort, as the Devil remained her constant antagonist.

John Stevenson, a farmer in Carrick in the early eighteenth century, composed a deathbed letter to his family that detailed a similar experience of fear and trembling at thoughts of sin and Satan. He wrote that once, while he was recalling the misdeeds of his youth, the Devil flooded his mind with fearful thoughts:

> [Satan] violently suggested to my soul that some time or other, God would suddenly destroy me as with a thunder clap. Which so filled my soul with fear and pain, that every now and then I looked about me to receive the divine blow, still expecting it was a coming; yea, many nights I durst not sleep, lest I had awakened in everlasting flames ...[65]

---

[61] Mistress Rutherford, 'Mistress Rutherford's Conversion Narrative', in David Mullan, ed., *Scottish History Society, Miscellany xiii* (Edinburgh: Scottish History Society, 2004), 146–88.

[62] Ibid., 153. R.A. Houston discusses the suicidal thoughts of Mistress Rutherford in *Punishing the Dead?*, 309–10.

[63] Some sins frequently considered eternal include the deliberate rejection of the mercy of God and ascribing the work of the Holy Spirit to the Devil. The basis for belief in eternal sins comes from Matthew 12:30–32. The sin against the Holy Spirit, which Calvin, Beza, James VI and many other theologians addressed, was the one sure sign that an individual was reprobate. On this point, see, for example, John Calvin, *A harmonie vpon the three Euangelists, Matthew, Mark and Luke* (London, 1584), and Theodore Beza, *Propositions and Principles of Divinity* (Edinburgh, 1591).

[64] Rutherford, 'Conversion Narrative', 166.

[65] John Stevenson, 'A Rare Soul-Strengthening and Comforting Cordial for Old and Young Christians: Being the last advice of John Stevenson, in the shire of Ayr, to his children

Elizabeth Blackadder, the daughter of a covenanting minister, spoke similarly of demonically induced sleepless nights and expectations of divine retribution. She told how, at the age of six, she would lay in bed but 'could not sleep but sorrow and weep under the fear of God's wrath'.[66] Whether these were truly the fears of a child or their interpretation by a self-conscious adult, these accounts illustrate the fear and hopelessness produced by a potent combination of demonic beliefs, Reformed theological ideas and pastorally encouraged introspection.

Amid such demonic struggles, Scottish self-writings often reveal lengthy explorations of the natural affinity between humans and Satan. On 5 July 1640, minister and former professor of divinity John Forbes of Corse wrote in his diary that 'because by sin [man] had lost his primitive dignitie ... so the whole posteritie of Adam is subject to the bondage of Satan, and the course of his world is to walk according to the prince of the power of the air ... He that commiteth sin is of the devil for the devil sinneth from the beginning'.[67] Adam, like Satan, fell from grace due to sin and foolish pride. Nearly a century later, John Stevenson told how he came to realize that man was 'the only creature, excepting devils, that ever disobeyed his holy, just, and good commandments, on which the depraved state of fallen man, and my own in particular, was more fully laid open to me than what I could well conceive before'.[68] The innate similarities between the Devil and humans, reiterated in both sermons and self-writings, reinforced an image of God as forgiving and merciful. If men and women were not so debased, God's grace would not have been so extraordinary. Reformed Protestantism was a faith in which the sovereignty of God reigned supreme, and it is unsurprising that ruminations of sin and Satan should serve not only to humble but also to exalt God.

Pastorally encouraged self-scrutiny and discussions of the relationship between Satan and human sin often directed how Scots reacted to trauma and allocated blame. In the late seventeenth century, Katharine Collace spoke of a moment of profound guilt after the accidental death of her young son. She reported that Satan had whispered in her ear that she herself had caused the babe's demise, upon which 'a hell arose in my conscience for blood-guiltiness ... I roared through the disquietness of my heart, and Satan was also let loose upon me ... Thus I continued in extremity for eight

---

and grandchildren', in W.K. Tweedie, ed., *Select Biographies* (Edinburgh: Wodrow Society, 1841), ii.427.

[66] Elizabeth Blackadder, 'A Short Account of the Lord's Way of Providence towards me in my Pilgrimage Journeys', in David Mullan, ed., *Women's Life Writing*, 387. Blackadder would have been six years old around 1665.

[67] NRS, CH12/18/6, Diary of John Forbes of Corse, 1624–47, f. 238.

[68] Stevenson, 'A Rare Soul-strengthening cordial', ii.417.

days, much without sleep, crying out against myself'.[69] The perception of demonic assaults compounded her already devastating loss, causing Collace, in her grief, to be overcome with anguish and self-reproach.

In a confession written in the late seventeenth century, a layman named James Gordon described all of the sins he had committed since his youth. The explicit purpose of such an account – written 'for the glory of God and my own conviction and self-abhorrence in the sight of a pure and holy God' – indicates from the outset that he had internalized admonitions about human depravity. Such ideas found easy expression in his discussions of sin and Satan. Gordon reported that his first 'heinous' sin occurred at the tender age of four:

> I being a young cheild was left at home on the Sabboath day and playing with the neighbouring children in the next house was caused by the eldest of them to imitate man and wife with a young femal cheild. Therefore ... I myself so early made to be one of Satans servants makes me to fear lest he have power given him by God to tempt me to this or the like sin.[70]

This was undoubtedly a traumatic and incomprehensible event for a four-year-old. Gordon attributed his actions to Satan (who was under the direction of a just God) and his own corruptions, with no blame placed on the older boy who orchestrated the whole thing. Belief in an intimate relationship between the Devil and human depravity, contrasted with the pure goodness of God, had shaped his hindsight and informed his interpretation of such an event.

The potential dangers of such introspection and demonic interaction did not go unnoticed by the ministry in Scotland. In 1688, Robert Rule delivered a revealing sermon that detailed how the Devil manipulated men and women's natural proclivity to fear and doubt. 'Of all the creatures', he began, 'man is apt to torment and afflict himself with fears'.[71] Rule explained that external threats were not 'so dangerous as the fears that arises from within a mans self', for the Devil used these internal tendencies to cast men and women 'into despondency, and unbelief and distrust of [God's] promises'.[72] The weakness of the mortal mind cooperated with Satan by allowing and even inviting such fears to enter. Only reliance on God could bring deliverance. R.A. Houston has argued that in Scotland, though invocations of the Devil were rare in understandings of actual suicide,

---

[69] Katharine Collace, 'Memoirs or Spiritual Exercises of Mistress Ross', in Mullen, ed., *Women's Life Writing*, 39–40. This entry was composed in the late seventeenth century, but a specific date is not given.
[70] NRS, GD248/616/9, Confession of James Gordon, f.1.
[71] NLS, MS 5770, Seventeenth- century sermons, f.3.
[72] Ibid.

it was not uncommon for Calvinist self-writings to contain discussions of suicidal thoughts.[73] According to Scottish divines, overcoming such thoughts served as a reflection not of the strength of the afflicted, but of the power of God's merciful intervention. The twenty-first-century reader cannot help but notice the irony in laying the blame for fears, anxieties and depressions at the feet of sinful men and women (in conjunction with the Devil), rather than recognizing that these despairing tendencies may have been inherent in and encouraged by Reformed theology and pastoral practice.

As historians have demonstrated, Satan also figured prominently in the internal experiences (and subsequently, the spiritual diaries) of the godly in England.[74] A dramatic yet telling example comes from John Bunyan's *Grace Abounding to the Chief of Sinners*, published in London in 1666 and in Scotland in 1697. *Grace Abounding* would be republished in Scotland no less than eight additional times over the course of the eighteenth century.[75] Here, Bunyan recounted his past wickedness and detailed the turmoil that wracked his heart as he wrestled with sin and Satan, especially in his youth. He wrote that often as a boy, after having 'spent this and the other day in sin', he would lay in bed 'greatly afflicted, while asleep, with the apprehensions of devils and wicked spirits'. 'I should', Bunyan wrote, 'at these years, be greatly afflicted and troubled with the thoughts of the fearful torments of hell-fire; still fearing, that it would be my lot to be found at last among those devils and hellish fiends, who are there bound down with the chains and bonds of darkness'.[76]

Driven to desperate episodes of psychological struggle against Satan, he wrote of crying out in bed for all hours of the night, until he was breathless and exhausted. 'Oh!', he lamented, 'The diligence of Satan! The desperateness of man's heart!'[77] Later in life, before his conversion, Bunyan became convinced he had sinned beyond redemption. He began 'to shake and totter under the sense of the dreadful judgment of God, that should fall on those that have sinned that most fearful and unpardonable

---

[73] See Houston, *Punishing the Dead*, esp. pp. 292–312.

[74] Johnstone, *The Devil and Demonism*, chapter 4 and Oldridge, *The Devil in Early Modern England*, chapter 3. On the genre of autobiography in Puritan England, see Watkins, *The Puritan Experience*; William Matthews, 'Seventeenth- Century Autobiography', in William Matthews and Ralph W. Rader, eds, *Autobiography, Biography, and the Novel* (Los Angeles, CA: William Andrews Clark Memorial Library, 1973); Elizabeth Botanaki, 'Seventeenth-Century English Women's Spiritual Diaries: Self-Examination, Covenanting and Account-Keeping', *Sixteenth Century Journal* 30 (1999): 3–21; Paul Seaver, *Wallington's World: A Puritan Artisan in Seventeenth-Century London* (Stanford, CA: Stanford University Press, 1985).

[75] John Bunyan, *Grace abounding to the chief of sinners: or, A brief and faithful relation of the exceeding mercy of God in Christ* (London, 1666).

[76] Ibid., paragraph 6.

[77] Ibid., paragraph 139.

sin'.[78] In both English and Scottish spiritual diaries, disturbing thoughts of atheism and other unpardonable sins often appeared in the minds of the godly in the midst of demonic experiences, leading them to obsess about grace and the threat of damnation.

Another noteworthy English example comes from the diary of navigator and surveyor Richard Norwood.[79] In it, he wrote that even after his conversion experience at the age of 26, Satan remained a constant antagonist. At one point, when considering the sins of his past, Norwood entered into a panic over his possible reprobation. His desperate state was exacerbated by the sense of Satan overcoming him physically as well as spiritually: 'It is hard to express the manner of it, but sometimes he [the devil] seemed to lean on my back or arms or shoulder, sometimes hanging on my cloak or gown'.[80] At one point, he questioned if he himself was 'a devil'.[81] Norwood's experiences with Satan made him worry that 'the Lord had or should utterly cast me off', exemplifying the extreme despair and estrangement from God that often characterized, albeit temporarily, the internalization of the demonic.[82]

Though surprisingly few diaries from seventeenth-century New England have survived, the ones that do are illustrative of the now-familiar concern with the Devil and his unwanted but inevitable interventions in human life.[83] As in Scotland, the relationship between Satan and the evil nature of men and women was pervasive. One passage from the first-generation New Englander and famed minister Thomas Shepard is particularly exemplary. Struck by the fear that he had committed 'hellish blasphemy' and 'the unpardonable sin' upon reading certain scriptures, Shepard 'had some strong temptations to run my head agaynst walls & braine & kill myself'. At the height of his despair, God bestowed the following meditation upon him: 'Be not discouraged because thou art so vile, but make this double use of it; 1. loathe thyself the more; 2. feele a greater need & put a greater price upon Jesus'. Shepard found this advice particularly useful in his struggles with the Devil, whom he beat 'as it were with his own weapons'. God, he said, had helped him to 'loathe myself in some great measure',

---

[78] Ibid, paragraph 164.

[79] Richard Norwood, *The Journal of Richard Norwood Surveyor of Bermuda*, eds. W.F. Craven and W.B. Hayward (New York: Pub. for the Bermuda Historical Monuments Trust by Scholars' Facsimiles & Reprints, 1945).

[80] Ibid., 93.

[81] Ibid., 95.

[82] Ibid., 101. On perceptions of the Devil in cases of religious melancholy in Calvinist England more broadly, see Jeremy Schmidt, *Melancholy and Care of the Soul: Religion, Moral Philosophy and Madness in Early Modern England* (Aldershot: Ashgate, 2007), 64–77. See also Johnstone, *The Devil and Demonism*, esp. chapter 4.

[83] Baird Tipson, 'The Routinized Piety of Thomas Shepard's Diary', *Early American Literature* 13 (1978), 65.

realizing that his inner nature was 'the greatest enemy, worse than the devil can be agaynst myself'.[84] This passage exemplifies how the obsession with sinfulness in conjunction with demonic activity pervaded many godly writings on both sides of the Atlantic.

A Devil Weakly Fettered[85]

As historians have long acknowledged, Reformed Protestantism set the bar for living very high. The challenge lay in not only controlling one's actions and words, but also one's thoughts. This was no easy task for Scots who had been constantly reminded, from a very young age, of their own moral and mental frailty. As Nathan Johnstone has argued, 'diabolic intrusion did not separate subversive thoughts from the conscience … Protestant writers never intended that it should, but rather that it should do the reverse, forcing a self-conscious and often sustained engagement with the experience of sin, guilt and the demonic'.[86] When Scottish men and women recorded their improper thoughts in self-writings, they did so with anxiety and often shame, regardless of whether these thoughts had demonic origins. They had heard many times from the pulpit that Satan and human corruption were two sides of the same coin, and many Scots spoke of the Devil operating in tandem with their evil hearts.[87] Their experiential engagement with Satan was thus creative and reflective of an uncompromising perception of the self as feeble, sinful and at worst, demonic.

As noted from the onset, there are obvious patterns in how Reformed Scots, as well as their counterparts in England and New England, wrote about their encounters with and responses to Satan. Such patterns were clearly adopted and adapted according to the cultural expectations prescribed from the pulpit and in print. Yet even if such demonic encounters were purposefully constructed along these lines, they none the less illustrate what the godly believed – and indeed felt, sometimes with great terror – about themselves and Satan's involvement in their hearts

---

[84] Thomas Shepard, *The Autobiography of Thomas Shepard* (Pierce and Parker, 1832), 26.
[85] This phrase comes from Robert Louis Stevenson and Fanny De Grift Stevenson, *More New Arabian Nights: The Dynamiter* (New York: Henry Holt and Company, 1885), 321.
[86] Johnstone, *The Devil and Demonism*, 129.
[87] See, for example, NLS, Adv. MS. 34.6.22, Marion Veitch, 'An account of the Lord's gracious dealing with me and of his remarkable hearing and answering my supplications', c. 1670–1680s, f.20; NRS, GD237/21/64, Part of an unnamed Scottish woman's spiritual diary, 1633, f.9.; NRS, CH12/18/6, Diary of John Forbes of Corse (1593–1648), 1624–47, f.114; James Nimmo, *The Narrative of Mr. James Nimmo: Written for his own Satisfaction to Keep in some remembrance the lords way dealing and kindness towards him, 1654–1709*, ed. W.G. Scott Moncrieff (Edinburgh: The Scottish History Society, 1889).

and souls. Moreover, the patterns in, and expectations of, such demonic experiences are themselves revealing of how Reformed men and women felt they should perceive and present their inner lives and their utmost fears.

In theory and in practice, the cycle of locating one's sins, repenting for them, and finally looking to God for relief occurred throughout the early modern world in a variety of guises. Stuart Clark has explained that according to preachers across Protestant Europe, the proper response to demonic affliction, and to misfortune more generally, ought to be an appraisal of recent and past sins that may have invited the specific misfortunes. Men and women facing any hardship should 'begin with reflections on faith and sin, move on to the twin therapies of repentance and patience, and conclude with requests for divine and clerical assistance'.[88] For godly Scots facing internal onslaughts from the Devil, however, it seems that the systematic taking of a moral inventory and ensuing acknowledgement of one's own sinful heart served as a crucial form of repentance in and of itself. Such internal repentance might be viewed as a dramatic corollary to the common punishment of standing in sackcloth and beseeching the local congregation for forgiveness.[89] To forgive one's fellow Christian, however, seems to have been a very different and perhaps simpler matter than forgiving oneself – especially after conceptions of human and demonic evil had been so conflated and dually experienced.

This is a despairing picture of the darker side of Reformed piety. It bears reiterating that internalizing the demonic was not a consistent, universal process. Not every godly Scot underwent this process to the same degree, or at all. Moreover, as the previous chapters explore at length, Reformed piety also entailed the comforting aspects of God's promise of victory and the unity embedded in both the highs and lows of election. Some Scots may have even found comfort in the knowledge that their internal struggles with Satan and the self, often popularized in printed spiritual diaries, were part of the larger communal plight of the elect. Because there was no recourse to good works as a means of achieving grace, the most that Reformed Scots could do was to examine themselves with fear and repentance, struggle against the assaults of Satan, and acknowledge that this was part of their godly fate.[90]

---

[88] Clark, *Thinking with Demons*, 445–56. In this chapter, tellingly titled 'Cases of Conscience', Clark also argues that Catholics would soon assume a similar understanding of the misfortune caused by witchcraft.

[89] On the performance of repentance in early modern Scotland, see Margo Todd, *The Culture of Protestantism in Early Modern Scotland* (New Haven, CT: Yale University Press, 2002), 38–9, 127–82.

[90] This point is also made about English Protestants in Schmidt, *Melancholy and Care of the Soul*, 54.

In recent years, historians have qualified and in some cases rejected the rather despairing interpretation of Reformed Protestantism that lay at the centre of this chapter, instead focusing on the hopeful, constructive side of demonic experiences.[91] Nathan Johnstone has argued that the experience of the Devil was 'far more differentiated than the historical emphasis on the darker psychological implications of predestinarian theology suggest'.[92] Jeremy Schmidt points out that despite the scholarly emphasis on the psychologically negative consequences of Calvinist predestinarianism, it should not be overlooked that for Protestants and Catholics alike, moments of despair were thought of as 'both common occurring features of the Christian life and as spiritually healthy, or at least health-inducing'.[93] Alec Ryrie has persuasively suggested that Protestants in Reformation Britain were even attracted to spiritual warfare against Satan because it brought with it the promise of absolute and final victory.[94]

Clearly, the hopeful, communal elements of spiritual warfare are crucial to understanding the varied realities of Protestant piety in Scotland. Nevertheless, the negative ways in which the Reformed emphasis on sin, Satan and salvation shaped lived experiences cannot be discounted. As Margo Todd has written, the problem of human sin created in the redeemed a tension through which 'puritan self-fashioning' was both a constructive and a destructive process; the creation of the godly self entailed the purging of the innately evil self.[95] For many early modern Scots, especially those who took the tenets of Reformed theology very seriously, this experiential 'purging' often entailed a heavy dose of self-scrutiny and self-loathing during traumatic encounters with the Devil. For a substantial cohort of the godly, the internalization of ideas about the relationship between Satan and human frailty produced demonic experiences that were both creative and reflective of their darkest conceptions of themselves.

It should not be assumed, moreover, that the majority of Reformed men and women, in the face of such despairing experiences, would have found solace in unity or the doctrine of election. Though the doctrine of predestination may have been intended by divines, as Lief Dixon has cogently argued, to be a source of 'comfort and contextualization' to anxious parishioners, messages of grace themselves were imbedded with uncertainty.[96] Conversions, demonic assaults and the innate desire to live

---

[91] See, for example, Johnstone, *The Devil and Demonism*; Ryrie, *Being Protestant*, and Schmidt, *Melancholy and Care of the Soul*.
[92] Johnstone, *The Devil and Demonism*, 108.
[93] Schmidt, *Melancholy and Care of the Soul*, 541.
[94] Ryrie, *Being Protestant*, 247.
[95] Margo Todd, 'Puritan Self-Fashioning: The Diary of Samuel Ward', *Journal of British Studies* 31:3 (1992): 262.
[96] See Dixon, *Practical Predestinarians*, 7.

a godly life were noteworthy signposts of election, but even with these assurances, grace was not a guarantee. For many lay and clerical Scots alike, the doctrine of predestination proved more psychologically taxing than spiritually comforting. Many Scots continued to struggle against Satan and doubt long after their conversion experiences. As demonstrated above, it was the acute awareness of one's own sinfulness as much as anxiety about election that led many of the godly into intense periods of personal despair and even suicidal thoughts.

Neither insecurity over salvation nor acknowledgement of personal depravity explains why some Scots experienced Satan more palpably and dramatically than others. The question of why the Devil drove some Scots to suicidal despair, troubled but did not confound others, while barely leaving a mark on the lucky ones begs further inquiry. What accounts for this variety of demonic experiences? Despite shared patterns in their encounters with Satan, one cannot discount the influence of personality, past experience and present affliction in informing how Scots perceived and responded to demonic assaults. Past trauma or illness, unsurprisingly, often attended many accounts of internalizing the demonic. Mistress Rutherford, a woman orphaned at a tender age, reported being very ill just before the worst of her encounters with Satan, as did James Nimmo. For Kathleen Collace, the height of her demonic anxiety occurred just after the untimely death of her young bairn. Undoubtedly, the combination of past and present suffering with periods of physical or mental weakness left some Scots especially susceptible to dangerous obsession with the Devil and human depravity.

Thanks to gendered cultural expectations and patterns, women also appear more apt to have recorded periods of emotional distress in greater detail, though in general their experiences of Satan had much in common with their male counterparts.[97] Moreover, many Scottish men and women experienced the height of their demonically induced angst and self-loathing in their delicate adolescent years, when they were both impressionable and insecure. As Louise Yeoman has pointed out, for a young person, especially 'a young girl in a covenanting atmosphere, at an age where the possibility of going to hell as a responsible adult, rather than an elect infant, was just beginning to dawn', any chance remark about hell or innate depravity might trigger the internal perception of demonic assaults, leaving behind lasting trauma that they might later reflect upon as a necessary part of their conversion process.[98]

---

[97] For a discussion of the role of introspection and self-doubt in women's self-writings, see Mullan, ed. *Women's Life Writing* and *Patricia Demers, Women's Writing in English: Early Modern England* (Toronto: University of Toronto Press, 2005).

[98] Yeoman, 'The Devil as Doctor: Witchcraft, Wodrow and the Wider World', 96.

Leif Dixon has argued, in reference to the spiritual anxiety often attributed to the doctrine of predestination, that no belief system 'can make a person feel depressed or happy'. He goes on to aver that 'few modern understandings of depression revolve around particular belief systems as a causative factor'.[99] His point is well taken, but it does not fully account for the importance of pastorally encouraged introspection and the cultural expectation of demonic struggle, which was especially prevalent in post-Reformation Scotland. Here, exposure over the course of a lifetime to dramatic sermons on Satan, spiritual depravity and damnation clearly informed the internalization of certain ideas. It is unsurprising that many of the Scots who encountered the Devil in the most dramatic fashions were the wives, children or members of the Scottish clergy. This was not only the literate group most likely to keep spiritual diaries, but also those most exposed both to discussions of theological issues and, in the later part of the seventeenth century, religious persecution.

This is not to say the internalization of demonological ideas was the only causal factor in episodes of angst and despair. Certainly, specific circumstances and personalities contributed a great deal. For those men and women unable to keep spiritual diaries, it is difficult to assess to what extent ideas about Satan influenced their conceptions of self. It seems unlikely, though, that the frequent sermonic discussions of the Devil's relationship to human depravity would have completely escaped the attention of ordinary and educated parishioners alike. What is clear is that for a significant number of individuals, introspective anxieties about sin, Satan and salvation collided, often dramatically, in the process of internalizing the demonic.

Was the process of internalizing the demonic unique, in kind or in quantity, to the Anglophone world? The French Protestant experience provides an optimal, albeit necessarily superficial, point of comparison.[100] France was a country with close cultural and religious ties to Scotland, and during their respective Reformations, French and Scottish Protestants shared educational institutions and theological ideas.[101] Yet despite this relationship, Reformed Protestantism took root differently in the two countries. Beyond totally distinct political situations, French Huguenots

---

[99] Dixon, *Practical Predestinarians*, 31.
[100] It should be noted from the outset that the following discussion of Huguenot France is based largely on the findings of other historians, and this book does not presume to make a general argument here about the nature of French piety. I do hope, however, to demonstrate that the effects of Reformed theology on ideas about Satan were far from uniform.
[101] For more on the relationship between Scottish and French reformers, see W. Stanford Reid, 'Reformation in France and Scotland: A Case Study in Sixteenth Century Communication', in W. Fred Graham, ed., *Later Calvinism: International Perspectives* (Kirksville, MO: Sixteenth Century Journal Publishers, 1994).

seemed to have lacked the introspective, personal piety epitomized by the writings of John Bunyan in England or Mistress Rutherford in Scotland. As Philip Benedict has pointed out, in contrast to British and North American Protestantism, 'Huguenot ministers, under constant pressure to defend their flock against Catholic controversialists seeking converts, inclined toward a more intellectualist and less experiential understanding of the nature of saving faith'.[102] Because external threats abounded, there may have been little time or impulse to turn inward.

David Mullan has examined the differences between French and Scottish Calvinism in order to test whether or not the versions of Reformed piety present in the British world 'might have encouraged a "hotter" type of Protestant, perhaps more energetic in the performance of personal duties, including an Augustinian, introspective self-analysis'.[103] While rightly rejecting any clear-cut delineation of 'hot' versus 'lukewarm' Protestantism, Mullan points out that French diaries and memoirs, even those produced during the Wars of Religion, reflected religious commitment but were 'not designed as self-examination nor as a means of revealing the inner person with all of its attendant conflicts'.[104] He goes on to discuss how, unlike their Scottish counterparts, Huguenot ministers do not appear to have 'exploited' this focus on introspection and its ensuing melancholy.[105] Moreover, as Benedict has pointed out, French Protestants lived in a 'well-structured minority community whose devotional culture ... made less insistent demands on its members'.[106]

The ostensible absence of an internal, melancholic turn in French Huguenot piety might be partly attributed to the books that educated Huguenots owned, read and discussed. Beyond the Bible, Calvin's writings and works on religious controversy by French theologians most often filled the shelves of private libraries. Comparatively absent were the guidebooks on how to live a godly life that pervaded the English and (the much smaller) Scottish literary markets during the seventeenth century.[107] This was not an

---

[102] Benedict, *Christ's Church*, 524.

[103] David Mullan, 'A Hotter Sort of Protestantism? Comparisons between French and Scottish Calvinisms', *Sixteenth Century Journal*, 39 (2008): 45–69.

[104] Ibid., 51.

[105] Mullan contends that ministers in England and Scotland capitalized upon religious melancholy, presumably in order to reaffirm their flocks' dependence on both God and the church. While melancholy was not absent from the Huguenot community, it was not a focus of its pastoral practice and was accordingly less of a presence in Huguenot narratives. See Mullan, ibid., 65–6.

[106] Ibid., 210.

[107] Philip Benedict, *The Faith and Fortunes of France's Huguenot, 1600–85* (Aldershot: Ashgate, 2001), 220. To identify the comparative dearth of literature on practical divinity in Huguenot France, Benedict used Louis Desgraves, *Repertoire bibliographique des livres imprimes en France au XVIIe siècle* (Baden-Baden: V. Koerner, 1978).

issue of literacy, as one might assume. Members of the French Huguenot community were as able, if not more so, to read printed works such as devotional guides.[108] Though literacy rates were on the rise in seventeenth-century Scotland, most people remained unable to actually read complex texts such as devotional guides and printed sermons.[109] Thus the focus on and proliferation of devotional works in England and Scotland cannot be attributed to greater literacy rates than in Huguenot France.

The explanation for the absence of the introspective turn and ensuing internalization of the demonic in Huguenot France appears to have been primarily ideological and political. Benedict has argued that he has found no evidence of Huguenot preachers trying 'to convince the members of their audience of the extent of their sinfulness under the Law'.[110] Of course, further research, beyond the scope of this chapter, is necessary to confirm such assertions. It is worth noting, however, that while Bayly's *Practice of Piety* underwent multiple editions in France, it was poorly received by Huguenot divines. Moses Amyraut, a prominent French Protestant theologian and author, wrote that 'piety should be supremely voluntary and practised with full alacrity of courage and even gaity'. *Practice of Piety*, as he put it, was 'an enemy of that peace and joy ... to feel scruples and remorse that importune one's conscience'.[111] This attitude could not have been more different than the mentality one finds in the Reformed Anglophone world, where intense soul-searching and surveillance was pastorally encouraged and personally cultivated throughout the early modern period.

Neither Benedict nor Mullan addresses the issue of demonic belief in their studies of Huguenot piety. The most extensive study of French demonology, Jonathan Pearl's *The Crime of Crimes: Demonology and Politics in France, 1560–1620*, provides very little discussion of French Protestant demonic belief or theology more generally.[112] Pearl focuses instead on the political inspiration for French ideas about Satan and

---

[108] Literacy rates were high amongst the minority French Protestant community, partly because of the Reformed emphasis on literacy but also due to the community's social makeup, largely drawn from the middling ranks of society: R.A. Houston, *Literacy in Early Modern Europe: Culture and Education, 1500–1800* (New York: Longman, 1988), 149.

[109] See R.A. Houston, *Scottish Literacy and the Scottish Identity: Literacy and Society in Scotland and England, 1660–1850* (Cambridge: Cambridge University Press, 1989). Houston, 'The Literacy Myth?: Illiteracy in Scotland, 1630–1760', *Past and Present* 96 (1982): 89–91; John Bannerman, 'Literacy in the Highlands', *The Renaissance and Reformation in Scotland: Essays in Honour of Gordon Donaldson*, eds Ian B. Cowan and Duncan Shaw (Edinburgh: Scottish Academic Press, 1983), 214–35.

[110] Benedict, *Faith and Fortunes*, 220–21.

[111] As quoted in ibid., 221.

[112] On the Devil and demonic possession in France, see also Sarah Ferber, *Demonic Possession and Exorcism in Early Modern France* (London: Routledge, 2004).

contends that the most extreme French demonology came from Catholics who accused the Huguenots of being in league with Satan.[113] He contends that 'pure demonology' – strictly theological works on the Devil and witches, unencumbered by political agendas and propagandistic purposes (as if these things occurred in a vacuum) – 'hardly existed in France'.[114] This assertion, which should not be accepted without qualifications, does accord with the larger hypothesis that the French were less obsessed with Satan except as a means to demonize their opponents.[115] This lack of 'pure' French demonology, especially among its Protestant community, may be reflected in the reported absence of introspective experiences with Satan in the spiritual diaries of the time.

All this is to say that Reformed Protestantism alone does not account for the nature of demonic belief in Scotland or elsewhere. Rather, Reformed theological ideas acted in conjunction with a complex set of socio-political and cultural factors to produce demonic beliefs and experiences. English Puritans and Scottish Covenanters faced their fair share of persecution, for example, but this did not result in the great bloodshed found in places like France where society was starkly divided between large groups of Protestants and Catholics. That France was a confessional battleground undoubtedly shaped Huguenot belief in Satan and the location of blame for individual and communal struggles. Upon initial appraisal, it might be argued that the search for the enemy within took a necessary backseat to warring against enemies without. Further comparative research into the demonic experiences of Reformed Protestants on the Continent could reveal fascinating insights about how and why Satan figured more prominently in certain early modern lives and communities than others.

Conclusion

The close relationship between Satan and human nature, often within the context of predestinarian thought, undergirded and necessitated the Reformed practice of intense introspection in early modern Scotland. The contemplation of ideas about the Devil, innate depravity and salvation resulted in powerful internal struggles and self-loathing, culminating in some individuals with internalizing the demonic. This process was not confined to Scottish borders; it occurred among Reformed Protestants in England and New England. Throughout the Anglophone world, an

---

[113] Jonathan L. Pearl, *The Crime of Crimes: Politics and Demonology in France, 1560–1620* (Ontario, Canada: Wilfred Laurier University Press, 1999).
[114] Ibid., 6.
[115] Curiously, Pearl barely acknowledges the writings of Lambert Daneau, the father of French demonology, who he terms 'France's one Protestant demonologist', ibid., 6.

obsession with Satan, human sin and the attending need for introspection was championed from pulpits and internalized by earnest Protestants anxious for security in an insecure world.

The unwavering emphasis on the intimacy of Satan and 'man's evil heart' profoundly shaped the religious experiences and personal identities of many in post-Reformation Scotland. When Robert Louis Stevenson wrote in 1885 that 'man is but a devil weakly fettered by some generous beliefs and impositions', he expressed a conviction recorded by his fellow Scots centuries before him: postlapsarian men and women would struggle with Satan throughout their lives on earth, not only as a necessary part of the path to salvation, but as an integral piece of their hidden, darkest selves.[116]

---

[116] Stevenson. *More New Arabian Nights*, 321.

CHAPTER 5

Wicked Words and Demonic Belief

This study has hitherto focused on the self-proclaimed godly in early modern Scotland, those who took Satan, and the attending Reformed preoccupations with sin and self, quite seriously. But what of the ordinary, uneducated Scots who left behind few traces of their ideas and experiences? These were the men and women who filled the pews of the churches, frequented the alehouses, farmed the fields, shopped the streets, took their troubles to court and left to posterity few accounts of their lives. What did they believe about the Devil?

Thanks to court records, historians can glimpse some of their otherwise irretrievable daily utterances. In various places, times and circumstances, ordinary Scots invoked the Devil to harm their neighbours, express personal grievances, reveal fears and anxieties and rebel against authorities. This chapter argues that the frequency and variety with which the Devil appeared in the speech of these men and women indicates that concern for Satan was not confined to educated elites. Wide swathes of Scottish society articulated interest in, and anxiety about, demonic incursions into daily life. Though ordinary Scots often retained traditional ideas about the Devil that may have set their demonic beliefs apart from the educated few, many also embraced the messages heard regularly in the post-Reformation church. The result was an active blending of belief within the framework of a surprisingly accommodating Protestant demonology.

Outside of cases of witchcraft, scholars of the Devil in early modern Europe have focused primarily on what the literate minority believed about Satan.[1] When it comes to the Devil, the voices of the people who filled the pews across Europe remain largely unheard. This focus on printed sources and elite beliefs has been due, understandably, to the dearth of written records left by ordinary early modern men and women. As Nathan Johnstone writes of English demonic belief, 'it is simply impossible to say with any certainty to what extent the Devil played a significant role in the lives of those who either lacked the education or the inclination to

---

[1] Chief among these studies is Stuart Clark's *Thinking with Demons: The Idea of Witchcraft in Early Modern Europe* (Oxford: Oxford University Press, 1997). More recently, Nathan Johnstone and Darren Oldridge have written very useful studies of the Devil in post-Reformation England. See Johnstone, *The Devil and Demonism in Early Modern England* (Cambridge: Cambridge University Press, 2006), and Oldridge, *The Devil in Early Modern England* (Stroud: Sutton, 2000).

record their experiences'.[2] While I would concur, with the addendum that historians cannot say much of anything with certainty, this fact should not discourage us from mining the historical records in hopes of recovering the ideas and experiences of those largely forgotten by history. Happily, in the case of early modern Scotland, the records of the local ecclesiastical court – the kirk session – provide, at the very least, valuable snippets of what ordinary Scots reportedly said (and perhaps, privately thought) about Satan.[3]

The Kirk Session

The records of the kirk session, perhaps more than any other source, afford an invaluable, if at times fractured, window into the demonic beliefs and experience of the Scottish people. The hallmark of Reformed polity in Scotland, the kirk session was established during the Reformation and charged with enforcing moral order and implementing discipline in local communities.[4] The sessions convened at least once and as many as four times a week and usually consisted of a minister and between a dozen and twenty-five lay elders from a variety of social positions. Because they recruited people from all levels of society to participate in the enforcement of reform – from the occasional witness to the session clerk to the influential farmer turned elder – kirk sessions imbued the community

---

[2] Johnstone, *Devil and Demonism*, 25.

[3] This importance of court records for understanding the beliefs of ordinary, uneducated people is exemplified by Margo Todd's *The Culture of Protestantism in Early Modern Scotland* (New Haven, CT: Yale University Press, 2002). This chapter has also benefited from David Cressy's study of scandalous speech in pre-modern England. While Cressy's focus is on subversive political speech, he makes a similar point about the importance of looking beyond traditional sources (in my case, those on religion; in his, those on popular politics) to gauge the opinions and experiences of ordinary early modern people. Both our projects seek to 'incorporate a more elusive body of utterance, including words that were never intended to be written down'. See Cressy, *Dangerous Talk: Scandalous, Seditious, and Treasonable Speech in Pre-Modern England* (Oxford: Oxford University Press, 2010), ix.

[4] Historians generally estimate that by the beginning of the seventeenth century, 80 per cent of the thousand or so parishes in Scotland had regular, working kirk sessions. See Todd, *Culture of Protestantism*, 8. On the history and purpose of the sessions, see also Jenny Wormald, *Court, Kirk and Community: Scotland, 1470–1625* (Edinburgh: University of Edinburgh Press, 1991); Michael. F. Graham, *The Uses of Reform: Godly Discipline and Popular Behavior in Scotland and Beyond, 1560–1610* (Leiden, Netherlands: E.J. Brill, 1996); Lesley M. Smith, 'Sackcloth for the Sinner or Punishment for the Crime: Church and Secular Courts in Cromwellian Scotland', in John Dwyer, Roger Mason and Alexander Murdoch, eds, *New Perspectives on the Politics and Culture of Early Modern Scotland* (Edinburgh: John Donald Publishers, Ltd, 1982), 116–32.

with a vested interest in the success of Protestantism.[5] Throughout the early modern period, sessions arbitrated a wide array of crimes that fell under the jurisdiction of the ecclesiastical courts, including fornication and adultery, swearing and blasphemy, and drinking on the Sabbath day.[6] Given this wide array of offences, most members of a Scottish community could expect to appear before the session as a defendant, an accuser or a witness at least once over the course of a lifetime.

Standing before the session elders of their local community, ordinary Scots espoused their varied ideas about the Devil, usually by invoking Satan in cases of interpersonal conflict or blasphemy. Loosely, I have termed such speech as 'demonic language' or 'demonic words'. Of course, the words that appear in the session minutes were those filtered through the hand of the session clerk and sometimes prompted by the session elders, and as such must be approached with some caution. This mediation of speech does not mean, however, that the voices that emerge from the session are inauthentic. As Margo Todd has pointed out, depositions were often read back to the deponents who then had to sign them for accuracy, and it is doubtful that these Scots would have signed statements that greatly distorted their words. Furthermore, the language of the session itself and the language of the deponents differ markedly, suggesting 'a significant degree of authenticity for the latter'.[7]

This chapter examines the minutes from over fifty kirk sessions and presbyteries selected from rural and urban areas in both the Lowlands and Highlands, ranging in date from 1559 to the early eighteenth century.[8] I have chosen this sample of the voluminous session volumes available

---

[5] On the meetings and makeup of the sessions, see Todd, *Culture of Protestantism*, 9–11, and Ian Cowan, *The Scottish Reformation: Church and Society in Sixteenth Century Scotland* (New York: St. Martin's Press, 1982), 135.

[6] Some of these 'moral crimes' were also considered criminal, the most important of these being witchcraft, which was made a criminal offence in 1563. On the Witchcraft Act of 1563, see Julian Goodare, 'The Scottish Witchcraft Act of 1563', *Church History* 74 (2005): 39–67. Blasphemy also became a criminal offence in 1661. For a discussion of the categorization of blasphemy, see Michael F. Graham, *The Blasphemies of Thomas Aikenhead: Boundaries of Belief on the Eve of the Enlightenment* (Edinburgh: Edinburgh University Press, 2008), 33–6. On the usually porous division between secular and ecclesiastical crimes, see Smith, 'Sackcloth for the Sinner', and Stephen J. Davies. 'The courts and the Scottish Legal System 1600–1747: The Case of Stirlingshire', in V.A.C. Gatrell, Bruce Lenman and Geoffrey Parker, eds, *Crime and the Law: the Social History of Crime in Western Europe since 1500* (London: Europa Publications Ltd, 1980), 120–54.

[7] Todd, *Culture of Protestantism*, 19. For a wider discussion of how historians must be cognizant of the fictionalized elements of archival sources, see Natalie Zemon Davis, *Fiction in the Archives: Pardon Tales and Their Tellers in Sixteenth Century France* (Cambridge: Cambridge University Press, 1987).

[8] A full list of kirk session records consulted here is listed in a separate section of this book's bibliography.

in Scottish archives for purposes of both economy and representation. To conduct a thorough statistical analysis of these references to the Devil in the kirk session records would be misleading for two main reasons. First, many of these records are nearly illegible due to damage by age and the elements, and some are no longer extant. Second, kirk sessions often changed clerks after a few years, and some were much more interested in recording detailed language than others. For example, the minutes of the Duffus kirk session in 1648–1690 recorded frequent instances of Scottish men and women summoned by the session for 'miscalling the name of God', but no details of what specifically was said were ever recorded. Similarly, the Kilconquhar kirk session recorded between the years of 1637 and 1666 many episodes of 'cursing and swearing', but failed to spell out what any of these curses were. We cannot know whether or not these cases involved demonic language, though many similar but more detailed offences did, as will be discussed below. In many session records, it seems that only when the reported language was especially egregious, as in the invocation of the Devil or the slandering of the session elders, did the clerk put the specific words of the offending utterances on paper.[9] A statistical analysis of references to the Devil in session minutes would therefore be both problematic and unrepresentative of historical reality.[10]

Despite these caveats, a few patterns are worth noting. References to the Devil appear most commonly in the session minutes from the second half of the seventeenth century, when sessions throughout Scotland had grown better equipped to both compose and maintain records.[11] The demonic language discussed below comes mostly from the Lowlands, particularly in the south and east, partly for the simple fact that more people lived in these areas.[12] The types of cases in which references to the Devil commonly occurred – cases of interpersonal, verbal conflict – were more likely to be heard, reported and recorded in areas with greater population density. Moreover, the Protestant Reformation ran a rockier, though not entirely ineffective, course in the Scottish Highlands.[13] This uneven reform,

---

[9] NRS, CH2/96/1 and CH2/210/1-2, respectively.

[10] On the difficulties in using the kirk session records for any sort of statistical analysis, see also Todd, *Culture of Protestantism*, 16–18.

[11] The most vigorous periods of session activity occurred during this time, particularly amid the covenanting years from 1640–1652, during the years immediately following the Restoration in 1660, and from 1695 to 1705. See Philip Benedict, *Christ's Church Purely Reformed: A Social History of Calvinism* (New Haven, CT: Yale University Press, 2002), 470.

[12] Todd has also noted that, in general, the kirk session minutes are more voluminous from urban areas, which is unsurprising given the fact that towns 'understandably organized sessions earlier than did rural areas and found regular meetings easier to achieve without extensive travel'. See Todd, *Culture of Protestantism*, 14.

[13] Historians have pointed to evidence of substantial recusancy in the Highlands to argue that the Reformation was not as successful to the north. On this point, see James

combined with a smaller population and more challenging travel logistics, led to the establishment of fewer kirk sessions in the Highlands than in the Lowlands. Accordingly, a smaller portion of references to the Devil cited below comes from session minutes north of the Highland line. These regional and chronological emphases notwithstanding, the kirk session minutes here consulted reveal significant themes and trends. What follows, then, is an illustrative sample of the ways in which ordinary men and women throughout early modern Scotland referenced the Devil in their daily lives.

The Devil and Interpersonal Conflict

Words about Satan often began as, or quickly became, a community affair. Such scandalous speech only appears in the session minutes if heard and relayed to the court by a witness or a person directly involved in the reported case. Accordingly, demonic references uttered during interpersonal conflicts most often reached the ears of the session elders. These conflicts usually played out in one of two ways: the act of 'flyting', a Scottish word denoting verbal scolding between two parties, and 'cursing', when only one party was heard verbally assaulting another. Flyting and cursing frequently occurred in public spaces – on the high street, outside the church, at a neighbour's house – and attracted the attention of gossips and the kirk session alike.

During such cases, both men and women rhetorically invoked the Devil to wish harm upon other members of their communities. The unhappy parties on the receiving end of such threats, curses and insults came before the kirk sessions to angrily report hurtful words, occasionally expressing fright over invocations of the Devil. In a case overseen by the Ferryport-on-Craig (better known as Tayport) kirk session in 1658, William Edisone reported that John Walker had 'bad him hang himself and wisht the divell that the house were in his womb'.[14] An appalled witness named Margaret Embry came forward to confirm the accusation, declaring that Walker 'cursed horriblie by the divell & prophaned god's name'. Walker appeared before the session the following day, apparently quite drunk, and received

---

Kirk, 'Jacobean Church in the Highlands, 1567–1625', in *The Seventeenth Century in the Highlands* (Inverness: Inverness Field Club, 1986) and James Kirk, ed., *The Church in the Highlands* (Edinburgh: Scottish Church History Society, 1998). More recent work has argued, conversely, that reform in the Highlands was more successful than once assumed. On the spread of Protestantism to the Highlands, see Jane Dawson, 'Calvinism and the Gaidhealtachd in Scotland', in Andrew Pettegree, Alastair Duke and Gillian Lewis, eds, *Calvinism in Europe, 1540–1620* (Cambridge: Cambridge University Press, 1994), 231–53. See also Todd, *Culture of Protestantism*, 14–16, for a brief discussion of the kirk sessions in the Highlands.

[14] NRS, CH2/150/1, f.181.

a thorough rebuking for his blasphemous words.[15] Alongside verbal reprimand, punishments for cursing and flyting usually involved public repentance, which sometimes required the offending party to stand before the local congregation in sackcloth, a coarsely woven garment intended to humiliate the wearer.[16]

In these cases of interpersonal conflict, Scots most often called on the Devil to physically assault another person. Common curses included the imperatives 'Divell breake your legge', 'divil ding out your harns [brains]' and 'devil rip [you] up'.[17] A pregnant Janet Walker reported to the Old Kirk kirk session in 1656 that Margaret Henrysone had 'bade the devill ryve [tear] my wombe whither I was with bairne or not'. The minister sternly rebuked Henrysone and Walker, who had been feuding for some time, and told them that if 'ever they war hard in such ane scandal heirafter they should be referred to the Baillie to be punished to his pleasour'.[18] In Kirkcaldy in 1659, the Abbottshall kirk session convicted Henry Wilson of saying to Gissell Dryburt 'the devill put you head in a tether' (a rope used to restrain animals).[19]

Ordinary Scots invoked Satan to do mental and spiritual harm as well. Marion Leach was convicted in 1661 of bidding the Devil to 'rugg the soul out of Elspeth Sympson'.[20] In 1668, the Lenzie Easter kirk session near Glasgow heard the case of Janet Wallace, who was accused of pushing her elderly father to the ground and bidding 'the devil tak him away for she had not a father'.[21] The session, upset by this act of paternal disrespect as much as the invocation of the Devil itself, ordered Wallace to perform public repentance before the pulpit on the upcoming Sabbath day.

The records occasionally reveal ordinary Scots speaking overtly of Satan as an instigator of sin and temptation, echoing contemporary sermons that commonly addressed the dangerous internal activities of the Devil. In the winter of 1600, David Kid reported that Isobell Henderson had called him 'Satan', claiming 'the judgments of God would overtake him'. While she denied calling him Satan, Henderson did admit that she had claimed 'Satan was stirring [Kid] up to tempt her'. After hearing witnesses and deliberating

---

[15] Ibid.

[16] On session punishments for crimes, particularly that of public repentance, see Todd, *Culture of Protestantism*, 38–9, 127–82. On the use of the sackcloth as punishment, see Lesley M. Smith, 'Sackcloth for the Sinner'.

[17] NRS, CH2/11/1, f.105; CH2/124/1, ff.173–7; CH2/225/1, f.81.

[18] NRS, CH2/133/1, f.57.

[19] NRS, CH2/24/1, f.63. Punishment for this case is not specified.

[20] NRS, CH2/276/4, f.55. Leach denied that she invoked the devil to 'rugg' (meaning to pull forcibly) out of Elspeth Sympson, but confessed that she had 'bad the ill man rug it out'. The session, because of the 'ambiguousness of the word ill man', called upon more witnesses to confirm the story, and Leach was eventually publicly rebuked before the congregation.

[21] NRS, CH2/237/1, f.24.

on the case, the session determined that Kid should 'give [not] reviling for reviling but rather to studie peace wt. all', and ordered Henderson 'to goe and be counciled wt all those with whom she was at variance', or else she would be further punished.[22] This case exemplifies that, beyond concern over demonic references or spiritual improprieties, the sessions first and foremost desired to keep the communal peace, which in and of itself was a necessary condition for the creation of a godly community.[23]

On occasion, more violent uses of demonic language appear in the records of the Privy Council. In one such case, Patrick Lindsay reported to the Council in March 1632 that Isabel Muretoun had 'shamefullie railed upon him' in the public market of Edinburgh, calling him 'menswome dog, perjured theefe of all theeves ... tratour to God and man'.[24] According to further testimony, Muretoun then wished for 'the heavie vengeance of God to be powred out upon him and all his, that the devill would take him both soul and bodie', and finished the harangue by threatening to 'washe her hands in his heart blood and to burne him and all his hous'.[25] When Lindsay told her to leave him, Muretoun 'despitefullie spatt thrice' in his face, and with a group of other such 'rascals', attempted to break into his home. The request for divine vengeance and demonic assaults, coupled with a rather colourful threat of physical harm and actual damages to property, likely prompted the local kirk session to hand this case off to the Privy Council.

At times, Scots also directed their injurious words at the session minister or elders. These men had often served on the session for many years as disciplinary figures, doling out punishments for beloved pastimes such as drinking and fornication. Unsurprisingly, they were not always the most popular members of the community. Nevertheless, their position on the session conferred a certain level of respect, and to ill-wish an elder using demonic language assaulted his communal authority and general godliness. In the first years of the Reformation, some Scots invoked the Devil to protest the transformation of the formerly Catholic church. In St. Andrews in 1559, where some of the earliest reform measures took place, John Lawe expressed his frustration at being debarred from communion by publicly exclaiming 'the Divell knok owt Johne Knox harness (brains), for, quhen he wald see him hanget, he wald get his sacrament'.[26] That same year, another St Andrews

---

[22] NRS, CH2/150/1, f.207. It is also noteworthy that Henderson used the biblical term 'Satan' rather than the more common 'devil'.

[23] That the kirk sessions were concerned primarily with keeping the peace in their communities has been explored at length by Todd, *Culture of Protestantism*, 227–64.

[24] *Records of the Privy Council of Scotland, 1630–32*, 2nd series, 4 vols, eds D. Masson and P. Hume Brown (Edinburgh, 1899–1906), iv.427.

[25] Ibid.

[26] *St Andrews Kirk Session Register 1559–1600* (Edinburgh: Scottish History Society, 1889), i.36. It is unclear precisely why Lawe had been debarred from the Lord's Supper, but

resident, William Petillok, was convicted of saying 'The Divell cayre (rake up) the kyrk!'[27] The words of these two men reveal dissatisfaction with certain consequences of the Reformation, and both reached for demonic language to express these sentiments and to publicly challenge church authority.

In the mid-seventeenth century, Agnes Wallas stood accused of abusing one of the Edinburgh session elders by saying 'the devill drawe his puddings & guttes downe through his legges, and feet'. For her offence, the session referred Wallas to the higher court of the presbytery for punishment.[28] In 1654, the Newburgh kirk session summoned an obstinate Henry Beat for cursing and speaking wicked words while publicly drunk.[29] When the local minister had tried to end his game of dice, Beat apparently said to him, 'what the divel have ye to doe with our playing, since it is not upon the saboth day?' Growing increasingly agitated, Beat then cursed the minister, calling upon the Devil to 'pull his guts out at his broad side'. Witnesses confirmed the story, and the session ordered Beat to appear before the pulpit to publicly 'endure his grief for his blasphemous speeches and his unmannerly behaviour to the session'.[30]

As an interesting aside, that demonic language could be used to insult or wish harm on figures of authority or other members of the community appeared in a satirical broadside published in Scotland in the early twentieth century. The broadside enumerated rules and regulations 'for the purpose of putting down all forms of sin and vice'.[31] One of the rules satirically imposed on the Scottish community read:

> Any man or woman heard using strong language in the presence of a Policeman, such as 'Pip! Pip!' 'Sugar and Tongs', or, 'Go to the Devil!' shall be immediately proclaimed a dangerous lunatic; and the said policeman shall have the power of ordering a straight jacket, so that the said offender may be taken off to a padded room.

Clearly, the use of such demonic language, though it would have meant something quite different to a more modern audience, had remained

---

based on his subsequent comments it seems that he had been resistant to the practical reforms that were being implemented at St Andrews.

[27] Ibid. The minutes did not specify the session's punishment for these two men, but presumably they were strongly rebuked for their words, made to perform public repentance and possibly pay a fine.

[28] NRS, CH2/383/1, f.68. 'Puddings' refers to the bowels, entrails, or guts of a person or animal. A similar case occurred in Dunblane in 1659, when Andrew Kev was convicted of striking his father and bidding the 'divell drall his puddings among his feett'. See CH2/101/1, f.112.

[29] NRS, CH2/277/1, f.51.

[30] Ibid., ff.52–3.

[31] NLS, *By Royal Command* (Edinburgh, c.1905–1910).

imprinted in Scottish culture as a common insult. The extreme reaction by authorities to such language was here the subject of ridicule intended to provoke laughter in readers amused by satire of the harsher aspects Scottish discipline.[32]

Some Scots went so far as to explicitly claim that they would be willing to become a servant of Satan in order to avenge a wrong done to them by other members of their community. The Culross kirk session summoned John Westwatter in 1636 for stating that he would 'bee content to serve the devil to have amends of James Huton', an apparent enemy.[33] In 1650, the Liberton kirk session received a report that Agnes Aldinston had publicly cursed Margaret Reed, claiming she 'would be the devills servant to have ane mends of her'. The session quickly referred this case upwards to the Edinburgh Presbytery, which ordered Reed to 'mak publick satisfactione in sackcloth and declare herself penitent before the pulpit' on the next Sabbath day.[34] In Elgin in 1622, Marjorie Bonyman called Grissell Urrall a witch, and Urrall responded that she 'would not commit hir caus to God bot to the Devill', in order to seek revenge on Bonyman for her slanderous words.[35] The promise to serve Satan for any reason, even issued as a rhetorical threat, offended the session and community as a whole by impeding spiritual progress and disturbing the peace. The fact that demonic servitude laid at the heart of the demonic pact, which was both the inversion of a covenant with God and a precondition for witchcraft, only heightened the severity of such claims.[36] Private apologies before the session or small fines would not suffice for such offences, and public repentance in sackcloth was the standard punishment for these dangerous words.

While Scots of all sorts called upon Satan to physically or mentally harm others, women in particular tended to invoke the Devil as a general source of revenge and an agent of retribution. In the Highland town of Alves in 1688, for example, Grissell Duff became convinced that her neighbour had killed her rooster. She had wished, in response, for 'as manie crows as her cocke should have given, so mainie Devills take them to hell who killed him'.[37] In 1658, an irate Elizabeth Spittall, feeling that unidentified

---

[32] Ibid.

[33] NRS, CH2/77/1, f.49. As punishment, Westwater was called to appear at the pulpit the next Sabbath and make a public confession in front of the whole congregation.

[34] NRS, CH2/383/1, f.90.

[35] *The records of Elgin 1234–1800*, ed. William Cramond (Aberdeen: New Spalding Club, 1908), 172. The outcome of this case is unknown.

[36] On the demonic pact and its role in Scottish witchcraft, see Christina Larner, *Enemies of God: The Witch-Hunt in Scotland* (Baltimore, MD: Johns Hopkins University Press, 1981), esp. pp. 10, 11, 145–9, and Brian Levack, *Witch-hunting in Scotland: Law, Politics and Religion* (New York: Routledge, 2008), 34–9.

[37] NRS, CH2/11/1, f.227. For these words, the session sentenced Duff to public repentance before the congregation.

townsfolk had deceived her, publicly asked the Devil to 'tak the lyars and fiend blow them up in the aire'.[38] In Ferryport-on-Craig in 1660, Elspet Poutie found that someone had destroyed the plants outside her house. She reportedly responded by bidding 'the divell to rug them asunder' who had ruined her garden, and followed this request up with a number of 'other abominable oaths'.[39]

Early modern Scotland was a very hierarchical society. Men generally controlled the religious, economic and political realms, while female power often remained confined to domestic spaces. Yet as studies of Scotland and Europe more broadly have also demonstrated, early modern women were rarely passive members of society.[40] They frequently participated in public disturbances, using their words and even their fists to assert their opinions and avenge their grievances.[41] Nevertheless, because they lacked the same social and political clout or physical prowess as their male counterparts, Scottish women may have been more likely to invoke the Devil for aid or revenge because they felt powerless to control or avenge situations themselves. As John G. Harrison has argued, in Scottish cases of verbal assault, men most often threatened direct physical violence, while women tended to hope or demand that ill would befall their adversaries through non-human means such as the demonic intervention discussed above.[42] Here exists a fascinating parallel to early modern accusations of witchcraft, which often involved the notion that poor, older, less powerful women would be more apt to serve Satan in exchange for protection or

---

[38] NRS, CH2/315/8, f.44. For this outburst, Spittall was rebuked publicly the next Sabbath day.

[39] NRS, CH2/150/1, ff.211–13. The session rebuked Poutie for her behaviour (the records do not specify if this occurred publicly or privately).

[40] For more on how early modern women expressed grievances verbally, in Scotland and beyond, see Elizabeth Ewan, '"Many Injurious Words": Gender and Defamation in Late Medieval Scotland', in R.A. MacDonald, ed., *History, Literature and Music in Scotland, 700–1560* (Toronto: University of Toronto Press, 2002), 163–86; John G. Harrison, 'Women and the Branks in Stirling, c. 1600–c.1730', *Scottish Economic and Social History* 18 (1998): 114–31; Leah Leneman and Rosalind Mitchison, *Sin in the City: Sexuality and Social Control in Urban Scotland, 1160–1780* (Edinburgh: Scottish Cultural Press, 1998); Laura Gowing, *Domestic Dangers: Women, Words and Sex in Early Modern London* (Oxford: Clarendon Press, 1996); Jane Kamensky, *Governing the Tongue: The Politics of Speech in Early New England* (Oxford: Oxford University Press, 1999); James Farr, *Authority and Sexuality in Early Modern Burgundy, 1550–1730* (Oxford: Oxford University Press, 1995); Peter Rushton, 'Women, Witchcraft, and Slander in Seventeenth-century England', *Northern History*, 18 (1982): 116–32; Joy Wiltenburg, *Disorderly Women and Female Power in the Street Literature of Early Modern England and Germany* (Charlottesville: University of Virginia, 1992).

[41] See Yvonne Galloway Brown and Rona Ferguson, eds, *Twisted Sisters: Women, Crime and Deviance in Scotland since 1400* (Edinburgh: Tuckwell, 2002); Elizabeth Ewan, 'Disorderly Damsels? Women and Interpersonal Violence in Pre-Reformation Scotland', *Scottish Historical Review* 228 (2010): 153–71.

[42] Harrison, 'Women and the Branks in Stirling'.

vengeance through magical means.[43] If some unexpected ill had befallen an individual on the receiving end of such demonic invocations or insults, it is very probable that serious accusations of *maleficium* and sorcery would have followed.

Despite such patterns, however, the invocation of the Devil during interpersonal conflicts should not be seen as a specifically female act. As the kirk session minutes reveal, many men called on Satan to harm enemies in the midst of disputes and faced similar punishments, usually public repentance, to their female counterparts. Some historians have insinuated, especially when discussing the prosecution of sexual crimes, that godly discipline in Scotland was 'gender-blind', holding all individuals equally responsible for their own behaviour.[44] Others have argued against this gender-neutrality, citing that because of the belief that women were inherently sources of temptation, the 'war on sin was first and foremost a war on women'.[45] While this debate lies beyond the scope of this book, when it came to dealing with the use of demonic language, the gender of the accused does not appear to have substantially influenced the punishment received. The session's response was determined, above all, by precisely what was said, the reputation of the accused, the status of the person or persons offended and the necessity of keeping the peace.

Blaspheming by the Devil

Perhaps the most intriguing references to the Devil found in the kirk session minutes appear in cases of blasphemy. Blasphemy was not made an official criminal offence in Scotland until 1661, when the Privy Council passed a statute that made the 'horrible cryme of blasphemy' punishable

---

[43] On the role of perceived vengeance in witchcraft accusations, see Robin Briggs, *Witches and Neighbors: The Social and Cultural Context of European Witchcraft* (New York: Viking, 1996), esp. chapter 8.

[44] Michael Graham has argued that 'by holding individuals – men as well as women – primarily responsible for their own behaviour, [the kirk] mitigated against the maintenance of any double standard in the area of sexual ethics'. See Michael Graham, 'Women and the Church Courts in Reformation-Era Scotland', in E. Ewan and M. Meikle, eds, *Women in Scotland, c.1100–c. 1700* (East Linton: Tuckwell Press, 1999), 195–6.

[45] This position has been taken by Gordon DesBrisay, 'Twisted by Definition: Women under Godly Discipline in Seventeenth Century Scottish Towns', in Brown and Ferguson, eds, *Twisted Sisters*, esp. 137–8. Both Graham and DesBrisay's arguments have considerable merit. In early modern Scotland, women were certainly seen as sources of temptation, and more likely to serve the Devil through witchcraft. At the same time, both men and women could fall prey to Satan's temptations and assaults, as both were averred to be inherently, innately sinful. On the lives of Scottish women in both rural and urban areas in the late seventeenth and eighteenth centuries, see the works of Leah Leneman and Rosalind Mitchison, including *Sexuality and Social Control: Scotland 1660–1780* (Oxford: Blackwell, 1989).

by death. This statute was little used, however, and cases of blasphemy continued to be tried by the kirk sessions.[46] The sessions considered wicked words as blasphemies when someone went beyond usual curses by uttering subversive and sacrilegious statements that questioned the authority of the Scottish church as well as God. There existed, of course, much overlap with other categories of offence: some sessions issued convictions of 'cursing and blasphemous speech' and others of 'profaning and blaspheming'.[47] Unlike cases of cursing and flyting, however, Scots usually directed their blasphemous words broadly at the session or at no one in particular, as general statements of frustration, distrust or rebellion. The session reacted strongly to such words, often assigning the harshest punishments at their disposal and referring the blasphemer to the presbytery or secular courts for further punishment.

Ordinary men and women most commonly made blasphemous references to the Devil in order to question the spiritual authority and communal worth of the local session. A prime example of such disrespectful speech comes from 1656, when a witness reported that David and Gillies Murdowe of Fife had been drunkenly making profane statements about the kirk session. Specifically, the witness heard Gillies Murdowe say she 'wold not give a strawe for the session and for all yt were in it', and David Murdowe said 'the divell be in the sessione'. The session, 'considering that ryott, drunkennesse, swearing, shameless scolding, and reproachfulle speaking the sessione', appointed them both to stand in sackcloth in the jougs in order to repent for 'their grievous sines'.[48] The sessions usually reserved the joug – an iron neck-collar chained to the kirk wall or door and an uncomfortable and humiliating form of repentance – for those who deliberately (and often repeatedly) rebelled against church authority.

On occasion, sessions convicted a blasphemer for directly and impudently questioning key religious doctrines. As surprising as these

---

[46] It was not until the General Assembly of 1694 that ministers began to call for the 1661 statute, and the sentence of death, to be applied to blasphemers. Graham, *Blasphemies of Thomas Aikenhead*, 33–6.

[47] See, for examples of combined labels, *Rothesay Parish Records: The Session Book of Rothesay 1658–1750*, 48, 63–4; NRS, CH2/62/1, 129–31; NRS, CH2/278/1, 137–9. In discussing the use of demonic words in blasphemy cases, I have generally utilized the labels employed by the kirk sessions themselves. For a historical discussion of blasphemy in Scotland, see Graham, *Blasphemies of Thomas Aikenhead*, esp. chapter 2; in Europe, see David Nash, *Blasphemy in the Christian World: a History* (Oxford: Oxford University Press, 2007); Alain Cabantous, *Blasphemy: Impious Speech in the West from the Seventeenth to the Nineteenth Century*, trans. Eric Rauth (New York: Columbia University Press, 2002); Francisca Loetz, *Dealings with God: From Blasphemers in Early Modern Zurich to a Cultural History of Religiousness* (Farnham: Ashgate, 2009).

[48] NRS, CH2/150/1, f.113. This case was officially labelled as 'flyting', but that the session refers to the Murdowes' actions as 'blasphemous' in the text of the minutes.

blasphemous words seem to modern eyes, they must have been much more shocking and frightening to early modern ears. A particularly provocative example comes from 1602, when the Elgin kirk session convicted John Nauchtie of 'speiking blasphemeis agains God's ministrie, saying that the devill had as great power as God, and that they who served him were in as good case as they who served God'.[49] To say that the power of the Devil equalled that of God denied the doctrine of divine sovereignty, which underpinned much of Reformed theology. The session ordered Nauchtie to pay a penalty and stand for three days in sackcloth, with the warning that he would be banished from the parish if he committed the offence again.

Scots also referenced the Devil in order to publicly question the salvation of their adversaries. Beyond being incredibly incendiary and a threat to public peace, such remarks could be considered accusations of reprobation and thus presumptions of divine knowledge.[50] Accordingly, sessions tended to treat such utterances as cases of blasphemy rather than cases of cursing or flyting. This occurred in Rothesay in 1686, when Gillies Crawford reported that Margaret M'lachlan had said to her that 'she was the devills childe and that her father was so too, that she and her father had Satans image and resemblance, that the soul of her father was in hell and that her black soul would be there too'.[51] Though M'lachlan confessed to these statements and displayed shame for 'very unchristian abuse of the memory of the dead and reputation of the living', the session did not take her irreverent speech lightly. Finding her actions 'exceeding odious', the session, along with doling out the usual sentence of public repentance, sent M'lachlan to civil judge for additional punishment.[52]

The act of drinking to the Devil's health was another of the more scandalous acts of blasphemy. In the summer of 1680, a group of sailors in Fife reported that their shipmate James Anderson had been toasting the Devil's health while at sea. According to their account, while the men were drinking one evening, Anderson raised his glass to the Devil and did 'most horribly curse and swear so that the companie wer afraid to

---

[49] *The Records of Elgin*, 102.
[50] According to Reformed theology, God – and God alone – knew who was saved and who was damned. As Calvin and others had averred, man ought to accept the realities and justice of election and reprobation without extensive questioning, for it was 'indeed in reality a labyrinth, from which the mind of man can by no means extricate itself'. See John Calvin, *Commentaries on the Epistle of Paul the Apostle to the Romans* (1539), trans. Revd John Owen (Edinburgh: Calvin Translation Society, 1849), 353. Beza, too, had echoed this unknowability of salvation when he wrote that the reasons behind and means of predestination out were 'to be left unto God'. See Theodore Beza, *Propositions and Principles of Divinity* (Edinburgh, 1591), 22.
[51] *Session Book of Rothesay*, 63–4.
[52] Ibid., 64.

hear him'.[53] Shocked at hearing his demonic toast, the other men asked 'Are ye not afraid that evil spirit [will] take yow away?' Anderson replied 'I love him, therefore I'll drink to him', after which he threw his drink down and defiantly bade the Devil 'take that'. The Aberdour kirk session, the local ecclesiastical court, strongly rebuked Anderson for his blasphemous words. When he refused to acknowledge the sinfulness of his actions, the session referred him to the higher court of the presbytery for punishment.[54]

While a remarkable case in some respects, Anderson's demonic salute was not an isolated event. In 1677, the minister of Carnwarth had reported that various members of his parish had been seen 'drinking to the devils good health'.[55] Sometimes kirk sessions felt unable to adequately punish the blasphemer for such a serious offence and deferred to the secular courts for harsher sentences. This occurred in 1671, when the Lords of the Court of Justiciary, the supreme criminal court in Scotland, found Marrion M'Caul of Ayr guilty of 'drinking the good health of the Devill and all his servantis'.[56] The Court of Justiciary ordered that M'Caul be taken from the tollbooth of Ayr to the Mercat Cross of Edinburgh, where proclamations were made and punishments carried out, 'to be scourged (beaten) by the hand of the hangman and commone executioner'. Ultimately, the court banished M'Caul from Ayr for her blasphemous words, with the warning that should she attempt to return, it would be 'under the pains of death'.[57]

A Shared Spectrum of Belief

This chapter has detailed two broad, sometimes overlapping, categories in which Scottish men and women publicly referenced or invoked the Devil: cases of interpersonal conflict and cases of blasphemy. The most common of these involved accounts of men and women calling on the Devil to harm an enemy or avenge a wrong done to them. A host of questions arises from the terse and often perplexing use of demonic language in such cases: why did these Scots publicly ask the Devil for assistance, rather than God? Were they speaking flippantly, in jest, in moments of intense anger, or was there a literal request behind their words? Definitive intent remains unknowable, but such speech about the Devil does suggest patterns in how these Scots viewed the nature of Satan and his involvement in the human world.

---

[53] NRS, CH2/3/1 f.146.
[54] The outcome of this case is unknown, as the presbytery records are not extant.
[55] NLS, Wod. Qu. XXXVII, 293r.
[56] *Analecta Scotica. Collections Illustrative of the Civil, Ecclesiastical, and Literary History of Scotland*, ed. James Maidment (Edinburgh: Thomas Stevenson, 1837). 167.
[57] Ibid.

Clearly, there are some important differences in how elite and ordinary Scots – at least those called before the court for scandalous speech – understood and interacted with the Devil in their daily lives. To state the rather obvious, Scots consumed by concern about personal wickedness and Satan would not have been apt to speak about the Devil with abandon or to invoke him to do their bidding – an act that they would have considered a sin in and of itself. When calling on the Devil to commit bodily or spiritual harm to others, ordinary men and women often failed to first acknowledge the sovereignty of God, an omission that most Scottish divines would have been loath to make. An exception to this trend is seen in the case of Isobel Muretoun, a Scottish woman who verbally assaulted Patrick Lindsay by wishing for 'the heavie vengeance of God to be powred out upon him and all his, that the devill would take him both soul and bodie'.[58] Voicing something usually absent in the demonic utterances of ordinary Scots, here Muretoun made a clear connection between divine judgement and demonic actions, dual themes of many contemporary sermons.

On occasion, ordinary Scots attributed powers to Satan that their elite counterparts would likely not have dared, such as the ability to raise the dead from their graves. In Carrington in 1664, witnesses reported that Agnes Didope had cursed the deceased Barbara Steill for stealing some cloth from her, saying 'devell bring her out of her grave, that she may tell whether shee tooke that cloath or not', a crime for which she was ordered to pay a fee and publicly repent.[59] Agnes Henderson, in a small village in Fife in 1655, was insulted by Janet Simpson, and in response bid Satan to 'swell' Simpson and called her a whore and a thief. Simpson rebutted with 'prove it', to which Henderson replied 'the devill pull your mother out of the grave and she will prov it'.[60] The point here is that raising the dead was usually understood as a creative power restricted to God, and attributing this ability to Satan might seem to suggest a lack of concern for divine sovereignty, or a misunderstanding of the relationship between demonic activity and divine vengeance.

In their public utterances about the Devil, ordinary Scots usually characterized Satan as being with the power to do bodily harm. This emphasis on Satan's physical nature differs from that of Protestant reformers, who focused on the demonic powers of temptation and subversion, and from the spiritual experiences of educated Scots, who

---

[58] *Records of the Privy Council of Scotland, 1630–32*, iv.427.
[59] NRS, CH2/62/1, ff.141–3. For another example of a similar request, see CH2/150/1, ff.146–51.
[60] NRS, CH2/150/1, ff.146–51. This case goes on for some time in the records, and eventually Henderson was ordered to make public repentance before the congregation. Simpson's punishment for flyting is not specified. The next year, the session forbade Henderson to teach schoolchildren, indicating that the session considered her a perpetual troublemaker.

wrote primarily about wrestling with the internal assaults of the Devil. As John Brown warned his congregation in 1660, Scots must beware of the 'lying Injections and temptations of Satan', who was 'too great a Sophist and Disputer for us'.[61] For the elders leading the kirk sessions, the internal assaults of Satan were evidenced by the seeming abundance of demonically induced sin in early modern Scotland. When John Auchterlouny of West Seaton was convicted of repeated adultery in 1666, for example, a minister of the Presbytery was sent to him to see if it was 'possible to recover such a wretch led captive by Satan'.[62] Such temptations of Satan, rather than his physical prowess, remained the primary concern of Scottish divines.

At times, the session obviously phrased ideas about Satan as a tempter and prompted ordinary Scots to confirm them, as in the case of Rothesay resident Allan Orre. In 1701, Orre confessed to fathering a woman's illegitimate child. It was recorded that the minister

> ... represented to [Orre] the heinousness of his sin and how great advantage the divel had gotten of him and how loth the divel was to part with any grip he once got and how much he now stood in need to be eminent in his repentance as he was eminent in his sin ... At which exhortation the said Allan gave verie good symptoms of remorse and contrition and earnestlie begged both ministers and elders wold pity his fall ... .[63]

Orre's case, in which the ideas about demonic temptation clearly belonged to the minister, makes for an interesting comparison to another in Rothesay four years prior. In 1697, Janet Glases gave birth to a child out of wedlock. When interrogated, she revealed that a man named Ferchar M'Ilvray had illegitimately fathered her bairn. Confronted before the session, M'Ilvray testified that he was 'heartily grived that the divel got such advantage over him, first to make him fall with that woman and again to deny that he was father to her child, which now he owns to be his'.[64] Here the session likely encouraged or directed M'Ilvray to recognize the demonic root of his actions, or perhaps the clerk recorded his confession in terms that conformed to certain ideas about Satan. This does not mean, however, that Scots like M'Ilvray or Orre did not ascribe to the belief in Satan as an instigator of sin. Because these men would have been an audience to frequent sermons on the topic of demonic temptations, they may have

---

[61] John Brown, *Christ in believers the hope of glory being the substance of several sermons* (Edinburgh, 1694), 90. Probably delivered in 1660.

[62] NRS, CH2/15/1, f.79.

[63] *Session Book of Rothesay*, 101. The session then reported that it 'was verie weil pleased and dismissed him, appointing him to appear in publick before the congregation the nixt Lord's day'.

[64] Ibid., 124.

truly believed – or, with prompting, come to believe – that the Devil had indeed led them astray.

Diversity of emphasis regarding the powers and nature of Satan does not mean, moreover, that continued belief in the physicality of Satan was at odds with Reformed demonological ideas. An interpretive barrier should not be artificially placed between the demonic power to commit physical harm and the internal powers of temptation. Sermons and spiritual diaries, along with the kirk session minutes, reveal that these roles were not mutually exclusive, but rather mutually reinforcing. In the minds and experiences of elite and uneducated Scots alike, fear of a physical Devil persisted alongside growing concerns over Satan's internal threats.[65] Ministers commonly described the Devil in very tangible ways to reify Satan's unrelenting spiritual assaults, and spiritual diaries recorded how internal interactions with Satan often entailed physical manifestations such as fevers, shakes, fainting, pain, suicidal thoughts and, on rare occasion, possession. Moreover, while many of the godly understood the Devil to be a primarily internal foe, they did not altogether abandon the idea that Satan could also have a physical reality.[66] In post-Reformation Scotland, notions of a powerful Devil walking on earth were not divorced from concepts of his psychological arsenal. Scottish divines never intended them to be, for physical threat of Satan served to intensify the broader concern for the Devil amongst the laity.

While the coexistence of internal and physical notions of Satan in Scottish culture is evident enough, this does not explain why ordinary Scots spoke about Satan as a force of vengeance and bodily harm. It could seem, at first glance, that the invocations of the Devil during the aforementioned cases of interpersonal conflict were merely tropes or sayings, in the way that a modern person might say 'what the Devil?' or 'oh my God!' in a moment of surprise. Yet meanings of and attitudes towards speech are historically relative rather than historically constant. Unlike the language of slander, ill-wishes invoking the Devil were not particularly formulaic, though certain curses like 'devil rive you' and 'devil swell you' appear

---

[65] Though Protestant theologians tended to challenge the concept of the Devil as a 'material creature existing in ordinary material space and time', they did not reject his actual ability to, with the permission of God, cause bodily harm. See Oldridge, *Devil in Early Modern England*, 30.

[66] In their self-writings, Scots usually described Satan in the intangible form of an apparition or an illusion, but it was only in retrospect that they came to this conclusion. In actual moments of encountering Satan, they were often convinced that he had appeared physically before them, seeking to drag them away to hell. Alec Ryrie has made the important observation that while the Protestant Devil may have been more of a spiritual tempter, 'earnest Protestants were as liable to terrifyingly vivid encounters with the Devil as anyone else': Ryrie, *Being Protestant in Reformation Britain* (Oxford: Oxford University Press, 2013), 245.

in the minutes more common than others.[67] Because the Devil appears with variety and frequency in these cases of flyting and cursing, it seems that ordinary Scots genuinely viewed Satan as an agent of fear and pain. Through demonic insults, threats and curses, Scottish men and women articulated their belief in a Devil with profound physical and spiritual powers to avenge wrongs and punish sin.

Though the Devil may seem an unlikely agent of justice, this role actually accorded with a range of theological ideas espoused in Scotland and beyond. The problem of reconciling the evils of the world and the actions of Satan with the sovereignty and goodness of God had long preoccupied Catholic and Protestant scholars alike. Most believed God to be incapable of committing evil, and the popular term 'God's Hangman' characterized the Devil's role as enforcer of divine justice and God's agent of wrath. As John Calvin wrote in 1539, 'Satan is the minister of God's wrath, and as it were the executioner, so he is armed against us, not through the connivance, but by the command of his judge'.[68] In keeping with divine sovereignty, Reformed Protestants in Scotland contended that God willed the Devil to enact certain evils against the reprobate and the godly alike, which might also include physical harm. Satan was, as John Knox called him, 'an executer of God's will', and thus could be viewed as an avenger on earth.[69]

This is not to say that the Scots who invoked the Devil to harm others were doing so because they understood the nuances of theodicy. However, it seems that many Scots did view Satan as a more tangible, physical and even accessible figure than God. Through death, war, famine, witch-trials and the like, they felt a demonic earthly presence acutely and often. The Devil in Scotland thus possessed a surprisingly quotidian nature, though this did not render Satan any less dangerous or less disconcerting. As one historian has put it, the Devil in early modern Scotland was 'more effective disguised in domesticity than disgust'.[70] Due to this ubiquity and familiarity, ordinary Scots may have understood the Devil to be a likely and responsive avenger. As they had heard so often from the pews, Satan was both a daily reality and a dangerous arbiter of divine wrath.

---

[67] For cases of the wishing the Devil to 'swell' or 'rive' another, see, for example, NRS, CH2/150/1, ff.146 and 211; CH2/277/1, f.123; CH2/24/1, f.77. On the formulaic language of slander in Scotland, see Todd, *Culture of Protestantism*, 240–41.

[68] Calvin, *Commentaries on the Epistle of Paul*, 77.

[69] Knox, *An answer to a great number of blasphemous cauillations written by an Anabaptist, and aduersarie to Gods eternal predestination* (Edinburgh, 1560), 159.

[70] Joyce Miller, 'Men in Black: Appearances of the Devil in Early Modern Scottish Witchcraft Discourse', in Julian Goodare Lauren Martin and Joyce Miller, eds, *Witchcraft and Belief in Early Modern Scotland* (Basingstoke: Palgrave MacMillan, 2008), 154.

In cases of blasphemy, it is impossible to know precisely why some Scottish men and women choose to speak, often publicly, irreverent words about the Devil. Perhaps they felt frustrated by the actions of the kirk sessions, disliked a certain elder, were struggling to understand and express their own beliefs, or were just belligerently drunk. Cases of extreme blasphemy occurred much less frequently that the invocation of the Devil for physical harm or vengeance, and it is more difficult to identify clear patterns in such cases. In the absence of documentary evidence, one can only speculate about why these Scots spoke about the Devil in heretical ways. Still, blasphemous words, like those found in cases of interpersonal conflict, can help historians piece together the cultural role of the Devil in Scotland and the extent to which ordinary Scots adopted the ideas about Satan so often espoused from the pulpit.

Those Scots who spoke blasphemously about Satan clearly articulated an understanding of the world as divided into the camps of Good and Evil. John Nauchtie, by sacrilegiously stating that the power of Satan equalled that of God and that those who serve the Devil are as worthy as those who served God, demonstrated a basic knowledge of the prescribed ideas of sovereignty, service and righteousness to which he was issuing a challenge. When Margaret M'lachlan called Gillies Crawford a child of the Devil with a 'black soul', she echoed the sentiments of theologians who wrote at length on predestination and the eternal conflict between the children of the Devil and the children of God. The frightened reaction of those who heard James Anderson toast to the Devil's health and asked 'Are ye not afraid that evil spirit [will] take yow away?' reveals a common awareness that the Satan was not resting on his laurels in Scotland and was actively seeking to drag the impious to hell. These are not, of course, exclusively Protestant ideas about the Devil, but they were regular themes of post-Reformation sermons attended by Scots of all sorts. They suggest, at the very least, some level of reception among the Scottish people.

The above examples make apparent the difficulty in making absolute statements about the common ground or lack thereof between 'popular' and 'elite' demonic belief. Tracing the precise influence of Reformed ideas on the demonic beliefs of those who could or did not record their ideas and experiences is a slippery task, especially because Catholic and Protestant demonology shared much common ground. Because the kirk sessions were established during the Reformation, historians of Scotland lack a comparable source to access the demonic beliefs of ordinary Scots prior to the introduction of Protestantism. This challenge is quite exacerbated by the fact that we only have the words about Satan uttered by those Scots brought to court for behaviour deemed aberrant by the session and worthy of report by their peers. Yet a precise teasing-out of influences ought not be the primary aim when seeking to understand the role of the Devil in the mental worlds of ordinary Scots. Medieval, folk and elite demonological ideas never existed as categories in isolation from one another. Nor did Scottish reformers intend, or at least strive, for this to be the case. While they clearly wanted to eradicate many vestiges of 'superstitious' Catholic practices from their religious worlds, there was very little attempt to control *what* exactly was said about Satan. Diverse beliefs about Satan existed in concert along a shared spectrum, and this coexistence only reinforced the importance and awareness of Satan in Scottish society, which was precisely the goal of post-Reformation divines.

The Devil and Heated Speech in England and New England

The appearance of the Devil in the kirk session records poses an important comparative question: were the demonic references, invocations and commands publicly uttered by ordinary Scots unique to Scotland? During the early modern period, Protestant communities in New England and England also produced copious secular and ecclesiastical court records. Numerous historians have mined the language of these court records to answer key questions about early modern crime, gender and politics.[71] Many of these works, though they are not concerned specifically with ideas about the Devil, focus on slander, swearing and other forms of scandalous speech. They thus lend themselves to the question of if and how demonic language was employed by ordinary folk south of the Border and across the Atlantic.

Studies of slanderous speech in England rarely detail English men and women referring to Satan in their daily lives. The historian and anthropologist Alan Macfarlane has explicitly noted the absence of the words 'devil' and 'evil' in the parish records of Essex, 'despite very full ecclesiastical and equity court records where people were frequently abusing each other'.[72] James Sharpe makes no mention of the Devil appearing in the church court records he consulted for his study of defamation and

---

[71] This list includes David Cressy, *Dangerous Talk*; Laura Gowing, *Domestic Dangers*; James Sharpe, *Defamation and Sexual Slander in Early Modern England: The Church Courts at York* (York: Bothwick Papers no. 58, 1980); Martin Ingram, *Church Courts, Sex, and Marriage in England, 1570–1640* (Cambridge: Cambridge University Press, 1987); Christopher Haigh, 'Slander and the Church Courts in the Sixteenth Century', *Transactions of the Lancashire and Cheshire Antiquarian Society* 78 (1975): 1–13; Robert St. George, '"Heated" Speech and Literacy in Seventeenth-Century New England', in David D. Hall and David Grayson Allen, eds, *Seventeenth Century New England* (Boston: The Colonial Society of Massachusetts, 1984), 275–322.

[72] Alan Macfarlane, 'The Root of All Evil', in David Parkin, ed., *The Anthropology of Evil* (London: Blackwell, 1985), 57–75.

sexual slander in early modern York.[73] In her exploration of sexual insult in early modern England, Laura Gowing mentions the Devil just three times, detailing a demonic invocation in only one example.[74] In his work on slanderous speech directed at the state in pre-modern England, David Cressy cites a few brief instances of demonic language appearing in the English secular court records the assizes or quarter sessions, but references to the Devil do not feature prominently in his analysis.[75]

As none of these studies of English court records are concerned specifically with speech about Satan, it is quite possible that the authors overlooked demonic language in favour of other sorts of slanderous words. Nevertheless, the relative lack of references to the Devil in studies of English court records markedly contrasts the findings of the historian Robert St. George in his article on the use of 'heated speech' in Essex County, Massachusetts. In his brief study, which is primarily concerned with the gendered dimensions of insult, St. George details multiple references to the Devil uttered by Puritan men and women. In the records from 1640 to 1680, he identifies seven variant ways to insult someone by calling them a 'devil'.[76] Beyond demonic epithets, New Englanders also referenced Satan when ill-wishing their families and neighbours. In 1661, for example, Beatrice Canterbury of Salem was accused of abusing her son-in-law with 'wicked and reviling speeches'. Apparently she believed that he was not a fit husband for her daughter, and a witness reported that Canterbury had said of the son-in-law 'the divel should picke his bones before she would owne him to be her son'.[77] According to St. George, curses in seventeenth-century New England usually included wishes for God to 'visit pestilence on the victim' or that he or she 'be taken by the Devil'.[78] While not written to assess belief in the Devil, this article indicates that demonic words played an important role in the 'heated speech' of ordinary New Englanders.

---

[73] Sharpe, *Defamation and Sexual Slander*, 32.

[74] In 1611, Felix Chambers beat his wife Anne for what he claimed was 'just cause'. Chambers reported that he 'did ... beate or strike the said Anne and curse her and wished the devill to take her ... ': Gowing, *Domestic Dangers*, 219–20.

[75] The 1642 Quarter Sessions reported the account of a man who wished 'the devil to take parliament'. Oliver Cromwell found himself the specific target of such slander, as one Yorkshireman wished for 'the devil confound Cromwell'. Englishmen also took aim at Charles II, a man with colourful and questionable proclivities, occasionally bidding him 'to the devil'. See Cressy, *Dangerous Talk*, 194, 202, 213.

[76] For men, the words 'black', 'foresworn', 'Gurley-gutted', and 'old' were used to modify the epithet 'devil', while women were often called 'base devil', 'little devil', or 'lying devil': St. George, 'Heated Speech', 320–21.

[77] Ibid., 277–8. See *Records and Files of the Quarterly Courts of Essex County, Massachusetts*, 8 vols, ed. George Francis Dow (Salem, MA.: Essex Institute, 1911–1921), ii.340.

[78] Ibid., 299.

When compared to Scotland and New England, English court records seem to reveal a populace of men and women less vocal about the Devil and his role in their world. The lack of demonic references does not, as Alan Macfarlane has suggested, indicate that ordinary English parishioners had little interest in the role of the Devil in their lives. As Nathan Johnstone convincingly points out, 'such an absence is only significant if those records can be accepted to fully encompass all other important aspects of early modern culture'.[79] Still, the comparative similarities between how Scots and New Englanders spoke about the Devil are striking. So too is the fact that Satan also played a crucial role in many of the witch-trials of New England and Scotland, while diabolism only became a prominent feature of English witch-hunting during the 'Puritan moment' of the Civil War.[80] These observations suggest a correlation between the ways that ordinary, uneducated men and women thought about Satan and the prominence of Reformed theology in Anglophone communities. In all likelihood, the atmosphere of apocalyptic anticipation, intense desire for salvation, and required communal involvement in a program of reform – while certainly present amongst the 'hotter sort of Protestants' in England – had by the seventeenth century penetrated deeper into the lives of ordinary Scots and New Englanders and promoted an increased perception of demonic involvement in human lives. Further comparative research is needed to better understand how and why the Devil appeared more commonly in the daily utterances of some early modern individuals and communities than in others.

Conclusion

In the early modern world, wicked words carried a profound ability to do social, political and spiritual damage, as those who uttered them were well aware. As David Cressy has put it, '"words are but wind" was a popular expression, but speech could hurt as hard as sticks and stones ... Malicious tongues caused dispute between neighbours. Seditious words endangered the state. Scandalous and impious language disturbed the

---

[79] Johnstone, Devil and Demonism, 25.

[80] See Levack, *Witch-Hunting in Scotland*, esp. chapter 4. The role of the Devil in Scottish witch-trials has been challenged by a number of historians, most directly by Stuart MacDonald: 'In Search of the Devil in Fife', in Julian Goodare, ed., *The Scottish Witch-hunt in Context* (Manchester: Manchester University Press, 2002), 33–50. The reference to the 'Puritan moment' comes from William Hunt's excellent work on the religious underpinnings of the English Revolution, *The Puritan Moment: The Coming of Revolution in an English County* (Cambridge, MA: Harvard University Press, 1983).

community of believers'.[81] In his 1698 spiritual diary, James Murray, a young Presbyterian minister, explicitly named the use of demonic language as something frightful and offensive to God. During his teenage years, he began to feel increasingly concerned about the various transgressions committed by himself and his friends. 'About this time', he reported, 'soveraign grace took me up from many common evils that others were daily involved in, thinking it a fearfull thing, quhen any that were good scholars would name the devill or any such like word by way of imprecation or execration, having always a horrour of these terrible cursings by the name of God ... Tho' alas!' Murray lamented, 'too often I would have uttered in my anger and rage the name of fiend or devill'.[82] The use of, and concern for, demonic language cut across social divides and offended the ears of ministers, session elders and ordinary parishioners alike.

When Janet Meichie and Janet Keller came before the Aberdour Kirk Session on 6 October 1661 for flyting on the Sabbath day, they were made to crave God's pardon on their knees for 'breack of Sabbath and spending it so in the devills service'.[83] Any act of profane speech was seen as motivated by Satan; in one case of cursing, a man confessed to 'his sin in taking the divell in his mouth'.[84] Accordingly, the kirk sessions concerned themselves less with correcting any seemingly erroneous demonic beliefs and more with the eradication of subversive speech itself. Except in cases of obvert blasphemy, the sessions generally overlooked unorthodox demonic beliefs in order to concentrate on rooting out behaviours that threatened the stability and godliness of a community – behaviours that were themselves considered to be provoked by the Devil. As the historian Robert St. George put it, 'speech was a principal sign of the progress in the ongoing battle between God and Satan in which all men were soldiers. It both conveyed the Word of God and belched forth the flames of hell'.[85] The very acts of flyting, cursing and blasphemy posed a spiritual threat to the Scottish public as a whole, representing unrest, conflict and moral laxity among parishioners and indicating that the Devil and his minions were increasingly active on earth. The use of the Devil in these cases thus drove a double-edged sword into the heart of the kirk's reforming mission: demonic language both disturbed the peace and profaned the sacred, inviting the wrath of God on the entire community.

In assessing the terse and sometimes perplexing speech of ordinary Scots, a few conclusions can be drawn about belief in Satan across the spectrum of Scottish society. An interpretive barrier should not be artificially placed

---

[81] See Cressy, *Dangerous Talk*, x.
[82] NLS, MS. 3045, 'Diary of James Murray, c. 1698',. 5v.
[83] NRS, CH2/3/1, f.88.
[84] NRS, CH2/150/1, f.171.
[85] St. George, 'Heated Speech', 321.

between the demonic power to commit physical harm and the internal powers of temptation. Sermons and spiritual diaries, along with the kirk session minutes, reveal that these roles were not mutually exclusive, but rather mutually reinforcing. Though the demonic beliefs of ordinary Scots could and at times did differ markedly from those of the educated few, this did not mean that these beliefs existed in opposition or were not drawn from a 'shared pool of cultural meanings'.[86] References to the Devil appear in the kirk session minutes often and in a wide variety of ways, illustrating that ordinary Scots believed in a palpable, dynamic Devil, one who could be experienced physically, mentally and spiritually. For Scots of all sorts, even amid their distinctive demonic beliefs, the Devil was a potent and persistent reality.

In interpreting the words of the past, we in the twenty-first century should bear in mind that the meanings of speech are far from historically constant. Language was an immensely powerful tool in the early modern world, and certainly ordinary Scots knew the weight that their injurious speech about the Devil carried. From the pulpit, local ministers waxed on about Satan and his activities on earth. News of witchcraft trials, murders and political turmoil circulated through parishes, spreading the word that the Devil was alive and well in Scotland. Though the men and women in the pews may not have spent their time arguing the finer points of demonology, through their subversive speech and demonic words, ordinary Scots were actively contributing to a compelling communal discussion about the powers and earthly presence of the Devil.

---

[86] This phrase is Annabel Gregory's, in 'Witchcraft, Politics and "Good Neighborhood" in Early Seventeenth Century Rye', *Past and Present* 131 (1991), 52.

CHAPTER 6

The Devil as Master

Between 1661 and 1662, nearly seven hundred men and women were accused of witchcraft during one of the largest and most intense witch-hunts in Scottish history.[1] At the time, witchcraft was considered not only a criminal offence punishable by death, but also an egregious sin in the eyes of both God and the community. One of the witches accused during the summer of 1661 was Bessie Wilson, a woman from a town just outside of Edinburgh. In her confession before the Court of Justiciary at Edinburgh, she reported that the Devil had 'appeared to her clothed in black lyk a gentleman coming from Mortoun [an area south-east of Edinburgh] homeward ... and asked quhar [where] she was going'.[2] Wilson told him that 'she was going home', to which the Devil replied, 'thee art a poor pudled [confused, bewildered] body, will thee be my servant, and I will give the abundance, and thee sall never want'. She acquiesced, and six weeks later, Satan came to her at night when she was sleeping. The Devil 'lay with her and he bad her put one hand to her head, another to the foot, and give him all betwix with the renouncing of her baptisme, which she did'.[3] At the end of her confession, Wilson named two other women she had seen at a hillside meeting with Satan.

The case of Bessie Wilson exemplifies the demonic ideas characteristic of many Scottish witch-trials: the Devil's appearance as a man, at night; the promise of wealth and well-being; copulation with the Devil; the renunciation of one's baptism and entrance into demonic servitude, and the identification of fellow witches. This chapter examines these characteristics in depth, assessing the role of Satan in cases of Scottish witchcraft as well as demonic possession. It contends that in Scotland, cases of witchcraft depicted a composite Devil produced by the active blending of Reformed theology with traditional notions about the physicality of Satan. This blending rendered the Devil at once frightening

---

[1] For an analysis of the witch-hunts of 1661–1662, see Brian Levack, 'The Great Scottish Witch Hunt of 1661–1662', *Journal of British Studies* 20 (1980): 90–108.
[2] NRS, JC 26/27/5 and JC 2/10, ff. 18v–20r. The Court of Justiciary was the highest criminal court in Scotland, usually held in Edinburgh. The Court of Justiciary could dole out punishments, such as sentences of death, which were beyond the jurisdiction of local secular and ecclesiastical courts. This case is transcribed in Christina Larner, ed., *A Source-book of Scottish Witchcraft* (University of Glasgow, 1977), 258–9.
[3] Ibid.

and surprisingly quotidian, and all the more dangerous because of his daily pervasiveness. This immanence of Satan is also reflected in the relative dearth of possession cases in early modern Scotland. In a society where Satan's presence was ingrained and assumed, individuals had less impetus to act out that presence in a physical and extraordinary way.

None of the various ways in which the Devil pervaded early modern Scottish culture has received more scholarly consideration than in the accusation and persecution of witches.[4] Between the mid-sixteenth and early eighteenth centuries, nearly four thousand individuals in Scotland were accused of witchcraft. Of these, 84 per cent were women.[5] The witch-hunts in Scotland have attracted a considerable amount of historical attention in the last few decades, as part of a larger investigation of witch-beliefs and prosecution of witches throughout the early modern world.[6] The question of how belief in the Devil informed the Scottish witch-hunts has been a vital part of this inquiry since the 1981 publication of Christina Larner's *Enemies of God: The Witch-hunt in Scotland*, a work that brought Scottish witch-hunting to the forefront of witchcraft historiography.[7] Since

---

[4] On the role of the Devil in Scottish witch-trials, see in particular Joyce Miller, 'Men in Black: Appearances of the Devil in Early Modern Scottish Witchcraft Discourse', and Edward Cowan, 'Witch Persecution and Popular Belief in Lowland Scotland: the Devil's Decade', in Julian Goodare, Lauren Martin and Joyce Miller, eds, *Witchcraft and Belief in Early Modern Scotland* (Basingstoke: Palgrave Macmillan, 2008); Laura Martin, 'The Devil and the Domestic: Witchcraft, Quarrels and Women's Work in Scotland', and Stuart MacDonald, 'In Search of the Devil in Fife', in Julian Goodare, ed., *The Scottish Witch-hunt in Context* (Manchester: Manchester University Press, 2002).

[5] Julian Goodare, Lauren Martin, Joyce Miller and Louise Yeoman, 'The Survey of Scottish Witchcraft, 1563–1763', http://www.arts.ed.ac.uk/witches/. On the relationship between women and witch-hunting, see Julian Goodare, 'Women and the witch-hunt in Scotland', *Social History* 23 (1998), and Lauren Martin, 'Witchcraft and family: what can witchcraft documents tell us about early modern Scottish family life?' *Scottish Tradition* 27 (2002).

[6] For general studies of witchcraft, see Bengt Ankarloo and Gustav Henningsen, eds, *Early Modern European Witchcraft: Centres and Peripheries* (Oxford: Clarendon Press, 1990); Robin Briggs, *Witches and Neighbours: The Social and Cultural Context of European Witchcraft* (New York: Viking, 1996); Stuart Clark, *Thinking with Demons: The Idea of Witchcraft in Early Modern Europe* (Oxford: Oxford University Press, 1999); Joseph Klaits, *Servants of Satan: The Age of the Witch Hunts* (Bloomington: Indiana University Press, 1985); Brian P. Levack, *The Witch-Hunt in Early Modern Europe*, 3rd edn (London: Longman, 2006); Walter Stephens, *Demon Lovers. Witchcraft, Sex, and the Crisis of Belief* (Chicago, IL: University of Chicago Press, 2003); Robert W. Thurston, *Witch, Wicce, Mother Goose: The Rise and Fall of the Witch Hunts in Europe and North America* (London: Longman, 2001). For a discussion of recent trends in witchcraft historiography, see Malcolm Gaskill, 'The Pursuit of Reality: Recent Research into the History of Witchcraft', *Historical Journal* 51 (2008): 1069–88.

[7] Christina Larner, *Enemies of God: the Witch-Hunt in Scotland* (Baltimore, MD: Johns Hopkins University Press, 1981).

its publication, scholars in and outside of Scotland have cultivated the growing field of Scottish witchcraft studies.[8]

Like examinations of witch-hunting elsewhere, this corpus of work demonstrates the multi-causal nature of the trials in Scotland, which emerged from a combination of political, legal, social and religious factors that coalesced into an environment disposed to witch-hunting. As Brian Levack has argued, the localized judicial system and the use of torture in Scotland undoubtedly facilitated the large-scale witch-hunts.[9] Crucially, thanks to the passage of the 1563 Witchcraft Act, witchcraft in Scotland was considered both a moral sin and a dangerous, secular crime that could be prosecuted at a variety of ecclesiastical and civil levels.[10] More broadly, the ardent desire for a godly society – a product of the influence of Reformed Protestant theology – led to a general intolerance for deviation from behavioural orthodoxy. This reforming zeal combined with the constant fear of the Devil's involvement in earthly affairs to produce a religious culture ripe for witchcraft accusations and prosecutions.

Widespread concern for, and vigilance against, the Devil does not explain, in and of itself, the severity of Scottish witch-hunting.[11] Nevertheless, elite concern for Satan's machinations in the shadow of the Apocalypse added much fuel to the fire of witch-hunting. That the terrible crime of witchcraft was caused by demonic activity and servitude also fit within the larger spectrum of demonic belief held by the Scottish people, the bulk of whom were conditioned from childhood to expect a world beset by struggles

---

[8] For general studies of witchcraft and witch-hunting in Scotland, see Brian P. Levack, 'The Great Scottish Witch Hunt of 1661–1662', *Journal of British Studies* 20 (1980): 90–108; Levack, *Witch-Hunting in Scotland: Law, Politics and Religion* (New York: Routledge, 2008); Julian Goodare, 'The Aberdeenshire Witchcraft Panic of 1597', *Northern Scotland* 21 (2001): 1–21; Goodare, ed., *The Scottish Witch-Hunt in Context* (Manchester, 2002); Goodare, 'The Scottish Witchcraft Act', *Church History* 74 (2005): 39–67; Goodare, 'John Knox on Demonology and Witchcraft', *Archiv für Reformationsgeschichte* 96 (2005): 221–45; Goodare, Martin and Miller, eds, *Witchcraft and Belief in Early Modern Scotland*; Goodare, ed., *Scottish Witches and Witch-Hunters* (Basingstoke: Palgrave, 2013); Stuart MacDonald, *The Witches of Fife: Witch-Hunting in a Scottish Shire, 1560–1710* (East Linton: Tuckwell, 2002); Lizanne Henderson, ed., *Fantastical Imaginations: the Supernatural in Scottish History and Culture* (East Linton: Tuckwell, 2009); Larner, *Witchcraft and Religion: the Politics of Popular Belief* (Oxford: Oxford University Press, 1984); Lawrence Normand and Gareth Roberts, *Witchcraft in Early Modern Scotland: James VI's Demonology and the North Berwick Witches* (Exeter: University of Exeter Press, 2000).

[9] On the judicial use of torture, see also Levack, 'Judicial Torture in Scotland during the Age of Mackenzie', in Hector L. MacQueen, ed., *Miscellany IV* (Edinburgh: Stair Society, 2002), 185–98.

[10] On the legal designation of witchcraft as a secular crime as well as a moral sin, see Julian Goodare, 'The Scottish Witchcraft Act', *Church History* 74:1 (March 2005): 39–67.

[11] This point is most strongly made by Stuart MacDonald who has asserted that 'the devil and belief in the demonic pact can no longer be used to explain the severity of the Scottish witch hunt'. See MacDonald, 'In Search of the Devil in Fife', 46.

with the Evil One. Even the accused witches themselves would have been apt to see the crime of witchcraft as fundamentally diabolical in nature, thanks to the focus of Scottish preachers on the Devil's earthly activities and frequent interactions with humans.[12]

Scottish Witchcraft and the Demonic Pact

The demonic pact was central to the accusation and conviction of many Scottish witches. The pact, which revolved around the witch's renunciation of Christian baptism and entrance into a contract with Satan, often included the receipt of the Devil's mark and copulation with Satan. The cases of the witches of Libberton in 1661 provide descriptions of the demonic pact that typify those found in Scottish witchcraft cases. One accused woman, Janet Gibson, confessed that

> ... the divel did appear to her as she was going to the Carthall about the twilight in the evening and asked what she did want and bad her renounce her savior, and one night she confessed the divell did ly with her in her bed. She thought his nature was cold and that he had carnall dealling with her and caused her renounce her baptisme by laying her own hand on her head; and the other hand on the sole of her foot.[13]

Another witch claimed that the Devil told her 'he should tak her away soul and body', after which she renounced her baptism in the same fashion as Gibson and received the Devil's mark in the form of a nip on her shoulder. Promises of material wealth and personal satisfaction often preceded this entrance of the witch into the demonic pact. These promises were described in a wide variety of ways, ranging from clothing and money to the vague but enticing offer of 'all the pleasure of the earth'.[14] During or after the pact, the Devil often entered into some sort of sexual activity, usually intercourse, with his newly minted (and marked) servant.

This pact with Satan represented the inversion of two related and common practices in early modern Scotland: banding and covenanting. Bands, usually made by men as oaths of fidelity or friendships, had a long history in Scotland.[15] Covenants, to simplify a complex legal and

---

[12] Brian Levack makes this point about the differences between English and Scottish witches in *Witch-Hunting in Scotland*, 11.

[13] NRS, JC2/10, ff. 18v–20r. Also transcribed in Larner, ed., *A Source-book of Scottish Witchcraft*, 257–8.

[14] Ibid.

[15] On banding, see Ian Cowan, *The Scottish Reformation: Church and Society in Sixteenth Century Scotland* (London: Weidenfeld and Nicolson, 1982); Jenny Wormald,

theological term, were religious, and often political, manifestations of this process of banding. A religious covenant was a contractual agreement made voluntarily between an individual and God that, according to the tenets of Reformed Protestantism, could be interpreted as confirmation of predetermined salvation.[16] In Scotland, covenants were also documents by which individuals committed themselves to maintaining the Reformed doctrine and Presbyterian polity, as exemplified by the National Covenant of 1638. Sometimes authorities described the pact with the Devil as a covenant in wicked reverse, as in the 1650 case of Archibald Watt, who was accused of 'making covenant with the devil' and having attended 'many meetings since his covenant keeped with the devil'.[17] Thus the pact with Satan that lay at the heart of Scottish witchcraft belief was both an affirmation and inversion of a familiar practice in early modern Scotland. In an atmosphere of grave concern for the Devil and his actions during what seemed to be the Last Days, the pact with Satan entailed a dangerous charge indeed. Here the local Reformed Protestant clergy often instigated the prosecutions in an attempt to establish a godly kingdom and weed out any members of the community who might have entered into demonic servitude.

How did the pact with Satan become central to witch-belief in Scotland? Though Christina Larner has argued that James VI imported ideas about the pact to Scotland from Denmark in 1590, evidence suggests that elites in Scotland had believed in the threat and reality of the demonic pact since the scholastic condemnation of ritual magic during the fourteenth century.[18] The Scottish Witchcraft Act of 1563 did not contain an explicit mention of the demonic pact, but a deal with the Devil was implicit in the act's denunciation of necromancy.[19] The North Berwick witch-hunts of 1590–91, and their influence on Scottish society as a result of the publication of *Newes From Scotland* (1592) and James VI's *Daemonologie* (1597), cemented the demonic pact as a mainstay of Scottish witch-

---

Lords and Men in Scotland: Bonds of Manrent (Edinburgh: Edinburgh University Press, 1985).

[16] It is important to note, however, that a personal covenant was not a contract that bound God to any obligation; this would have been a constraint placed upon the absolute sovereignty of God.

[17] *Registers of the Presbytery of Lanark, 1623–1719*, ed. John Robertson (Edinburgh: Abbotsford Club, 1839), 80.

[18] For two divergent views on James and the demonic pact, see Christina Larner, 'King James VI and I and Witchcraft', in her *Witchcraft and Religion* (Oxford: Blackwell, 1984), who argues that James imported the idea of the pact from Denmark, and Jenny Wormald, 'The Witches, the Devil and the King', in Terry Brotherstone and David Ditchburn, eds, *Freedom and Authority: Scotland, c.1050–c.1650* (2000), who cites the earlier origins of the pact. On this point also see Goodare, 'Scottish Witchcraft Act', 58–9.

[19] Ibid., 64.

hunting, at least in the minds of the prosecutors. Agnes Sampson, standing before the king in 1590, was asked how she had come to serve the Devil. After initial refusals likely followed by torture, she 'confessed that after the death of her husband the devil appeared to her in the likeness of a man and commanded her to acknowledge him as her master and to renounce Christ'.[20] Others convicted in North Berwick confessed to a similar recognition of Satan as their master, as well as to meeting with him in large numbers and performing servant rituals such as kissing the Devil on his buttocks. This was a far cry from the orgies and cannibalistic infanticide that characterized the witches' sabbats of Continental Europe.[21] Nevertheless, the Devil was an undeniable and formative presence in these early prosecutions of the women accused of collaborating with Satan to harm the Scottish king.[22]

The events of 1590–91 inspired the composition of the pamphlet *Newes from Scotland* by the minister James Carmichael, who according to James Melville wrote a history of the North Berwick cases 'with their whole depositions', which no longer exists.[23] *Newes from Scotland* was published in London in 1592 'according to the Scottish copy', and summarized the testimonies from the North Berwick witches, which were given in the presence of James VI. This pamphlet articulated from the outset what would increasingly become a key component of witchcraft in Scotland: the demonic pact, demonstrated physically on the witch's body by the Devil's mark. Carmichael described the witches who joined forces against the King as individuals 'who suffering themselves to be allured and inticed by Divell whom they served, and to whome they were privatelye sworne; entered into the detestable Art of witchcraft'.[24] *Newes from Scotland* also politicized the pact by making the North Berwick witches, along with their demonic master, the overt enemies of James's physical and spiritual persona. Carmichael claimed that when the witches had asked Satan why 'he did beare such hatred to the King', he answered that 'the King is the greatest enemy he hath in the worlde'.[25] A bit of royal pandering as well as a genuine recognition of James's devout status, this rejoinder added to the perception that no one, least of everyone the King, was exempt from Satan's malice.

---

[20] NRS, JC 26/2; reprinted in Normand and Roberts, *Witchcraft in Early Modern Scotland*, 145.

[21] For an especially colourful and lurid example of a Sabbath, see Pierre de Lancre's *Tableau de l'inconstance des mauvais anges et demons* (Paris, 1612).

[22] On the hunts of the 1590s and James's role therein, see especially Normand and Roberts, *Witchcraft in Early Modern Scotland*.

[23] Carmichael's composition of a 'history' of the 1591 cases was described in the diary of James Melville. See *Memoirs of Sir James Melvil of Hal-hill* (London, 1683), 194–5.

[24] James Carmichael, *Newes from Scotland* (London, 1592).

[25] Ibid.

The King's involvement in the North Berwick trials led directly to his publication of *Daemonologie* in the final years of the sixteenth century.[26] The first and only demonological treatise published by a European monarch, *Daemonologie* further politicized the crime of witchcraft and solidified the demonic aspects of witch-belief in Scotland.[27] Initially published in Edinburgh in 1597, *Daemonologie* underwent two London editions in 1603 with later translations into Latin, French and Dutch. This work, as Stuart Clark has pointed out, was 'neither original nor profound', and it reinforced an image of the Devil mostly shared by Protestants and Catholics.[28] *Daemonologie*'s broader significance lay partly in its status as the first defence of Continental witch-beliefs in the English language, directed against sceptics Johann Weyer and Reginald Scot.[29] James's specific beliefs, though they had a distinctly Reformed flavour, were largely unremarkable. The articulation and promotion of such ideas by a monarch, however, were singular. Thanks to the writings and influence of James at the turn of the sixteenth century, Satan became solidified as a concern not only of the Scottish church and the godly Scot, but of the State as well.

In his discussion of witchcraft, James set out to prove in no uncertain terms that Satan constituted a very real and active presence in the world. In his introduction, he called the possibilities of the Devil's power 'infinite', while also carefully clarifying that those powers were given to Satan by God alone. 'But one thing I will pray thee to obserue in all these places, where I reason upon the deuils power', James hastened to add, is 'that God as the first cause, and the Devill as his instrument'.[30] He went on to list three groups who could suffer these internal demonic assaults:

> ... the wicked for their horrible sinnes, to punish them in the like measure; The godlie that are sleeping in anie great sinnes or infirmities and weakenesse in faith, to waken them vp the faster by such an vncouth forme: and euen some of the best, that their patience may bee tryed before the world, as JOBS was. For why may not God vse anie kinde of extraordinarie punishment, when it pleases him.[31]

---

[26] James VI and I, *Daemonologie* (Edinburgh, 1597). Here I have used the original 1597 Edinburgh edition. The best modernized version is printed in Normand and Roberts, *Witchcraft in Early Modern Scotland*, 353–425. For a discussion of the relationship between *Newes from Scotland* and James VI's *Daemonologie*, see Rhodes Dunlap, 'King James and Some Witches: the Date and Text of the Daemonologie', *Philological Quarterly* 54 (1975): 40–46.
[27] Levack, *Witch-Hunting in Scotland*, 42–3.
[28] Stuart Clark, 'King James's Daemonologie: Witchcraft and Kingship', in Sydney Anglo, ed., *The Damned Art: Essays in the Literature of Witchcraft* (London: Routledge and Kegan Paul, 1977), 156.
[29] Ibid.
[30] James VI and I, *Daemonologie*, xiv.
[31] Ibid.

He explained that the Devil 'knowes well inough how to perswade the corrupted affection of them whom God will permit him so to deale with'.[32] Satan, under divine direction, could and indeed would exploit the existing sinfulness of men and women of every sort. Anyone – royalty included – might easily fall victim to the dual threat of the Devil and their own depravity. For any that might question such an unrelenting and obvious threat, James warned that 'doubtleslie who denyeth the power of the Deuill, woulde likewise denie the Power of God, if they could for shame. For since the Devill is the verie contrarie opposite to God there can be no better way to know God, then by the contrarie'.[33]

Here James was setting up a straw man of sorts, as virtually no one at the time was likely to outright deny the power of the Devil. Yet the King had a great deal of personal investment not only in the project of witch-hunting, but also in fashioning himself as an unflinching antagonist of Satan. By building up the threat of the Devil, James augmented his own religious clout. That he saw demonic witchcraft as such a great personal threat was equally bound up in his identity as the monarch. Just as witches and Satan were affronts to God, so they were to the person of the King, who believed he derived his political power from divine and secular forces alike. As Daniel Fischlin points out, James's characterization of witchcraft as 'high treason against God's Majesty' purposefully conflated 'God' and 'Majesty' to demonstrate both the source of his power and the unity of his earthly aims with those of God.[34]

This was not, however, mere political posturing in the face of a church increasingly hostile to his Erastian leanings. James's investment in witch-hunting stemmed not simply from a fear of witches, but also from a personal engagement with the Devil that grew out of his Reformed Protestant convictions and his desire to assert his status as a divine and ideal monarch.[35] As both *Newes from Scotland* and *Daemonologie* made clear, James's personal faith – and his displays of this power from the throne – caused him to believe he was a prime target of demonic assaults. This was a threat made all the more frightening by the nearing of 'the consummation of the Worlde', which, as he wrote in *Daemonologie*, made 'Sathan rage the more in his instruments, knowing his Kingdome to be so near an ende'.[36]

One should not credit the North Berwick trials or the work of James VI with introducing demonological ideas to Scottish witchcraft. Belief in the demonic pact was present in Scotland some two hundred years prior to the

---

[32] Ibid., 45.
[33] James VI and I, *Daemonologie*, 44.
[34] Daniel Fischlin, '"Counterfeiting God": James VI (I) and the Politics of Daemonologie (1597)', *Journal of Narrative Technique* 26 (1996), 4.
[35] Clark, 'King James's Daemonologie', 158.
[36] James VI and I, *Daemonologie*, 81.

North Berwick witch-hunts. Trials that occurred before 1590 – particularly the trial of Bessie Dunlop in 1576 – already contained key demonological ideas.[37] Thanks to active kirk sessions, frequent sermons and news of witch-trials outside Scotland, these ideas had spread to, and been adopted by, Scots across the social spectrum.[38] The significance of the North Berwick trials to Scottish demonic belief thus lay in the wide publicity they generated and the publications they informed. *Newes from Scotland* and *Daemonologie* conveyed to a varied audience not just the events that transpired in these early trials, but the demonological ideas such as the pact that would come to define much of Scottish witch-hunting, which were endowed with further credibility by the involvement of the monarch.

Appearances of Satan

The relationship between Satan and the witch raises the question of whether witch-trial documents present a type of demonic belief marginal to or consistent with the place of the Devil in mainstream Scottish theology and experience. The most compelling evidence for the existence of a conception of Satan particular to the witch-trials derives from the fact that accused witches – and their accusers – often claimed that the Devil appeared as a physical being. Following the Reformation in Scotland, theologians and educated elites focused almost exclusively on the Devil's psychological prowess. Only rarely did the demonic manifest physically in Scottish sermons and spiritual diaries. In their sermons, ministers sometimes described the Devil as a beast, usually citing passages from the New Testament that depicted Satan as a lion, dragon or serpent, but almost never as an explicitly human figure. In their self-writings, Scots occasionally described the Devil as an intangible apparition, and very infrequently as a black man or animal.[39] Even in the cases of flyting, cursing and blasphemy

---

[37] For the records of Dunlop's trial, see *Ancient Criminal Trials in Scotland*, ed. Robert Pitcairn, 3 vols (Edinburgh: Printed for the Maitland Club, 1833), iii.602–15.

[38] Normand and Roberts, *Witchcraft in Early Modern Scotland*, 81.

[39] Two examples will suffice here: in her conversion narrative, Mistress Rutherford described in her diary, after her grandfather's death, she began to see apparitions of him for twenty straight days, which she believed to be 'the devil in his likeness': Mistress Rutherford, 'Mistress Rutherford's Conversion Narrative', in David Mullan, ed., *Miscellany xiii* (Edinburgh: Scottish History Society, 2004), 153. In 1684, Elizabeth Blackadder wrote that when she was young, she was perpetually terrified of apparitions or spirits. She reported that once she was 'lying into a room alone, and there came into the chamber a great black dog, which I was tempted to believe this was the devil': Elizabeth Blackadder, 'A Short Account of the Lord's Way of Providence towards me in my Pilgrimage Journeys', in David Mullan, ed., *Women's Life Writing in Early Modern Scotland: Writing the Evangelical Self, c. 1670–1730* (Aldershot: Ashgate, 2003), 387.

found in the kirk-session records of early modern Scotland, ordinary Scots depicted Satan as a being with physical powers and prowess, but failed to give any detailed descriptions of the Devil's bodily appearance.

In cases of witchcraft, however, Satan frequently appeared in very material, corporal terms. In the famed North Berwick witchcraft trials, a witness reported sighting Satan speaking from the pulpit of a local church and described him thus: 'His face was terrible, his nose was like the beak of an eagle ... his hands and legs were hairy, with claws upon his hands and feet like a griffin and he spoke with a rough, deep voice'.[40] Only occasionally, however, do the records reveal such detailed imagery in accounts of Satan. Far more often, accused witches described the Devil as appearing as a man, and commonly as an animal.[41] To name a few of the many variations, Satan might manifest as 'ane pretty boy in grein clothes', a man in brown clothing and a black hat or a black cat or dog.[42] Agnes Sampson, for example, confessed that the Devil had come to her at various times as a dog, a deer, a haystack and a man, all of these black in colour.[43] These simple and commonplace descriptions of clothing and form – human or animal – made up the majority of demonic depictions found in witchcraft cases.

Tales of copulation with Satan further reified the physicality of the Devil in cases of witchcraft. In the trial of Janet Barker in Edinburgh in 1643, Barker confessed to sex with the Devil, whom reportedly had lay 'heavie abone hir lyk an ox and noucht lyk an uther man'.[44] In one of Scottish witch-hunting's most unusual and colourful episodes, Isobel Gowdie characterized Satan as a 'meikle black roch man' with a very large and cold 'nature'. Gowdie went so far as to aver that certain young women had 'veerie great pleasure in their carnall cowpulation with him, yea much mor than with their awin husbandis'.[45] This case, while equal parts amusing and atypical, illustrates the notably physical and occasionally sexual role of Satan in Scottish witch-trials.[46]

---

[40] As quoted in MacDonald, 'In Search of the Devil in Fife', 34.

[41] According to the 'Survey of Scottish Witchcraft', out of the 392 references to demonic beings found in the witchcraft trials, 276 cite human forms. Animals account for 60 of those demonic forms. See Goodare et al., 'Survey of Scottish Witchcraft'.

[42] NLS, MS 905; see also NRS, JC2/11; JC2/10 ff.10v–17v; CH2/722/6; MS 1945. For a detailed description of the size, clothing, and general appearance of the demonic beings cited in witch-trials, see Miller, 'Men in Black', 149–52.

[43] NRS, JC26/2; printed as the 'Examination and Confession of Agnes Sampson', in Normand and Roberts, *Witchcraft in Early Modern Scotland*, 141–59.

[44] NRS, JC2/8, ff.347–9.

[45] *Ancient Criminal Trials in Scotland*, ed. Pitcairn, iii.602–15.

[46] For more on the case of Isobel Gowdie, see Emma Wilby, *The Visions of Isobel Gowdie: Magic, Witchcraft and Dark Shamanism in Seventeenth-Century Scotland* (Brighton: Sussex Academic Press, 2010).

More striking is the fact that the Devil usually appeared in witchcraft confessions as a human.[47] Most often he appeared as a man in black or some variation on that image.[48] In 1591, Janet Stratton depicted Satan as 'standing in likeness of a black priest, with black clothes like a hair mantle' – an obvious inversion of a godly minister.[49] In 1673, Janet M'Nicoll colourfully described the Devil as appearing to her 'in the likenes of ane gross lepper faced man'.[50] A number of possible reasons account for the Devil's appearance as a human rather than a beast. First, in cases of witchcraft involving the demonic pact, the Devil almost always appeared as a man just prior to the witches' entrance into a pact. The pact consisted of a range of activities – the giving of the Devil's mark through a physical impression of some sort, the demand that a witch renounce his or her baptism, the receipt of a new name, the ensuing copulation with Satan – that Scots apparently envisioned as being performed by two human figures. In part, this assumption reflects the familiarity of Scottish society with the practice of banding, which involved a covenant among humans. Sex and conversation should occur between two people, and the Devil necessarily appeared in human form to perform the acts associated with the pact.

Another possible explanation is that the physical, male personification of Satan reflected the affinity of humans and the Devil so often emphasized in post-Reformation sermons. As Samuel Rutherford claimed in 1645, 'the Devil and sinful Men are both broken Men, and Out-laws of Heaven, and of one Blood ... '.[51] In theory, Satan was a non-human other. In pastoral discussions and experiential reality, however, the Devil shared much with the spiritually frail men and women whom he constantly assaulted. The ubiquity and peril of demonic temptations, so often highlighted in Scottish sermons, may have also influenced reports of the Devil as a man, for Satan could take no form more dangerous or evasive than a human one.

Historians of the Devil in early modern England have suggested that the physical descriptions of Satan found in cases of English witchcraft, and in popular culture more generally, indicate the persistence of

---

[47] According to the witch-trial records, spirit beings – fairies, ghosts and others – often appeared to Scots as in male human form as well, appearances which interrogators quickly interpreted as demonic in origin. See Julian Goodare, 'Boundaries of the Fairy Realm in Scotland', in Karin E. Olsen and Jan R. Veenstra, eds, *Airy Nothings: Imagining the Otherworld of Faerie from the Middle Ages to the Age of Reason* (Leiden, Netherlands: E.J. Brill, 2014), 139–69.

[48] On appearances of Satan in cases of witchcraft, see Joyce Miller's fittingly titled 'Men in Black'.

[49] Pitcairn, ed. *Ancient Criminal Trials*, i.246; NRS, JC/26/2.

[50] *The Justiciary Records of Argyll and The Isles 1664–1705*, ed. John Cameron (Edinburgh: Printed for the Stair Society, 1949), 20.

[51] Samuel Rutherford, *The Trial and Triumph of Faith* (Edinburgh, 1645), 39.

medieval demonological ideas among the laity.[52] Belief in a corporal Devil certainly endured in Scotland, but it is important not to draw rigid boundaries between demonic physicality and internality where they did not actually exist in lived experience. Medieval and post-Reformation demonology, though shaped by divergent theologies and emphases, were not incompatible. It was not only the common folk who believed that in cases of witchcraft, the Devil was apt to appear in physical form. James VI himself specified in *Daemonologie* that 'to some of the baser sorte of them he [Satan] oblishes him selfe to appeare at their calling vpon him, by such a proper name which he shewes vnto them, either in likenes of a dog, a Catte, an Ape, or such-like other beast'.[53] Theologians did not have a singular, definitive depiction of Satan's being or appearance. Just as Scripture called the Devil by numerous names – Satan, Lucifer, The Prince of this World, The Wicked One – and depicted him in an array of guises – fallen angel, serpent, dragon – so too did Scots of all sorts. Nor did the Scottish divines and lay elites who conducted the witch-trials regularly attempt to influence exactly how ordinary Scots portrayed Satan, even though they were often the ones to introduce demonological ideas into the trials. The Devil's appearance, physicality or choice of apparel was largely irrelevant, as concern for Satan centred on how he and his servants might hinder the creation of a godly community and damage the well-being – primarily spiritual but also bodily – of that community's members.

More interesting than the question of demonic physicality is the fact that, despite his apparent ability to harm, the Devil found in witchcraft cases was rarely monstrous or obviously frightening. Rather, the accused witches recounted their interactions with the Devil in a matter-of-fact fashion, far removed from the now popular image of the hellish red beast with horns. As Joyce Miller has put it, 'it seems that in popular culture the Devil was more effective disguised in domesticity than disgust'.[54] Most obviously, the Devil usually appeared as a familiar animal or as a man wearing common clothing. Alongside the typically bland physical descriptions of Satan's facade, the interactions with the Devil testify to his surprising ordinariness.

These interactions, ranging from copulation to exchange of money to conversation, could have all occurred between any Scottish man and woman. Even dancing with the Devil was a tame affair. In a 1597 Aberdeen case, Thomas Leyis and other witches detailed how Satan had played music before them 'on his kynd of instruments' for 'ane long

---

[52] In particular, see Darren Oldridge, *The Devil in Early Modern England* (Stroud: Sutton, 2000), esp. chapters 4 and 7.
[53] James VI and I, *Daemonologie*, 19.
[54] Miller, 'Men in Black', 154.

space of tyme'. All present engaged in dancing and revelry.[55] Beyond the involvement of Satan, nothing outlandish characterized this demonic ceilidh. Exchanges of goods and money between Scots and Satan occurred in a quotidian fashion, as they would during a routine business exchange. The convicted sorcerer James Reid claimed to have learned his healing abilities from his master the Devil, who gave him 'thrie penneis at ane tyme' when they met.[56] Scottish men and women accused of witchcraft reported exchanging words with the Devil, striking only because of their conversation partner. North Berwick witch Agnes Sampson, for example, confessed to asking the Devil to cure Robert Cass of an illness. When the Devil refused to grant her request, Sampson demanded of him, 'I man (must) have it!'[57] One of the witches involved in an outbreak at Stirling in 1658 was heard ordering Satan to get out of her bed.[58] Even the names that Satan bestowed upon the witches following the renunciation of their baptisms were usually conventional: to name a few, Janet Couper became 'Nikkie Clark', Elspet Blackie was deemed 'Jonet Dalry', and Jonnet Man simply became 'Bessie'.[59]

Of course, the seemingly routine nature of these interactions with Satan occurred in tandem with heinous or supernatural acts like infanticide, the creation of effigies, shape-changing and the occasional broomstick ride.[60] Yet these elements, however fascinating, did not typify Devil-witch interactions in Scotland. As Lauren Martin points out, the very foundation of demonic involvement in witchcraft, the pact with Satan, recalled Scottish marriage as 'a heterosexual, contract-like union between the witch and the Devil'.[61] The Devil found in the context of witch-belief was generally an unremarkable being that often appeared in human form. The Scottish people had come to expect Satan's earthly presence and attending involvement in negative events such as witchcraft. As a consequence, the Devil's appearance was rarely shocking because of the very fact that it was assumed.

---

[55] *Miscellany of the Spalding Club*, 5 vols, ed. John Stuart (Aberdeen: The Spalding Club, 1841–52), i.97–8.
[56] Pitcairn, ed. *Ancient Criminal Trials*, ii.420.
[57] Normand and Roberts, *Witchcraft in Early Modern Scotland*, 152.
[58] NRS, CH2/722/6, ff.89–99. The particular witch ousting the devil from her bed was Janot Black.
[59] NRS, CH2/40/1 f. 161; JC26/27/5.
[60] For a very detailed and fantastic, though atypical, Scottish witchcraft case, see the 1662 trial of Isobel Gowdie, in Pitcairn, ed., *Ancient Criminal Trials*, iii.602–15.
[61] Martin, 'The Devil and the Domestic', 74.

'Popular' vs 'Elite' Demonologies

Understanding the role of Satan in the witchcraft trials is particularly useful for teasing out differences in the demonic beliefs of Scots from across the social spectrum. An abundance of sources – theological writings, sermons, spiritual diaries and the like – demonstrate what elite, educated Scots believed about Satan. Yet even with the clues provided by the kirk session records, what ordinary, less-educated Scots thought and said about the Devil remains more elusive. The testimonies found in cases of witchcraft, though they must be approached with necessary interpretive caution, offer another crucial source for retrieving the demonic beliefs of the common people. As Christina Larner suggested in *Enemies of God*, by using the evidence from Scottish witch-trials, historians know more about how ordinary folks viewed the Devil than how they viewed God.[62]

Though witchcraft records are replete with descriptions of Satan, the demonic beliefs found in witchcraft cases are far from straightforward. When the courts, both ecclesiastical and civil, interrogated suspected witches about their relationship with the Devil, they sometimes received elaborate descriptions of the physical appearance of Satan, the signing of the demonic pact and even copulation with the Devil. The problem, however, is that the origins of these demonic beliefs are generally quite hazy. Did the authorities elicit this information about the Devil through leading questions because it is what they wanted to hear and because it conformed to their demonological expectations? The answer, in many cases, is probably yes, especially when torture was applied or threatened in order to solicit confessions. Similarly, one wonders if the demonic motifs found in the confessions of ordinary Scots differ markedly from those in elite Scottish demonology.[63] This query is further exacerbated by the fact that the demonic beliefs of ordinary Scots, to the extent that they can be accessed at all, were consistently moderated through the hand of the literate individual who recorded them.

Scottish witch-trials, like those throughout early modern Europe, generally consisted of two elements: *maleficium*, meaning harmful magic, and diabolism, the assertion that witches worshipped the Devil in a variety of ways. These two elements were linked by the belief that it was the Devil who initially bestowed witches with magical powers. Many historians have demonstrated that at the accusatory level, ordinary Scots concerned themselves with *maleficia* rather than diabolism. Though these Scots believed in the Devil, their primary concern remained the health of themselves, their families and their crops, which might be compromised

---

[62] Larner, *Enemies of God*, 134.
[63] These questions have also been explored in Miller 'Men in Black'.

by the harmful magic of witches. Thus some scholars have persuasively argued that the demonic aspects of witch-trials were introduced primarily by elites who had a specific understanding of witchcraft derived from Continental demonologies.[64] Others have gone as far as to argue that the witch-hunts and their demonic elements constituted an attack on folk culture more generally.[65]

These arguments revolve around the premise that the witch-trials furthered a trend begun by the Reformation, in which the logic and implementation of Protestantism increasingly polarized the worldviews of the elites and the peasantry. One main reason for this polarization was that at the time of the Scottish Reformation, the worldviews of many Scots allowed for the existence of a grey zone between good and evil, in which fairies, ghosts, elves, witches and the like could exist without operating as direct servants of God or the Devil.[66] In the closing decades of the sixteenth century, theologians insisted on relegating such creatures to either 'superstition' or the dominion of the Devil – and often both.[67] As Knox put it plainly, 'In religioun thair is na middis: either it is the religioun of God ... or els it is the religioun of the Divill'.[68] At least initially, and certainly during the early phases of the witch-trials, this demonization of fairies and the like occurred from the top down, at the hands of the zealously reforming clergy.

As Julian Goodare has recently pointed out, in going through the historical record it is challenging to identify the distinctiveness of fairies and other middling beings in early modern Scotland from descriptions of demons.[69] In the remarkably detailed case of Bessie Dunlop in 1572, for example, Dunlop recounted her relationship with Reid, a spirit whom she had encountered while taking her cow out to a field. She described Reid as an elderly, grey-bearded man wearing a grey coat. He wore a black bonnet on his head and carried a white wand in his hand.[70] Reid took Dunlop to meet the fairy queen and her people, whom he described to her as 'the good wichtis that wer rydand in middil-zerd'.[71] At no point did

---

[64] See MacDonald, *The Witches of Fife*, and Cowan, 'Witchcraft Persecution and Folk Belief'. Julian Goodare has also made this point in *Witchcraft and Belief*, 27.
[65] See Cowan, 'Witch Persecution and Folk Belief'.
[66] Lizanne Henderson and Edward J. Cowan, *Scottish Fairy Belief: A History* (East Linton: Tuckwell, 2001), 116.
[67] On the impact of the Reformation on both demonic belief and superstition, see Euan Cameron, *Enchanted Europe: Superstition, Reason and Religion, 1250–1750* (Oxford: Oxford University Press, 2010).
[68] John Knox, *Works*, 6 vols, ed. David Laing (Edinburgh: Wodrow Society, 1846–64), iv.232.
[69] Goodare, 'Boundaries of the Fairy Realm in Scotland', 139–69.
[70] Pitcairn, ed., *Ancient Criminal Trials*, ii.52.
[71] Ibid.

Dunlop explicitly equate Reid or the fairies/spirits she met with Satan, despite prodding by the interrogators. However, her description of Reid as wearing a black bonnet and carrying a white wand was almost identical to the Devil described in *Newes from Scotland* as appearing before John Fian, 'appareled all in blacke, which a white wand in his hand'.[72] The ordinary, quotidian discussions between Dunlop and Reid about topics like 'the evill weddir that was to cum' mirrored how other witches claimed to have talked to Satan.[73]

The late sixteenth-century case of Alison Pierson describes a similar encounter with fairies and a man 'cled in grene clathe'. The man, who Pierson does not specify as either the Devil or a fairy, reportedly 'said to hir gif scho wald be faithfull, he wald do hir guid'.[74] He appeared again, this time as a 'lustie mane, with mony mene and women'.[75] Pierson discussed her interaction with this man and the fairies in a situation markedly similar to a witches' sabbath. She even received a mark from the fairies that was 'blae and ewill sarrit [discolored and ill-looking]'.[76] The appearance of a man in green who asked Pierson to be faithful, the large gatherings, the receipt of an unsightly mark on the body – these accorded completely, as discussed above, with the concept of the relationship between Satan and the Scottish witch.

One cannot know definitively whether accused witches like Bessie Dunlop and Alison Pierson believed or came to believe that the beings that they described were in fact demonic. Certainly the authorities thought so. Yet ordinary Scots, who had long coexisted with fairies and other supernatural and semi-natural beings, appear to have conflated or fused their pre-existing ideas about fairies or spirits with their beliefs in Satan. While elites tended to interpret all middling beings depicted in folk culture as inexorably demonic, the boundaries of the fairy world among ordinary Scots were often, as Julian Goodare has pointed out, actively indeterminate.[77] Authorities doubtlessly read or imposed demonic activities like the pact and the sabbath onto beliefs about fairies and spirits, but ordinary Scots may have simultaneously incorporated 'elite' demonology into their own conceptions of the supernatural world.

More specifically, and despite the leading questions of the interrogators, the use of torture and even the filter of the court clerk's hand, the possibility remains that uneducated Scots had adopted some of the demonological ideas promoted from the pulpit and by their neighbours about the

---

72 Carmichael, *Newes From Scotland*.
73 Pitcairn, ed. *Ancient Criminal Trials*, ii.52.
74 Ibid., 163.
75 Ibid.
76 Ibid.
77 Goodare, 'Boundaries of the Fairy Realm in Scotland'.

relationship between Satan and the witch. At least by the beginning of the seventeenth century, and probably earlier, the rampant activities of the Devil in the world would have been familiar to Scots of all sorts who were exposed to frequent and passionate sermons on the topic. The spread of knowledge of the witch-trials, in print, by word of mouth and in public executions, also popularized the concept of demonic witchcraft. While it is often difficult to tease out exactly when, where and from whom diabolism entered the witch-trials, this does not mean that accused witches did not believe the veracity of claims they had been persuaded, often under duress, to make. More obviously, those from across the social spectrum who read or heard about such confessions of copulation with the Devil and other horrifying acts had little reason not to believe them. Even when details of recounted cases made it explicit that torture had been used to obtain confessions, and though some of the details of demonic interaction would have shocked early modern ears, audiences would not have been surprised to learn of Satan's attempts and successes in luring weak-hearted individuals into dreadful acts of sin.

To explore more closely how ordinary folks understood the relationship between witchcraft and Satan, it is useful to look beyond the documents of the witch-trials themselves, to sources such as the day-to-day records of the kirk session. During cases of flyting and cursing, Scots often made references to the Devil in the context of witch-belief, even when no actual witch-trial was involved or even tangentially related. In Culross in 1654, for example, William Dryld reported that Margaret Wither had accused him of being a witch on whom 'the dewill laid his mark'.[78] A witness confirmed this report, saying that Wither had indeed called Dryld a 'witchburd whose master was the dewill'.[79] Despite the obvious reference to the demonic pact, the Culross kirk session regarded the case as one of slander, probably based on the reputation of Margaret as a troublemaker and the fact that no evidence of witchcraft was presented. Clearly, though, both Wither and Dryld understood two key components of Scottish witchcraft often promoted by educated elites – that witches were servants of the Devil, and that this servitude could be identified by a mark left on the body by Satan.

In 1654 in Edinburgh, witnesses reported that Issobell Anderson had said to Mareon Rutherford that she hoped she 'should die in the devills armes as her fathers sister did'.[80] Another witness elaborated on this claim, detailing how Issobell had 'called Mareon Rutherfurd a devill', and said that 'all the geir she [Mareon] had was by the Art of the devill, and that

---

[78] NRS, CH2/77/2, f.115.
[79] Ibid.
[80] NRS, CH2/141/2, f.42.

her fathers sister was burnt and she hoped she should goe the same gate'.[81] Further witnesses provided similar reports, and the case was sent to the presbytery.[82] It is unclear whether Rutherford's aunt had in fact been accused of and executed as a witch, or if Anderson was creatively describing her wish that Rutherford 'go to hell'. If indeed this was a reference to a witch-trial in Rutherford's family, Anderson's slanderous words displayed knowledge that through the demonic pact, witches received material gains in exchange for their service of Satan.

These brief examples suggest that, beyond actual cases of witchcraft, ordinary Scots could and did understand concepts such as demonic servitude and the Devil's mark, without any obvious official prompting. In their study of the texts of the North Berwick witch-hunt, Lawrence Normand and Gareth Roberts point out that 'the elite/popular distinction should not obscure the fact that there was exchange among different social levels concerning the cultural formations that found their way into accounts of witchcraft'.[83] When these accounts emerged into the public sphere, they 'were meaningful to people from a wide social range, educated as well as uneducated'.[84] Witch-hunting remained, above all, a community affair. By identifying convicted witches, who were often publicly executed, as servants of Satan, 'good' Scots could identify themselves by pointing to precisely what they were not. Even if elites *originally* introduced the demonic elements to witch-trials or attempted to recast fairy belief in accordance with Protestant demonology, it is clear that through the discussion of witchcraft in sermons, pamphlets, court records and (albeit unrecoverable) personal conversation, by the mid-seventeenth century many Scots understood that the Devil and the witch went hand in hand.

Nathan Johnstone has insisted that, in the case of demonic belief in early modern England, witchcraft was marginal compared to more general perceptions of the Devil.[85] While this is a debatable claim in the case of England, witchcraft in Scotland certainly did not exist outside the pervasive demonic beliefs of clerical or lay Scots. The cases of witchcraft may have displayed a greater emphasis on the physicality of the Devil than did other contemporary sources, but this did not render them incompatible with the demonic belief found throughout the sermons, diaries, treatises and commonplace books of early modern Scotland. In *Newes from Scotland*, for example, the warlock Doctor Fian refused to confess his interactions with the Devil even under severe torture. The author interpreted Fian's choice to remain mum as a sure sign of how 'deeply had the devil entered into

---

[81] Ibid., f.43.
[82] Ibid., f.45.
[83] Normand and Roberts, *Witchcraft in Early Modern Scotland*, 68.
[84] Ibid.
[85] Johnstone, *Devil and Demonism*, 12–18.

his heart'.[86] The frequent sermons on the subject of demonic temptation and human sinfulness, paired with the manifest examples of these twin threats found in printed spiritual diaries, murder stories and dying accounts, conditioned Scots to believe in and expect such occurrences. Though elites may have introduced and promulgated such ideas, they became part of a shared religious culture that devoted much time and energy to thinking about the Devil. The result was a population that, on the whole, could find a common enemy in Satan and share in an awareness of their own susceptibility to temptation, delusion and even demonic servitude.

In 1826, over a century after the last Scottish witch was executed, a broadside was published in Edinburgh detailing the crimes of witchcraft that had plagued Scotland in the late sixteenth and seventeenth centuries.[87] The anonymous author first cited Agnes Sampson of the famed North Berwick trials in 1590 who, along with her fellow witches, had 'raised storms, and kissed the devil's a–e'.[88] The broadside then recounted how others committed crimes such as meeting with Satan and renouncing their baptisms. For their sinful actions, these women and men were strangled before being burned at the stake. According to the author, the last person was brought to the stake in Scotland in 1722, and 'the devil has never been seen in Scotland since'.[89] Generations removed from the last witch-hunt, the collective memory of witchcraft remained firmly wedded to Satan. Despite the claim that the Devil was last seen in Scotland in 1722, his early modern appearances – physically before witches and internally in the minds of Scots of all sorts – left a lasting and consequential mark on Scottish society.

The Devil and Witch-belief in the British World

Witchcraft throughout the early modern British world has long been a subject of scholarly and popular fascination, and historians have pointed out a number of important differences between patterns of witch-hunting north and south of the Border and across the Atlantic.[90] Despite the

---

[86] Carmichael, *Newes from Scotland*.
[87] According to the central court records, the last execution for witchcraft took place in Scotland in 1706, and the last trial occurred in 1727. In 1736, the British Parliament repealed the Scottish witchcraft statute of 1563. See Levack, *Witch-Hunting in Scotland*, 131.
[88] NLS, *An account of the most remarkable Trials and Executions which took place in Scotland for above 300 years* (Glasgow, 1826). This broadside also discusses, to a lesser extent, cases of fornication and adultery.
[89] Ibid.
[90] For witch-hunting in England, see Gregory Durston, *Witchcraft and Witch Trials: a History of English Witchcraft and its Legal Perspectives, 1542 to 1736* (Chichester: Barry Rose Law Publishing, 2000); Malcolm Gaskill, *Witchfinders: A Seventeenth-Century English*

attempts by divines such as William Perkins to make the demonic pact into a premise for witch-hunting in England, English witch-trials generally lacked the diabolical association found in Scotland.[91] In England, witchcraft was not strictly defined in religious terms as it was in Scotland, explaining in part the comparatively mild nature of English witch-hunting. According to Brian Levack, a Scottish woman was 'twelve times more likely than her English counterpart to be executed for witchcraft'.[92] The only time when the patterns of witch-hunting in England and Scotland converged, as Levack has argued, was in revolutionary Britain, when England experienced its only mass witch-hunt. In a period of remarkable political, social and religious unrest, the rise in Puritan sentiment led to increased commitment to moral reform and to the creation of a godly society.[93] As a consequence, the Devil and his minions – political enemies, papists and witches – became central targets of the English church and government. Amid the turmoil of war, criminal trials were also often conducted by inexperienced local authorities at the quarter sessions rather than by assize justices, which allowed for unprecedented use of torture. During the 1640s, English witch-hunting more closely resembled the Scottish witch-trials than any previous English trials.[94]

This height of demonic belief in England, and the corresponding witch-hunting fervour, was relatively short lived. By the second half of the seventeenth century, intellectuals in England became increasingly sceptical about witchcraft. Unprecedented debate about the Devil's ability to

---

Tragedy (London: John Murray, 2005); Alan Macfarlane, *Witchcraft in Tudor and Stuart England* (London: Routledge & Kegan Paul, 1970); James Sharpe, *Instruments of Darkness: Witchcraft in Early Modern England* (Philadelphia: University of Pennsylvania Press, 1997); Keith Thomas, *Religion and the Decline of Magic* (New York: Scribner, 1971); Owen Davies, *Witchcraft, Magic and Culture, 1736–1951* (Manchester: Manchester University Press, 1999). On witchcraft in New England, see John Demos, *Entertaining Satan: Witchcraft and the Culture of Early New England* (Oxford: Oxford University Press, 1982); Mary Beth Norton, *In the Devil's Snare: The Salem Witchcraft Crisis of 1692* (New York: Knopf, 2002); Paul Boyer and Stephen Nissenbaum, *Salem Possessed: The Social Origins of Witchcraft* (Cambridge, MA: Harvard University Press 1974); Richard Godbeer, *The Devil's Dominion: Magic and Religion in Early New England* (Cambridge: Cambridge University Press, 1992); Peter Hoffer, *The Devil's Disciples: The Makers of the Salem Witchcraft Trials* (Baltimore, MD: Johns Hopkins Press, 1996); Carol F. Karlsen, *The Devil in the Shape of a Woman: Witchcraft in Colonial New England* (New York: W.W. Norton and Co., 1987); Elizabeth Reis, *Damned Women: Sinners and Witches in Puritan New England* (Ithaca, NY: Cornell University Press, 1997).

[91] William Perkins, *A Discourse of the Damned Art of Witchcraft* (London, 1608). The close composition dates and content of Perkins' *Damned Art* (written in 1602) and James VI's *Daemonologie* in 1597 suggest that the Scottish adoption of Continental demonology was equally influential for Puritans in England.

[92] Levack, *Witch-Hunting in Scotland*, 1–2.

[93] Ibid., 55–80.

[94] Ibid.

operate in the world ensued amid scientific developments and an increasing emphasis on empirical proof.[95] This was not, however, a straightforward, linear or complete 'decline of magic', nor does an intellectual explanation fully account for why the trials in England and elsewhere ended.[96] The sceptical voices in England had little impact on the actual trials themselves; it was not until the trials had already declined or ended that most elites began to reject the idea of witchcraft itself.[97] Moreover, the sharp decrease and eventual end of witch-trials should not be understood uncritically as a reflection of private beliefs about the Devil and his witches. Theologians and ordinary people continued to believe in the reality of Satan well into the eighteenth and nineteenth centuries.[98]

Nonetheless, partly as a reaction to the actual decline of the witch-trials, in early modern England intellectuals did begin to call into question the capacity of the Devil to affect human life in tangible ways, especially by means of witchcraft.[99] Reformed theology did not satisfy many who wanted more concrete answers than the assertion that some mysteries are beyond man's comprehension. In late seventeenth-century Scotland, conversely, Satan continued to hold prominence of place in the minds of Scots of all sorts. Scotland experienced a major witch panic in 1661–62 that resulted in the accusation of at least 660 persons, after which Scottish witch-hunting began a slow, uneven decline that continued until the last prosecution in 1727.[100] When the trials did come to an end, witchcraft

[95] See Oldridge, *Devil in Early Modern England*, 163–64.

[96] Until recently, many scholars of witchcraft uncritically accepted Keith Thomas's explanation of the end of the witch-trials and the more general decline of magic in Europe: that the rise of rationalism and scientific thinking among European elites resulted in the rejection of previously held demonological ideas. Jonathan Barry has argued in his recent work on witchcraft and demonology during the supposed period of 'decline', from 1640 to 1789, that we cannot accept this idea of the decline of magic uncritically. Through the assessment of six cases of witchcraft and magic in late seventeenth- and eighteenth-century south-west England, Barry concludes that there was no teleological decline of magic, but rather a complex amalgamation of folk and intellectual belief contingent upon the specific circumstances of different areas in England. See Jonathan Barry, *Witchcraft and Demonology in South-West England, 1640–1689* (Basingstoke: Palgrave Macmillan, 2012).

[97] For a recent account of the decline of witch-belief, see Edward Bever, 'Witchcraft Persecutions and the Decline of Magic', *Journal of Interdisciplinary History*, 40 (2009), 264. See Levack, *Witch-Hunting in Scotland*, 132.

[98] On the persistent belief in the supernatural, see Owen Davies, *Witchcraft, Magic, and Culture, 1736–1951* (Manchester: Manchester University Press, 1999).

[99] Jonathan Barry has pointed out that beginning in the seventeenth century and increasingly thereafter, 'witchcraft cases raised specific problems for those defending and describing the world of spirits' which 'made them increasingly less attractive as stories compared to other forms of spirit activity', such as ghosts. When they were published, the point was not to defend the existence of witches or even the devil, but rather the spirit world and God himself. See Barry, *Witchcraft and Demonology*, 262.

[100] See Levack, 'The Great Scottish Witch Hunt', 90.

was still considered a reality. The sceptical voices of the Englishman Reginald Scot or the Dutchman Balthasar Bekker found no counterparts in Scotland, where the few critics of witch-hunting were unwilling to challenge witch-belief itself.[101] Rather, legal caution and the reduction of torture led to the end of witch-hunting, without an attending challenge to orthodox demonology.

The preoccupation with the Devil that propelled much of Scottish, but not English, witch-hunting was also pervasive in the witch-panic that consumed Salem and other parts of New England during the 1690s. The period of witch-hunting in the English colonies in North America, concentrated almost exclusively in New England, highlights the affinity between Scottish and New England demonic belief. The famous trials in Salem were set in motion by initial 'fits' of three young girls and the ensuing accusation of nearly two hundred persons for witchcraft. Diabolism rather than *maleficium* lay at the heart of the definition of New England witchcraft, a capital crime defined as 'solemn compaction or conversing with the Devil', 'fellowship by covenant with a familiar spirit', or commonly as 'giving entertainment to Satan'.[102]

Certainly, as many historians have argued, social, economic and political tensions actuated the witch-trials in Salem and elsewhere.[103] The Salem court's allowance of spectral evidence was, for example, key to the implication of a large number of suspects.[104] Without the tense religious environment created by strict Puritanism and the attending demonic belief, however, the witch-trials in Salem would have never reached their now-famous fever pitch. As in Scotland, New England divines desired to create a godly community, a New Jerusalem to serve as a 'city upon a hill'. As part of this mission, witches and other deviants in league with Satan would have to be persecuted, and the New England clergy were eager to conduct

---

[101] Levack, *Witch-Hunting in Scotland*, 133.

[102] The first definition comes from the Plymouth Statute of 1636, printed in Samuel G. Drake, *Annals of Witchcraft in New England* (New York, 1869), 56; the second comes from the 1641 'laws of judgment' of Southampton, Long Island, reprinted in George R. Howell, *The Early History of Southampton, L.I., New York* (Albany, NY, 1887). Sources as quoted in Demos, *Entertaining Satan*, 23. Richard Godbeer explains that prior to the Salem trials, courts had difficulty actually proving the demonic pact, around which the definition of the crime centred, and thus of the 61 cases of witchcraft prior to Salem, only 26.2 per cent of the accused were convicted and executed: Godbeer, *Devil's Dominion*, 158–9.

[103] For such socio-economic interpretations of the witch-trials in New England, see the still influential Boyer and Nissenbaum, *Salem Possessed*, and more recently, Mary Beth Norton, *In the Devil's Snare*, which considers the Indian Wars on the Maine–New Hampshire border as a key precipitate of the Salem witch-trials.

[104] This point is made in Levack, *Witch-hunt in Early Modern Europe*, 205. For a thorough appraisal of the legal context of the Salem witchcraft trials, see Paul Hoffer, *The Salem Witchcraft Trials: A Legal History* (Lawrence: University of Kansas Press, 1997).

these prosecutions.[105] This clerical leadership characterized the witch-trials in New England and in Scotland, but not in England, where the centralized government at Westminster tightly held the reins of the prosecutions.[106] Beyond the legal and political constraints placed upon the English clergy, the obsession with the creation of a godly community through the combat of Satan was mitigated by dissent in the English church.

Demonic belief was just one component of complex, layered situations that led to fervent and deadly witch-hunting in Scotland, New England and throughout early modern Europe. Yet without the demonic pact, which comprised the very definition of the crime of witchcraft in these areas, the witch-trials in Scotland and New England would have lacked the urgency that Satan instilled. England, on the other hand, generally lacked this demonically induced fervour, with the exception of witch-hunting during the English Civil War. A brief survey of witch-hunting in New England, England and Scotland thus illustrates the profound influence that ideas about Satan had on the definition and prosecution of witchcraft, as well as the general affinity of Scottish and New England demonic belief.

Demonic Possession

While cases of witchcraft abounded in early modern Scotland, the oft-related phenomenon of demonic possession did not.[107] This near-absence of possession cases sets early modern Scotland apart from many other European countries. Throughout the sixteenth and seventeenth centuries in Europe, men, women and children from France to Germany to Russia experienced fits of possession.[108] Only in 1696 with the notorious case

---

[105] As in Scotland, New England clerics were careful to temper discussions of the Devil's involvement in witchcraft with the assertion that the will of an all-sovereign God lay behind all the actions of Satan and his servants. As John Demos explains that 'the ultimate triumph of the Almighty God was assured. But in particular times and places Satan might achieve some temporary success – and claim important victims ... God, meanwhile, opposed this onslaught of evil – and yet He also permitted it. For errant men and women there was no more effective means of chastening'. See Demos, *Entertaining Satan*, 10.

[106] Levack, *Witch-Hunting in Scotland*, 32

[107] Demonic spirits were said to enter victims in two ways: the spirit could possess the body on its own, with God's permission, or possession could occur at the command of a witch. Thus, witches were often accused of having caused demonic possession. Still, it is important to remember that demonic possession and witchcraft were also two very distinct phenomena. This was particularly true in Scotland, where the vast majority of the witch-trials had no connection whatsoever to cases of possession. See Levack, *Witch-Hunting in Scotland* (New York: Routledge, 2008), 115–30; Levack, 'Demonic Possession in Early Modern Scotland', in Goodare, Martin, and Miller, eds, *Witchcraft and Belief in Early Modern Scotland*, 166–84.

[108] On demonic possession in early modern Europe, see Erik Midelfort, 'The Devil on the German People: Reflections on the Popularity of Demonic Possession in Sixteenth-century

of demoniac Christian Shaw did possession become an important component – and product – of Scottish demonic belief. Shaw was an eleven year-old Renfrewshire girl possessed by a demonic spirit in typical fashion: she had fits, her head twisted around, her tongue stuck out of her mouth with remarkable length, she vomited hair, gravel, pins, bones and feathers, and she was reportedly carried through her house with her feet off the ground.[109] In the midst of her fits, Shaw accused two women, a maid and a neighbour, of causing her possession by means of witchcraft. She subsequently added others to the list of witches responsible for her afflicted state, and in the end, a total of twenty-four people were indicted for witchcraft. Seven of these were eventually convicted and executed.[110]

The subsequent series of possession cases that spanned the eight-year period from 1696 to 1704 were closely linked to the Shaw case and its popularization in *A True Narrative of the Sufferings and Relief of a Young Girl*.[111] Two years after Shaw's possession, Margaret Murdoch and Margaret Laird accused more than twenty individuals of causing them demonic affliction through witchcraft.[112] These cases involved both girls demonstrating symptoms typical of demonic possession and closely resembling that of Shaw's case, including contortions, spitting out pins and other foreign objects, uncontrolled thrashing, and accusations of various tormentors.[113] These girls had grown up in the same area as Shaw and had likely heard details of her affliction. In the case of the 1704 possession of sixteen-year-old Patrick Morton, the minister Patrick Cowper had actually read Shaw's account to the teen when his fits began.[114] Clearly, then, the case of Christian Shaw provided a script for demoniacs in Scotland to follow in experiencing their possession.

The Salem witchcraft trials and the cases of demonic possession that attended them also influenced the string of possessions in late seventeenth- and early eighteenth-century Scotland. Cotton Mather's account of the *Memorable Providences Relating to Witchcrafts and Possessions*, which detailed the possessions of the Goodwin children at the hands of washerwoman Mary Glover in 1688, was published in Scotland in 1697.

Germany', in Susan Ozment, ed., *Religion and Culture in the Reformation* (Kirksville, MO: Sixteenth Century Journal Publishers, 1989); Christine Worobec, *Possessed: Women, Witches, and Demons in Imperial Russia* (Dekalb: Northern Illinois University Press, 2001); see Levack, *The Devil Within; Demonic Possession in Early Modern Europe* (New Haven, CT: Yale University Press, 2013).

[109] *A True Narrative of the Sufferings and Relief of a Young Girle* (Edinburgh, 1698), reprinted in *A History of the Witches of Renfrewshire* (Paisley, 1877).
[110] Levack, 'Demonic Possession', 172.
[111] For details of these cases, see ibid., 169–71.
[112] NLS, Wod. Fol. XXVIII, ff.168r–174v.
[113] Ibid.
[114] Levack, *Witch-Hunting in Scotland*, 121.

A slightly amended account of the Goodwin children's possession had been published in London in 1691, and English copies likely circulated throughout Scotland prior to the publication of the Edinburgh edition.[115] No doubt the interest in possession generated by Shaw's case the year prior prompted this later printing of *Memorable Providences* in Scotland.

The descriptions of the Goodwin children's bewitching included tongues hanging out of their mouths 'to a prodigious length', bulging eyes and contorted necks, bouts of deafness and dumbness interspersed with shrieking and the 'most pitteous out-cries'.[116] A rapid best-seller in New England, *Memorable Providences* directly influenced the performance and interpretation of possession during the Salem witch-trials. A ten-page narrative of the possession of the group of young girls at Salem, Deodat Lawson's *A Brief and True Narrative of Some Remarkable Passages Relating to Sundry Persons Afflicted by Witchcraft, at Salem Village* was published in Boston in 1692.[117] Christian Shaw's story, printed as *A True Narrative of the Sufferings and Relief of a Young Girl* in 1698, bore noteworthy resemblance in style and content to the text of Lawson's narrative.[118] Ideas about demonic possession in Scotland were thus part of a larger transatlantic conversation about Satan's earthly interventions.

Brian Levack has rightly argued that demonic possession ought to be viewed as reflective of the specific religious cultures in which they occurred, regardless of the individual causes of possession.[119] In the case of Scotland, the scarcity and belatedness of possession reveal more about the role of Satan in Reformed Scottish society than do the cases themselves. Scottish theologians believed in the possibility of possession as much as their Catholic and Protestant counterparts throughout Britain and on the Continent did.[120] James VI himself had acknowledged the Devil's ability to possess humans in *Daemonologie*, though he rejected the traditional methods of exorcism in favour of the Protestant rituals of fasting and prayer.[121] The belated and sparse nature of demonic possession

---

[115] The title of the version published in London was *Late memorable providences relating to witchcrafts and possessions clearly manifesting, not only that there are witches, but that good men (as well as others) may possibly have their lives shortned by such evil instruments of Satan*. This version includes a preface by English Puritan clergyman Richard Baxter, but the text of Mather's original *Memorable Possessions* is the same.

[116] Cotton Mather, *Memorable Providences Relating to Witchcrafts and Possessions* (orig. Boston, MA, 1689; Edinburgh, 1697).

[117] Deodat Lawson, *A Brief and True Narrative of Some Remarkable Passages Relating to Sundry Persons Afflicted by Witchcraft, at Salem Village* (Boston, MA, 1692).

[118] Hugh V. McLachlan, ed. *The Kirk, Satan and Salem: A History of the Witches of Renfrewshire* (Glasgow: Grimsay Press, 2006), 491.

[119] Levack, *The Devil Within*.

[120] Levack, *Witch-Hunting in Scotland*, 122.

[121] Ibid.

in Scotland can be explained not by scepticism about possession, but by certain elements of Reformed Protestantism and the attending Reformed demonic belief.

First, the doctrine of double predestination rendered possession a very risky occurrence, as demoniacs would have likely been assigned moral responsibility for their own possession. As we have seen in Scottish sermons and personal writings, men and women held primary culpability for falling victim to the temptations of Satan. They had failed to safeguard their hearts and minds against his assaults; their bodies were no different. In a culture ripe with apocalyptic anxiety about salvation, Scots were hesitant to behave in ways that might demonstrate to themselves and to others any sign of reprobation. It was not until the doctrinaire emphasis on double predestination declined in the late seventeenth century that possession cases became a viable expression of Scottish demonic belief. Equally crucial, during this period Reformed Protestant ministers stopped assigning moral blame to demoniacs, and instead looked to cases of possession as an opportunity to prove the existence of spirits amid new debates within British demonology.[122]

The emphases on human depravity and demonic ubiquity, mainstays of Scottish sermons, provide a second possible explanation for the missing demoniacs. Scottish sermons consistently asserted that the Devil already had a natural, innate possession of many men and women's hearts, and that he gained an easy possession of their minds through temptation and the implantation of doubt. This was, of course, not the physical, outwardly manifest demonic possession as displayed in the case of Christian Shaw. Still, both the clergy and ordinary Scots may have assumed that Satan already partly possessed most postlapsarian men and women (the reprobate) in an internal, spiritual way. Evidence of this possession was made manifest in witchcraft, murder, political turmoil and so on. The Devil also held a natural sway over the elect, at least in terms of their innate inclinations. Individuals were accordingly less inclined to dramatically perform this partial possession because it was an assumed part of spiritual warfare and even the conversion process.[123] For these reasons, for much of the early modern period, outward physical possession did not have a place in the cultural script in Scotland. Due to the emphasis on innate depravity and the belief in predestined reprobation, demonic possession was, in a subtle, spiritually intrinsic sense, a constant component of Reformed Protestantism.

---

[122] Levack, *Witch-hunting*, 125.

[123] On connections between the despair experienced in the initial phase of conversion and accusations of witchcraft or possession, see Yeoman, 'The Devil as Doctor: Witchcraft, Wodrow and the Wider World', *Scottish Archives* 1 (1995); 93–105.

When a limited number of possessions began to occur in Scotland in the late seventeenth century, the vast majority of Scottish demoniacs were adolescents or youths between the ages of eleven and seventeen. As conversion accounts, personal covenants and spiritual diaries attest, these were the years when individuals first became cognizant of their fallen state and began to agonize over salvation. Mistress Rutherford's narrative, a model of this adolescent angst, detailed at length her despair in considering Satan and her own sinfulness during her teenage years. Believing that she was doomed to hell, 'the sight and sense of these things put my soul in such torment as is inexpressible, finding myself guilty of every tribunal of God and my own conscience'.[124] When Katherine Collace entered into a personal covenant with God at the age of fourteen, she was paralysed by 'a violent fit of sickness', perceiving that Satan had set about 'the breaking of [her] body'.[125] At the age of thirteen, James Fraser of Brea lay in bed one night thinking of past sins and was struck 'with great horror' by 'a number of blasphemies and cursings' running through his mind. Momentarily, he believed that the Devil was within him.[126] While none of these Scots actually became demoniacs, their adolescent struggles with Satan suggest why, when possession became a more viable option for expressing demonic struggles in the 1690s, Scottish adolescents found themselves the most vulnerable.

Conclusion

The comparatively small number of possession cases in Scotland indicates that in a society where Satan's presence was immanent and assumed, individuals may have been less likely to experience that presence in a physical and extraordinary way. Witchcraft trials also demonstrate a paradoxical aspect of Satan in Scotland: his ubiquity rendered him a very threatening, but also very ordinary, figure. This constant presence of the Devil suggests that Reformed demonological ideas had become a key part of the cultures and identities of Scots of all sorts who had been conditioned to expect a world constantly beset by the assaults of Satan and his human followers, with whom the Devil shared a natural affinity. By examining descriptions of Satan in cases of witchcraft, it also becomes apparent that there was no clear-cut, singular Devil in early modern Scotland. As Joyce Miller has pointed out, there seems to have been no attempt by authorities

---

[124] Mistress Rutherford, 'Conversion Narrative', 163.
[125] Collace, 'Memoirs or Spiritual Exercises', 45.
[126] James Fraser of Brea, 'Memoirs of James Fraser of Brea', in W.K. Tweedie, ed., *Select Biographies*, 2 vols (Edinburgh: Wodrow Society, 1841), 103.

to promote a definitive, Reformed Protestant image of Satan.[127] The Devil appeared in an assortment of guises, from insect to man to fairy-like, all of which were deemed probable and dangerous by authorities and ordinary Scots alike.

Regardless of what form Satan took, the danger of the Devil remained the powers of coercion and spiritual delusion, and it was upon these powers that the actions of witches themselves were predicated. The Devil did not need to appear as a physically intimidating monster to be intensely threatening, to individuals or to Scottish society as a whole. His actions, even in cases of witchcraft, remained primarily spiritual and internal. Through the act of convincing to-be witches to enter into a pact and effectively renounce their baptism, Satan overturned the most central and sacred element of Reformed Protestantism in Scotland: the covenant with God. Nothing could be more dangerous for a society seeking godly conformity in anticipation of the Last Days.

---

[127] Miller, 'Men in Black', 149.

CHAPTER 7

Satan on the Streets

In 1724, Margaret Dickson was convicted of infanticide and hanged in the Grassmarket of Edinburgh. According to legend, while her body was en route to Musselburgh for burial the driver heard banging from inside the coffin. He opened the lid to find, much to his surprise, that the recently hanged Dickson was very much alive. Scottish officials decided that because the sentence of hanging had already been carried out, she could not be legally executed again. Dickson supposedly went on to live a long and happy life, and a pub commemorating the tale of 'Half-hangit Maggie' now stands in the Grassmarket.[1]

Before her failed execution, an anonymous poem titled 'A Warning to the Wicked' was composed and printed for consumption by the Scottish public. It began with a dramatic invocation: 'Ye Sons of Satan, Candidates of Hell, Listen unto the serious Truths I tell'. The poetic broadside went on to warn readers to avoid the well-trod path to sin and Satan followed by its subject. It read,

> This Ignorance, the Source of all our Evil
> Made her a faithful Factor to the Devil
> For when the Heart's not bolted against Sin
> It let's the Devil and Damnation in ...
> Seeds of all Sins are in our Nature sown
> And conquer'd by the Grace of God alone
> On him depend, walk in holy Ways
> And then a pleasant Death will end your Days.[2]

---

[1] This story is recounted, among other places, in John Maclaurin Dreghorn, ed., *Arguments and decisions, in remarkable cases: before the High Court of Justiciary, and other supreme courts, in Scotland* (Edinburgh: J.Bell, 1774), 71–2. The indictment papers for Margaret Dickson can be found at the NRS, JC 3/12/115–74.

[2] NLS, *A Warning to the Wicked, or, Margaret Dickson's Welcome to the Gibbet* (Edinburgh, 1724). See also NLS, *Margaret Dickson's Penetential Confession* (Edinburgh, 1728). The story of Margaret Dickson would be retold in an English broadside published in 1813, NLS, *Particulars of the Life, Trial, Character, and Behaviour of Margaret Dickson* (Derby, 1813). On the crime of infanticide in eighteenth-century Scotland, see Deborah A. Symonds, *Weep Not for Me: Women, Ballads, and Infanticide in Early Modern Scotland* (College Park: The Pennsylvania State University Press, 1997) and Anne-Marie Kilday, *Women and Violent Crime in Enlightenment Scotland* (Woodbridge: Boydell & Brewer, 2007), chapter 4.

In recounting the sad story of Maggie Dickson's downfall, this murder ballad articulated three clear points that had become mainstays of demonic belief in post-Reformation Scotland: Satan was the ultimate tempter; the human heart was by nature sinful and open to demonic assaults; and God's grace alone could provide deliverance from hell.

This chapter explores the role of Satan in Scottish broadsides recounting murders and the last words of criminals destined for the hanging tree, as well as dying accounts immortalized in cheap print.[3] These sources demonstrate the blending of demonic beliefs that occurred across the social spectrum and the varied yet shared concept of Satan that shaped Scottish culture and identity. They illustrate how the Devil, and his theological and experiential relationship to humanity, had become central to how individuals and communities alike understood murder, guilt and death. In turn, broadsides covering crime and dying reiterated to the public the constant and consequential presence of Satan in daily life and in weak human hearts.

Two questions underpin the analysis of the role of the Devil in Scottish broadsides. First, how did printed reports of murders, narratives of executions and dying accounts reflect the ways in which ideas about Satan were disseminated, absorbed and altered by the wider Scottish public? Second, to what extent did ideas about the Devil found in printed accounts of crime and death accord with the portrayals of Satan at theological, personal and institutional levels? This chapter argues that the portrayal of the Devil in such works reified the universality of demonic temptation and made manifest to a wide audience the admonitions about Satan and sin so often disseminated from the pulpit and experienced in spiritual diaries. The broader purpose of these broadsides was to instil a sense of collective and corrective guilt in the reading public. To this aim, Satan proved instrumental.

Cheap Print in Early Modern Scotland

Affordable and available to many Scots, and far less complicated reads than theological treatises and sermons, broadsides served as the sensationalist tabloids of the day and vehicles for espousing religious ideas and didactic warnings. These broadsides certainly promoted specific moral norms and expectations, as many were probably composed by clergymen, but they also pandered to the interests of a wider audience in order to sell in the first place. Peter Lake has memorably likened the crime stories of early modern

---

[3] For an examination of the role of Satan in English broadsides, see Owen Davies, 'Talk of the Devil: Crime and Satanic Inspiration in Eighteenth-Century England', in http://herts.academia.edu/OwenDavies, 2007.

England to a John Carpenter film; they had to titillate to sell.[4] But sell to whom? The question of audience is one that has long fascinated historians of print culture. In Scotland, the literacy of the public grew slowly over the course of the early modern era. At the beginning of the eighteenth century, male literacy was high as 75 per cent in many areas, while only 25–30 per cent of women could be deemed literate.[5] It should be kept in mind, however, that being able to write is not the same thing as being able to read, and evidence suggests that reading was taught before writing in Scottish schools.[6] Officially literate or not, by the late seventeenth and early eighteenth centuries, more and more Scots were able to consume cheap print recounting tales of murder, last words and death – tales in which the Devil, and his cooperation with human sin, often played a starring role.

According to the National Library of Scotland's digital collection of Scottish broadsides, most broadsides 'were just about within the means of most working people, whereas quality prints ... were well beyond the means of the working class and even lower middle class artisans. Some ballads cost as little as half a penny'.[7] Despite the ability of the working class to purchase them, Scottish broadsides ought not to be viewed as directed at a specific group of people. Usually sold in bustling urban areas such as Edinburgh and Glasgow, but also distributed in more rural areas by travelling merchants known as hawkers, these works reached a wide array of men and women throughout Scotland.[8] Tessa Watt has persuasively argued that in England, cheap print served as 'an instrument of social cohesion, as more people were brought into the reading public, and as stories, images and values permeated the multiple tiers of English society'.[9] Scottish broadsides served a similar function with regard to cultural understandings of Satan, as they informed, integrated and reflected ideas about the Devil held by Scots from across the social spectrum. Moreover, as print that bridged the gap between religious and secular works,

---

[4] Peter Lake, 'Deeds Against Nature: Cheap Print, Protestantism and Murder in Early Seventeenth Century England', in Kevin Sharpe and Peter Lake, eds, *Culture and Politics in Early Stuart England* (Stanford, CA: Stanford University Press, 1993), 259.

[5] Bob Harris, 'Communicating', in Elizabeth Foyster and Christopher A. Whatley, eds, *A History of Everyday Life in Scotland, 1600–1800* (Edinburgh: Edinburgh University Press, 2010), 167. See also R.A. Houston, 'The Literacy Myth?: Illiteracy in Scotland, 1630–1760', *Past and Present* 96 (1982): 81–102; John Bannerman, 'Literacy in the Highlands', in Ian B. Cowan and Duncan Shaw, eds, *The Renaissance and Reformation in Scotland: Essays in Honour of Gordon Donaldson* (Edinburgh: Scottish Academic Press, 1983), 214–35.

[6] This point has also been made by Margaret Spufford, 'First Steps in Literacy: the Reading and Writing Experiences of the Humblest Seventeenth-Century Autobiographers', *Social History* 4 (1979): 407–35, and Tessa Watt, *Cheap Print and Popular Piety in England* (Cambridge: Cambridge University Press, 1993), 7.

[7] NLS, 'The Word on the Street', http://digital.nls.uk/broadsides.

[8] Ibid.

[9] Watt, *Cheap Print*, 5.

broadsides demonstrate both the continuity and evolution of ideas about Satan consistently promoted in the generations following the Reformation.

The ability of cheap print to cross social categories is precisely what renders the study of broadsides crucial to understanding the place of the Devil in wider Scottish culture. That the Scottish people had developed a taste for salacious broadsides by the early eighteenth century is apparent; what is less obvious is the extent to which the appearance of the demonic in street literature reflected or informed public sentiment about Satan. Moralizing about the Devil in broadsides not only served the didactic purpose of the oft-anonymous authors, but also illustrated the complex and shared demonic beliefs of the Scottish public. The powerful presence of the Devil in cheap print reveals how pervasive Reformed demonic ideas, beyond the walls of the church, had become in Scottish society. These ideas cemented the distinction between good and evil members of society while simultaneously making manifest the ubiquity of the Devil and the danger of his temptations for all men and women. These broadsides, while executed in a more entertaining and digestible fashion, served a similar purpose as early modern Scottish sermons and spiritual diaries: to persuade readers to choose a 'good' path and identity for themselves by vigilantly protecting their weak hearts from the incursions of Satan.

The majority of the Scottish broadsides examined here date from the late seventeenth and early eighteenth centuries.[10] Printing slowly flourished in Scotland following the Reformation in 1560, as religious tracts, prayers and sermons increasingly circulated throughout the country, reflecting the reforming zeal of the newly Protestant nation.[11] Political proclamations, commentaries and satire were also increasingly published in pamphlet form, amid the turmoil of events such as Mary Queen of Scots' death, the Union of the Crowns in 1603 and the wars of the covenanting era.[12] As the seventeenth century progressed, these religious and political works began to be accompanied by the printing of broadsides recounting of murder, infanticide and other sensationalist crimes to a growing, albeit slowly, body of literate Scots.

---

[10] The research for this chapter has relied primarily on broadsides from the National Library of Scotland's digital broadside collection, which holds over 1,800 broadsides from 1650 and 1910. In conducting research for this chapter, I read over fifty that discuss the role of the Devil in crimes, primarily from the century between 1650 and 1750. Unless otherwise noted, the broadsides cited in this chapter come from this NLS collection and were composed by an anonymous author.

[11] Alasdair J. Mann, 'The Anatomy of the Printed Book in Early Modern Scotland', *Scottish Historical Review* 80 (2001), 187.

[12] For a discussion of political satire in sixteenth-century Scottish broadsides, see Tricia A. McElroy, 'Imagining the "Scottis Natioun": Populism and Propaganda in Scottish Satirical Broadsides', *Texas Studies in Literature and Language* 47 (2007): 319–39.

The popular broadsides examined here, though not entirely absent in the sixteenth and early seventeenth centuries, were vastly overshadowed by religious works such as sermons and psalms. The domination of explicitly religious literature in Scotland is especially noteworthy when compared to England, where stories of murder, witchcraft and other crimes pervaded the English pulp press, becoming by the second half of the sixteenth century a staple of London print culture.[13] The situation was quite different in Scotland, where, according to Aldis's *List of Books Published in Scotland before 1700*, Robert Sempill's *Deploration of the cruell murther of James Earle of Moray* (1570) was the only murder pamphlet published in Scotland until 1679, when *A Narrative of the murther of the Archbp. of St. Andrews* was published in Edinburgh. Aldis's list is not indicative of all the works circulated in Scotland, as it only includes those works that contained 'some definite indication of Scottish origin'.[14] Doubtlessly works of foreign origin, especially those from England, were disseminated widely in Scotland. Still, the relative absence of Scottish crime literature until the late seventeenth century, especially compared to the fairly voluminous publication of sermons, catechisms and other religious works alongside royal and parliamentary proclamations, demonstrates the rather late proliferation of sensationalist street literature in Scotland.[15]

Part of this late proliferation was logistical, as Scottish printing itself greatly expanded in the seventeenth century, when ten times as many books, pamphlets and newspapers were printed than in the previous hundred years.[16] Purchasing power grew among ordinary Scots grew during the late seventeenth and early eighteenth centuries, augmenting market demand for cheap literature. Yet the dearth of sensationalist cheap print in the generations immediately following the Reformation may indicate that, beyond the preferences and outputs of printers, the literate Scottish public lacked a taste for such tabloid literature. Until the early eighteenth century, the educated elite dominated the market for print in Scotland, the majority of whom were zealous Protestants more interested in reforming sermons

---

[13] A significant number of important studies have been written of such crime literature in early modern England. See, for example, Malcolm Gaskill, *Crime and Mentalities in Early Modern England* (Cambridge: Cambridge University Press, 2000); James Sharpe, *Crime in Early Modern England 1550–1750* (London: Longman, 1984); Peter Lake, 'Deeds Against Nature'; Frances E. Dolan, *Dangerous Familiars: Representations of Domestic Crime in England, 1550–1700* (Ithaca, NY: Cornell University Press, 1994).

[14] Harry Gildney Aldis, *List of Books Published in Scotland before 1700: Including those Printed furth of the Realm for Scottish Booksellers*, revised edition (Edinburgh: National Library of Scotland, 1970), xvi.

[15] Ibid, 144.

[16] Mann, 'Anatomy of the Printed Book', 188. Mann bases this number on the Aldis *List of Books Printed in Scotland before 1700*. In the eighteenth century, this number of printed works grew even more, especially with the intellectual contributions of the Scottish Enlightenment.

than salacious murder stories. George Penny, looking back from the 1830s, recalled of the later seventeenth century that even the reading of the common people 'was limited to a few books of a religious character, such as the Bible, Confessions of Faith, Shorter Catechism; Bonston's, Bunyan's and Willison's works and a few sermons'.[17] Even amid the rising literacy of the eighteenth century, the most popular and widely circulated works remained religious ones.[18] It should come as no surprise, then, that when broadsides and ballads did come belatedly to the fore of the Scottish print market, they blurred the lines of spiritual and secular themes – a blurring that made them all the more salacious and relevant to their readers.

'A Murderer from the Beginning'[19]

Satan appeared often in the baleful accounts of murders and executions that were printed and sold on Scottish streets. Early modern Scots firmly believed that the influence of the Devil lay at the heart of earthly events, ranging from minor cases of slander to heinous crimes like patricide and infanticide. R.A. Houston has suggested that the lack of demonic agency in cases of suicide in early modern Scotland indicates that 'the Scots were sparing in attributing any bad things to the Devil'.[20] This assertion, though accurate in cases of suicide, does not hold true for the role of Satan in Scottish culture more generally. Throughout the early modern period and into the eighteenth century, Scots of all sorts pointed to Satan as the orchestrator of temptation and harm, instigating both individual and communal transgressions. This is not to say that crimes were explained with a simple 'the Devil made me do it'. Rather, belief in the Devil's ability and proclivity to lure people to sin stemmed from a dynamic combination of biblical foundations, personal experiences and affirmations of human frailty. These demonic ideas suffused reports of murder that were published in broadsides and sold to an audience eager to read about the dark and scandalous deeds of others.

Often the language of crime literature borrowed heavily from Scripture and mirrored that of early modern Scottish sermons, which focused on the ability of Satan to infiltrate the hearts and minds of men and women. That many broadsides shared these themes is unsurprising considering

---

[17] George Penny, *Traditions of Perth* (1836), 39.
[18] Harris, 'Communicating', 174.
[19] John 8:44 of the King James Version (1611) recounts Jesus' debate with the Pharisees, in which he said to them: 'Ye are of *your* father the devil, and the lusts of your father ye will do: he was a murderer from the beginning, and abode not in the truth, because there is no truth in him. When he speaketh a lie, he speaketh of his own: for he is a liar, and the father of it'.
[20] See Houston, *Punishing the Dead: Suicide, Lordship, and Community in Britain, 1500–1800* (Oxford: Oxford University Press, 2010), 293.

that many of their authors were probably clergymen. The first murder story published in early modern Scotland appeared in the form of a poem written by poet and Protestant controversialist Robert Sempill on the occasion of the murder of James Stewart, 1st Earl of Moray, in 1570.[21] The poem began with a reference to the story of Cain and Abel, from whom 'this haill warld did discend'. In describing the man who murdered Moray, Sempill lamented that 'come neuer ane gude byrde of the Deuillis eg', insinuating that the assassin was a reprobate in league with Satan. As always, the murderer would receive due punishment in the afterlife, as

> The tyme sall cum, that he sall weip and murne
> Quhen hiddeous hell with greuous gloward gleims
> Baith body and saule for euer mair sall burne.[22]

Such sermonic admonitions about hell found compelling expression in the stories of the most heinous earthly actions and terrible ends of the reprobate.

Nearly a century-and-a-half later, in 1717, Dublin resident Owen Brady murdered his two children. The story quickly reached Edinburgh and was printed in a broadside that portrayed the murder, and the Devil's involvement therein, in biblical terms: 'The Devil as a Roaring Lion goes continually about seeking whom he may Devore, he is constantly in his Watch, ready to seize his unguarded Prey, and to seduce unhappy inconsiderate Men into Everlasting Ruin, and yet we Live as if there were no Danger ...'.[23] Brady's murderous actions confirmed the warning about the Devil's tirelessness issued in 1 Peter 5:8, a familiar passage from contemporary sermons throughout the British Isles. The brief text of the broadside closed with a warning to others 'to give no way to Jealousy the Fiend of Hell, and to Teach us tho' we are Poor not to distrust God's Mercy's, which are great and boundless: least he in His Anger shou'd justly give us over to Hell and destruction'.[24] In this admonition, the rages of Satan and the spiritual poverty of humanity were contrasted with the sovereignty and greatness of God, without whom many individuals would meet the same tragic end as Brady had.[25]

---

[21] Robert Sempill, *Deploration of the cruell murther of James Earle of Moray* (Edinburgh, 1570).
[22] Ibid.
[23] *A Full and True Account of A most Horrid, Barbarous, and Bloody Murther Committed by Owen Brady* (Dublin and Edinburgh, 1717).
[24] Ibid.
[25] It is worth noting that at the time this pamphlet was published in Ireland, English Protestants dominated the government and the printing press in Ireland, explaining the dominance of Protestant ideas in a murder story such as this one. That said, the reference

A pamphlet detailing the murders committed by William Bolamgall reiterated the influence of the Devil on the abhorrent actions of men and women. In 1721, Bolamgall killed three victims staying in his father's home near Edinburgh. The only motive given for these murders was 'the Devil entering into the Heart of the said William Bolamgal, Tempting him to commit these horrid Murders upon three Innocent Persons'.[26] That Satan entered his heart, rather than his mind or soul, reflects the common rhetoric of the need to protect one's heart from demonic incursions and the general danger of the Devil's internal, personal presence. The tale of the murder also included the suggestion that had it not been for the 'LORD'S Providence', the same fate might have befallen the whole house. Divine subversion of satanic wiles, too, recalls the hope for eventual victory found in many post-Reformation self-writings and sermons.[27]

One of the more sensationalized murder cases of the early eighteenth century was that of Mr Robert Irvine, executed in 1717 for the murder of John and Alexander Gordon, two of his students. Three separate broadsides recounting the sordid details of the crime were published in Edinburgh. Two of these detailed the last confession of Irvine, and the third laid out the facts of the murder, trial and execution. In these broadsides, Irvine provided two related answers for why he had committed such heinous crimes. When initially interrogated as to what 'induced him to commit so horrid Wickedness', he claimed that 'it was a Temptation of the Devil'.[28] At the same time, however, Irvine acknowledged that to succumb to the temptations of the Devil was his own active choice. He confessed to ministers before his death that 'he could distinguish between Good and Evil, been a great Sinner, and had never spent so much as one Day as he ought to have done'.[29]

Upon further prodding, Irvine provided an additional explanation for his crime. According to the report of his last confession

> ... after he had been often asked what prompted him to so monstrous a crime ... he said before many Witnesses, That the Predestinarian Principles had led him into it. And being ask'd where he learned these Principles, he said from a Book

---

to 1 Peter 5:8 and the belief that Satan lay behind some of the heinous actions of men and women should not be seen as exclusive to Protestantism.

[26] *An Account of a Horrid and Bloody Murder* (Edinburgh, 1720).

[27] See, for example, John Brown, *Christ in believers the hope of glory being the substance of several sermons* (Edinburgh, 1694); William Thompson, *The churches Comfort, or a Sermon on John XVI* (Edinburgh, 1661), Zachary Boyd, *The balme of Gilead prepared for the sicke* (1629); Robert Blair, *The Life of Mr. Robert Blair*, ed., Thomas M'Crie (Edinburgh: Wodrow Society, 1848); John Welwood, 'Letters, 1675–77', in *Protestant Piety*; Diary of Marion Veitch, Adv. MS 34.6.22.

[28] *The Whole Trial, Confession and Sentence, OF Mr. Robert Irvine* (Edinburgh, 1717).

[29] *The Last Confession of Mr. Robert Irvine* (Edinburgh, 1717).

he had out of the College Library. And being ask'd what Book that was, he answered, one of Flavel's.[30]

John Flavel, a late seventeenth-century English Presbyterian clergyman, had published extensively on the tenets of Reformed Protestant theology, including 'the Predestinarian Principles' cited by Irvine.[31] What is fascinating here is that Irvine explicitly cited the concept of predestination, along with Satan, as an impetus for committing murder. Unfortunately, the broadside's author moved immediately from this admission to Irvine's pre-death expressions of guilt about his crime, so precisely how the 'predestinarian principles' influenced his actions remains cloudy. Irvine was clearly an educated man, a tutor of some sort, but he was far from a man of the cloth.[32] Though his specific interpretation of predestination is unclear, it seems likely that he believed salvation to be out of his hands. At the Devil's provocation, he acted on his basest instincts, possibly believing that he was already damned. This is conjecture, of course, but nevertheless Irvine's admission is a compelling example of how this particular element of Reformed Protestantism, with its emphasis on the power of demonic temptation, may have incited a spiritually insecure man to action.

Beyond Satan's involvement in tempting individuals to sin, broadsides recounting murders consistently implicated the Devil in causing the moral backslide of the Scottish community as a whole. In a particularly tragic 1721 account of the brutal death of John Halden, a poor boy seeking work in Edinburgh, the anonymous author singled out Satan as a source of not only the boy's violent end, but also of Scotland's general moral decay.[33] This blame for the murder did not originate solely with Satan, but equally with the actions of the fallen Scottish community. The author expressed hope that the murder of Halden would 'quicken Christians to Repentance and induce us to lay seriously to Heart our horrid Provocations, which tempts God to give up so many Persons to the Conduct of Satan and their own Lusts'.[34] In keeping with the Reformed belief in divine sovereignty, the

---

[30] Ibid.

[31] John Flavel's principle works included *Navigation Spiritualized* (London, 1671); *The Fountain of Life, in forty-two Sermons* (London, 1672); *The Method of Grace* (London, 1680); *Pneumatologia, a Treatise on the Soul of Man* (London, 1698); *A Token for Mourners; Husbandry Spiritualized* (London, 1699). The majority of Flavel's works were also published in Edinburgh during the late seventeenth century.

[32] Robert Chambers refers to Irvine as a 'licentiate of the church' who was considered 'of respectable attainments, but remarked for a somewhat melancholic disposition'. See Chambers, *Domestic Annals of Scotland: From the Revolution to Rebellion*, Vol. 3 (Edinburgh, 1824), 422.

[33] *A Faithful Narrative of The Circumstances of the Cruelty committed upon the Body of John Halden* (1721).

[34] Ibid.

author credited God with allowing Satan to influence the actions of Scots. Most striking about this particular broadside was the implication of the whole community in the murder of John Halden, as if all of Edinburgh – or even Scotland – had contributed to his destruction. As Nathan Johnstone points out in his discussion of crime literature in England, 'exposes of the Devil's agency were often also exposes of society's negligence in opposing it'.[35] According to this broadside, both the Devil and a spiritually negligent public had incited the barbarous actions of the murderer.

The account of the murder of James Campbell in 1723, killed by his cousin in a drunken brawl, reiterated this larger influence of the Devil on Scottish society. Here the author used the murder to chastise a morally lax public. The broadside began with a description of how Scotland was once a beacon of morality, calling it 'a Land irradiate with Gospel-light whose native Off-spring is Peace, the vital Grace of Religion'. The author then detailed how Satan had usurped the place of prior godliness. 'Did not daily Experience too plainly evidence', the author implored, 'that Hell is broke loose 'mongst nominal Christians, who poisoned by his [Satan's] infernal Philters commit Murder in the Face of the Sun?'[36]

In the author's chastising of those who behaved as Christians in name only, he mimicked the language of a sermon delivered by Covenanter Andrew Cant nearly a century before, in 1638:

> Long ago our gracious God was pleased to visit this nation with the light of His glorious Gospel, by planting a vineyard in, and making His glory to arise upon Scotland … .But alas! Satan envied our happiness, brake our ranks, poisoned our fountains, mudded and defiled our streams. Truth is fallen in the streets, our dignity is gone, our credit lost, our crown is fallen from our heads; our reputation is turned to imputation.[37]

Both Cant's sermon and the broadside detailing the murder of James Campbell contrasted the imagery of the 'sun' or 'light' of God with Satan's 'poisoning' of the Scottish community. Concern for this poisoning of the true faith, and the individuals and communities that held this faith, had clearly preoccupied the Scottish clergy from the early days of the Scottish Reformation. Through sermons, kirk sessions and eventually broadsides, this concern for Satan seeped into and shaped the culture of a nation ripe with apocalyptic anticipation.

---

[35] Nathan Johnstone, *The Devil and Demonism in Early Modern England* (Cambridge: Cambridge University Press, 2006), 152.

[36] *A True and distinct Account Of the Murder of James Campbel of Lawers* (Edinburgh, c. 1723).

[37] James Kerr, ed. *The Covenants And The Covenanters: Covenants, Sermons, and Documents of the Covenanted Reformation*. (Edinburgh: R.W. Hunter, 1895), 77–8.

In 1723, in a parish east of Edinburgh, Elizabeth Murray was brutally murdered by her husband. This tragedy was recorded and published in the form of a poetic elegy, which began with a lamentation of the sad spiritual state of Scotland and the rampant activities of the Devil:

> So, there are terrible unlucky Times
> (For Providence corrects enormous Crimes)
> When Satan spreads Contagion in the Mind,
> With Mischief, and with Madness damns Mankind
> The Venom or the Asp, with Tumors swell,
> And turgide grows and ripens unto Hell ...
> When Villany it's impious Head shall rear,
> In Querpo, strut and Satan's Liv'ry wear ;
> And this we by a sad Experience know,
> We feel th' Effects of Sin, and Heav'ns weighty blow:
> Mens Principles, and Practices contend,
> The Devil's Empire for to recommend:
> It's hard to say (the Times are so accurs'd)
> If our Opinions, or our Deeds are worst?[38]

The poem focused on the ability of Satan to infiltrate and corrupt the spiritually unguarded and highlighted the Reformed obsession with controlling both words and deeds. The broadside did not detail the specific murder itself, but rather the sinfulness of the community, for whom 'A thousand Devils in the Conscience dwell' – a line which recalls the sermonic language of Satan being within the hearts and minds of all men.[39] This depiction of Satan collaborating with collective human frailty reiterated the goals espoused from pulpits across early modern Scotland: to instil in the Scottish community awareness of an eminent and often internal enemy, along with a shared sense of responsibility in the face of demonic assaults.

Satan and the End of Life

In tandem with these murder stories, the Devil dominated broadsides detailing the last words of those executed for such heinous crimes, as well as stories of those who died of natural causes. Death was often a public affair in early modern Scotland. Executions often drew large crowds eager to watch the morally fallen pay for their crimes and produced broadsides

---

[38] *Elegy* (Edinburgh, 1723).
[39] Ibid.

that recounted the last words of the criminals facing death. These printed speeches, usually dictated to or drafted by anonymous scribes, were often formulaic. The amount of actual input from the subjects themselves is difficult to pinpoint, as authors usually muddled together specific biographical and case details with prescribed expressions of repentance. In the face of death, the men and women likely expressed some of the sentiments found in such speeches, but their words were also often interpreted by an experienced author attuned to public tastes. Thus these last words and dying speeches represent a complex mix of personal belief and community expectations. Like cases of murder, dying accounts and last words of criminals focused on the themes of sin and its consequences, with the Devil looming large as the instigator of wrongdoings in collaboration with spiritual depravity of humankind.

In these last words, the criminal act and the execution itself usually took a backseat to moralizing about the nature of sin and the human heart. The case of Janet Hutchie, who was convicted in 1721 of infanticide and executed in the Grassmarket of Edinburgh, exemplifies the prevalence of these themes. After lamenting her sad spiritual state for the bulk of her final speech, Hutchie (or, at the least, the author of her words) expressed hope that despite her wrongdoing, she might still be granted salvation:

> Oh that now I may be made a singular Monument of the unsearchable Riches and Free Mercy, and Grace of GOD ... not having my own Righteousness, which is nothing, but that of his imputed to me, which yet can make me clean before that great Tribunal, for as black as the Devil, Hell and my own Corruptions have made me.[40]

In her last words, Hutchie articulated both an acknowledgement of her internal corruptions and a desire for mercy from the only available source: God's grace. The language of 'the Devil, Hell and my own corruptions' appeared in a number of printed final speeches, mirroring the references to the dual threat of 'the devil and an evil heart' so often found in the spiritual diaries and sermons.[41]

Another broadside published in 1723 detailed 'The Last speech and dying words of John Treplecock', a man executed for murder but apparently guilty of numerous other crimes. In his last words, Treplecock blamed Satan and his own weak heart as the source of his many transgressions:

---

[40] *The Last Speech and Dying Words of Janet Hutchie* (Edinburgh, 1721).

[41] See, for example, NLS Adv. MS. 34.6.22: Marion Veitch, 'An account of the Lord's gracious dealing with me and of his remarkable hearing and answering my supplications', f.20; James Nimmo, *The Narrative of Mr. James Nimmo: Written for his own Satisfaction to Keep in some rememberance the lords way dealing and kindness towards him, 1654–1709*, ed. W.G. Scott Moncrieff (Edinburgh: The Scottish History Society, 1889), 9.

'Sins gradually introduced themselves, one after another, and the wicked Heart of mine soon betray'd me into by the cuning Insinuations of the Devil'.[42] As they did again and again in sermons and self-writings, lamentations of this intimate relationship between Satan and the spiritually feeble human heart appeared regularly in popular murder and dying accounts of the late seventeenth and early eighteenth centuries. As Alexander Henderson had explained in a 1638 sermon, men and women were to blame for not guarding their hearts against Satan: 'be that we had a right heart, then Satan nor his temptations would not prevail over us. But it is a pitiful thing that he has darts, and shoots them at poor souls, and we are ready to receive them'.[43] The appearance of this theme in broadsides reflects not only a common belief in the cooperation between Satan and the individual heart, but a desire on the part of the reading public to have that relationship confirmed in printed stories of those who had let their baser inclinations get the best of them.

In a 1702 broadside ballad, Jannet Riddle confessed that as she contemplated the murder of her only child, 'the Div'l helpt me to go on, and paved out the way/How I should make my Child begon, which 'twixt my Sides long lye'.[44] Her tale ends with the interesting assertion that the public should be happy to hear of the supposed author's execution:

> Farewel O People, be you fil'd
> with Joy, for I do Die
> For Murthering of my only Child
> which 'twixt my Sides did lye.[45]

Though this last confession, as with many others, was written entirely from a first-person perspective, a professional broadside writer likely composed it. Still, an early modern audience long educated in the dangers of Satan's temptations would have readily accepted the demonic instigation of a crime as contemptible as infanticide. The Devil's involvement, however, was not intended to mitigate the guilt of the criminal, whose 'many Sins' drove her to deserve 'the Cru'lest Death that e're was known'.[46]

Last words often concluded with advice to the reader about the threat of Satan and the means of resisting him. One telling example comes from the last words of John Webster, who in the early eighteenth century murdered a fourteen-year-old girl for whom he had 'unclean thoughts', purportedly

---

[42] *The Last speech and dying words of John Treplecock* (Edinburgh, 1723).
[43] Alexander Henderson, *Sermons, prayers and pulpit addresses of Alexander Henderson*, ed. Martin R. Thomson (Edinburgh: John Maclaren, 1867), 215.
[44] *The last Speech and Confession of Jannet Riddle* (Edinburgh, 1702).
[45] Ibid.
[46] Ibid.

induced by the Devil.[47] After recounting a troubled childhood marred by the death of his parents and lack of religious education, Webster lamented the terrible error of his ways: 'O! the Evil of Sin? What can be expected; when all Fear of GOD is cast off, his Worship Forsaken, and the Service of the Devil engaged into; as alas! I have done'.[48] The murder of the young girl, he claimed, stemmed from his initial abandonment of the godly path, which led to his submission to Satan. In his final words, Webster told his reader to 'be humble and beg of GOD that ye be not given up to the Temptations of the Devil and these powerful Corruptions that dwell in the Heart of the Children of the Son of Men by Nature'.[49] Again, because the exact author is unknown, it is hard to discern the origins of this theological and experiential relationship between Satan and the depraved nature of men and women. Regardless, the moralizing that dominated the last-word genre of broadsides must have found a receptive audience in early eighteenth-century Scotland, reflecting the prevalence of such ideas among the authorial elite and their internalization by the wider Scottish public.

Letters sent by loved ones to those awaiting execution occasionally made their way into printed broadsides. Unlike last words, these letters were less likely to be composed by anonymous scribes. They may, then, present a more straightforward window into individual demonic belief, though it is sometimes uncertain whether or not the authors of such letters initially knew that their words would find a public audience. One particularly evocative example comes from 1720, when Lady Boghall mailed a letter to her son, Nichol Mushet, who was imprisoned in the tollbooth of Edinburgh for the murder of his wife.[50] After thoroughly admonishing her son for his act of 'Unparalled Barbarity', Boghall told him that he deserved 'the Holy and Righteous GOD to Wrath against thy poor Soul', for having shown 'that thy only Pleasure and Delight was in Doing the Works of the Devil and Reproaching thy Maker, by Sinning presumptuously against him'.[51] Here her letter expressed the familiar inability of individuals to escape Satan's grasp on their own, as the evil of the Devil and human evil operated as two sides of a sinful coin. She closed her letter with a prayer that Nichol might be among the elect – 'a Wonder of the Riches of Free Grace and Mercy in being plucked as a Brand out

---

[47] *The last Speech And Dying Words of John Webster Gardiner at Greenhill* (Edinburgh, 1722).
[48] Ibid.
[49] Ibid.
[50] The murder of Margaret Hall by Nicol Mushet was recounted in a broadside a year later. See *Elegy: On the deplorable Death of Margaret Hall* (Edinburgh, 1721). In this broadside, Satan was cited as the chief orchestrator of the violent murder, as it was 'he [Mushet] and Satan who had form'd the Plot'.
[51] *A true Copy of a Letter Tent by the Lady Boghall to her Son Nicol Mushet, Prisoner within the Tolbooth of Edinburgh, for the Murder of his own Wife* (Edinburgh, 1720).

of the Fire ... a poor loft Sheep plucked by the Shepherd out of the Jaws of that Devouring Lyon the Devil' – an end that would remain ultimately unknowable for the grieving mother.[52]

The belief that the end of one's life would be marked by a painful awareness of past sins and general human depravity continued well beyond the early modern period. An 1819 account of the death of James Mossat, a notorious thief, detailed how the 'retrospective part of his life furnished such a view of consummate villainy and wickedness, that, in his last moments, he exhibited such a picture of agony, that it appeared as if the terrors of another world had seized upon him before he had actually quitted this'.[53] The 'terrors of another world' referred here, of course, to Hell, and in his last moments, Mossat reportedly felt profound horror in contemplating a future in Satan's final kingdom:

> When the mind reverted on past enormities, he became afraid of himself and felt pain not to be uttered; particularly during the night season he used to, fight with his arms, and to shake his limbs; under those paroxysms he swore and exclaimed bitterly, frequently crying out, 'Depart from me ye Devils, ye monsters and companions of my guilt' ... as he lived, so he appeared to die without God and without hope.[54]

The purpose of such descriptions of both anticipating and realizing hell was to discourage the audience from a life of sin by demonstrating the consequences of a heart open to demonic temptation. The supposed cry of 'Depart from me ye Devils' implies that, even if Mossat had not actually uttered this, the author perceived the residence of Satan in the corrupted heart of the criminal.

On occasion a piece of 'last advice' was composed from the viewpoint of a fictional criminal, usually written by a clergyman and published with the intent of providing specific moral and spiritual warnings. One such example is the 1720 broadside entitled *Robert Johnston's Ghost OR, His last ADVICE to the Gipsies, and other Gangs of Robbers and Murderers in Scotland*. Written from the perspective of a recently deceased criminal suffering eternal punishment, the poem advised deviants in Scotland to repent while they still could. Satan appeared in this advice as the archetype for the evil behaviour of the criminals. Johnston's ghost conflated humans and the Devil, accusing prospective criminals of acting 'the Devil in a human Shape' and propagating 'Hell's Works of Lust and Hate'. The overarching theme of this poem, however, was the wrath of a mighty God:

---

[52] Ibid.
[53] *Life and Memoirs of James Mossat* (Edinburgh, 1819).
[54] Ibid.

> O ! did you know the Terrors of his Face,
> How would you prize the Offers of his Grace ?
> If your blind Eyes could him behold on high,
> Clothed with Power and awful Majesty,
> Judge of the Quick and Dead, great King of Heav'n,
> Whose awful Frown to Hell hath Sinners driv'n,
> You'd soon recal your Time so vainly spent,
> And all your Sins with heavy Tears repent.[55]

It was not the Devil that the ghost told his audience to fear, but rather the revenge of a just God who would not tolerate deviant behaviour. While earthly justice was doled out by the courts, for unredeemed sinners, a much harsher divine justice awaited.

Two things about the advice of the fictional Robert Johnston are worth further noting. First, here belief in predestination carried less weight than the idea of repentance while on earth. Though the broadside did not explicitly mention good works, the author subtly lent some agency to the intended audience in controlling their fate. This seems to be consistent with other broadsides of the early eighteenth century, in which the Reformed Protestant themes of sin and Satan stood front and centre, while the concept of predestination, so prevalent in the late sixteenth and seventeenth centuries, was at times noticeably absent. This likely reflects the larger splintering of opinion between Presbyterians and Episcopalians over doctrine and piety that occurred during the waning years of the Stuart era, and a more general step back from a focus on predestination.[56] These shifts were articulated not only in religious and polemical tracts, but subtly in popular print. Second, in this poem, Satan was not portrayed as an aggressive tempter as he was in many other contemporary broadsides. Rather, this last advice focused one hypothetical man's active choice to live in the path of Satan and 'propagate Hell's Works of Lust and Hate'.

The involvement of Satan in crime literature thus existed on a spectrum. On one end stood the Devil as the maestro of the crime, and on the other the pull of humanity's innately evil tendencies, with an increasingly porous division between the two. As in sermons, spiritual diaries and cases of witchcraft, Satan and human depravity always worked in tandem, and the emphasis on human evil increasingly came to the fore in broadsides as time progressed.

---

[55] *Robert Johnston's Ghost OR, His last ADVICE to the Gipsies, and other Gangs of Robbers and Murderers in Scotland* (Edinburgh, 1720).

[56] On the confessionalization of Scottish religious cultures after 1660, see Alasdair Raffe, 'Presbyterians and Episcopalians: the Formation of Confessional Cultures in Scotland, 1660–1715', *English Historical Review* CXXV (514), and Raffe, *The Culture of Controversy: Religious Arguments in Scotland, 1660–1714* (Woodbridge: Boydell Press, 2012).

For those who died of natural causes, death could also be a public affair. Accounts of natural deaths circulated in early modern Scotland in both printed and manuscript form, sharing the words uttered by final breaths in final moments. Such accounts, often recorded by a minister and occasionally by an educated family member, displayed the piety of the recently deceased and the comfort delivered by God. Throughout, Satan appeared to tempt the dying with doubts about salvation. In the 1640 account of the death of Mary Rutherford, the minister Archibald Porteous described how the Devil assaulted the lady's mind in her final hours. He observed that 'it is a hard and difficult Work to cure a troubled Soul, Satan opposing it with all his Might (for he would always have you looking to Sense, or else he would make you believe there is no Mercy for you) and feeling Satan's Policy is so great that none can rebuke these Storms and Waves'.[57] Prayer, he wrote, provided the only answer to Lady Rutherford's struggles. In accordance with the necessity of dependence on God, he told her to say the following short prayer when troubled: 'Lord, hold Satan off me, and give me not leave to the doubt of thy Love, or to believe any Thing that comes out of Satan's mouth'.[58] In the end, with this prayer as armour against the Evil One, Mary Rutherford died a peaceful death.[59]

In his *Historie of the Kirk of Scotland*, John Row recorded the story of the death of Martha Barron, the pious first wife of the minister Patrick Simpson. According to Row's account, in the weeks before her death, Martha was 'visited with sicknes', not of the body, but of the heart and mind. She told her husband that 'the divill had often suggested to her, and cast in her teeth that he should be about with hir, and that she should be given over in his hand'.[60] Her husband assured her that she had an abundance of the marks of grace, which would 'certainlie be objects of Satan's malice and hatred; but the gates of hell cannot prevail against the Kirk, or so neither agains any member thereof'.[61]

Soon after, on a Sabbath day in August, Martha began to speak with uncharacteristic irreverence to her husband and to God. Simpson interpreted this strange behaviour as a product of Satan's assaults, calling it a 'distraction', though notably not a possession. He prayed for his wife and claimed to all those in the house that 'for all the devill's malice and

---

[57] Archibald Porteus, *The Spiritual Exercise of Soul and Blessed Departure of Dame Mary Rutherford Lady Hundaly, and Mary M'Konnel, cousin to the said lady; which fell out in the year 1640; both died in London.* (Edinburgh, 1745), 8.
[58] Ibid.
[59] For a discussion of the role of prayer in Protestant spiritual warfare, see Alec Ryrie, *Being Protestant*, 243–7.
[60] John Row, *History of the Kirk of Scotland* (Edinburgh: Wodrow Society, 1842), 433.
[61] Ibid.

crueltie agains this infirme person, he shall get a shamefull foyle'.[62] Simpson went to pray alone and secretly in a garden, where he saw a vision of angels that 'revealled the Lord's mind to him concerning the condition of his wife'.[63] He returned to his wife's bedside and delivered a prayer on Genesis 32, when Jacob wrestled with an angel and was renamed Israel. Upon hearing of Jacob's wrestling, his wife sat up in her bed with renewed life and told her husband that she had been delivered from Satan: 'And thou art Jacob today, who hast wrestled and prevailed ... for I am now pulled out of the hands of Satan, and he shall have no more power or dominion over me'.[64] Martha then remained at peace until she died, a week later. The narrative of this dying account followed the same pattern of the wrestlings with Satan in spiritual diaries, only here Row portrayed Simpson as an intermediary and even a conduit for God to bring Martha relief from the Devil.

In his 1679 dying testimony, published as a pamphlet the following year, John King, a field preacher, lamented the evil of his being: 'I have no righteousness of my owne, all is vyle and lyke filthie rags. But blessed be god, that ther is a savior and advocate Jesus Chryst the righteous and I doe believe that Jesus Chryst is come into the world to save sinners off who I am cheife'.[65] He closed his testimony with the assertion that through his faith in Christ, he hoped for 'a happie victorie over sin, Satan, hell, and death'.[66] Echoing the language of sermons and spiritual diaries, King emphasized man's total dependence on God for deliverance from Satan. Such dying accounts were not always printed in broadside form, and many thus constitute a different genre of writing with its own cultural expectations and functions. However, like tales of murder and executions, they provided the author an opportunity to contrast the sinfulness of humanity and the evil of Satan with the goodness of God, presenting a personal, individual manifestation of the messages popularized in Scottish cheap print.

Satan on the Streets in Early Modern Britain

Though most of the works addressed here date from the early eighteenth century and comprise a smaller pool of sources than those available to

---

[62] Ibid., 434.
[63] Ibid., 435.
[64] Ibid.
[65] Wod. Qu. XCIX Dying Testimony of John King, field preacher, chaplain to Lord Cardross. Aug 12 1679. f.216v; *The last speeches of the two ministers Mr. John King, and Mr. John Kid* (Edinburgh, 1680).
[66] Ibid.

historians of England, comparison between the role of Satan in English and Scottish street literature remains a fruitful way to better understand demonic belief in Scotland.[67] In early modern English murder ballads in particular, the Devil held a central role. Peter Lake has pointed out that nearly every one of the English murder stories he consulted from 1580 to 1640 contained such phrases as 'by the fury and assistance of the devil'.[68] Similarly, Owen Davies has used eighteenth-century English crime literature to demonstrate that 'the Devil's grip on society was firmer, more pervasive and lasted longer than is usually thought'.[69] He points out that long after the decriminalization of witchcraft in England, Satan remained a significant presence in the discourse on crime, as thieves and murderers, seeking to explain their sordid actions, regularly cited the Devil in their dying speeches.[70]

In English works, some written by members of the clergy and others by educated laymen, authors referenced Satan with the didactic purpose of instilling in readers the perception of an external, 'all pervasive malice' that preyed upon man's innate weakness.[71] Lake has also argued that English pamphlets did not consistently or overtly condemn such crimes, though they certainly did not condone them either. The main purpose of salacious, detailed murder stories was 'not merely to edify but also to shock, titillate and engender that *frisson* of horror laced with disapproval which allows both pleasure and excitement at the enormities described to be combined with a reconfirmed sense of the reader's own moral superiority'.[72] Even in heavily moralized accounts in which Satan featured prominently, the relationship of these pamphlets to their subject matter was more exploitative than didactic.

Due to shared Protestant origins, as well as circulation in both countries, street literature in England and Scotland share many similarities in purpose and presentation. There are, however, some important

---

[67] Historians of early modern England as well as Europe have looked to print culture to interrogate the relationship between new Protestant ideas and the persistence of traditional culture. See Johnstone, *The Devil and Demonism*, and Darren Oldridge, *The Devil in Early Modern England* (Stroud: Sutton, 2000). On the relationship between print culture and religious belief, the best are Tessa Watt's *Cheap Print and Popular Piety, 1540–1650* and Robert Scribner, *For the Sake of Simple Folk: Popular Propaganda for the German Reformation* (Cambridge: Cambridge University Press, 1981). On the role of the Devil in eighteenth-century English crime literature, see Owen Davies, 'Talk of the Devil: Crime and Satanic Inspiration in Eighteenth-Century England', in http://herts.academia.edu/OwenDavies, 2007.

[68] Lake, 'Deeds against Nature', 268.
[69] Davies, 'Talk of the Devil', 2.
[70] Ibid.
[71] Lake, 'Deeds against Nature', 268–9.
[72] Ibid.

differences in how the Devil featured in such works. One obvious contrast is that while English broadsides often contained woodcut images of Satan, those in Scotland almost never did.[73] The lack of any visual depiction of Satan is consistent with the overall dearth of images produced in early modern Scotland and the Protestant de-emphasis of the physicality of the Devil in Scottish sermons and spiritual diaries. Scottish crime literature not only lacks the images but also the *imagery* found in English cheap print. Many English murder pamphlets contained extensive descriptions of the 'bizarre, bloody, and grotesque killings' that occurred across a wide range of social levels.[74] Scottish murder pamphlets, however, often glazed over the gory details in order to devote more space to discussions of the sinfulness of the criminal and, in the case of last words, to the anguished repentance of individuals facing death. In Scottish pamphlets, unlike those in England, the judgement of criminals was also overt and didactic. This was particularly true of last words, which seem to have been more popular in Scotland than the murder cases themselves.

Scottish and English crime literatures both reflect the influence of Protestantism in the early modern British world, though to differing degrees. Broadsides in both countries depicted a world polarized between the forces of divine goodness and demonic evil. On one side of this battle, at once earthly and cosmic, stood the potent combination of Satan and human sin. On the other were the forces of divine providence, grace and final justice, which would ultimately and always prevail.[75] Within this divided structure, there was little room left for positive human agency. According to Lake, English murder pamphlets and the providential view of the world they presented 'lent themselves to a Protestant reading and thus offered Protestant authors an opening or series of openings which they could use to bring the Protestant message to a wider audience'.[76] This was not an exclusively or even explicitly Calvinist agenda, as Lake points out, but could be readily co-opted by authors of the Puritan persuasion who desired to advance their ideals within a wider audience.

The extent to which Protestant ideas such as reprobation affected the average English reader is another issue. As Lake puts it, 'it was, in short, one thing to believe that somewhere there were desperate sinners so evil as to have been abandoned even by God himself; it was quite another to wake up at night wondering whether you were such a sinner'.[77] The extremity of the events in these pamphlets, he contends, allayed the possibility of

---

[73] For a discussion of images of Satan in English pamphlet literature, see Johnstone, *Devil and Demonism*, 145–7.
[74] Lake, 'Deeds against Nature', 259.
[75] Ibid., 277.
[76] Ibid.
[77] Ibid., 283.

personal internalization of Protestant messages.[78] That is, because the depicted events were so gruesome and dramatic, this prevented most people from seeing any of themselves in the murder stories. Yet despite the extra-ordinariness of the actual crimes committed, the offences that led up to the murder were completely commonplace. These popular sins included fornication, lust, drunkenness and Sabbath-breaking. The ordinariness of the deeds of the criminals – up until their ultimate and worst act – made these murder stories and their exhortations applicable to virtually everyone. As both Lake and Nathan Johnstone have pointed out, every man and woman was a sinner and susceptible to the demonically induced temptations that might ultimately lead to murderous acts. By discussing the most extreme consequences of a near-universal experience, 'the pulp press gave far wider transmission to the dominance of internal temptation in demonism'.[79]

The influence of Scottish print culture on the promotion and reception of Reformed Protestant ideas, with regard to the Devil or otherwise, has received less attention than its southern neighbour. This is largely due to the fact that historians of the Scottish Reformation do not have a comparable body of 'cheap print' from which to draw these conclusions. The actions of the local kirk sessions, along with the proliferation of oral, manuscript and printed sermons, were the most important mechanisms for reform in Scotland.[80] Moreover, the Scottish Reformation occurred over forty years after Luther and nearly thirty after the English crown officially severed ties with Rome. This late date means that Reformed Protestant ideas had been circulating in Scotland for a generation before the Reformation actually occurred. This lent new theological ideas, including those about Satan, a long gestation period. This, in conjunction with the localized actions of the kirk sessions, explains the relative success of the Scottish Reformation and suggests why there was not an immediate flood of broadsides attempting to convey the messages of Protestantism.

Despite the late date of Scottish cheap print, these works still have much to say about the Scottish public's reception of Protestant ideas about Satan, particularly the persistence of Reformed demonic belief and the relationship of this belief to Scottish culture and identity. In Scotland, the Reformed Protestant agenda seems to have been promoted more forcefully by broadsides than in England, which is unsurprising given the Reformed influence on the Scottish church and the community at large, even amid the theological debates of the late seventeenth and early eighteenth centuries.

---

[78] Ibid.
[79] Johnstone, *Devil and Demonism*, 143.
[80] For the best study of the role of the kirk sessions in spreading the Reformation, see Margo Todd, *The Culture of Protestantism in Early Modern Scotland* (New Haven, CT: Yale University Press, 2002).

Murder stories, last words and dying accounts collectively demonstrate the continued ways in which the Reformed concepts of temptation, sin and human frailty commingled with belief in the Devil. Noticeably absent in early eighteenth-century broadsides, however, were discussions of the relationship of Satan to the issue of predestination, which had been a key theme of seventeenth-century sermons and spiritual diaries. As suggested above, this move away from the orthodox Reformed preoccupation with double predestination coincided with the larger shifts in the Scottish church that had occurred during the later Stuart years.[81] Still, broadsides detailing murders and deaths display the remarkable continuity of formative elements of Reformed Protestantism in shaping demonic belief.

As in England, the ubiquity of temptation and sin allowed the ordinary Scottish reader to relate to the criminal while also being appalled by his or her actions. Johnstone has argued that because of this ordinariness of sins discussed in English murder stories, there was no concerted attempt to 'other' the murderers, who generally retained their humanity. To the extent that they were demonized, it was through the process of temptation, which according to Johnstone 'affected to bring ordinary people closer to the Devil'.[82] As a result, he contends

> ... demonisation actually discouraged the belief that intimate demonic experience was an aberration which clearly identified society's marginalized enemies. Every man and woman had experienced the same temptations that led some to murder and witchcraft; thus the gap that separated them from these 'incarnate devils' was very small.[83]

This process of highlighting the common sinfulness of all, from the occasional drunk to a violent murderer, also occurred in Scottish broadsides, exemplifying key ideas already promoted from the pulpit.

Johnstone also demonstrates that murder narratives 'highlighted the unseen demonic hold over the will' and presented English criminals as

---

[81] There are many works that deal with religious controversy in late seventeenth-century Scotland. To name a few: Alasdair Raffe, *Culture of Controversy*; Clare Jackson, *Restoration Scotland, 1660–1690: Royalist Politics, Religion, and Ideas* (Woodbridge: Boydell Press, 2003); David Mullan, *Episcopacy in Scotland and Scottish Puritanism, 1590–1638* (Oxford: Oxford University Press, 2000); John Morrill, ed., *The Scottish National Covenant in its British Context, 1638–51* (Edinburgh: Edinburgh University Press, 1991); David Stevenson, *The Covenanters* (Edinburgh: Edinburgh University Press, 1988); Tim Harris, *Restoration: Charles II and His Kingdoms, 1660–1685* (New York: Penguin, 2005); Elizabethanne Boran and Crawford Gribben, eds, *Enforcing Reformation in Ireland and Scotland, 1550–1700* (Aldershot: Ashgate, 2006).

[82] Johnstone, *The Devil and Demonism*, 174.

[83] Ibid., 143.

'merely mediating the devil's agency'.[84] This is a key point in which Scottish murder narratives differ, as they generally presented deviants who, though moved to act by demonic temptation, were responsible for allowing their own evil hearts to go unchecked.[85] Though these Scots could never totally repress their baser ways, they did have some agency in allowing Satan to move them to sin. This difference between the involvement of the Devil in English and Scottish crime literature, though subtle, indicates the greater emphasis in Scotland on the innate depravity of all people alongside the role of the Devil as a master manipulator of human nature.

Some historians have argued that the early modern period marked the swan song of Satan's dominance in Christian theodicy, as the Protestant emphasis on divine sovereignty and predestination effectively downgraded the Devil to a tool of God and little else. Euan Cameron has contended that, as the sowing of erroneous religious ideas became the Devil's main weapon, over time this caused Satan 'to gradually and imperceptibly slide into the area of metaphor and symbol'.[86] As the above chapters have demonstrated, however, the theoretical decline of Satan's physical prowess did not mitigate the profound and frightening reality of the Devil in the religious lives of Protestants in Scotland. As witchcraft records and the occasional spiritual diary reveal, the broader focus on an internal Devil did not negate the possibility that many Scots might see and experience Satan in corporeal form or experience bodily consequences of internal assaults. As Scottish crime stories attest, that the Reformed experience of Satan was primarily internal did not mitigate the genuine threat that the demonic posed for Scots of all sorts – both individually and communally – well into the eighteenth century.

Conclusion

Though one cannot know for certain how Scottish readers and hearers interpreted the role of the Devil found in these broadsides, there was clearly a profitable market for moralizing murder and dying accounts. The Scots who purchased such broadsides were probably more interested in the sensational tales of crime and punishment than in the sermonic musings about sin and Satan. Yet the fact that such ideas about the Devil found a

---

[84] Ibid., 149–50.
[85] Ibid., 150.
[86] Euan Cameron, *Enchanted Europe: Superstition, Reason and Religion, 1250–1750* (Oxford: Oxford University Press, 2010), 216. Jeffery Burton Russell has also argued that Protestantism marked the decline of the Devil's role in the Christian world. See Russell, *Mephistopheles: The Devil in the Modern World* (Ithaca, NY: Cornell University Press, 1986), esp. 66–76.

place in these broadsides – the very ideas refined by theological writings, communicated by sermons and articulated in self-writings – indicates the Reformed Devil had indeed become an assumed presence in the Scottish worldview. Furthermore, descriptions of the actual crimes or executions often took a backseat to discussions of the dangerous cooperation between Satan and human sin. Using the language of community and collective responsibility, these broadsides depicted the murderers, slaves to Satan, as the worst of Scottish society, but not as individuals whose demonic struggles were especially unique.

Scots of all sorts clearly believed they were living with the enemy, an enemy made all the more manifest in cheap print. Far from being an external, foreign other, the Devil shared more than spiritual and physical space with the Scottish people. He infiltrated their minds, tempted their hearts and helped to shape their identities by pointing out who they were not, while simultaneously warning them about the darker parts of who they were. The Devil who appeared in Scottish broadsides thus affirmed pre-existing Protestant conceptions of sin and human frailty. Stories of murder, executions and natural deaths also provided the Scottish public with something that theological works and sermons could not: concrete and immediate examples of the consequences of allowing Satan to run amok amongst the weak hearts of men and women.

Conclusion: Of Monsters and Men

From the Reformation through the seventeenth century, beliefs about Satan shaped Scottish culture and identity in numerous ways. Scots invoked the Devil's name from the pulpit, in print, on the street, in the courtroom and in their personal writings. Sermonic discussions of Satan conveyed the complex nuances of Reformed Protestant theology, such as divine sovereignty, double predestination and innate depravity, to audiences of ordinary Scottish men and women. The Devil existed as a potent experiential force for the godly who sought to understand themselves and their fates through demonic engagement, sometimes with dangerous consequences. The demonic components of witchcraft rendered the Devil a tangible concern for all sorts of Scots involved in the communal project of witch-hunting. The ubiquity of Satan, espoused from the pulpit and demonstrated by his role in the witchcraft trials, self-writings, crime literature and cases of interpersonal violence, rendered the Devil at once frightening and quotidian. Well into the eighteenth century, sermons and popular broadsides depicted to an interested public a Devil ever-active in his quest to tempt the godly and the unregenerate alike into sin.

Four main factors determined the nature and pervasiveness of Satan in early modern Scotland: the introduction, adoption and promotion of Reformed Protestantism during and long after the Scottish Reformation; a unique blend of theological continuity in the context of a fluid, flexible spectrum of demonic belief; the primacy of place given to Satan in Scottish sermons; and the influence of an introspective and anxiety-ridden process that I have termed 'internalizing the demonic'. This process – both a precipitant and a product of demonic belief in Scotland and throughout the Anglophone world – paired with Scotland's specific religious and political situation to render Satan a formative component of Scottish culture and society. The internalization of the demonic in the early modern British world demonstrates the power of religious belief, and specifically the belief in evil, to profoundly influence the ways in which people conceptualize themselves and the world around them.

What does this role of Satan in post-Reformation Scotland tell us about the larger place of the Devil in the early modern world? In a study of Protestantism, one must inevitably include a discussion of Max Weber's famous argument that the Protestant Reformation, particularly in its Calvinist guise, occasioned a 'disenchantment of the world' as science and modernity usurped supernatural beliefs of their authority.[1] The Weberian thesis has been adopted by a number of historians, most importantly Keith Thomas, who have emphasized the 'essential unity' of the Reformation and the Enlightenment and implied that Protestantism paved the way for a more modern society.[2]

In recent decades, this aspect of the Weber/Thomas thesis has been challenged and largely overturned, most convincingly by historians following in the footsteps of Robert Scribner who have discredited Protestantism of any sort of 'modernizing' or desacralizing influence.[3] Even historians who ascribe to a relatively modernizing view of the Reformation acknowledge that the 'evidence of continuing Protestant belief in a meaningful cosmos is copious and indisputable'.[4] Scholars studying the eighteenth and nineteenth centuries have also demonstrated in recent years the powerful persistence of beliefs in ghosts, angels, demons and the like in both Protestant and Catholic Europe.[5] Thanks to this elucidating scholarship, one can now confidently argue that Protestantism did not, at least in any immediate sense, remove the importance of the supernatural in the lives of both elite and ordinary early modern men and women. Whether or not the Reformation eventually or conclusively secularized society over the long haul is still a subject of considerable debate, as the arguments of and responses to Brad Gregory's most recent book have attested.[6]

---

[1] In Weber's *The Protestant Ethic and the Spirit of Capitalism*, first published in 1904–1905, he argued that the Reformation was part of a 'great historic process' which he later called 'the disenchantment of the world'. This argument has long been the subject of historical debates, which have been recently summarized in Alexandra Walsham's historiographical essay 'The Reformation and "The Disenchantment of the World" Reassessed', *Historical Journal* 51: 2 (2008): 497–528.

[2] Keith Thomas, *Religion and the Decline of Magic* (London: Weidenfeld & Nicolson, 1971).

[3] See Robert Scribner, 'The Reformation, Popular Magic, and the "Disenchantment of the World"', *Journal of Interdisciplinary History*, 23 (1993): 475–94. In this article, Scribner points out parallels to the supernaturalism of Catholicism found in Protestant culture and faith.

[4] Euan Cameron, *Enchanted Europe: Superstition, Reason and Religion, 1250–1750* (Oxford: Oxford University Press, 2010), 11.

[5] See, for example, Owen Davies, *Witchcraft, Magic and Culture, 1736–1951* (Manchester: Manchester University Press, 1999); Jane Shaw, *Miracles in Enlightenment England* (New Haven, CT: Yale University Press, 2006); Sasha Handley, *Visions of an Unseen World: Ghost Beliefs and Ghost Stories in Eighteenth-Century England* (London: Pickering & Chatto, 2007); Owen Davies and Willem de Blécourt, eds, *Beyond the Witch Trials: Witchcraft and Magic in Enlightenment Europe* (Manchester: Manchester University Press, 2004).

[6] Brad Gregory, *The Unintended Reformation: How a Religious Revolution Secularized Society* (Cambridge, MA: Harvard University Press, 2012). See the book review forum on Gregory's provocative book in *Church History* 81:4 (December 2012), 912–42. See also Alec Ryrie's review in 'Moderation, Modernity and the Reformation', *Past & Present* 223:1 (2014): 271–82.

While many of these issues lay beyond the scope of this book, the records of post-Reformation Scotland have provided ample opportunity to examine the ways in which Protestantism influenced the concept of Satan in theory and in experiential reality. Some historians looking at Europe more broadly have suggested that due to the Protestant obsession with the sovereignty and immutability of God, the Reformation usurped the Devil of independent agency. Satan, while retaining his innately evil nature, was downgraded to 'a helpless tool in the hands of the Almighty'.[7] Jeffery Burton Russell has accordingly seen the early modern period as the Devil's last stand, the final era when Satan dominated Christian theodicy.[8] Certainly Protestantism was, in many respects, the project of consolidating mystical, supernatural power into the Godhead alone. The emphasis on divine providence, while not an attempt to remove mysticism from the Christian world, made God the sole owner and dictator of all things mystical and enchanting. A dog on a divinely grasped leash, Satan lacked any agency or will of his own.

In many respects, Reformed Protestantism, with its emphasis on a remote, immutable God and the removal of intermediaries between humans and the deity, widened the gulf between the supernatural and natural realms. At the same time, however, innate human depravity emphasized the closeness of postlapsarian individuals to Satan. In turn, God's total control of Satan pushed him toward men and women, as the Devil increasingly operated as an earthly instrument of wrath and internal temptation. Ordinary Scots consistently invoked the Devil during interpersonal conflicts; Satan appeared in quotidian, often human, fashion in cases of witchcraft; the internalization of the demonic, in part, rendered actual demonic possession obsolete in Scotland through most of the early modern period. Though remaining a supernatural entity, Satan increasingly occupied the void between the human world and the cosmos. In Scotland, this presence was most profoundly felt and frequently confirmed by the self-identified or would-be godly, who expended great energy and angst searching their hearts and minds for signs of demonic intrusion and personal sin.

Though stripped of his previous ability to hinder salvation, Satan's constant presence in the human realm as an instrument of God made him an all-the-more evident and frightening force. The relegation of the Devil to the hands of the almighty meant that his sole function was as 'God's hangman', a vehicle for divine wrath. In this way, Satan came to represent something more terrible than pure, independent evil. Evidence of

---

[7] Cameron, *Enchanted Europe*, 16.
[8] Jeffery Burton Russell, *Mephistopheles: The Devil in the Modern World* (Ithaca, NY: Cornell University Press, 1986), 36.

demonic activities in the world meant that a wrathful, all-powerful God was enacting his just anger on a deserving world. In an era of apocalyptic fervour, augmented by the Reformation in both Catholic and Protestant Europe, this meant that the Day of Judgement was nigh. The need to purify the world, overcome Satan, and avoid the apocalyptic rage of God was more urgent than ever before.

Regarding the notion of Protestantism as a desacralizing force, Jeffery Burton Russell has also argued that early modern Europe witnessed 'a profound shift in the center of gravity of perceptions of evil, from the world of spirits to the world of man'.[9] While his interpretation is marred by a linear teleology and lack of contextualization, he here puts his finger on one of the most important effects of Reformed theology. The doctrine of double predestination effectively wrested from Satan the ability to hinder salvation, and to many Protestants, struggles against the Devil no longer affected the fate of individuals. While the godly should find comfort in the promise of eventual victory, they, like the Devil, could do nothing to guarantee salvation. Their energies, therefore, ought to be applied exclusively and exhaustively to challenges of their present lives. The once-cosmic battle between Good and Evil was thus relocated to the human realm, as warring with Satan became inherent in godly life while on earth.

Dying rituals provide perhaps the most evident manifestation of this Reformed Protestant emphasis on battling Satan in the here-and-now. Reformed worship removed the graveside rituals, songs and prayers that characterized Catholic deaths and burials. The focus became preparation for the despair and demonic assaults that inevitably followed the godly through their lives and onto their deathbeds.[10] As Philip Benedict has noted, these changes to graveside ceremony were

> ... among the most radical of all breaks with pre-Reformation religious practice, for it meant an end to the economy of prayer for remembered relatives and spiritual kin and to the community between the living and the dead that were among the most prominent features of the late medieval spiritual landscape.[11]

---

[9] Ibid., 25.

[10] On death and dying in post-Reformation Europe, see Peter Marshall, *Beliefs and the Dead in Reformation England* (Oxford: Oxford University Press, 2002); Bruce Gordon and Peter Marshall, eds, *The Place of the Dead: Death and Remembrance in Early Modern Europe* (Cambridge: Cambridge University Press, 2000); Keith Luria, 'Separated by Death? Burials, Cemeteries, and Confessional Boundaries in Seventeenth Century France', *French Historical Studies* 24 (2001):185–222.

[11] Benedict, *Christ's Church Purely Reformed: A Social History of Calvinism* (New Haven, CT: Yale University Press, 2002), 506.

Under the doctrine of predestination, prayers for the already dead had little merit or utility. They might commemorate the deceased or comfort the living, but the souls of the dead went immediately to their preordained, eternal home.[12] Satan and sin, however, remained adversaries until the very last breath. Combating demonically induced doubt and despair thus became the most important deathbed ritual.

This relocation of the demonic battleground to the terrestrial realm does not mean that the early modern period ought to be viewed as some sort of cosmic halfway-house on the way to the Enlightenment and the disenchantment of the world. This interpretation is often misguided by hindsight and risks neglecting the persistence of belief in the supernatural long after the climax of the Enlightenment came and went. Yet the contention that, after the Reformation, evil was increasingly attributed to humanity contains a good deal of truth and insight. Certainly Satan retained supernatural status, and early modern men and women continued to view him as a powerful non-human entity. But it does seem, at least in the case of post-Reformation Scotland, that Reformed Protestantism, in theology and in practice, eroded the once-rigid divide between the supernatural evil of Satan and the natural evil of humankind. As evidenced by the process of internalizing the demonic, the two were wedded in Reformed theology and experience. Evil in the world did not shift seamlessly from the world of spirits to the world of man. Rather, Protestants in Scotland increasingly attributed evil to the internal cooperation and coexistence of Satan and the sinful human heart.

For Reformed Protestant Scots, then, the battle against Satan was not taking place in the cosmos, with God and the Devil vying for human souls. The war between the forces of Good and Evil, between God and Satan, raged on as it always had. But more than ever, this war was an earthly one, and the vulnerable human heart provided a fertile battleground. It is quite possible that this rhetorical and experiential focus on the demonic struggle that occurred in the heart paved the way for the evangelical, emotional brand of Scottish piety that took root in the late seventeenth and early eighteenth centuries and greatly influenced American religious revivalism.[13] It may also be worth considering the extent to which the Scottish Enlightenment, with its vigorous attempt to understand human nature, was in part a reaction to the fact that Reformed Protestantism had thrust the spotlight onto the activities of Satan in the human heart and mind. Whatever the after-effects of this demonic belief may have been, the influence of Satan in early modern Scotland can hardly be overstated.

---

[12] On this point, see Marshall, *Beliefs and the Dead*, esp. 66–92.
[13] See Leigh Eric Schmidt, *Holy Fairs: Scottish Communions and American Revivals in the Early Modern Period* (Princeton, NJ: Princeton University Press, 1989).

The belief in a ubiquitous, earthly Devil, one who infiltrated and even resided in the hearts of men and women, indelibly shaped how Scots of all sorts perceived their communities and themselves.

Bibliography

Manuscript Sources

National Records of Scotland, Edinburgh

CH2/3/1	Aberdour (Fife) Kirk Session Minutes, 1649–1682.
CH2/11/1	Alves North Kirk Session Minutes, 1649–1700.
CH2/15/1	Presbytery of Arbroath Minutes, 1659–1689.
CH2/20/1	Auchterader Kirk Session Minutes, 1675–1712.
CH2/21/5	Auchterderran Sermon Notes.
CH2/23/1	Auchterhouse Kirk Session Minutes, 1656–1677.
CH2/24/1	Auchtermuchty Kirk Session Minutes, 1649–1658.
CH2/40/1	Presbytery of Brechin Minutes, 1639–1661.
CH2/56/2	Carluke Kirk Session Minutes and Accounts, 1694–1703.
CH2/62/1	Carrington Kirk Session Minutes, 1653–1683.
CH2/77/1–2	Culross Abbey Kirk Session Minutes, 1630–1646, 1646–1657.
CH2/84/2	Dalkeith Kirk Session Minutes and Accounts, 1653–1667.
CH2/96/1–2	Duffus Kirk Session Minutes, 1631–48, 1648–1690.
CH2/97/1	Dumbarton Kirk Session Minutes, 1667–1691.
CH2/100/2	Dunbarney Kirk Session, 1655–1682.
CH2/101/1	Dunblane (Cathedral) Kirk Session, 1652–1688.
CH2/121/1	Presbytery of Edinburgh Minutes, 1586–1593.
CH2/124/1	Corstophine Kirk Session Minutes, 1646–1685.
CH2/133/1	Old Kirk Session Minutes, 1655–1659.
CH2/141/1–3	Trinity College (Edinburgh) Kirk Session Minutes, 1626–1666.
CH2/145/4	St Giles Kirk Session (Elgin) Minutes, 1622–29.
CH2/150/1	Ferryport-on-Craig (Tayport) Kirk Session Minutes, 1640–1674.
CH2/168/1–2	Trinity Gask Kirk Session Minutes, 1643–1661, 1669–1679.
CH2/210/1–2	Kilconquhar Kirk Session Minutes, 1637–1653, 1653–66.
CH2/225/1	Kirkcaldy (Abbotshall) Kirk Session, 1650–1660.

CH2/229/1	Kirkliston Kirk Session Minutes, 1659–1687.
CH2/237/1	Lenzie Easter Kirk Session Minutes, 1666–1688.
CH2/276/1–2, 4	Newbattle Kirk Session Minutes, 1616–1628, 1643–1649, 1653–1673.
CH2/277/1	Newburgh Kirk Session Minutes, 1652–1697.
CH2/278/1	Newburn Kirk Session Minutes, 1628–1687.
CH2/293/1	Oyne Kirk Session Minutes, 1663–1688.
CH2/315/8	Rutherglen Old Kirk Session Minutes, 1658–1688.
CH2/326/11	Scoonie (Leven) Kirk Session Minutes, 1666–1687.
CH2/377/1	Yester Kirk Session Minutes, 1613–1643.
CH2/383/1	Liberton (Edinburgh) Kirk Session Minutes, 1639–1671.
CH2/400/1	Falkirk Kirk Session Minutes, 1617–1640.
CH2/406/1	Kinglassie Kirk Session Minutes, 1648–1774.
CH2/418/1	Kinnaird Kirk Session Minutes, 1633–1683.
CH2/636/34	Kirkcaldy, Old, (St. Bryce) Kirk Session Minutes, 1614–1645.
CH2/722/6	Stirling Presbytery Records, 1654–1661.
CH2/1020/1	Aberdeen (Old Machar) Kirk Session Minutes, 1621–1639.
CH2/1142/1	Fraserburgh Kirk Session Minutes, 1612–1623.
CH2/1173/1	Kelso, Old, Kirk Session Minutes, 1622–1647.
CH12/18/6	Diary of John Forbes of Corse (1593–1648), 1624–1647.
CH12/20/9	Religious diary, 1679–1692.
CH12/20/11	Poems and hymns from the early eighteenth century.
GD1/395/6	Notes on Andrew Ramsay sermons, 1614–1642.
GD 18/20/93	Sir John Clerk's 'personal covenantings with the Lord' and renewals thereof, 1692–1708.
GD237/21/64	Part of an unnamed Scottish woman's spiritual diary, 1633.
GD248/616/9	Confession of James Gordon, late seventeenth or early eighteenth century.
JC 2/1	Justiciary Court, Books of Adjournal.
JC 26/2, 24–27	Justiciary Court Processes.
JC 3/12/115–174	Indictment papers for Margaret Dickson.

National Library of Scotland, Edinburgh

Adv. MS 5.2.6 1693	Anonymous sermon, 'The champlain's vade mecum: or the art of prayer and devotion', given at King James's College (University of Edinburgh) in 1693.

BIBLIOGRAPHY

Adv. MS 17.2.3	Part of a journal, possibly of minister Thomas Forrester, 1673–1678.
Adv. MS 31.1.1–1a	Extracts from the Records belonging to the Church at Perth.
Adv. MS 34.6.22	Marion Veitch, 'An account of the Lord's gracious dealing with me and of his remarkable hearing and answering my supplications', c. 1670–1680s.
Adv. MS. 34.6.30	Hugh Cameron, 'Remarks on Providences and the Lords dealings with me in my tender years, and progressively carried on since', 1746–1763.
MS 905	Extracts from trials of witches in Orkney and Shetland.
MS 1945	Transcription of the Records of the High Court of Justiciary, 1585–1723.
MS 2206	Sermon preached by Mr James Webster In the Tolbooth Church of Edinburgh, February 1700.
MS 2824	Commonplace book, mostly poems, 1692.
MS 3008	Commonplace book, letters and notes on sermons, early eighteenth century.
MS 3045	'Diary of James Murray, c. 1698'.
MS 3150	Diary of Sir George Maxwell of Pollock, 1655–1656.
MS 5769	Seventeenth-century sermons, c. 1655.
MS 5770	Collection of seventeenth-century sermons.
MS 8187	Anonymous seventeenth-century theology book
MS 8483	Collection of unpublished sermons by Hugh Anderson of Udol, Presbyterian minister of Cromarty, late seventeenth century.
Wod. Fol. XXVIII	Circuit Court Procognition, 1699.
Wod. Fol. XLVIII	Sermons, 1638–1643.
Wod. Oct. XXXI	Part of the diary of Sir John Chiesly, 1667; Personal Covenant of Marion Stewart. Edinburgh, 10 March 1716.
Wod. Qu. XVII	James Guthrie, 'The Waters of Sihor', 1653.
Wod. Qu. XXIV	Sermon, 1639.
Wod. Qu. XXVIII	'An account of the exercise of a Christian', 1698: a letter explaining how to deal with obsessive blasphemous thoughts.
Wod. Qu. XXXVI	Two letters from John Gilry, 1683; letter from James Corsan to his wife, 1679.
Wod. Qu. XXXVII	'Ane account of some sufferings in the parish of Carnwarth', 1677–1688.
Wod. Qu. LXVII	John Livingstone, 'The gold and growth of the New Testament saints and service', 1661.

Wod.Qu. LXXV	Accounts of covenanting preachers and martyrs from a letter from David Walker to Robert Wodrow, May 1716.
Wod. Qu. LXXXII	Thomas Locke, 'To the parents of the children of Eastwood', c. 1706.
Wod. Qu. LXXXIII	Extracts of the records of the kirk session of Ayr.
Wod. Qu. XCIX	Conversion account, 1628, by Arthur Myrton, minister of Crail; Dying Testimony of John King, field preacher, 12 August 1679.
Wod. Th. MSS. 5	Notebook of Professor James Wodrow, 1673–1691.

Folger Shakespeare Library, Washington, DC

MS V.a.415	Anonymous sermon notebook, seventeenth century, Bothwell.

Printed Primary Sources

Abbot, George. *An exposition upon the prophet Jonah Contained in certaine sermons, preached in S. Maries church in Oxford*. London, 1600.

An Account of a Horrid and Bloody Murder. Edinburgh, 1720.

An Account of the Most Remarkable Trials and Executions which took place in Scotland for above 300 years. Glasgow, 1826.

Analecta Scotica. Collections Illustrative of the Civil, Ecclesiastical, and Literary History of Scotland. ed. James Maidment. Thomas Stevenson: Edinburgh, 1837.

Ancient Criminal Trials in Scotland, 3 vols, ed. Robert Pitcairn. Edinburgh: Printed for the Maitland Club, 1833.

The Annals of Banff, 2 vols, ed. William Cramond. Aberdeen: The New Spalding Club, 1893.

Anon. *The sacrifice of a Christian soule conteining godlie prayers, and holy meditations for sundry purposes; drawne out of the pure fountaines of the sacred Scriptures*. Edinburgh, 1591.

Anon. *Two prayers to be taught unto children at school*. Edinburgh, 1672.

Aquinas, St Thomas. *The De Malo of Thomas Aquinas*, trans. Richard Regan, ed. Brian Davies. Oxford: Oxford University Press, 2001.

———. *Summa Theologica*, 61 vols, ed. David Bourke. Cambridge: Cambridge University Press, 2006.

Augustine of Hippo. 'A Treatise on the Predestination of the Saints', in *A Select Library of the Nicene and Post-Nicene Fathers of the Christian Church*, ed. Philip Schaff. Grand Rapids, MI: William B. Eerdmans, 1886–1890.

Baillie, Robert. *Satan the Leader in chief to all who resist the reparation of sion*. London, 1643.

———. *The Letters and Journals of Robert Baillie, 1637–1662*, 3 vols, ed. David Laing. Edinburgh: The Bannatine Club, 1841.

Bayly, Lewis. *Practice of Piety, Directing the Christian how to walk that he may please God*. London, 1611.

Becon, Thomas. *The Workes of Thomas Becon*. London, 1564.

Beza, Theodore. *Christian Meditations upon Eight Psalmes of the Prophet David*. London, 1583.

———. *Maister Bezaes houshold prayers translated out of French into English*. London, 1603.

———. *Propositions and principles of diuinitie*. Edinburgh, 1591.

Blackadder, Elizabeth. 'A Short Account of the Lord's Way of Providence towards me in my Pilgrimage Journeys', in Mullan, ed., *Women's Life Writing*, 384–409.

Blair, Robert. *The Life of Mr. Robert Blair*, ed. Thomas M'Crie. Edinburgh: Wodrow Society, 1848.

Birrell, Robert. 'The Diary of Robert Birrel', in J.G. Daylell, ed. *Fragments of Scottish History*. Edinburgh: A. Constable, 1798.

Boyd, Zachary. *The balme of Gilead prepared for the sicke*. Glasgow, 1629.

Broadside concerning a man who became possessed by an evil spirit. Glasgow, c.1810–1830.

Brodie, Alexander. *The Diary of Alexander Brodie of Brodie, and of his Son, James Brodie*. Aberdeen: Spalding Club, 1863.

Brown, John. *An apologeticall relation of the particular sufferings of the faithfull ministers & professours of the Church of Scotland*. Edinburgh, 1665.

———. *Christ in believers the hope of glory being the substance of several sermons*. Edinburgh, 1694.

———. *From Christ in believers the hope of glory being the substance of several sermons*. Edinburgh, 1694.

Bruce, Michael. *Soul-Confirmation*. Edinburgh, 1709.

———. *The Rattling of Dry Bones*. Edinburgh, 1672.

Bruce, Robert. *Sermons*, ed. William Cunninghan. Edinburgh: Wodrow Society, 1843.

Bunyan, John. *Grace abounding to the chief of sinners: or, A brief and faithful relation of the exceeding mercy of God in Christ*. London, 1666.

Cadwell, James. *The Countesse of Marres Arcadia, or Sanctuarie*. Edinburgh, 1625.

Calvin, John. *Calvin's commentary on the epistle of James*. Aberdeen: J. Chalmers and Co., 1797.

———. *The catechisme or maner to teache children the Christiane religion*. Edinburgh, 1578.

———. *Commentaries on the Epistle of Paul the Apostle to the Philippians, Colossians, and Thessalonians*, trans. John Pringle. Grand Rapids, MI: Eerdmans, 1948.

———. *Commentaries on the Epistle of Paul the Apostle to the Romans* (1539), trans. Revd John Owen. Edinburgh: Calvin Translation Society, 1849.

———. *Commentaries on the Last Four Books of Moses, Arranged in the Form of a Harmony*, 4 vols, trans. and ed. C.W. Bingham. Edinburgh: Calvin Translation Society, 1950.

———. *Commentary on Psalms*, trans. Revd James Anderson. Edinburgh: Calvin Translation Society, 1849.

———. *A harmonie vpon the the three Euangelists, Matthew, Mark and Luke*. London, 1584.

———. *The Institutes of the Christian Religion*, 2 vols, ed. J.T. McNeill. Philadelphia, PA: Westminster John Knox Press, 1960.

———. *Letters*, 4 vols, ed. David Constable. Edinburgh: Thomas Constable and Co., 1855.

Capel, Richard. *Tentations: their nature, danger, and care*. London, 1633.

Carmichael, James. *Newes from Scotland*. London, 1592.

Chambers, Robert. *Domestic Annals of Scotland: From the Revolution to Rebellion*, Vol. 3. Edinburgh, 1824.

Church of Scotland. *The National Covenant of the Kirk of Scotland and the Solemn League and Covenant of the three kingdoms*. Edinburgh, 1660.

———. *Statutes of the Scottish Church 1225–1559*, ed. David Patrick. Edinburgh: Scottish History Society, 1907.

Clerk, James. Covenant of Sir. James Clerk of Penicuik; 'An Account of the Particular Soliloquies and Covenant Engagements, past betwixt Mrs. Janet Hamilton, the defunct Lady of Alexander Gordon of Earlstoun', in Tweedie, ed., *Select Biographies*, i.495–508.

Cochrane, Arthur C., ed. *Reformed Confessions of the Sixteenth Century*. Philadelphia, PA: Westminster Press, 1966.

Collace, Katharine. 'Memoirs or Spiritual Exercises of Mistress Ross', in Mullan, ed. *Women's Life Writing*, 39–94.

Cotton, John. *An exposition upon the thirteenth chapter of the Revelation*. London, 1656.

Craig, John. *A shorte summe of the whole catechisme, wherein the question is proponed and answered in few wordes, for the greater ease of the commoune people and children*. Edinburgh, 1581.

Dick, Quinton. 'A Brief Account,' in David Mullan, ed. *Protestant Piety in Early Modern Scotland: Letters, Lives and Covenants, 1650–1712*, 167–96. Edinburgh: Scottish History Society, 2008.

Dickson, Margaret. *Margaret Dickson's Penetential Confession.* Edinburgh, 1728.

Downame, John. *The Christian Warfare.* London, 1634.

Dreghorn, John Maclaurin, ed. *Arguments and decisions, in remarkable cases: before the High Court of Justiciary, and other supreme courts, in Scotland.* Edinburgh: J. Bell, 1774.

Duncan, Henry. 'The most memorable passages of the life of Mr. Henrie Duncan, late minister of the gospel at Dunsyre, c. 1710', in Mullan, ed,. *Protestant Piety in Early Modern Scotland*, 213–80.

Durham, James. *The great corruption of subtile self, discovered, and driven from it's lurking-places and starting-holes.* Edinburgh, 1686.

Elegy. Edinburgh, 1723.

Elegy: On the deplorable Death of Margaret Hall. Edinburgh, 1721.

Erskine, Ebenezer. *The Life and Diary of the Reverend Ebenezer Erskine*, ed. Donald Fraser. Edinburgh: W. Oliphant, 1831.

A Faithful Narrative of The Circumstances of the Cruelty committed upon the Body of John Halden. Edinburgh, 1721.

Fergusson, David. *Ane answer to ane epistle written by Renat Benedict the Frenche doctor.* Edinburgh, 1563.

Fraser, James. 'Memoirs of James Fraser of Brea', in Tweedie, ed., *Select Biographies.*

A Full and True Account of A Most Horrid, Barbarous, and Bloody Murther Committed by Owen Brady. Dublin and Edinburgh, 1717.

Mistress Goodall, 'Memoir', in Tweedie, ed. *Select Biographies.*

Goodwin, Thomas. *Childe of Light Walking in Darknes: Or a Treatise Shewing the Causes, by which the Cases, wherein the Ends, for which God Leaves his Children to Distresse of Conscience.* London, 1636.

Gordon, William. 'Personal Covenant of William Gordon', in Mullan, ed., *Protestant Piety in Early Modern Scotland*, 76–7.

Gray, Andrew. *Directions and instigations to the duty of prayer how, and why the heart is to be kept with diligence.* Edinburgh, 1669.

———. *Great precious promises.* Edinburgh, 1667.

Hammond, Charles. *God's Eye from Heaven.* Edinburgh, 1671.

Hay, Andrew. *The Diary of Andrew Hay of Craignethan*, ed. Alexander George Reid. Edinburgh: Scottish History Society, 1901.

Henderson, Alexander. *Sermons, prayers and pulpit addresses of Alexander Henderson*, ed. Thomas R. Martin. Edinburgh: John Maclaren, 1867.

Hume, Alexander. *Ane treatise of conscience Quhairin divers secreits concerning that subiect, are discovered, as may appeare, in the table following.* Edinburgh, 1594.

James VI and I. *Daemonologie.* Edinburgh, 1597.

———. *The essayes of a prentise, in the diuine art of poesie.* Edinburgh, 1584.

———. *The fathers blessing: or, counsaile to his sonne*. London, 1624.

———. *Ane fruitfull meditatioun contening ane plane and facill expositioun of ye 7.8.9 and 10 versis of the 20 chap. of the Reuelatioun in forme of ane sermon*. Edinburgh, 1588.

———. *Ane meditatioun vpon the xxv, xxvi, xxvii, xxviii, and xxix verses of the XV chapt. of the first buke of the Chronicles of the Kingis*. Edinburgh, 1589.

Johnston, Archibald. 'Diary', in Mullan, ed., *Protestant Piety in Early Modern Scotland*, 31–46.

The Justiciary Records of Argyll and The Isles 1664–1705, ed. John Cameron. Edinburgh: Printed for the Stair Society, 1949.

Kerr, James, ed. *The Covenants and The Covenanters: Covenants, Sermons, and Documents of the Covenanted Reformation*. Edinburgh: R.W. Hunter, 1895.

Knox, John. *An admonition or vvarning that the faithful Christia[n]s in London, Newcastel Barwycke [and] others, may auoide Gods vengeau[n]ce bothe in thys life and in the life to come*. London, 1554.

———. *An answer to a great number of blasphemous cauillations written by an Anabaptist, and aduersarie to Gods eternal predestination*. Edinburgh, 1560.

———. *A fort for the afflicted VVherin are ministred many notable & excellent remedies against the stormes of tribulation*. London, 1580.

———. *A sermon preached by Iohn Knox minister of Christ Iesus in the publique audience of the Church of Edenbrough*. Edinburgh, 1566.

———. *Works*, 6 vols, ed. David Laing. Edinburgh: Wodrow Society, 1846–1864.

Kramer, Heinrich. *The Malleus Maleficarum*, ed. P.G. Maxwell-Stuart. Manchester: Manchester University Press, 2007.

The Last Confession of Mr. Robert Irvine. Edinburgh 1717.

The Last Speech and Confession of Jannet Riddle. Edinburgh, 1702.

The Last Speech and Dying Words of Janet Hutchie. Edinburgh, 1721.

The Last Speech and Dying words of John Treplecock. Edinburgh, 1723.

The Last Speech and Dying Words of John Webster Gardiner at Greenhill. Edinburgh, 1722

The Last Speeches of the Two Ministers Mr. John King, and Mr. John Kid. Edinburgh, 1680.

Lawson, Deodat. *A Brief and True Narrative of Some Remarkable Passages Relating to Sundry Persons Afflicted by Witchcraft, at Salem Village*. Boston, MA, 1692.

———. *Christ's Fidelity the Only Shield Against Satan's Malignity*. London, 1714.

Lindsay, Henrietta. 'Her Diary', in Mullan, ed. *Women's Life Writing*, 204–353.

Luther, Martin. *On the Bondage of the Human Will* (1525), eds J.I. Packer and O.R. Johnson. Old Tappan, NJ: Revell, 1957.
Mather, Cotton. *Memorable Providences Relating to Witchcrafts and Possessions*. Boston, MA, 1689; Edinburgh, 1697.
———. *The Wonders of the Invisible World*. Boston, MA, 1693.
Melville, James. *The Autobiography and Diary of Mr. James Melville*, ed. Robert Pitcairn. Edinburgh: Wodrow Society, 1842.
———. *Ane fruitful and comfortable exhortatioun anent death*. Edinburgh, 1597.
———. *Memoirs of Sir James Melvil of Hal-hill*. London, 1683.
———. *Spirituall propine of a pastour to his people*. Edinburgh, 1598.
Mildmay, Grace. 'Lady Mildmay's Meditations', in L.A. Pollock, ed., *With Faith and Physic: The Life of a Tudor Gentlewoman*. London: Collins & Brown, 1993.
Miscellany of the Spalding Club, 5 vols, ed. John Stuart. Aberdeen: The Spalding Club, 1841–1852.
Mossat, James. *Life and Memoirs of James Mossat*. Edinburgh, 1819.
Nimmo, James. *The Narrative of Mr. James Nimmo: Written for his own Satisfaction to Keep in some rememberance the lords way dealing and kindness towards him, 1654–1709*, ed. W.G. Scott Moncrieff. Edinburgh: Scottish History Society, 1889.
Norwood, Richard. *The Journal of Richard Norwood Surveyor of Bermuda*, eds W.F. Craven and W.B. Hayward. New York: Scholars' Facsimiles & Reprints, 1945.
Parliament of Scotland. *Charles I. Parl. 3. Sess. An Act of the Parliament of the Kingdom of Scotland, approving and establishing the Directory for Publick Worship*. Edinburgh, 1645.
Particulars of the Life, Trial, Character, and Behaviour of Margaret Dickson. Derby, 1813.
Penny, George. *Traditions of Perth*. Perth, 1836.
Perkins, William. *A Case of Conscience, the greatest that euer was; how a man may know whether he be the child of God or no*. London, 1592.
———. *A Discourse of the Damned Art of Witchcraft*. London, 1608.
———. *The Foundation of Christian Religion Gathered Into Six Principles*. London, 1641.
———. *A Golden Chaine or Description of Theologie*. Edinburgh, 1592.
Pethane, Alexander. *The Lord's Trumpet sounding an Alarm Against Scotland*. Edinburgh, 1682.
Porteus, Archibald. *The Spiritual Exercise of Soul and Blessed Departure of Dame Mary Rutherford Lady Hundaly, and Mary M'Konnel*. Edinburgh, 1745.
The records of Elgin 1234–1800, ed. William Cramond. Aberdeen: New Spalding Club, 1908.

Records and Files of the Quarterly Courts of Essex County, Massachusetts, 8 vols, ed. George Francis Dow. Salem, MA.: Essex Institute, 1911–1921.

The Records of the Kirk of Scotland, ed. Alexander Peterkin. Edinburgh: P. Brown, 1838.

Records of the Privy Council of Scotland, 1630–32, 2nd series, 4 vols, eds D. Masson and P. Hume Brown. Edinburgh, 1899–1906.

Registers of the Presbytery of Lanark, 1623–1719, ed. John Robertson. Edinburgh: Abbotsford Club, 1839.

Register of the Privy Council of Scotland, 1569–1578, Series 1, Vol. 2, eds J.H. Burton and David Masson. Edinburgh: H.M. General Register House, 1878.

Register of the Privy Council of Scotland, 1638–1643, Series 2, Vol. 7, ed, P. Hume Brown. Edinburgh: H.M. General Register House, 1906.

Renwick, James. *Christ Our Righteousness*. Glasgow, 1776.

Robert Johnston's Ghost OR, His last ADVICE to the Gipsies, and other Gangs of Robbers and Murderers in Scotland. Edinburgh, 1720.

Row, John. *History of the Kirk of Scotland*. Edinburgh: Wodrow Society, 1842.

Rothesay Parish Records: The Session Book of Rothesay 1658–1750, ed. and trans. Henry Paton. Edinburgh: Bute Scottish Record Series, 1931.

Rutherford, Mistress. 'Mistress Rutherford's Conversion Narrative', in David Mullan, ed., *Miscellany xiii*, 146–88. Edinburgh: Scottish History Society, 2004.

Rutherford, Samuel. *Christ Dying and Drawing Sinners to Himself*. Edinburgh, 1842.

———. *Fourteen Communion Sermons*, ed. Andrew Bonnar. Glasgow, 1877.

———. *Joshua Reivivus, or Mr. Rutherford's Letters*, ed. Robert McWard. Edinburgh, 1664.

———. *The Trial and Triumph of Faith*. Edinburgh, 1645.

St Andrews Kirk Session Register 1559–1600, ed. David H. Fleming. Edinburgh: Scottish History Society, 1889.

The Scots Confession, 1560, ed. G.D. Henderson. Edinburgh, 1937.

Sempill, Robert. *Deploration of the cruell murther of James Earle of Moray*. Edinburgh, 1570.

Shepard, Thomas. *The Autobiography of Thomas Shepard*. Boston, MA: Pierce and Parker, 1832.

Sibbes, Richard. *The Saints Safetie in Evill Times*. London, 1643.

Stevenson, John. 'A Rare Soul-Strengthening and Comforting Cordial for Old and Young Christians: Being the last advice of John Stevenson, in the shire of Ayr, to his children and grandchildren', in Tweedie, ed. *Select Biographies*.

Thompson, William. *The Churches Comfort, or a Sermon on John XVI*. Edinburgh, 1661.
A True Copy of a Letter Tent by the Lady Boghall to her Son Nicol Mushet. Prisoner within the Tolbooth of Edinburgh, for the Murder of his own Wife. Edinburgh, 1720.
A True and distinct Account Of the Murder of James Campbel of Lawers. Edinburgh, c.1723.
A True Narrative of the Sufferings and Relief of a Young Girle. Edinburgh, 1698.
Tweedie, W.K., ed. *Select Biographies*, 2 vols. Edinburgh: Wodrow Society, 1841.
A Warning to the Wicked, or, Margaret Dickson's Welcome to the Gibbet. Edinburgh, 1724.
Welsh, John. *Forty-Eight Select Sermons*. Edinburgh, 1744.
Welwood, John. 'Letters, 1675–77', in Mullan, ed., *Protestant Piety in Early Modern Scotland*, 78–139.
West, Elizabeth. *Memoirs, or Spiritual Exercises of Elisabeth West*. Edinburgh, 1724.
The Whole Trial, Confession and Sentence, OF Mr. Robert Irvine. Edinburgh, 1717.
Woodward, Daniel. *An Almanac but for one Day, or the Son of Man reckoning with Man*. Glasgow, 1671.

Select Secondary Sources

Aldis, Harry Gildney. *List of Books Published in Scotland before 1700: Including those Printed furth of the Realm for Scottish Booksellers*. Edinburgh: National Library of Scotland, 1970.
Anglo, Sydney, ed. *The Damned Art: Essays in the Literature of Witchcraft*. London: Routledge and Kegan Paul, 1977.
———. 'Evident Authority and Authoritative Evidence: The Malleus Maleficarum', in idem, ed., *The Damned Art*, 1–31.
Ankarloo, Bengt and Gustav Henningsen, eds. *Early Modern European Witchcraft: Centres and Peripheries*. Oxford: Clarendon Press, 1990.
Bailey, Michael David. *Battling Demons: Witchcraft, Heresy, and Reform in the Late Middle Ages*. University Park, PA: Penn State University Press, 2003.
Bannerman, John. 'Literacy in the Highlands', in Ian B. Cowan and Duncan Shaw, eds, *The Renaissance and Reformation in Scotland: Essays in Honour of Gordon Donaldson*, 214–35. Edinburgh: Scottish Academic Press, 1983.

Bargett, Frank D. *Scotland Reformed: The Reformation in Angus and the Mearns*. Edinburgh: John Donald Publishers, 1989.
Barry, Jonathan. *Witchcraft and Demonology in South-West England, 1640–1689*. Basingstoke: Palgrave Macmillan, 2012.
——— and Owen Davies. *Palgrave Advances in Witchcraft Historiography*. Basingstroke: Palgrave MacMillan, 2007.
Bauckham, Richard. *Tudor Apocalypse: Sixteenth-Century Apocalyptism, Millenarianism and the English Reformation*. Oxford: Oxford University Press, 1978.
Benedict, Philip. *Christ's Church Purely Reformed: A Social History of Calvinism*. New Haven, CT: Yale University Press, 2002.
———. *The Faith and Fortunes of France's Huguenot, 1600–85*. Aldershot: Ashgate, 2001.
Bever, Edward. 'Witchcraft Persecutions and the Decline of Magic', *Journal of Interdisciplinary History* 40 (2009): 263–93.
Blench, J.W. *Preaching in England in the Late Fifteenth and Sixteenth Centuries: a Study of English Sermons 1450–1600*. Oxford: Oxford University Press, 1964.
Boran, Elizabethanne and Crawfod Gribben, eds. *Enforcing Reformation in Ireland and Scotland, 1550–1700*. Aldershot: Ashgate, 2006.
Botanaki, Elizabeth. 'Seventeenth-Century English Women's Spiritual Diaries: Self-Examination, Covenanting, and Account-Keeping', *Sixteenth Century Journal* 30 (1999): 3–21.
Bouswma, William. *John Calvin: A Sixteenth Century Portrait*. New York: Oxford University Press, 1988.
Boyer, Paul and Stephen Nissenbaum. *Salem Possessed: The Social Origins of Witchcraft*. Cambridge, MA: Harvard University Press, 1974.
Briggs, Robin. *Witches and Neighbours: The Social and Cultural Context of European Witchcraft*. London: Harper-Collins, 1996.
Brock, Michelle. 'Internalizing the Demonic: Satan and the Self in Early Modern Scottish Piety', *Journal of British Studies* 54:1 (2015): 23–43.
Broedel, Hans Peter. *The Malleus Maleficarum and the Construction of Witchcraft*. Manchester: Manchester University Press, 2003.
Brown, Yvonne Galloway and Rona Ferguson, eds. *Twisted Sisters: Women, Crime and Deviance in Scotland since 1400*. Edinburgh: Tuckwell, 2002.
Burrell, Sidney. 'The Apocalyptic Vision of the Early Covenanters', *Scottish Historical Review*, 43 (1964): 1–24.
Cabantous, Alain. *Blasphemy: Impious Speech in the West from the Seventeenth to the Nineteenth century*, trans. Eric Rauth. New York: Columbia University Press, 2002.
Cameron, Euan. *Enchanted Europe: Superstition, Reason and Religion, 1250–1750*. Oxford: Oxford University Press, 2010.

———. 'Frankfort and Geneva: The European Context of John Knox's Reformation', in Roger A. Mason, ed., *John Knox and the British Reformations*, 51–73. Aldershot: Ashgate, 1998.

Cañizares-Esguerra, Jorge. *Puritan Conquistadors: Iberianizing the Atlantic, 1550–1700*. Stanford, CA: Stanford University Press, 2006.

Capp, Bernard. 'The Political Dimension of Apocalyptic Thought', in Patrides and Wittreich, eds, *The Apocalypse in English Renaissance Thought and Literature*.

Cervantes, Fernando. *The Devil in the New World: The Impact of Diabolism in New Spain*. New Haven, CT: Yale University Press, 1994.

Christianson, Paul. *Reformers and Babylon: English Apocalyptic Visions from the Reformation to the Eve of the Civil War*. Toronto: University of Toronto Press, 1978.

Clark, Stuart. 'Inversion, Misrule, and the Meaning of Witchcraft', *Past and Present*, 87 (1980): 98–127.

———. 'King James's Daemonologie: Witchcraft and Kingship', in Anglo, ed., *The Damned Art*, 156–81.

———. 'Protestant Demonology: Sin, Superstition and Society', in Ankarloo and Henningsen, eds, *Early Modern European Witchcraft*, 45–82.

———. *Thinking with Demons: The Idea of Witchcraft in Early Modern Europe*. Oxford: Oxford University Press, 1997.

———. *Vanities of the Eye: Vision in Early Modern European Culture*. Oxford: Oxford University Press, 2007.

Clouse, Robert. 'John Napier and Apocalyptic Thought', *Sixteenth Century Journal* 1 (1974): 101–14.

Coffey, John. 'The Impact of Apocalypticism during the Puritan Revolutions', *Perichoresis* 4 (2006): 117–47.

———. 'The Problem of "Scottish Puritanism", 1590–1638', in Boran and Gribben, eds, *Enforcing Reformation in Ireland and Scotland, 1550–1700*, 66–90.

Cohen, Charles L. *God's Caress: The Psychology of Puritan Religious Experience*. New York: Oxford University Press, 1986.

Cohn, Norman. *Europe's Inner Demons: The Demonization of Christians in Medieval Christendom*. Chicago, IL: University of Chicago Press, 1975.

Collinson, Patrick. 'A Comment: Concerning the Name Puritan', *Journal of Ecclesiastical History* 31 (1980): 483–8.

Cowan, Edward J. 'Witch Persecution and Popular Belief in Lowland Scotland: the Devil's Decade', in Goodare, Martin and Miller, eds, *Witchcraft and Belief in Early Modern Scotland*, 71–94.

Cowan, Edward J. and Lizanne Henderson. *Scottish Fairy Belief: A History*. East Linton: Tuckwell, 2001.

Cowan, Ian. *The Scottish Reformation: Church and Society in Sixteenth Century Scotland*. New York: St. Martin's Press, 1982.

Cressy, David. *Dangerous Talk: Scandalous, Seditious, and Treasonable Speech in Pre-Modern England*. Oxford: Oxford University Press, 2010.
Davies, Owen. 'Talk of the Devil: Crime and Satanic Inspiration in Eighteenth-Century England', in http://herts.academia.edu/OwenDavies, 2007.
——. *Witchcraft, Magic and Culture, 1736–1951*. Manchester: Manchester University Press, 1999.
—— and Willem de Blécourt, eds. *Beyond the Witch Trials: Witchcraft and Magic in Enlightenment Europe*. Manchester: Manchester University Press, 2004.
Davies, Stephen J. 'The Courts and the Scottish Legal System 1600–1747: The Case of Stirlingshire', in V.A.C. Gatrell, Bruce Lenman and Geoffrey Parker, eds, *Crime and the Law: the Social History of Crime in Western Europe since 1500*, 120–54. London: Europa Publications Ltd, 1980.
Davis, Natalie Zemon. *Fiction in the Archives: Pardon Tales and Their Tellers in Sixteenth Century France*. Cambridge: Cambridge University Press, 1987.
Dawson, Jane. 'Calvinism and the Gaidhealtachd in Scotland', in Andrew Pettegree, Alastair Duke and Gillian Lewis, eds, *Calvinism in Europe, 1540–1620*, 231–53. Cambridge: Cambridge University Press, 1994.
——. *John Knox*. New Haven, CT: Yale University Press, 2015.
——. *Scotland Re-formed, 1488–1587*. Edinburgh: Edinburgh University Press, 2007.
——. 'Trumpeting Resistance: Christopher Goodman and John Knox', in Roger A. Mason, ed., *John Knox and the British Reformations*. Aldershot: Ashgate, 1998.
Demers, Patricia. *Women's Writing in English: Early Modern England*. Toronto: University of Toronto Press, 2005.
Demos, John. *Entertaining Satan: Witchcraft and the Culture of Early New England*. Oxford: Oxford University Press, 1982.
DesBrisay, Gordon. 'Twisted by Definition: Women under Godly Discipline in Seventeenth Century Scottish Towns', in Brown and Ferguson, eds, *Twisted Sisters*, 137–55.
Desgraves, Louis. *Repertoire bibliographique des livres imprimes en France au XVIIe siècle*. Baden-Baden: V. Koerner, 1978.
Dixon, Leif. *Practical Predestinarians in England, c. 1590–1640*. Farnham: Ashgate, 2014.
Dolan, Frances E. *Dangerous Familiars: Representations of Domestic Crime in England, 1550–1700*. Ithaca, NY: Cornell University Press, 1994.
Donaldson, Gordon. *The Faith of the Scots*. London: Batsford, 1990.

———. *Scottish Church History*. Edinburgh: Scottish Academic Press, 1985.
Drake, Samuel G. *Annals of Witchcraft in New England*. New York, 1869.
Drinnon, David. 'The Apocalyptic Tradition in Scotland', PhD Thesis, University of St Andrews, 2013.
Dye, Sierra. 'To Converse with the Devil? Speech, Sexuality, and Witchcraft in Early Modern Scotland', *International Review of Scottish Studies* 37 (2012): 9–40.
Dunlap, Rhodes. 'King James and Some Witches: the Date and Text of the Daemonologie', *Philological Quarterly* 54 (1975): 40–46.
Durston, Gregory. *Witchcraft and Witch Trials: a History of English Witchcraft and its Legal Perspectives, 1542 to 1736*. Chichester: Barry Rose Law Publishing, 2000.
Edington, Carol. 'John Knox and the Castillians: A Crucible of Reforming Opinon?', in Mason, ed., *John Knox and the British Reformations*, 29–50.
Ewan, Elizabeth. 'Disorderly Damsels? Women and Interpersonal Violence in Pre-Reformation Scotland', *Scottish Historical Review* 228 (2010): 153–71.
———. '"Many Injurious Words": Gender and Defamation in Late Medieval Scotland', in R.A. MacDonald, ed., *History, Literature and Music in Scotland, 700–1560*, 163–86. Toronto: University of Toronto Press, 2002.
Farr, James. *Authority and Sexuality in Early Modern Burgundy, 1550–1730*. Oxford: Oxford University Press, 1995.
Firth, Katharine R. *The Apocalyptic Tradition in Reformation Britain, 1530–1645*. Oxford: Oxford University Press, 1979.
Fischlin, Daniel. '"Counterfeiting God": James VI (I) and the Politics of Daemonologie (1597)', *Journal of Narrative Technique* 26 (1996): 1–29.
Ford, James Thomas. 'Preaching in the Reformed Tradition', in Taylor, ed., *Preachers and People in the Reformations and Early Modern Europe*, 65–88.
Foster, Walter Roland. 'A Constant Platt Achieved: Provision for the Ministry, 1600–1638', in Shaw, ed., *Reformation and Revolution*.
———. *The Church before the Covenants: The Church of Scotland 1596–1638*. Edinburgh: Scottish Academic Press, 1975.
Gaskill, Malcolm. *Crime and Mentalities in Early Modern England*. Cambridge: Cambridge University Press, 2000.
———. 'The Pursuit of Reality: Recent Research into the History of Witchcraft', *Historical Journal* 51 (2008): 1069–88.
———. *Witchfinders: A Seventeenth-Century English Tragedy*. London: John Murray, 2005.

Godbeer, Richard. *The Devil's Dominion: Magic and Religion in Early New England*. Cambridge: Cambridge University Press, 1992.
Goodare, Julian. 'The Aberdeenshire witchcraft panic of 1597', *Northern Scotland* 21 (2001): 1–21.
———. 'Boundaries of the Fairy Realm in Scotland', in Karin E. Olsen and Jan R. Veenstra, eds, *Airy Nothings: Imagining the Otherworld of Faerie from the Middle Ages to the Age of Reason*, 139–70. Leiden, Netherlands: Brill, 2014.
———. 'The Cult of the Seely Wights in Scotland', *Folklore*, 123 (2): 198–219.
———. 'John Knox on Demonology and Witchcraft', *Archive for Reformation History*, 96 (2005): 221–45.
———. 'Review of Margo Todd's *Culture of Protestantism in Early Modern Scotland*', *Albion* 36 (2004): 376.
———. 'The Scottish Witchcraft Act', *Church History* 74 (2005): 39–67.
———,. ed. *The Scottish Witch-Hunt in Context*. Manchester: Manchester University Press, 2002.
———,. ed. *Scottish Witches and Witch-Hunters*. Basingstoke: Palgrave, 2013.
———. 'Women and the Witch Hunt in Scotland', *Social History* 23 (1998): 31–57.
Goodare, Julian, Lauren Martin and Joyce Miller, eds. *Witchcraft and Belief in Early Modern Scotland*. Basingstoke: Palgrave MacMillan, 2008.
——— and Louise Yeoman, eds. 'The Survey of Scottish Witchcraft, 1563–1763', http://www.arts.ed.ac.uk/witches/.
Gordon, Bruce. *Calvin*. New Haven, CT: Yale University Press, 2009.
———. 'Preaching and Reform of the Clergy in the Swiss Reformation', in Andrew Pettegree, ed., *The Reformation of the Parishes*. Manchester, Manchester University Press, 1993.
——— and Peter Marshall, eds. *The Place of the Dead: Death and Remembrance in Early Modern Europe*. Cambridge: Cambridge University Press, 2000.
Gowing, Laura. *Domestic Dangers: Women, Words and Sex in Early Modern London*. Oxford: Clarendon Press, 1996.
Graham, Michael F. *The Blasphemies of Thomas Aikenhead: Boundaries of Belief on the Eve of the Enlightenment*. Edinburgh: Edinburgh University Press, 2008.
———. 'The Civil Sword and the Scottish Kirk, 1560–1600', in Graham, ed., *Later Calvinism: International Perspectives*, 237–66.
———, ed. *Later Calvinism: International Perspectives*. Kirksville, MO: Sixteenth Century Journal Publishers, 1994.
———. 'Social Discipline in Scotland, 1560–1610', in Mentzer, ed., *Sin and the Calvinists*, 129–57.

———. 'Women and the Church Courts in Reformation-Era Scotland', in Elizabeth Ewan and Maureen Meikle, eds, *Women in Scotland, 1100–1700*, 187–98. East Linton: Tuckwell, 1999.

———. *The Uses of Reform: 'Godly Discipline' and Population Behavior in Scotland and Beyond, 1560–1610*. Leiden, Netherlands: E.J. Brill, 1996.

Greaves, Richard L. 'The Puritan-Nonconformist Tradition in England: Historiographical Reflections', *Albion* 17 (1985): 449–86.

———. *Theology and Revolution in the Scottish Reformation: Studies in the Thought of John Knox*. Grand Rapids, MI: Christian University Press, 1980.

Gregory, Annabel. 'Witchcraft, Politics and "Good Neighborhood" in Early Seventeenth Century Rye', *Past and Present* 133 (1991): 31–66.

Haigh, Christopher. 'Slander and the Church Courts in the Sixteenth Century', *Transactions of the Lancashire and Cheshire Antiquarian Society* 78 (1975): 1–13.

Hall, David D. *The Faithful Shepherd; A History of the New England Ministry in the Seventeenth Century*. Chapel Hill: University of North Carolina Press, 1972.

Handley, Sasha. *Visions of an Unseen world: Ghost Beliefs and Ghost Stories in Eighteenth-Century England*. London: Pickering & Chatto, 2007.

Harris, Bob. 'Communicating', in Foyster, Elizabeth and Christopher A. Whatley, eds, *A History of Everyday Life in Scotland, 1600–1800*. Edinburgh: Edinburgh University Press, 2010.

Harris, Tim. *Restoration: Charles II and his Kingdoms, 1660–1685*. Harmondsworth: Penguin, 2005.

Harrison, John G. 'Women and the Branks in Stirling, c. 1600–c.1730', *Scottish Economic and Social History* 18 (1998): 114–31.

Haykin, M. and M. Jones, eds. *Drawn into Controversie: Reformed Theological Diversity and Debates within Seventeenth-Century British Puritanism*. Göttingen: Vandenhoeck and Ruprecht, 2011.

Hazlett, W. Ian P. 'The Scots Confession 1560: Context, Complexion and Critique', *Archiv für Reformationsgeschichte (Archive for Reformation History)* 78 (1987): 287–320.

Helm, Paul. *John Calvin's Ideas*. Oxford: Oxford University Press, 2005.

Henderson, Lizanne, ed. *Fantastical Imaginations: the Supernatural in Scottish History and Culture*. Edinburgh: John Donald Publishers, Ltd, 2009.

——— and Edward J. Cowan. *Scottish Fairy Belief: A History*. East Linton: Tuckwell, 2001.

Hoffer, Paul. *The Salem Witchcraft Trials: A Legal History*. Lawrence: University of Kansas Press, 1997.

Hoffer, Peter. *The Devil's Disciples: The Makers of the Salem Witchcraft Trials*. Baltimore, MD: Johns Hopkins Press, 1996.

Holwerda, David. 'Eschatology and History: A Look at Calvin's Eschatological Vision', in idem, ed., *Exploring the Heritage of John Calvin*, 110–39. Grand Rapids, MI: Baker Academic, 1976.
Houston, Robert A. *Literacy in Early Modern Europe: Culture and Education, 1500–1800*. New York: Longman, 1988.
———. 'The Literacy Myth?: Illiteracy in Scotland, 1630–1760', *Past and Present* 96 (1982): 81–102.
———. *Punishing the Dead: Suicide, Lordship, and Community in Britain, 1500–1800*. Oxford: Oxford University Press, 2010.
———. *Scottish Literacy and the Scottish Identity: Literacy and Society in Scotland and England, 1660–1850*. Cambridge: Cambridge University Press, 1989.
Hunt, William. *The Puritan Moment: The Coming of Revolution in an English County*. Cambridge, MA: Harvard University Press, 1983.
Ingram, Martin. *Church Courts, Sex, and Marriage in England, 1570–1640*. Cambridge: Cambridge University Press, 1987.
Jackson, Clare. *Restoration Scotland, 1660–1690: Royalist Politics, Religion, and Ideas*. Woodbridge: Boydell Press, 2003.
Jensen, Peter. 'Calvin and Witchcraft', *Reformed Theological Review* 34 (1975): 76–86.
Johnstone, Nathan. *The Devil and Demonism in Early Modern England*. Cambridge: Cambridge University Press, 2006.
———. 'The Protestant Devil: The Experience of Temptation in Early Modern England', *Journal of British Studies* 43 (2004): 173–205.
Kamensky, Jane. *Governing the Tongue: The Politics of Speech in Early New England*. Oxford: Oxford University Press, 1999.
Karlsen, Carol F. *The Devil in the Shape of a Woman: Witchcraft in Colonial New England*. New York: W.W. Norton and Co., 1987.
Kellar, Claire. *Scotland, England, and the Reformation, 1534–1561*. Oxford: Oxford Historical Monograph Series, 2004.
Kilday, Anne-Marie. *Women and Violent Crime in Enlightenment Scotland*. Woodbridge: Boydell & Brewer, 2007.
Kirk, James, ed. *The Church in the Highlands*. Edinburgh: Scottish Church History Society, 1998.
———. 'Jacobean Church in the Highlands, 1567–1625', in Inverness Field Club, ed., *The Seventeenth Century in the Highlands*. Inverness: Inverness Field Club, 1986.
———. *Patterns of Reform: Continuity and Change In The Reformation*. Edinburgh: T. & T. Clark, 1989.
———. 'The Scottish Reformation and the Reign of James VI: A Select Critical Biography', *Records of the Scottish Church History Society (RSCHS)*, 23 (1987).

Klaits, Joseph. *Servants of Satan: The Age of the Witch Hunts*. Bloomington: Indiana University Press, 1985.
Kyle, Richard. 'The Divine Attributes in John Knox's Concept of God', *Westminster Theological Journal* 48 (1986): 161–72.
———. 'John Knox and Apocalyptic Thought', *Sixteenth Century Journal* 15:4 (1984): 449–70.
———. 'John Knox's Concept of Divine Providence and its Influence on his Thought', *Albion* 18 (1986): 395–410.
———. *The Mind of John Knox*. Lawrence, KS: Coronado Press, 1984.
Lake, Peter. 'Deeds Against Nature: Cheap Print, Protestantism and Murder in Early Seventeenth Century England', in Kevin Sharpe and Peter Lake, eds, *Culture and Politics in Early Stuart England*. Stanford, CA: Stanford University Press, 1993.
Lamont, Stuart. *The Swordbearer: John Knox and the European Reformation*. London: Hodder and Stoughton, 1991.
Larner, Christina. *Enemies of God: The Witch-Hunt in Scotland*. Baltimore, MD.: Johns Hopkins University Press, 1981.
———. *Witchcraft and Religion: the Politics of Popular Belief*. Oxford: Oxford University Press, 1984.
Leneman, Leah and Rosalind Mitchison. *Sexuality and Social Control: Scotland 1660–1780*. Oxford: Blackwell, 1989.
———. *Sin in the City: Sexuality and Social Control in Urban Scotland, 1160–1780*. Edinburgh: Scottish Cultural Press, 1998.
Lesnick, Daniel R. *Preaching in Medieval Florence: the Social World of Franciscan and Dominican Spirituality*. Athens: University of Georgia Press, 1989.
Levack, Brian. 'Demonic Possession in Early Modern Scotland', in Goodare, Martin and Miller, eds, *Witchcraft and Belief in Early Modern Scotland*, 166–84.
———. *The Devil Within: Demonic Possession in Early Modern Europe*. New Haven, CT: Yale University Press, 2013.
———. 'The Great Scottish Witch Hunt of 1661–1662', *Journal of British Studies* 20 (1980): 90–108.
———. 'Judicial Torture in Scotland during the Age of Mackenzie', in *Miscellany IV*, 185–98. Edinburgh: Stair Society, 2002.
———. *The Witchcraft Sourcebook*. New York: Routledge, 2004.
———. *The Witch-Hunt in Early Modern Europe*, 3rd edn. London: Longman, 2006.
———. *Witch-Hunting in Scotland: Law, Politics and Religion*. New York: Routledge, 2008.
Loetz, Francisca. *Dealings with God: From Blasphemers in Early Modern Zurich to a Cultural History of Religiousness*. Farnham: Ashgate, 2009.

Luria, Keith. 'Separated by Death? Burials, Cemeteries, and Confessional Boundaries in Seventeenth Century France', *French Historical Studies* 24 (2001):185–222.

Luttmer, Frank. 'Persecutors, Tempters and Vassals of the Devil: The Unregenerate in Puritan Practical Divinity', *Journal of Ecclesiastical History* 51 (2000): 37–68.

Lynch, Michael. 'Calvinism in Scotland, 1559–1638', in Prestwich, ed., *International Calvinism, 1541–1715*, 225–56.

———. 'Preaching to the Converted?', in Alan MacDonald, Michael Lynch and Ian Cowan, eds, *The Renaissance in Scotland: Studies in Literature, Religion, History, and Culture*, 307–14. Leiden, Netherlands: Brill, 1994.

MacDonald, Alan. *The Jacobean Kirk 1567–1625: Sovereignty, Polity, and Liturgy*. Aldershot: Ashgate, 1998.

———. 'Welsh, John (1568/9–1622)', *Oxford Dictionary of National Biography*. Oxford: Oxford University Press, 2004.

MacDonald, Fiona A. *Mission to the Gaels: Reformation and Counter-Reformation in Ulster and the Highlands and Islands of Scotland 1560–1760*. Edinburgh: Scottish Cultural Press, 2006.

Macdonald, Michael and Terence Murphy, *Sleepless Souls: Suicide in Early Modern England*. Oxford: Oxford University Press, 1990.

MacDonald, Stuart. 'In Search of the Devil in Fife', in Goodare, ed., *The Scottish Witch-hunt in Context*, 33–50.

———. *The Witches of Fife: Witch-Hunting in a Scottish Shire, 1560–1710*. East Linton: Tuckwell, 2002.

Macfarlane, Alan. 'The Root of All Evil', in Parkin, David, ed., *The Anthropology of Evil*. London: Blackwell, 1985.

———. *Witchcraft in Tudor and Stuart England*. London: Routledge & Kegan Paul, 1970.

Macinnes, Allan. 'Catholic Recusancy and the Penal Laws, 1603–1707', *Records of the Scottish Church History Society (RSCHS)* 24 (1992): 27–63.

Maggi, Armando. *Satan's Rhetoric: A Study of Renaissance Demonology*. Chicago, IL: University of Chicago Press, 2001.

Mann, Alasdair J. 'The Anatomy of the Printed Book in Early Modern Scotland', *Scottish Historical Review* 80 (2001): 181–200.

Marshall, Joseph and Sean Kelsey, 'Weldon, Sir Anthony (*bap*. 1583, *d*. 1648)', *Oxford Dictionary of National Biography*, Oxford: Oxford University Press, 2004; online edn, 2008.

Marshall, Peter. *Beliefs and the Dead in Reformation England*. Oxford: Oxford University Press, 2002.

Martin, Lauren. 'The Devil and the Domestic: Witchcraft, Quarrels and Women's Work in Scotland', in Goodare, ed., *The Scottish Witch-hunt in Context*, 73–89.

———. 'Witchcraft and Family: What can Witchcraft Documents tell us about Early Modern Scottish Family Life?', *Scottish Tradition* 27 (2002).

Marcus, Leah. *Childhood and Cultural Despair: A Theme and Variations in Seventeenth-Century Literature*. Pittsburgh, PA: University of Pittsburgh Press, 1978.

Marshall, Peter. *Beliefs and the Dead in Reformation England*. Oxford: Oxford University Press, 2002.

Mason, Roger A., ed. *John Knox and the British Reformations*. Aldershot: Ashgate 1998.

———. 'Usable Pasts: History and Identity in Reformation Scotland', *Scottish Historical Review* 201 (1997): 54–68.

Matthews, William. 'Seventeenth-Century Autobiography', in William Matthews and Ralph W. Rader, eds, *Autobiography, Biography, and the Novel*. Los Angeles, CA: William Andrews Clark Memorial Library, 1973.

McCallum, John. *Reforming the Scottish Parish: The Reformation in Fife, 1560–1640*. Aldershot: Ashgate, 2010.

McElroy, Tricia A. 'Imagining the "Scottis Natioun": Populism and Propaganda in Scottish Satirical Broadsides', *Texas Studies in Literature and Language* 47 (2007): 319–39.

McGrath, Alister. *A Life of John Calvin: A Study in the Shaping of Western Culture*. Chicago, IL: Blackwell, 1990.

McKim, Donald K, ed. *Cambridge Companion to John Calvin*. Cambridge: Cambridge University Press, 2004.

McLachlan, Hugh V, ed. *The Kirk, Satan and Salem: A History of the Witches of Renfrewshire*. Glasgow: Grimsay Press, 2006.

McNeill, John T. *The History and Character of Calvinism*. New York: Oxford University Press, 1954.

Mentzer, Raymond, ed. *Sin and the Calvinists: Morals Control and the Consistory in the Reformed Tradition*. Kirksville, MO: Truman State University Press, 1994.

Midelfort, Erik. 'The Devil on the German People: Reflections on the Popularity of Demonic Possession in Sixteenth-century Germany', in Susan Ozment, ed., *Religion and Culture in the Reformation*. Kirksville, MO: Sixteenth Century Journal Publishers, 1989.

Miller, Joyce. 'Men in Black: Appearances of the Devil in Early Modern Scottish Witchcraft Discourse', in Goodare, Martin and Miller, eds, *Witchcraft and Belief in Early Modern Scotland*, 144–65.

Moore, R.I. *The Formation of a Persecuting Society*. New York: Blackwell, 1987.

Morrill, John, ed. *The Scottish National Covenant in its British Context, 1638–51*. Edinburgh: Edinburgh University Press, 1990.

Morrissey, Mary. 'Interdisciplinarity and the Study of Early Modern Sermons', *Historical Journal* 42 (1999): 1111–23.
Muessig, Carolyn. *Preacher, Sermon and Audience in the Middle Ages*. Leiden, Netherlands: Brill, 2001.
Mullan, David. *Episcopacy in Scotland and Scottish Puritanism, 1590–1638*. Oxford: Oxford University Press, 2000.
———. 'A Hotter Sort of Protestantism? Comparisons between French and Scottish Calvinisms', *Sixteenth Century Journal* 39 (2008): 45–69.
———. *Narratives of the Religious Self in Early-Modern Scotland*. Farnham: Ashgate, 2010.
———, ed. *Protestant Piety in Early Modern Scotland: Letters, Lives and Covenants, 1650–1712*. Edinburgh: Scottish History Society, 2008.
———, ed. *Religious Controversy in Scotland, 1625–1639*. Edinburgh: Lothian Print for the Scottish Historical Society, 1998.
———. *Scottish Puritanism, 1590–1638*. Oxford: Oxford University Press, 2000.
———. 'Theology in the Church of Scotland, 1618–1640: a Calvinist consensus?', *Sixteenth Century Journal*, 26 (1995), 595–617.
———, ed. *Women's Life Writing in Early Modern Scotland: Writing the Evangelical Self, c. 1670–1730*. Aldershot: Ashgate, 2003.
Muller, Richard A. *After Calvin: Studies in the Development of a Theological Tradition*. Oxford: Oxford University Press, 2003.
———. *Calvin and the Reformed Tradition: On the Work of Christ and the Order of Salvation*. Grand Rapids, MI: Baker Academic, 2012.
———. *Christ and the Decree: Christology and Predestination in Reformed Theology from Calvin to Perkins*. Grand Rapids, MI: Baker Academic, 1988.
———. 'John Calvin and Later Calvinism', in David V.N. Bagchi and David Curtis Steinmetz, eds, *The Cambridge Companion to Reformation Theology*, 130–49. Cambridge: Cambridge University Press, 2004.
Nash, David. *Blasphemy in the Christian World: a History*. Oxford: Oxford University Press, 2007.
Normand, Lawrence and Gareth Roberts. *Witchcraft in Early Modern Scotland: James VI's Demonology and the North Berwick Witches*. Exeter: University of Exeter Press, 2000.
Norton, Mary Beth. *In the Devil's Snare: The Salem Witchcraft Crisis of 1692*. New York: Knopf, 2002.
Oldridge, Darren. *The Devil in Early Modern England*. Stroud: Sutton, 2000.
O'Malley, John W. *Religious Culture in the Sixteenth Century: Preaching, Rhetoric, Spirituality, and Reform*. Aldershot: Ashgate, 1993.
Pagels, Elaine. *The Origin of Satan*. London: Allen Lane, 1996.

Patrides, C.A. and J. Wittreich, eds. *The Apocalypse in English Renaissance Thought and Literature: Patterns, Antecedents and Repercussions*. Manchester: Manchester University Press, 1984.

Pearl, Jonathan. *The Crime of Crimes: Demonology and Politics in France, 1560–1620*. Waterloo, Ontario: Wilfrid Laurier University Press, 1999.

Pocock, J.G.A. 'British History: A Plea for a New Subject', *Journal of Modern History* 47:4 (December, 1975): 601–21.

Prestwich, Menna, ed. *International Calvinism, 1541–1715*. Oxford: Clarendon Press, 1985.

Raffe, Alasdair. *The Culture of Controversy: Religious Arguments in Scotland, 1660–1714*. Woodbridge: Boydell Press, 2012.

———. 'Presbyterians and Episcopalians: the Formation of Confessional Cultures in Scotland, 1660–1715', *English Historical Review*, CXXV(514).

Reid, W. Stanford. 'Reformation in France and Scotland: A Case Study in Sixteenth Century Communication', in Graham, ed., *Later Calvinism: International Perspectives*, 195–214.

———. *Trumpeter of God: A Biography of John Knox*. Grand Rapids, MI: Baker Academic, 1974.

Reis, Elizabeth. *Damned Women: Sinners and Witches in Puritan New England*. Ithaca, NY: Cornell University Press, 1997.

Roach, Andrew P. *The Devil's World: Heresy and Society 1100–1300*. Harlow: Pearson, 2005.

Rosen-Zvi, Ishay. *Demonic Desires: 'Yetzer Hara' and the Problem of Evil in Late Antiquity*. Philadelphia: University of Pennsylvania Press, 2011.

Ross, Christina J. 'Scottish Demonology in the Sixteenth and Seventeenth Centuries and Its Theological Background', PhD Thesis, University of Edinburgh, 1962.

Rushton, Peter. 'Women, Witchcraft, and Slander in Seventeenth-century England', *Northern History*, 18 (1982): 116–32.

Russell, Jeffrey B. *Lucifer: The Devil in the Middle Ages*. Ithaca, NY: Cornell University Press, 1984.

———. *Mephistopheles: The Devil in the Modern World*. Ithaca, NY: Cornell University Press, 1986.

———. *The Prince of Darkness: Evil and the Power of Good of History*. Ithaca, NY: Cornell University Press, 1988.

Ryrie, Alec. *The Origins of the Scottish Reformation*. Manchester: Manchester University Press, 2006.

———. *Being Protestant in Reformation Britain*. Oxford: Oxford University Press, 2013.

———. 'Moderation, Modernity and the Reformation', *Past & Present*, 223:1 (2014): 271–82.

St. George, Robert. '"Heated" Speech and Literacy in Seventeenth-Century New England', in David D. Hall and David Grayson Allen, eds, *Seventeenth Century New England*, 275–322. Boston: The Colonial Society of Massachusetts, Boston, 1984.

Sanderson, Margaret H.B. *Ayrshire and the Reformation: People and Change 1490–1600*. East Lothian: Tuckwell Press, 1997.

———. 'Catholic Recusancy in Scotland in the Sixteenth Century', *The Innes Review* 21 (1970): 87–107.

Schmidt, Jeremy. *Melancholy and Care of the Soul: Religion, Moral Philosophy and Madness in Early Modern England*. Aldershot: Ashgate, 2007.

Schmidt, Leigh Eric. *Holy Fairs: Scottish Communions and American Revivals in the Early Modern Period*. Princeton, NJ: Princeton University Press, 1989.

Seaver, Paul. *Wallington's World: A Puritan Artisan in Seventeenth-Century London*. Stanford, CA: Stanford University Press, 1985.

Shagan, E. 'Beyond Good and Evil: Thinking with Moderates in Early Modern England', *Journal of British Studies* 49 (2010): 488–513.

Sharpe, James. *Crime in Early Modern England 1550–1750*. London: Longman, 1984.

———. *Defamation and Sexual Slander in Early Modern England: The Church Courts at York*. York: Bothwick Papers no. 58, 1980.

———. *Instruments of Darkness: Witchcraft in Early Modern England*. Philadelphia: University of Pennsylvania Press, 1997.

Shaw, Duncan, ed. *Reformation and Revolution*. Edinburgh: St Andrews Press, 1967.

Shaw, Jane. *Miracles in Enlightenment England*. New Haven, CT: Yale University Press, 2006.

Smith, Lesley M. 'Sackcloth for the Sinner or Punishment for the Crime: Church and Secular Courts in Cromwellian Scotland', in John Dwyer, Roger Mason and Alexander Murdoch, eds, *New Perspectives on the Politics and Culture of Early Modern Scotland*, 116–32. Edinburgh: John Donald Publishers, Ltd, 1982.

Spencer, H. Leith. *English Preaching in the Late Middle Ages*. Oxford: Oxford University Press, 1993.

Spufford, Margaret. 'First Steps in Literacy: the Reading and Writing Experiences of the Humblest Seventeenth-Century Autobiographers', *Social History* 4 (1979): 407–35.

Stachniewski, John. *The Persecutory Imagination: English Puritanism and the Literature of Religious Despair*. Oxford: Clarendon Press, 1991.

Stauffer, Richard. 'Calvinism in Geneva in the time of Calvin and of Beza', in Prestwich, ed., *International Calvinism, 1541–1715*.

Stephens, Walter. *Demon Lovers. Witchcraft, Sex, and the Crisis of Belief*. Chicago, IL: University of Chicago Press, 2003.
Stevenson, David. *The Covenanters*. Edinburgh: Edinburgh University Press, 1988.
Stevenson, Robert Louis and Fanny De Grift Stevenson. *More New Arabian Nights: The Dynamiter*. New York: Henry Holt and Company, 1885.
Stout, Harry S. *The New England Soul: Preaching and Religious Culture in Colonial New England*. Oxford: Oxford University Press, 1986.
Taylor, Larissa, ed. *Preachers and People in the Reformations and Early Modern Europe*. Leiden, Netherlands: Brill, 2001.
———. *Soldiers of Christ : Preaching in Late Medieval and Reformation France*. Oxford: Oxford University Press, 1992.
Teall, John L. 'Witchcraft and Calvinism in Elizabethan England: Divine Power and Human Agency', *Journal of the History of Ideas* 23 (1962): 21–36.
Thomas, Keith. *Religion and the Decline of Magic*. New York: Scribner, 1971.
Thurston, Robert W. *Witch, Wicce, Mother Goose: The Rise and Fall of the Witch Hunts in Europe and North America*. London: Longman, 2001.
Tipson, Baird. 'The Routinized Piety of Thomas Shepard's Diary', *Early American Literature* 13 (1978): 4–80.
Tipson, Lynn B. Jr. 'The Development of a Puritan Understanding of Conversion', PhD Dissertation, Yale University, 1972.
Todd, Margo. *The Culture of Protestantism in Early Modern Scotland*. New Haven, CT: Yale University Press, 2002.
———. 'Puritan Self-Fashioning: The Diary of Samuel Ward', *Journal of British Studies* 31:3 (1992).
Toon, P. *Puritans, the Millennium and the Future of Israel: Puritan Eschatology 1600–1660*. Cambridge: Cambridge University Press, 1970.
Walsham, Alexandra. 'Invisible Helpers: Angelic Intervention in Post-Reformation England', *Past and Present* 208 (2010): 77–130.
———. 'The Reformation and "The Disenchantment of the World" Reassessed', *Historical Journal* 51:2 (2008): 497–528.
———. *The Reformation of the Landscape: Religion, Identity and Memory in Early Modern Britain and Ireland*. Oxford: Oxford University Press, 2011.
Wandel, Lee Palmer. 'Switzerland', in Taylor, ed., *Preachers and People*.
Watkins, Owen C. *The Puritan Experience: Studies in Spiritual Autobiography*. New York: Schocken, 1972.
Watt, Jeffery, ed. *From Sin to Insanity: Suicide in Early Modern Europe*. Ithaca, NY: Cornell University Press, 2004.

Watt, Tessa. *Cheap Print and Popular Piety in England*. Cambridge: Cambridge University Press, 1993.

Wendel, François. *Calvin: Origins and Development of His Religious Thought*. New York: Harper and Row, 1963.

Wilby, Emma. *The Visions of Isobel Gowdie: Magic, Witchcraft and Dark Shamanism in Seventeenth-Century Scotland*. Brighton: Sussex Academic Press, 2010.

Williamson, Arthur. *Scottish National Consciousness in the Age of James VI: The Apocalypse, the Union and the Shaping of Scotland's Public Culture*. Edinburgh: John Donald Publishers, 1979.

Wormald, Jenny. *Court, Kirk and Community: Scotland, 1470–1625*. Toronto: University of Toronto Press, 1981.

———. 'Godly Reformer, Godless Monarch: John Knox and Mary Queen of Scots', in Mason, ed., *John Knox and the British Reformations*, 220–41.

———. *Lords and Men in Scotland: Bonds of Manrent*. Edinburgh: Edinburgh University Press, 1985.

———. 'The Witches, the Devil and the King', in Terry Brotherstone and David Ditchburn, eds, *Freedom and Authority: Scotland, c.1050-c.1650*. East Linton: Tuckwell, 2000.

Worobec, Christine. *Possessed: Women, Witches, and Demons in Imperial Russia*. Dekalb: Northern Illinois University Press, 2001.

Wright, Shawn D. *Our Sovereign Refuge: The Pastoral Theology of Theodore Beza, Studies in Christian History and Thought*. Carlisle: Paternoster, 2004.

Yeoman, Louise. 'Heart-Work: Emotion, Empowerment and Authority in Covenanting Times', PhD Thesis, University of St Andrews, 1991.

———. 'The Devil as Doctor: Witchcraft, Wodrow and the Wider World', *Scottish Archives* 1 (1995): 93–105.

Young, John. 'The Covenanters and the Scottish Parliament, 1639–51: The Rule of the Godly and the 'Second Scottish Reformation', in Boran and Gribben, eds, *Enforcing Reformation in Ireland and Scotland, 1550–1700*, 131–58.

Zakai, Avihu. *Exile and Kingdom: History and Apocalypse in the Puritan Migration to America*. Cambridge: Cambridge University Press, 1992.

Index

Abjuration Oath 72
Amyraut, Moses 121
Anglo, Sydney 31
Antichrist
    Calvin on 42
    Pope as 44
apocalypticism
    and the Devil 41–2, 44
    James VI, King of Scotland 44
    Knox on 42–3
    Last Days 41, 46, 70, 71
        Fergusson on 43
        Knox on 42
Aquinas, Thomas, St 30
Arminianism 3
Augustine, St 41, 102
    City of God 41

Baillie, Robert 58, 62, 66, 71, 106
Bayley, Lewis, *Practice of Piety* 121
    popularity 104
Benedict, Philip 120, 121, 204
Beza, Theodore 19, 23
    on the Devil 27
    on reprobation 24
    supralapsarianism doctrine 24
    works
        Propositions and Principles of Divinity 24
        Tabula praedestinationis 24
Bishops' Wars (1639/40) 38, 57
Blackadder, Elizabeth 80, 81, 83, 111
Blair, Robert 89
blasphemy
    as a criminal offence 135–6
    references to The Devil 136–8
Book of Revelation 70
Boyd, Zachary 55, 72–3
broadsides
    audience for 178–9
    bibliography 181
    The Devil in 178, 179–80, 182, 187–200
    last words in 187–94
    murders in 182–7
Brown, John 58, 59, 66, 69, 72, 140
Bruce, Michael 69, 72
Bruce, Robert 39, 55, 106–7
    on human depravity 37, 105–6
Bunyan, John, *Grace Abounding to the Chief of Sinners* 113

Calvin, John 19, 24, 103
    on the Antichrist 42
    on demons 26–7
    on the Devil 16, 22, 24–8, 32, 142
    on God 22–3
    Knox, relationship with
        correspondence 35
        influence on 22
    on predestination 23–4
    The Institutes of the Christian Religion 21–2, 22, 23, 26, 28, 81
Calvinism, French/Scottish, comparison 120–21
Cameron, Euan 32, 199
Cameron, Hugh 84
Cameronians 66
Cant, Andrew, on the Devil 67–8, 186
Carmichael, James, *Newes from Scotland* 153, 154, 156, 157, 164, 166
Catholic Reformation 5, 9
Cervantes, Fernando 13
Charles I, King 66, 105
Charles II, King 66, 72, 91
Chiesly, John, Sir 78, 88–9
church attendance, compulsory 48, 83
Clark, Stuart 30, 32, 45, 116
    Thinking with Demons 12–13
Clifford, George 94
Coffey, John 3
Collace, Katharine 79, 84, 111–12, 118, 175
covenants, with God 87–8
    see also Scottish Covenanters

Craig, John 35
Cressy, David 145, 146
cursing 129, 130, 133
    see also blasphemy

Davies, Owen 195
Day of Judgement 42, 43, 90–91, 204
demonic possession 83–4, 108–15, 203
    cases 172
    Christian Shaw episode 172
    and double predestination 174
    Goodwin children 172–3
    Scotland, infrequency 171, 173–4, 175
demonology
    Catholic/Protestant, comparison 30–32
    studies 13–14
demons, Calvin on 26–7
Devil (Satan), The
    and apocalypticism 41–2, 44
    as apparition 80–81
    appearances 157–61, 176
    at large 40–46
    belief in, popular and elite 142–4, 162–7
    biblical sources 56
    and binary oppositions 100–101
    blasphemous references to 136–8
    bodily harm, cause of 79–80, 139, 141, 148, 199
    in broadsides 178, 182, 183–4, 185–200
    Calvin on 16, 22, 24–8, 32, 142
    Christ, temptation of 59–60
    corporality 80, 199
    dancing with 160–61
    didactic uses of 32, 48
    in dreams 85, 86
    England, references, lack of 145, 146
    Essex, Massachusetts, insulting references 145
    and fairies 163–4
    and God, relationship 24–5, 57
    as God's agent 57–8, 91, 142, 203–4
    Gordon on 83, 112
    historiography 12–15

Huguenot France, references 122
and human depravity 60–64, 78–9, 82, 86, 97, 108, 115, 122, 192, 203
human personification 159–60, 161
images of 17
    woodcut 196
internal assaults by 140, 141, 148, 199
and interpersonal conflict 129–35
invocations of 129–31, 133–4, 139, 141–2
justice, agent of 142
kirk sessions, references 127, 128–30, 148
Knox on 34–5, 36, 100, 142
in last words 187–94
master of deception 58–9
as mental construct 7, 77
as mental threat 14
New England, references 145, 146
in the night 84–5
and ordinary people 125–6
pictures of, lack 93
poem about 187
and political conflict 66–7
Pope as instrument of 65
possession by see demonic possession
prayer against 39–40
preaching about 105–8
in Protestant Britain 91–4
and Reformed Protestantism 2–6, 29, 52, 198, 203, 205–6
and salvation 29, 77, 203
in *The Scots Confession of the Faith* 34, 37–8, 101
and Scottish identity 37–8, 76, 94–5
and Scottish society, sources 10–12
and self-examination 97–123
    process 98–9
and self-surveillance 102, 106
in self-writings 75–7, 98, 111
in sermons 37, 47–8, 52, 54–5, 59, 74
sex with 152, 158, 159, 165
in street literature 194–9

struggle against 81–6, 94, 98
and suicidal thoughts 118
supernatural status 205
and temptation 140–41
toasting the health of 137–8
ubiquity 1, 142, 150, 180, 195, 201
visual forms of 92–3
and will of God 35
and witchcraft 17, 45, 80, 152–7, 168–9
diary keeping 103–4, 114
Dick, Quinton 66–7
Dickson, David 53
Dickson, Margaret
  failed execution 177
  poem about 177
Directory of Public Worship 67
discipline, and sin 1–2
Dixon, Leif 23, 72, 117, 119
Downame, John 103
dreams, The Devil in 85, 86
Duncan, Henrie 85
Durham, James 107

Edington, Carol 41
election 28, 30, 34, 37, 56, 75, 89, 109, 118
  and attendance at sermons 49
  demonstration of 49
  doctrine 29, 73, 101, 117
  predestined 16, 47, 70, 95
  promise of 72, 88, 94, 116
  unknowability of 101
  see also predestination
England, Devil references, lack of 145, 146
evil
  and human nature 1
  problem of 25

fairies, and the Devil 163–4
Fergusson, David
  on the Devil 36, 39
  on Last Days 43
flyting 129, 147
Forbes, John 111
Ford, James 50

Fraser, James 77–8, 79, 109, 175
French Protestantism 22
  features 119–20

General Assembly of the Church of Scotland 70
Gilry, John 89
God
  Calvin on 22–3
  covenants with 87–8
  and The Devil, relationship 24–5, 57
  goodness of 86–7
  invocation of 139
  trust in 89–90
  will of, and The Devil 35
Goodare, Julian 163, 164
Goodare, Julian & Miller, Joyce, *Witchcraft and Belief in Early Modern Scotland* 6
Goodwin children, demonic possession 172–3
Goodwin, Thomas 107–8
Gordon, Bruce 23
Gordon, James, on the Devil 83, 112
Gordon, William 88
Gowing, Laura 145
Graham, John 72
Gray, Andrew 61, 67, 70, 107
Gregory, Annabel 12
Gregory, Brad 202

Hammond, Charles 60–61
Hay, Andrew 75
Hazlett, Ian 34
Henderson, Alexander 56–7, 59, 62, 68, 106, 189
Highlands, Lowlands, dichotomy 8–9, 128–9
Houston, R.A. 112–13, 182
Huguenot France, Devil references 122
human depravity 5
  Bruce on 37, 105–6
  and the Devil 60–64, 78–9, 82, 86, 97, 108, 115, 122, 192, 203
  obsession with 102
  in Reformed theology 86
human nature, and evil 1

Hume, Alexander 107

identity *see* Scottish identity

James VI, King 105
   apocalypticism 44
   works
      Ane fruitfull meditation 43–4
      Daemonologie 44, 160, 173
Jesus Christ, temptation by the Devil 59–60
Johnstone, Archibald 62–3
Johnstone, Nathan 87, 91, 93, 95, 115, 117, 125–6, 146, 166, 198
   The Devil and Demonism in Early Modern England 14

Kendall, R.T. 23
kirk sessions
   and the communal peace 131, 147
   crime adjudication 127
   Devil references 127, 128–30, 148
   elders, animosity towards 131–2
   frequency 126
   punishments 130, 136
   purpose 126
   records 11, 126–9
Knox, John 21, 33, 163
   on apocalypticism 42–3
   Calvin
      correspondence with 35
      influence on 22
   Catholic Church, hostility to 38
   on the Devil 34–5, 36, 100, 142
   on Last Days 42
   works
      Fort for the Afflicted 36
      Godly Letter to the Faithful of London 38
Kramer, Henrich, *Malleus Maleficarum* 31, 32

Lake, Peter 178–9, 195
Larner, Christina 9
   Enemies of God: The Witch-hunt in Scotland 150, 162
Last Days *see under* apocalypticism

Laud, Archbishop 66
Lawson, Deodat, *A Brief and True Narrative* 173
Levack, Brian 151, 168, 173
Lindsay, Henrietta 91
Lindsay, John 33
Livingstone, John 54, 65, 74
Locke, Thomas 63, 103
Luther, Martin 19
Lynch, Michael 37

McCallum, John 49
Macfarlane, Alan 144, 146
Martin, Lauren 9, 161
Mary of Guise 33
Mary Queen of Scots 38
Mather, Cotton
   Memorable Providences Relating to Witchcrafts and Possessions 172–3
   The Wonders of the Invisible World 68
Maxwell of Pollock, George, Sir 85
Melville, James 37, 82
Miller, Joyce 9, 160, 175
ministers, qualifications 53–4
Mullan, David 76, 120
Muller, Richard 24
murders
   in broadside narratives 182–7
   The Devil in 178, 182, 183–4, 185–99
   and predestination 185
Murray, James 147

Napier, John, *A Plaine Discovery of the Whole Revelation of Saint John* 44–5
National Covenant (1638) 53, 56–7, 65
   see also Covenanters
New England, Devil references 145, 146
night, The Devil in 84–5
Nimmo, James 63, 118
   on the Devil 82–3, 86
Normand, Lawrence & Roberts, Gareth 166
North Berwick, witch-trials 93

Norwood, Richard 114

Oldridge, Darren 79, 91, 93–4
  The Devil in Early Modern England 13–14

Pagels, Elaine 99–100
Pearl, Jonathan, *The Crime of Crimes* 121–2
Perkins, William 103–4, 168
  A Case of Conscience 104
Pethane, Alexander 70–71
Pocock, J.G.A. 14
political conflict, and The Devil 66–7
Pope
  as Antichrist 44
  as instrument of the Devil 65
popery, Scottish fear of 38
preaching, about the Devil 105–8
predestination 39, 46, 101, 104, 117, 192
  Calvin on 23–4
  double 3, 14, 16, 19, 198, 201
    and demonic possession 174, 198
    doctrine 23, 24, 63, 79, 101, 204
  and murders 185
  and prayers for the dead 205
Presbyterianism 15
Prestwich, Menna 23
print culture, Scotland 179, 181, 197
Privy Council (Scotland) 38, 131
Protestantism
  as desacralizing force 204
  and modernism 202
  and persistence of the supernatural 202
  Weber on 201–2
  see also Reformed Protestantism

Raffe, Alasdair 4
Reformed piety 116, 117
Reformed Protestantism 15, 33, 50, 197, 201
  images, lack of 93
  and role of the Devil 2–6, 29, 52, 198, 203, 205–6
Reformed theology 17, 29, 41, 73, 205

human depravity in 86
  themes 201
Renwick, James 69
reprobation 23, 24, 47, 99, 114, 137, 174, 196
Rogers, John 92
Row, John 33
  Historie of the Kirk of Scotland 193
Rule, Robert 62, 112
Russell, Jeffrey B. 203, 204
Rutherford, Mistress, demonic possession 78, 80, 87, 110, 118, 175, 193
Rutherford, Samuel 61, 74, 107, 159
  on the Devil 69
  'The Malice of the Devil' 57
Ryrie, Alec 4, 92, 117

St Bartholomew's Day Massacre (1572) 38
St George, Robert 145, 147
Salem, witch-trials 170, 172
  narratives 173
salvation
  and The Devil 29, 77, 203
  insecurity about 29–30, 78
Satan *see* [The] Devil
Schmidt, Jeremy 117
Scotland
  apocalypticism in 40–41, 46
  Catholicism 9
  popery, fear of 38
  post-Reformation religious debates 3–4
  print culture 179, 181, 197
The Scots Confession of the Faith 33
  the Devil in 34, 37–8, 101
Scottish Covenanters 3, 65, 72, 90
Scottish identity
  and The Devil 76, 94–5
  and fighting the Devil 37–8
Scottish Reformation 5, 20, 21, 33, 51, 197, 201
Scribner, Robert 202
self-surveillance, and The Devil 102, 106
self-writings, The Devil in 75–7, 98, 111
Sempill, Robert 183

sermons
   attendance at
      as demonstration of election 49
      as mark of godliness 49
   The Devil in 37, 47–8, 52, 54–5, 59, 74
   and mass communication 48, 74
   as social events 50–51
   structure 51–2
sex, with the Devil 152, 158, 159, 165
Sharp, James, Archbishop 66
Sharpe, James 144–5
Shaw, Christine
   A True Narrative of the Sufferings and Relief of a Young Girl 173
   demonic possession of 172
Shepard, Thomas 114–15
Sibbes, Richard 107
sin, and discipline 1–2
   see also human depravity
Spottiswoode, John 33
Stevenson, John 110, 111
Stevenson, Robert Louis 6, 123
street literature, The Devil in 194–9
   see also broadsides
supralapsarianism doctrine, Beza 24

Thomas, Keith 202
Todd, Margo 11, 117, 127

Union of the Crowns (1603) 8, 180

Veitch, Marion 89
Viret, Pierre 108

Wallington, Nehemiah 92
Walsham, Alexandra 84
Wandel, Lee Palmer 51
Wars of the Three Kingdoms (1639–51) 65
Watt, Tessa 179
Weber, Max, on Protestantism 201–2
Webster, James 58

Welsh, John 56, 57, 74, 105, 107
   on The Devil 47, 61
Welwood, John 55
   on the Devil 90–91
Williamson, Arthur 42
Willingham, David 61
   on the Devil 71
Willock, John 33
Wilson, Bessie, witchcraft trial 149
Wishart, George 21
witch-hunting 40
   English Civil War 171
witch-trials 11
   decline 169
   diabolism 162
   England/Scotland, comparison 168
   features 149
   harmful magic (*maleficium*) 162–3
   New England 146
   North Berwick 93
   Salem 170
witchcraft
   accusations of 150
   Bessie Wilson case 149
   and The Devil 17, 45, 80, 152–7
      appearances 157–61
      dancing with 160–61
      human personification 159–60, 161
      pact with 152–7
      scepticism about 168–9
      sex with 152, 158, 159
   and women 9, 134–5, 150
Witchcraft Act (1563) 151
women
   in public disturbances 134
   and witchcraft 9, 134–5, 150
Woodward, Daniel 69

Yeoman, Louise 98, 118

Zakai, Avihu 41

St Andrews Studies in Reformation History

Editorial Board: Andrew Pettegree, Bridget Heal and Roger Mason,
St Andrews Reformation Studies Institute,
Bruce Gordon, Yale Divinity School, USA,
Amy Nelson Burnett, University of Nebraska at Lincoln, USA,
Euan Cameron, Union Theological Seminary, New York, USA,
Kaspar von Greyerz, University of Basel, Switzerland,
Alec Ryrie, Durham University, UK,
Felicity Heal, University of Oxford, UK,
Jonathan Willis, University of Birmingham, UK,
Karin Maag, Calvin College, USA

Seminary or University?
The Genevan Academy and Reformed Higher Education, 1560–1620
Karin Maag

Marian Protestantism
Six Studies
Andrew Pettegree

Protestant History and Identity in Sixteenth-Century Europe
(2 volumes) edited by Bruce Gordon

Antifraternalism and Anticlericalism in the German Reformation
Johann Eberlin von Günzburg and the Campaign against the Friars
Geoffrey Dipple

Piety and the People
Religious Printing in French, 1511–1551
Francis M. Higman

The Reformation in Eastern and Central Europe
Edited by Karin Maag

The Magnificent Ride
The First Reformation in Hussite Bohemia
Thomas A. Fudge

Kepler's Tübingen
Stimulus to a Theological Mathematics
Charlotte Methuen

The Reformation and the Book
Jean-François Gilmont,
edited and translated by Karin Maag

'Practical Divinity'
The Works and Life of Revd Richard Greenham
Kenneth L. Parker and Eric J. Carlson

Frontiers of the Reformation: Dissidence and Orthodoxy in Sixteenth-Century Europe
Auke Jelsma

The Jacobean Kirk, 1567–1625
Sovereignty, Polity and Liturgy
Alan R. MacDonald

The Education of a Christian Society
Humanism and the Reformation in Britain and the Netherlands
Edited by N. Scott Amos, Andrew Pettegree and Henk van Nierop

Tudor Histories of the English Reformations, 1530–83
Thomas Betteridge

Poor Relief and Protestantism
The Evolution of Social Welfare in Sixteenth-Century Emden
Timothy G. Fehler

Radical Reformation Studies
Essays Presented to James M. Stayer
Edited by Werner O. Packull and Geoffrey L. Dipple

Clerical Marriage and the English Reformation
Precedent Policy and Practice
Helen L. Parish

The Faith and Fortunes of France's Huguenots, 1600–85
Philip Benedict

Penitence in the Age of Reformations
Edited by Katharine Jackson Lualdi and Anne T. Thayer

The Sixteenth-Century French Religious Book
Edited by Andrew Pettegree, Paul Nelles and Philip Conner

The Bible in the Renaissance
Essays on Biblical Commentary and Translation in the Fifteenth and Sixteenth Centuries
Edited by Richard Griffiths

Music as Propaganda in the German Reformation
Rebecca Wagner Oettinger

Christianity and Community in the West
Essays for John Bossy
Edited by Simon Ditchfield

John Foxe and his World
Edited by Christopher Highley and John N. King

Obedient Heretics
Mennonite Identities in Lutheran Hamburg and
Altona during the Confessional Age
Michael D. Driedger

Reformation, Politics and Polemics
The Growth of Protestantism in East Anglian
Market Towns, 1500–1610
John Craig

Usury, Interest and the Reformation
Eric Kerridge

Confessional Identity in East-Central Europe
Edited by Maria Crăciun, Ovidiu Ghitta and Graeme Murdock

The Correspondence of Reginald Pole
Volume 1. A Calendar, 1518–1546: Beginnings to Legate of Viterbo
Thomas F. Mayer

The British Union
A Critical Edition and Translation of David Hume of
Godscroft's De Unione Insulae Britannicae
Edited by Paul J. McGinnis and Arthur H. Williamson

Self-Defence and Religious Strife in Early Modern Europe
England and Germany, 1530–1680
Robert von Friedeburg

Penitence, Preaching and the Coming of the Reformation
Anne T. Thayer

Huguenot Heartland
Montauban and Southern French Calvinism during
the French Wars of Religion
Philip Conner

Reforming the Scottish Church
John Winram (c. 1492–1582) and the Example of Fife
Linda J. Dunbar

Baptism and Spiritual Kinship in Early Modern England
Will Coster

Charity and Lay Piety in Reformation London, 1500–1620
Claire S. Schen

Cultures of Communication from Reformation to Enlightenment
Constructing Publics in the Early Modern German Lands
James Van Horn Melton

The Construction of Martyrdom in the English Catholic
Community, 1535–1603
Anne Dillon

Sebastian Castellio, 1515–1563
Humanist and Defender of Religious Toleration in a Confessional Age
Hans R. Guggisberg, translated and edited by Bruce Gordon

The Front-Runner of the Catholic Reformation
The Life and Works of Johann von Staupitz
Franz Posset

The Correspondence of Reginald Pole
Volume 2. A Calendar, 1547–1554: A Power in Rome
Thomas F. Mayer

William of Orange and the Revolt of the Netherlands, 1572–1584
K.W. Swart, translated by J.C. Grayson

The Italian Reformers and the Zurich Church, c.1540–1620
Mark Taplin

William Cecil and Episcopacy, 1559–1577
Brett Usher

A Dialogue on the Law of Kingship among the Scots
A Critical Edition and Translation of George Buchanan's
De Jure Regni Apud Scotos Dialogus
Roger A. Mason and Martin S. Smith

Music and Religious Identity in Counter-Reformation
Augsburg, 1580–1630
Alexander J. Fisher

The Correspondence of Reginald Pole
Volume 3. A Calendar, 1555–1558: Restoring the English Church
Thomas F. Mayer

Women, Sex and Marriage in Early Modern Venice
Daniela Hacke

Infant Baptism in Reformation Geneva
The Shaping of a Community, 1536–1564
Karen E. Spierling

Moderate Voices in the European Reformation
Edited by Luc Racaut and Alec Ryrie

Piety and Family in Early Modern Europe
Essays in Honour of Steven Ozment
Edited by Marc R. Forster and Benjamin J. Kaplan

Religious Identities in Henry VIII's England
Peter Marshall

John Jewel and the English National Church
The Dilemmas of an Erastian Reformer
Gary W. Jenkins

Catholic Activism in South-West France, 1540–1570
Kevin Gould

Local Politics in the French Wars of Religion
The Towns of Champagne, the Duc de Guise, and
the Catholic League, 1560–95
Mark W. Konnert

Enforcing Reformation in Ireland and Scotland, 1550–1700
Edited by Elizabethanne Boran and Crawford Gribben

Philip Melanchthon and the English Reformation
John Schofield

Reforming the Art of Dying
The ars moriendi *in the German Reformation (1519–1528)*
Austra Reinis

Restoring Christ's Church
John a Lasco and the Forma ac ratio
Michael S. Springer

Catholic Belief and Survival in Late Sixteenth-Century Vienna
The Case of Georg Eder (1523–87)
Elaine Fulton

From Judaism to Calvinism
The Life and Writings of Immanuel Tremellius (c.1510–1580)
Kenneth Austin

The Cosmographia *of Sebastian Münster*
Describing the World in the Reformation
Matthew McLean

Defending Royal Supremacy and Discerning God's Will in Tudor England
Daniel Eppley

The Monarchical Republic of Early Modern England
Essays in Response to Patrick Collinson
Edited by John F. McDiarmid

Adaptations of Calvinism in Reformation Europe
Essays in Honour of Brian G. Armstrong
Edited by Mack P. Holt

Johann Sleidan and the Protestant Vision of History
Alexandra Kess

The Correspondence of Reginald Pole
Volume 4. A Biographical Companion: The British Isles
Thomas F. Mayer and Courtney B. Walters

Life Writing in Reformation Europe
Lives of Reformers by Friends, Disciples and Foes
Irena Backus

Patents, Pictures and Patronage
John Day and the Tudor Book Trade
Elizabeth Evenden

The Chancery of God
Protestant Print, Polemic and Propaganda against the Empire, Magdeburg 1546–1551
Nathan Rein

The Impact of the European Reformation
Princes, Clergy and People
Edited by Bridget Heal and Ole Peter Grell

Patents, Pictures and Patronage
John Day and the Tudor Book Trade
Elizabeth Evenden

The Reformation in Rhyme
Sternhold, Hopkins and the English Metrical Psalter, 1547–1603
Beth Quitslund

Defining Community in Early Modern Europe
Edited by Michael J. Halvorson and Karen E. Spierling

Humanism and the Reform of Sacred Music in Early Modern England
John Merbecke the Orator and The Booke of
Common Praier Noted *(1550)*
Hyun-Ah Kim

The Idol in the Age of Art
Objects, Devotions and the Early Modern World
Edited by Michael W. Cole and Rebecca Zorach

Literature and the Scottish Reformation
Edited by Crawford Gribben and David George Mullan

Protestantism, Poetry and Protest
The Vernacular Writings of Antoine de Chandieu (c. 1534–1591)
S.K. Barker

Humanism and Protestantism in Early Modern English Education
Ian Green

Living with Religious Diversity in Early-Modern Europe
Edited by C. Scott Dixon, Dagmar Freist and Mark Greengrass

The Curse of Ham in the Early Modern Era
The Bible and the Justifications for Slavery
David M. Whitford

Dealings with God
From Blasphemers in Early Modern Zurich to
a Cultural History of Religiousness
Francisca Loetz

Magistrates, Madonnas and Miracles
The Counter Reformation in the Upper Palatinate
Trevor Johnson

Narratives of the Religious Self in Early-Modern Scotland
David George Mullan

Church Music and Protestantism in Post-Reformation England
Discourses, Sites and Identities
Jonathan Willis

Reforming the Scottish Parish
The Reformation in Fife, 1560–1640
John McCallum

Commonwealth and the English Reformation
Protestantism and the Politics of Religious Change in the Gloucester Vale, 1483–1560
Ben Lowe

Heinrich Heshusius and the Polemics of Early Lutheran Orthodoxy
Confessional Conflict and Jewish-Christian Relations in North Germany, 1556–1597
Michael J. Halvorson

Humanism and Calvinism
Andrew Melville and the Universities of Scotland, 1560–1625
Steven J. Reid

The Senses and the English Reformation
Matthew Milner

Early French Reform
The Theology and Spirituality of Guillaume Farel
Jason Zuidema and Theodore Van Raalte

Catholic and Protestant Translations of the Imitatio Christi, *1425–1650*
Maximilian von Habsburg

Getting Along?
Religious Identities and Confessional Relations in Early Modern England – Essays in Honour of Professor W.J. Sheils
Edited by Nadine Lewycky and Adam Morton

From Priest's Whore to Pastor's Wife
Clerical Marriage and the Process of Reform in the Early German Reformation
Marjorie Elizabeth Plummer

George Buchanan
Political Thought in Early Modern Britain and Europe
Edited by Caroline Erskine and Roger A. Mason

Censorship and Civic Order in Reformation Germany, 1517–1648
'Printed Poison & Evil Talk'
Allyson F. Creasman

Private and Domestic Devotion in Early Modern Britain
Edited by Jessica Martin and Alec Ryrie

A King Translated
The Writings of King James VI & I and their Interpretation in the Low Countries, 1593–1603
Astrid Stilma

A Linking of Heaven and Earth
Studies in Religious and Cultural History in Honor of Carlos M.N. Eire
Edited by Emily Michelson, Scott K. Taylor and Mary Noll Venables

Worship and the Parish Church in Early Modern Britain
Edited by Natalie Mears and Alec Ryrie

Baal's Priests
The Loyalist Clergy and the English Revolution
Fiona McCall

The Early Reformation in Germany
Between Secular Impact and Radical Vision
Tom Scott

Practical Predestinarians in England, c. 1590-1640
Leif Dixon

The Search for Authority in Reformation Europe
Edited by Helen Parish, Elaine Fulton and Peter Webster

Following Zwingli
Applying the Past in Reformation Zurich
Edited by Luca Baschera, Bruce Gordon and Christian Moser

Andrew Melville (1545–1622)
Writings, Reception, and Reputation
Edited by Roger A. Mason and Steven J. Reid

Metrical Psalmody in Print and Practice
English 'Singing Psalms' and Scottish 'Psalm Buiks', c. 1547–1640
Timothy Duguid

Public Religious Disputation in England, 1558–1626
Joshua Rodda

The Sacralization of Space and Behavior in the Early Modern World
Studies and Sources
Edited by Jennifer Mara DeSilva

The Singing of the Strasbourg Protestants, 1523–1541
Daniel Trocmé-Latter

Dying, Death, Burial and Commemoration in Reformation Europe
Edited by Elizabeth C. Tingle and Jonathan Willis

Sin and Salvation in Reformation England
Edited by Jonathan Willis

Lord Burghley and Episcopacy, 1577–1603
Brett Usher